Racing Line

British motorcycle racing in the
golden age of the big single

More great motorcycle books from Veloce:

Speedpro Series
Harley-Davidson Evolution Engines, How to Build & Power
  Tune (Hammill)
Motorcycle-engined Racing Car, How to Build (Pashley)

Enthusiast's Restoration Manual Series
Beginner's Guide to Classic Motorcycle Restoration YOUR
  step-by-step guide to setting up a workshop, choosing a
  project, dismantling, sourcing parts, renovating & rebuilding
  classic motorcycles from the 1970s & 1980s, The (Burns)
Classic Large Frame Vespa Scooters, How to Restore (Paxton)
Ducati Bevel Twins 1971 to 1986 (Falloon)
How to restore Honda CX500 & CX650 – YOUR step-by-step
  colour illustrated guide to complete restoration (Burns)
How to restore Honda Fours – YOUR step-by-step colour
  illustrated guide to complete restoration (Burns)
Yamaha FS1-E, How to Restore (Watts)

Essential Buyer's Guide Series
BMW GS (Henshaw)
BMW X5 (Saunders)
BSA 350 & 500 Unit Construction Singles (Henshaw)
BSA 500 & 650 Twins (Henshaw)
BSA Bantam (Henshaw)
Ducati Bevel Twins (Falloon)
Ducati Desmodue Twins (Falloon)
Ducati Desmoquattro Twins – 851, 888, 916, 996, 998, ST4
  1988 to 2004 (Falloon)
Ducati Overhead Camshaft Singles, "The Book of the (Falloon)
Harley-Davidson Big Twins (Henshaw)
Hinckley Triumph triples & fours 750, 900, 955, 1000, 1050,
  1200 – 1991-2009 (Henshaw)
Honda CBR FireBlade (Henshaw)
Honda CBR600 Hurricane (Henshaw)
Honda SOHC Fours 1969-1984 (Henshaw)
Kawasaki Z1 & Z900 (Orritt)
Moto Guzzi 2-valve big twins (Falloon)
Norton Commando (Henshaw)
Peugeot 205 GTI (Blackburn)
Triumph 350 & 500 Twins (Henshaw)
Triumph Bonneville (Henshaw)
Triumph Thunderbird, Trophy & Tiger (Henshaw)
Triumph TR6 (Williams)
Triumph TR7 & TR8 (Williams)
Vespa Scooters – Classic 2-stroke models 1960-2008 (Paxton)

Those Were The Days ... Series
Alpine Trials & Rallies 1910-1973 (Pfundner)
Brighton National Speed Trials (Gardiner)
Café Racer Phenomenon, The (Walker)
Drag Bike Racing in Britain – From the mid '60s to the mid
  '80s (Lee)

General
Automotive A-Z, Lane's Dictionary of Automotive Terms
  (Lane)
BMW Boxer Twins 1970-1995 Bible, The (Falloon)
BMW Cafe Racers (Cloesen)
BMW Custom Motorcycles – Choppers, Cruisers, Bobbers,
  Trikes & Quads (Cloesen)
British 250cc Racing Motorcycles (Pereira)
BSA Bantam Bible, The (Henshaw)
BSA Motorcycles – the final evolution (Jones)
Ducati 750 Bible, The (Falloon)
Ducati 750 SS 'round-case' 1974, The Book of the (Falloon)
Ducati 860, 900 and Mille Bible, The (Falloon)
Ducati Monster Bible (New Updated & Revised Edition), The
  (Falloon)
Fine Art of the Motorcycle Engine, The (Peirce)
Funky Mopeds (Skelton)
Italian Cafe Racers (Cloesen)
Italian Custom Motorcycles (Cloesen)
Kawasaki Triples Bible, The (Walker)
Kawasaki Z1 Story, The (Sheehan)
Lambretta Bible, The (Davies)
Little book of trikes, the (Quellin)
Moto Guzzi Sport & Le Mans Bible, The (Falloon)
Motorcycle Apprentice (Cakebread)
Motorcycle GP Racing in the 1960s (Pereira)
Motorcycle Road & Racing Chassis Designs (Noakes)
Off-Road Giants! (Volume 1) – Heroes of 1960s Motorcycle
  Sport (Westlake)
Off-Road Giants! (Volume 2) – Heroes of 1960s Motorcycle
  Sport (Westlake)
Off-Road Giants! (volume 3) – Heroes of 1960s Motorcycle
  Sport (Westlake)
Scooters & Microcars, The A-Z of Popular (Dan)
Scooter Lifestyle (Grainger)
SCOOTER MANIA! – Recollections of the Isle of Man
  International Scooter Rally (Jackson)
Singer Story: Cars, Commercial Vehicles, Bicycles & Motorcycle
  (Atkinson)
Triumph Bonneville Bible (59-83) (Henshaw)
Triumph Bonneville!, Save the – The inside story of the
  Meriden Workers' Co-op (Rosamond)
Triumph Motorcycles & the Meriden Factory (Hancox)
Triumph Speed Twin & Thunderbird Bible (Woolridge)
Triumph Tiger Cub Bible (Estall)
Triumph Trophy Bible (Woolridge)
Triumph TR6 (Kimberley)
TT Talking – The TT's most exciting era – As seen by Manx
  Radio TT's lead commentator 2004-2012 (Lambert)
Velocette Motorcycles – MSS to Thruxton – New Third Edition
  (Burris)
Vespa – The Story of a Cult Classic in Pictures (Uhlig)

www.hubbleandhattie.com   www.battlecry-books.com

www.veloce.co.uk

For post publication news, updates and amendments relating to this book please visit www.veloce.co.uk/books/V4793

Front cover image: The usual suspects – Bill Ivy leads Paddy Driver, Derek Minter and John Cooper in a 500cc race at Brands Hatch in 1965. (Courtesy Mortons Archive)
First published in September 2015 by Veloce Publishing Limited, Veloce House, Parkway Farm Business Park, Middle Farm Way, Poundbury, Dorchester DT1 3AR, England.
Fax 01305 268864 / e-mail info@veloce.co.uk / web www.veloce.co.uk or www.velocebooks.com.
ISBN: 978-1-845847-93-7 UPC: 6-36847-04793-1 © 2015 Bob Guntrip and Veloce Publishing. All rights reserved. With the exception of quoting brief passages for the purpose of review, no part of this publication may be recorded, reproduced or transmitted by any means, including photocopying, without the written permission of Veloce Publishing Ltd. Throughout this book logos, model names and designations, etc, have been used for the purposes of identification, illustration and decoration. Such names are the property of the trademark holder as this is not an official publication. Readers with ideas for automotive books, or books on other transport or related hobby subjects, are invited to write to the editorial director of Veloce Publishing at the above address. British Library Cataloguing in Publication Data – A catalogue record for this book is available from the British Library. Typesetting, design and page make-up all by Veloce Publishing Ltd on Apple Mac. Printed in India by Replika Press.

RACING LINE

British motorcycle racing in the golden age of the big single

Bob Guntrip

VELOCE PUBLISHING
THE PUBLISHER OF FINE AUTOMOTIVE BOOKS

Contents

*To Bob Guntrip (senior), Bob Peck, Walter Peck, Bill Minchin and
Mr C J Washington: for showing us why and explaining how*

Foreword

The Sound of Magic

Turn right from the gate of my childhood home, and, after a quarter of a mile or so, there is a T-junction where Caldecott Road meets the old A34. As a boy I'd often pass that way when cycling home from school, and once in a while I'd stop at the corner, to look and to wonder. Away to the left lay Thruxton and Blandford and beyond them, in a hazy, distant world labelled foreign, the excitement of grand prix, the Continental Circus; to the right was everything else, spread in a deep arc from Castle Combe to Brands Hatch. In the far north lay the Heysham Ferry, and so the Island. To our family it was never the Isle of Man, still less Mona's Isle; and I don't recall anyone ever talking of the Mountain Course. It was just the Island.

From the south, the A34 dropped gently between thick hedgerows, angling slightly left and climbing gently to where I stood, before swinging left again, down and out of view towards the western edge of town. On the junction, opposite Caldecott Road, was an old weatherboard service station with a couple of petrol pumps and a few enamel signs. We knew it as Esso Garage. There had to be, I would tell myself, somewhere like this on the Island – around Glen Vine or Crosby, perhaps … *here comes McIntyre past Esso Garage, he's got the Gilera really flying now …*

The odd thing was, while I numbered among the family's third generation of motorcyclists, we were off-roading stock and given to scrambling, as it then was, grass track and trials. Sundays to us meant Aldworth, Stokenchurch, even the Land's End Trial. But that all changed for me one bleak Sunday morning in March 1967, when I wobbled up to the junction on my new 80cc Suzuki, flicked the indicator switch and turned right for Mallory Park. I was 16 and my hitherto fantasy world of road racing was about to acquire shape and colour; before the day was out I would be standing in a paddock crammed with British single-cylinder racing motorcycles and so come to discover the sound of magic.

I managed about 20 meetings over the next three or four years, mesmerised by what

I'd seen and heard, before life began to make more pressing demands. The first half of the 1970s is now a blur of other, non-racing images; I didn't get to another event until 1976 or so, when something called a Yamaha TZ750 was turning the world upside down. The racing was as intoxicating as ever. I watched Barry Sheene as he struggled in vain to contain Kenny Roberts, as the American dynasty established itself and ended, almost as abruptly, 15 years later. Today I derive as much pleasure from motorcycle sport, be it World Superbike, BSB or MotoGP.

This book is not about these things, and neither does it focus on the TT. The aim of *Racing Line* is to document a little of the 1960s, when short circuit racing dominated the calendar if not the headlines, when the last great generation of riding talent from Britain and its old Commonwealth rode Manx Nortons and G50 Matchless, 7R AJSs and Aermacchis to do battle with itself and the world. During the 1960s there were up to five major meetings every Easter and quality racing could be seen up and down the land on most weekends between March and October. It was the decade that began with Bob McIntyre wresting the 500cc British Championship from Mike Hailwood and ended with Dave Croxford beating Alan Barnett to the title; and the years in between saw the flowering of some of the finest talents in the history of the sport, from Derek Minter and Bill Ivy to John Cooper and Peter Williams.

Racing Line began to take shape in August 2012. I was due to turn in my regular column for *Cycle Torque* and decided to do something to mark the 50th anniversary of Bob McIntyre's death. I thought I'd write not about the 1957 TT, but about Mac's exploits at home; the number of British championships he'd won*, for example. It turned out to be far trickier than I'd have thought possible. The internet offered plenty of references to Gilera and to Libero Liberati, to Surtees, to Duke, to that lap of the Island at 101.12mph. There was rather less about Joe Potts, Pim Fleming or Razorblade frames, and little indeed about how Mac came to be at Oulton Park on 6 August 1962. There was more material on the bookshelves, of course, excellent works by Mick Walker and Colin Seeley among it; but the die was cast. I decided to work up my own modest tribute to the giants of my youth and this is the result.

For reasons of space I've confined myself to 350 and 500cc racing, and the larger-capacity classes as they began to emerge and take shape. The results section bears the same constraints. Oh, and Production, cap P, means Production racing which, as we all know, is a very different animal from the process and issue of production, small p.

As much as I'd like to believe otherwise, *Racing Line* will contain omissions and other errors of diverse kinds. Such horrors as there may be are my responsibility, and for these I crave your indulgence and invite your corrections. They should emphatically not be laid at the door of the helpful folk who have tried to keep me on the straight and narrow, among them the generous and accommodating John and Rosemary Cooper, who tolerated a complete stranger's plea to spend time with a champion; Dave Degens, who rolled back the years in his own rather different way; Michelle Duff, who answered my questions with patience and grace; Phil Read, who helped with his life before Yamaha; Tina May and her husband David, who added to my understanding of Tina's dad, the great Ray Petty; Chris and Sondra Pereira, who offered me hospitality and wisdom while confronting difficulties of their own; Gary James, for whom Tom Kirby really was Uncle Tom; Mike Redfern and Michael Thompson, who helped me with details of Ken Redfern's too-brief but incandescent career; Elwyn Roberts and Paul McElvie, who allowed me to plunder their photo files; Peter Chamberlain and his glimpse into the formative years of postwar racing at Haddenham; and Ken McIntosh for his help with Manx design. Long days at library desks were made the more pleasant by the attentive staffs of the New South Wales State Library and the British Library, the National Motorcycle Museum of Australia in the sleepy town of Nabiac, and particularly of the library of the Vintage Motorcycle Club in Burton-on-Trent where Vicky, Michelle and Peter – and Pam – offered proper tea, local knowledge and good humour as well as guidance through the groaning shelves of their fantastic resource. The VMCC library is the best of its kind and is open to anyone seeking answers; long may it prosper. My thanks are likewise due in full measure to Bill Snelling at FoTTofinders who helped me with images and works with great skill as custodian of the TT's photographic legacy; to Glenn Ducey for knowing everything; to Ross Hannan for explaining the value of aluminium cases; to the irrepressible Dennis Quinlan; and to Adrian Sellars, the present owner of Ray Petty's reverse-head 350 Manx, who offered his time, his technical expertise, his photographs, and a belief we share, that the Manx Norton is still an embodiment of beauty. Finally, and no less importantly, I thank Rod Grainger at Veloce for taking me on and the staff at Veloce for their patience and expertise; and must acknowledge two seers of the age, Sir Tim Berners-Lee and Bill Gates, for today making so much so easy. Slightly off-track, perhaps, I thank too the British Automobile Racing Club for moving to Thruxton and supplanting a series of ruined compromises with one of the most exciting tracks in the country. I've seen Jean-Claude Chemarin and Christian Leon deliver a long-distance demonstration of Gallic style there on a Honda RCB1000; I've seen Jochen Rindt win a Formula 2 race there; and what is more than either, I've seen Alan Barnett at his best there, and for that no thanks can be sufficient. Finally, to my beloved wife Sandy, without whose expert blend of cajolement, provocation and encouragement I'd achieve nothing, my everlasting gratitude.

Today the A34 takes a wide sweep west of the town on a new bypass, and I live far away. The junction is still there, though a road now runs through the site of the old service station; and I'll stand on that corner just the same, once in a long while, to think again of sunlight flashing off Bob Mac's howling Gilera, to feel anew that boyhood sense of wonder.

Bob Guntrip, Wentworth Falls

* Four – 1956: 250 and 500; 1960: 350 and 500

Chapter 1

Regeneration

They came under starter's orders again at noon on Good Friday, 19 April 1946. Cadwell Park's narrow three-quarter-mile track of rough concrete had not much deteriorated since it was last used for racing in 1939, and proved good enough for George Brown (499 Vincent) and sidecar ace Eric Oliver (596 Norton) to put in record-breaking performances, winning their events and slicing a neat two seconds off the lap record to leave the mark at 50 seconds even.

Britain had come out of the most destructive war in history with its cities ravaged, much of its industry laid waste, its people exhausted; yet within the first year of peace, motorcycle racing was back and moving, if hesitantly to begin with, into a new era. And if Louth & District MCC led the way at Cadwell, others soon followed: the Irthlingborough club hatched plans to run events on a half-mile track at a private park in Kettering; Cambridge University Aero Club ran meetings at Gransden Lodge and North Weald aerodromes in aid of RAF charities. From farther afield came word of meetings, rich in plunder, planned in Belgium, Switzerland and Spain, and hints that the Ulster Grand Prix, run over the formidable 16.5-mile Clady Circuit with its notorious Seven Mile Straight, might soon be restored to the racing calendar. The improbable was already happening; the TT, however, might take a little longer.

Fergus Kenrick Anderson, freshly demobbed from the Royal Navy; soon to become a trailblazer among stars of the Continental Circus before the term was even coined, had already packed his KTT Velocette and brooked the prevailing trend by heading south across the English Channel, celebrating the first anniversary of peace in Europe by winning the Brussels International Grand Prix.

The calendar of events thickened quickly: a grand prix was planned for Switzerland (where Maurice Cann won the 500cc race for Moto Guzzi), and an international at Albi in France (the itinerant and articulate Anderson claiming the laurels in the 350cc event). Meanwhile the big names of racing continued gradually to reappear in civilian life, exchanging wartime serge for demob suits and two-piece leathers: Sergeant Freddie Frith, Wing Commander Jock West, Home Guardsman Harold Daniell – his eyesight, famously too poor for army despatch work, kept the Isle of Man lap record holder at home – and Flight Lieutenant Leslie Graham DFC, long familiar with the pilot's seat of a Lancaster bomber, began the journey that would take him and AJS to the inaugural 500cc world championship.

The factories started making the switch to peacetime production. Norton had spent the war making close to 100,000 side-valve 16H singles and Big Four sidecar outfits for the armed forces. AMC's Plumstead works had contributed 80,000 G3 and G3L 350cc singles for the Don Rs of a dozen armies (by way of comparison, Harley-Davidson had made 90,000 WLAs). Triumph rebuilt itself at Meriden after its Coventry factory had been pounded to destruction during a series of air raids early in the war. In November 1946 Norton struck an optimistic note by publishing a price list of its 1947 street and competition bikes, largely for export, and then thought it prudent to take advertising space in the specialist press to mollify frustrated British buyers for whom new road bikes weren't available, much less racing hardware.

The recovery was under way, however slowly. At Norton, Joe Craig, aided a little later by the McCandless brothers, and later still by former Flight Lieutenant Leo Kuzmicki, was able for a time to restore the Manx Norton to the top step of the grand prix podium, while at AMC, Phil Walker and later Jack Williams plotted the development of the 7R AJS – the 'boy racer.'

In sunnier southern climes, another of the prewar giants was awakening. In the last season before Hitler's war, Dorino Serafini had won the European championship for Italy on Piero Remor's water-cooled, supercharged four-cylinder 500cc Gilera, trading agility and even reliability for enough speed to see off challengers from BMW, Moto Guzzi and Norton. With supercharging banned by the FIM from late in 1946, Remor, aided by Ottavio Milani and Federico Vertemati, designed a new, air-cooled engine to supplant the prewar powerhouse. A spate of engine seizures, traced to inadequate pistons, did nothing to conceal the speed of the new bike – nor its wayward high-speed handling. But when, in 1949, Remor took his talents to MV, together with those of chief mechanic Arturo Magni, to design a similar and ultimately much more successful machine, it seemed likely indeed that Britain's broke and broken factories would soon find the going tough in grand prix competition.

The way back

Austerity Britain was a harsh environment. The cost of war had taken the country to the brink of bankruptcy before 1941 was out, and it had since been heavily reliant on American aid through Lend Lease to sustain its people and its war. When Lend Lease ended abruptly in August 1945 with the cessation of hostilities, the immediate consequence for Britain was rationing tougher than at any time during the war, and the demand for exports on a massive scale to boost the nation's ailing balance of payments. The needs of motorcycle racing counted for little in comparison.

The range and quality of supplies available to a burgeoning racing community so bore the threadbare cast of war; nothing exemplified the problem more clearly than the take-it-or-leave-it supply of 'pool' 72-octane petrol with which, said Joe Craig, Norton's 500cc factory racers struggled to a peak compression ratio of 7.2:1, compared with 10.5:1 in 1938. But if speeds at the first postwar TT in 1947 were modest, the achievements of its competitors lacked nothing. Bob Foster hung out Velocette's shingle to win the Junior race on a 1939 factory bike and lead his team-mates into second and third, while Daniell repeated his 1938 Senior win for Norton (with team-mate Artie Bell backing up), albeit at a pace markedly reduced from his searing prewar victory.

The privateer engineers and tuners were starting to reopen for business. Steve Lancefield ("I am a racing engineer not a tuner, I do not tune pianos") and the stylish and patrician Francis Beart, late of Brooklands, had been scooped up by the aero industry during the war but now returned to their Manx Nortons, with Lancefield preparing bikes for Johnny Lockett while Beart looked after Dennis Parkinson and Cromie McCandless – with help from protégés Ray Petty and Phil Kettle. Back at their benches, all would coax performance from their engines that the factory had not exploited. Lancefield, notoriously secretive even to his sponsored riders, became a pioneer in the use of twin-plug heads and coil ignition. Bill Lacey, who prized reliability above all things, gained a particular reputation for fastidious preparation and getting the best from a stock engine. Later, he developed a massive flanged drive-side main bearing for the Manx Norton, to replace the highly stressed standard unit, and helped to develop a one-piece crankshaft running a plain big-end rod from a Jaguar. While Bill Stuart worked in the Norton race shop for a time, he would establish his own business in Warwickshire, fettling engines for talents as diverse as Geoff Duke and Dan Shorey and experimenting with coil valve springs for the Manx. Allen Dudley-Ward made his own one-piece Manx crank. Beart, closely associated with Norton's factory racing programme as the Rex McCandless Featherbed chassis was being developed, and keenly aware that it was a little too heavy, became notorious for trimming weight from his bikes, drilling components for lightness and even hollowing bolts. A Beart Norton, meticulously prepared and turned out, would rarely be subjected to the indignity of trackside repair, but returned to Beart's workshop for attention. The Surrey engineer's bikes were distinctively finished in Ford Ludlow Green and he would ultimately prepare a broader range of machines than many of his contemporaries – though no longer at his well-known Brooklands shed, initially opening new premises behind a friend's garage in Byfleet High Street.

Further north, Manchester Norton dealer Reg Dearden developed an early reputation on other marques, notably Velocette and Vincent, but became established as one of the leading Norton tuners, buying up much of the contents of the Norton race shop when the marque closed its Bracebridge Street, Birmingham premises at the end of 1962, and ultimately constructing his own short-stroke 500 Manx.

North of the border, and among the most innovative of the great names, was Glasgow tuner Joe Potts. Best known as sponsor of fellow Scots Bob McIntyre and Alistair King, Potts decided in the later 1950s to challenge the prevailing might of MV Agusta at grand prix level by building a Manx with desmodromic valve gear (independent of Norton's factory effort), which is designed to offer better valve control than springs, and particularly so of the heavy inlet and exhaust valves typical to the period. That the enterprise ultimately failed through want of an adequate chassis was hardly the fault of Potts, whose bikes propelled McIntyre and King to scores of wins through the 1950s and 60s.

Assorted machinery, musty riding kit, pool petrol – but racing for all that. Bemsee members prepare to enjoy the pleasures of peace at a meeting in 1949. (Courtesy haddenhamairfieldhistory.co.uk)

By the opening of the 1949 season, with the Hutchinson 100 restored to the top of the domestic calendar and the first world championships just around the corner, the sport was regaining a kind of shabby normality. Tommy Wood, Dave Whitworth and George Brown were winning at home and Norton had announced a factory team (Daniell, Bell and Lockett) for the coming championships. Meanwhile, another former despatch rider had been released by the army to make headlines: G E Duke (490 Norton) of St Helens had won the Derbyshire Trial. There was even talk of raising the octane rating of fuel to prewar levels, from 72 to 80, through the magic of a chemical booster catchily named tetraethyl lead.

Have bike, will travel

There were problems, naturally, and some more intractable than others. To begin with, the sport was effectively homeless and had been since Brooklands and Donington were requisitioned for military use at the start of the war. True, its soul reposed where it had for 40 years and more, in the Isle of Man – but that wasn't much use to an enterprising club in the midlands, or the south-east, that wanted access to a couple of miles of tarmac on a bank holiday to run a few races for its members. The root of the problem lay in the blanket ban on conducting motorsport over mainland roads, which had been in place since the late 1920s.

"Britain cannot afford to remain trackless while Italy has Monza, France Montlhéry, Germany Avus and the Nürburgring," growled Arthur Bourne, editor of 'the Blue 'un' – *The Motor Cycle* – as early as January 1946. In December of that year, the Air Ministry said it was considering the question of racing on its rapidly rising total of disused airfields, but its anguish was plain and, concerned about adequate control, it 'released' a number of airfields, but turned over all further responsibility for their racing use to the RAC.

Such airfield circuits, often a combination of perimeter tracks and runways (sometimes of disorientating width), came and went, and by force of circumstance racing eased into a nomadic, make-do-and-mend kind of existence. Clubs loaded up their stop watches, tapes and straw bales – perhaps even a little bunting and a loudhailer or two – and held meetings here in May, there in June, somewhere else in August.

Tougher times yet lay in wait during the decade before Prime Minister Harold Macmillan told the nation, in 1957, that "most of our people have never had it so good." Factories closed, racing budgets dried up, teams disbanded. By the middle years of the 1950s, Britain's racing status had declined dramatically in almost every particular. Early in 1955, Norton announced its new team, comprising John Surtees, John Hartle and Jack Brett, but added that it would contest only selected events, and that these would not amount to a full world championship campaign. A week later, AMC said its racing efforts would thereafter be confined to developing its production racers (the 7R AJS for the 350cc class and the G45 Matchless for 500cc events), that it would halt development on the AJS

Porcupine and 7R3, and that its riders for the year, Bill Lomas, Derek Ennett, John Clark and Peter Murphy would, like their opposite numbers in the Norton camp, largely be staying at home.

Italy, meanwhile, had gone from strength to strength. Gilera rider Umberto Masetti had won the 500cc World Championship in 1950 (winning two grands prix from six) and 1952 (winning two grands prix from eight) with its transverse air-cooled fours. These were still fast but wayward, and their uncertain handling made Craig's factory Nortons a better overall proposition, even at world championship level, from the middle of 1950 with the advent of the Featherbed chassis created by Rex McCandless and Artie Bell.

The inevitable was postponed – but only until Gilera signed three-time world champion Geoff Duke, together with Reg Armstrong and Dickie Dale, to spearhead its 1953 title bid. The Italian bikes took the first three places in the 500cc championship, Duke leading the way on a bike he'd transformed, a bike that could win anywhere. He'd hit it off with Gilera racing manager Piero Taruffi, and the pair collaborated successfully to give their bikes the benefits of a lower centre of gravity, sturdier suspension and a stiffer frame, attributes he understood from long experience of the pounding endured by man and machine during seven-lap, 264-mile races over the Isle of Man TT course. In 1954 Duke won five grands prix for Gilera; Rhodesian Ray Amm, in a doughty rearguard action for Norton, just two.

In the 350 class the names were different but the outcome the same: by 1953 Moto Guzzi's light, low and versatile singles had comprehensively seen off sometimes more powerful but invariably heftier British opposition. Norton again won two races that year, and in 1954 New Zealander Rod Coleman took the Junior TT for AJS – but these, in a wider context, were crumbs from the table; without major investment, British bikes would no longer be competitive at grand prix level. And the cash simply wasn't there.

Staying local

If Britain's position as a leading manufacturer of racing hardware was increasingly questionable, its status as a producer of quality riding talent was not. Between 1949 and 1960, British riders had dropped just four world championships in the major classes: in the 500cc class, three times to Gilera, with Masetti the winner in 1950 and 1952 and Libero Liberati in 1957; in the 350cc class the succession was unbroken, excepting – and to stretch a point – Australian Keith Campbell in 1957, who completed Moto Guzzi's impressive run of five championships in the class. And the stars kept coming. By the middle 1950s the first great postwar generation of riders had finished their national service and were collecting an early shelfload of tinware: Bob McIntyre and Derek Minter led the way, forsaking the inevitable BSA Gold Stars for more potent machines, and progressively giving rein to their talents. Indeed, McIntyre became Geoff Duke's anointed successor at Gilera and posted one impressive, if injury-marred, season before Gilera

**Last delivery: John Surtees during his final TT win, the 1960 Senior. At season's end he
went car racing, and Gary Hocking took his place at MV Agusta.
(Courtesy FoTTofinder Bikesport Photo Archives)**

joined fellow Italian manufacturers Moto Guzzi and Mondial in pulling out of grand prix
racing.

The withdrawal of the Italian factories meant that in just four seasons the number of
350 and 500cc factory rides had dwindled from upwards of a dozen to the few within the
gift of Count Domenico Agusta and a couple of smaller teams, and that's the way it would
stay, at least until small groups of men wearing red caps bearing the name Honda began to
appear at race tracks a year or two later.

For the lucky few, which in 1958 effectively meant John Surtees and John Hartle at
MV, world championship racing remained a practical, paying proposition. Others, lacking
factory hardware, would load their faithful Norton, AJS or Matchless into vans and
trucks of varying antiquity, and run away to join the Continental Circus, confident and
enthusiastic, expecting to make a living and hoping to be noticed.

Most would stay at home, however. Much had changed since that meeting at Cadwell
Park in April 1946: circuits had come and gone but a dozen had become a permanent part
of life; a handful of big events had disappeared from the calendar while others had been
restored and still more had been launched to become features of a packed domestic season

that extended from March to October. Loading two bikes into an unheated van at five on a bleak Sunday morning in March to drive 200 miles to the first national of the season no doubt felt far removed from the glamour of the world championships or the prestige of the TT; but there was a living to be made, titles and trophies to be won.

The better engineers and tuners had plenty of regular customers with whom to develop their craft and were making headlines in their own right, with summaries appearing in the press at the beginning of each season explaining how many engines each was preparing for whom, whether for short circuit racing, grand prix use or the TT. Meanwhile the British racing single, the tool of aspiring champions for half a century, was nearing the peak of its factory development. The works teams might have gone, taking with them their light and low, experimental short-stroke, three-valve and twin-cylinder engines; but for the present, Norton and AMC continued to make and to tweak the stock Manx Norton, the 7R AJS, and the newcomer and AMC rival for the Manx in 500cc events, the G50 Matchless.

With MV Agusta supreme at grand prix level and Honda's intervention just around the corner, the long, rich story of the British single as a race winner at international level was almost done, but it was a proven performer in national events, and would remain so for another decade – in some ways the most challenging in its history. In the years since World War II the air-cooled, overhead-cam thumper had developed into a fine instrument for settling domestic disputes.

Chapter 2

A Choice of Rivals

It began so well. By the end of 1949 Les Graham had become inaugural 500cc World Champion, taking the AJS E90 Porcupine to grand prix wins in Switzerland and Ulster, and to a crucial second place behind Nello Pagani's Gilera in Holland. Meanwhile, a favourable reaction from dealers and buyers, together with a growing list of solid results on the track, was making AJS's newly launched 350cc 7R 'boy racer' a success. AMC's racing programme clearly held promise for the decade ahead. All that was needed was a catalogue 500cc racer to stand alongside the 7R in showrooms and paddocks across the land.

There were two ways to fill the gap: to use the 7R as a basis on which to develop a purpose-built 500cc single, so creating a simpler, lower-maintenance equivalent of the 30M Manx Norton; or to modify a catalogue road bike, as Triumph had done with its Tiger 100-inspired Grand Prix. From marketing and promotional standpoints it made good sense to develop a road bike, and AMC had just the thing – the new Matchless G9 Super Clubman.

Enter AMC's chief development engineer, Ike Hatch, who went to work on the G9's twin-cylinder OHV engine. By the time the prototype racer was entered for the 1951 Manx Grand Prix the 179kg, 29bhp G9 roadster, its road gear swapped for largely 7R-derived cycle parts, had become the 145kg, 48bhp G45.

Early signs were hopeful. Robin Sherry took the bike to fourth in the 1951 event, with Derek Farrant doing well to win the 1952 Manx GP on the production model. When the

G45 went on sale in 1953 AMC found itself acquiring enthusiastic buyers ready to hand over the £390 necessary for the privilege of G45 ownership.

Meanwhile, in the 350cc class the 7R was proving its worth. While not consistently a threat to the factory Nortons, or particularly to Velocette's KTT singles at world championship level, the boy racer continued to perform well at the Manx Grand Prix, and had taken a catalogue of wins in more modest competition.

At its launch the 7R offered simple, sturdy reliability and performance at a price comparable to the equivalent long-stroke garden-gate Manx Norton. Its heart was Philip Walker's 74 × 81mm SOHC powerplant, which owed much to its prewar forebear, the R7. The engine was mated to an Amal 10TT carburettor, Burman four-speed gearbox and Lucas racing magneto. The newcomer boasted several advantages over its Bracebridge Street rival: a twin-cradle frame allied to swinging arm suspension. The Norton would be reliant on its plunger back end until the McCandless brothers came to the rescue with the Featherbed chassis. In its earliest form the 7R made 29bhp on the ubiquitous blight of the age, 72-octane pool petrol, which was enough to give it 100mph at 6600rpm.

Major changes began to appear from the 1950 model year. Modified valves, lightened flywheels and a sturdier conrod headed the list. Compression was boosted from 8.45:1 to 8.85:1, thanks to the newly available 80-octane petrol. Most important, perhaps, was the adoption of twin oil pumps, a system that delivered more oil to the cambox and reduced wear to cam and rocker pads. Externally, a new exhaust system broadened the engine's powerband. Burman, meanwhile, supplied a new gearbox that was both stronger and lighter than its predecessor.

The changes kept coming: a new cam profile, with uprated oil feeds to the camshaft, and a new piston, boosting compression to 9.4:1, headlined internal changes for the 1951 model. Most memorably, perhaps, AMC replaced the leaky, undersprung Candlestick rear suspension units with its leaky, underdamped Jampots.

There was no doubt, however, that the 7R was a winner.

Spring-heel Rex

Rex McCandless won the last prewar race in the British Isles, the 1940 Dublin 100, and then spent Hitler's war working in the Short Brothers aircraft factory in Belfast, a dozen miles from his native Hillsborough, in County Down. In the evenings he tinkered with his ideas on improving motorcycle chassis and rear suspension. Come the end of hostilities, McCandless, together with pal and collaborator Artie Bell, was ready to offer his ideas to the world.

McCandless' 'spring-heel' rear end – a swinging arm pivoting from the frame to mount the back wheel, with suspension struts between the swinging arm and the bolted-on rear subframe – represented a mighty improvement over the sprung hubs and plunger rear ends then in common use elsewhere.

18

Jack Williams of AMC tightly grips his pipe while Vic Willoughby, technical scribe of
***The Motor Cycle*, inspects the newcomer of the 1958 TT, the G50 Matchless.**
(Courtesy FoTTofinder Bikesport Photo Archives)

McCandless made the headlines with a successful rear-end conversion to Bill Nicholson's scrambles mounts as early as 1946 and he soon began a thriving business converting rigid-framed motorcycles at £25 a pop. Bell, meanwhile, had joined the Norton racing team alongside Geoff Duke; while McCandless added increasing numbers of scrambles and trials bikes to his list of successful conversions, Bell spread the word at Bracebridge Street.

Soon, McCandless was offered work on a freelance basis by Norton factory boss Bill Mansell. At first he worked on the 500T trials iron, but quickly attracted attention by making the blunt suggestion that he could design a far better frame for the Manx than the ageing unit then in use, and so revitalise the factory's faltering road racing programme. After their machines had taken a battering from AJS, Velocette and Gilera in the 1949 world championships, the good and the great at Bracebridge Street were ready to listen.

In just six months from autumn 1949, McCandless transformed the ailing Manx into a completely new proposition. Conceiving the chassis as a whole, he created a new duplex frame, cross-braced and gusseted at key points, which shifted more weight over the front wheel to sharpen the bike's steering. He added his own swinging arm rear end, and vertically mounted spring/damper units, with remote reservoirs to help keep the damping fluid free of air.

During testing at Montlhéry and in Britain, the McCandless-framed Manx drew praise from Norton team boss Joe Craig, while development rider Harold Daniell said the bike was "like riding a feather bed." The description stuck.

The new bike made its competition debut at Britain's first mainland postwar international at Blandford in April 1950, a venue borrowed for the weekend from the army. Duke had the only Featherbed Norton at the meeting, a 500, and won from an entry laden with talent, and which included an E90 AJS Porcupine. Just a week later, Johnny Lockett backed up Duke's victory by giving the 350cc version of the Featherbed a winning debut, in Ireland.

It was an encouraging start that gained real impetus at the Isle of Man a month later: Norton took all three podium places in both major events, Bell cleaning up in the 350cc race and Duke in the 500.

The Manx Norton was back in business. Duke would post another three grand prix wins during the 1950 season, but tyre delamination troubles forced him to wait until the following year to claim his first world championships, when he took the only 350/500cc title double of his career. Duke won the 350cc championship again in 1952, but the bigger class proved a tougher proposition. By now the Italians, led by Gilera, were beginning to find reliability and handling to match the raw power produced by their Remor-designed four-cylinder engines, and by late in the season were muscling aside the British singles and twins. Reg Armstrong took two GP wins for Norton in the premier class, at the TT and in Germany, while Umberto Masetti claimed a second 500cc world championship to add to the title he snatched from Duke by one point in 1950 – and Rex McCandless' brother, Cromie, won the Ulster Grand Prix … on a Gilera.

Momentum

Development engineer Jack Williams joined AMC from Vincent, following the death of Ike Hatch in October 1954, to find a racing department losing momentum. Its resources were being channelled into the E95 Porcupine and the three-valve (one inlet, two exhaust) variant of the 7R, designed by Hatch; and while the production 7R had received some attention (the 1953 model was fitted with a stiffer crankshaft assembly, slimmer crankcases, sturdier main bearings, and a new cylinder head with bigger-diameter valves and a better-flowing inlet tract), the G45 Matchless had been largely neglected, its sales falling as customer complaints mounted.

At its best the G45 offered a brisk turn of speed and good handling tempered by vibration, oil leaks and a narrow powerband. But there was worse; much worse.

"They were very quick in a straight line," a factory mechanic told writer Alan Cathcart many years later. "But you couldn't get them to stay together. The cam they used was much too vicious."

The writing, it seemed, was on the wall, and even after the official factory racing programme was shut down following the 1954 season, the G45 received little further development. Production finally stopped in 1957 after just four bikes of the year's planned run of 25 had been built. The 30M Manx Norton was, for the moment, the only game in town in the 500cc class – which might have been a problem, had not AMC acquired Norton Motors in 1952.

The engine of a '61 500 Manx in muscular profile. This is Adrian Sellars', which features include a twin-plug head and coil valve springs. Inside the gearbox housing is a PGT five-speed cluster. (Courtesy Adrian Sellars)

Meanwhile the 7R's status as AMC's quiet achiever gained further currency. While New Zealander Rod Coleman won the 1954 Junior TT on the 7R3, Manxman Derek Ennett claimed the Junior Manx Grand Prix for the company on a stock 7R, highlighting the bike's worth to privateers who wanted performance for their hard-earned racing budget.

When the factory bikes were wheeled quietly away following the closure of AMC's works racing teams, Williams was able to interest himself exclusively in the production bikes, turning his attention first to the 7R and for 1956 giving the bike its first full overhaul since its release eight years before.

Williams adopted the 75.5mm × 78mm engine dimensions of the factory 7R3, giving a freer-revving engine – though his later work would be more concerned with improving breathing than with more revs in an engine that already had as much inertial load as it was likely to cope with.

The major changes to the bottom end in the 1956 rebuild were lightened flywheels and a double-row timing-side main bearing, while top-end modifications included new piston rings, a revised inlet port angle, reworked exhaust valve guide and range of valve adjustment.

Changes to the chassis included new handlebars, footpegs and pedals and a narrower oil tank. The frame was strengthened, the Jampot rear units were at last discarded in favour of Girlings, and the brakes were modified to improve airflow.

Power output crept up. For 1957 the 7R was rated at 37.5bhp; a year later, with a new camshaft, another inlet port and a larger carb, the figure had risen to 39bhp with compression boosted to 10.25:1 and peak power being delivered between 7600 and 7800rpm. And the bike was still winning the Manx Grand Prix, with newcomer Alan Shepherd getting home first in 1958 with a new lap record at 90.58mph.

AMC was selling as many 7Rs as it could make (totalling some 800 bikes in 14 years' production). The AJS was easier to live with than the 40M Manx Norton through simpler maintenance; it was cleaner to run thanks to its enclosed valve gear, and was almost as fast and brisker in acceleration. The 7R had proven itself an inspired design that had improved with time; it was a pity it had no viable 500cc stablemate.

Short measures

The combination of Roadholder forks and Featherbed chassis had helped Joe Craig to maintain the Manx Norton's competitive edge at grand prix level for a little longer, but the writing was on the wall well before the closure of the factory team. By 1953 Moto Guzzi's lithe, lightweight singles were getting the better of Norton in the 350 class, particularly on fast tracks, while among the 500s Geoff Duke, now riding for Gilera, collected the Italian factory's third Senior world title and the Lancastrian's second, in his debut season on the Arcore multis.

Ray Amm, Norton's replacement for Duke, performed prodigies of excellence on the Manx, taking a TT double in 1953 and winning the 500cc event again the following year – keeping 'The Unapproachable Norton' in the public eye. These were the races that mattered to the generations of privateer entrants and riders who were Norton's principal customers, and who became the major beneficiaries of the advances made during the dying days of Norton's factory racing programme.

For the 1954 season the Manx got its first major overhaul since the arrival of the Featherbed frame, for private buyers, in 1951. Gone were the old long-stroke engines: the new dimensions for the 40M were 76 × 76.85mm, for 348cc; the 30M, 86 × 85.62mm, for 499cc. Both high-revving engines had new conrods, revised finning, a new cambox design and new valve springs. Principal change to the chassis was a works-type twin-leading-shoe front brake, adapted to fit the standard Manx conical hub. Both models cost £418 16s.

More innovations from the factory race shop came for 1956, including new cams and revised valve timing, a modified exhaust valve for more efficient cooling, a double-row ball timing-side main bearing and a new magneto. Compression ratios were up, to 9.72:1 for the smaller engine,

Spartan accommodation: the cockpit of a 350 Manx. This is the Ray Petty reverse-head special, built in 1963 for Derek Minter. Note 8500rpm redline. (Courtesy Adrian Sellars)

9.53:1 for the 500; the new motors weren't released until the 350 made 35bhp at 7200rpm, and the 500 47bhp at 6500rpm.

Also new for the 1956 season was a statement from Norton to the effect that individual customers were buying a motorcycle "equivalent to that used by the [John] Surtees, [John] Hartle, [Jack] Brett threesome at meetings where they had been factory entered."

In 1957, both models received a new-design conrod and crankpin, sodium-cooled valves and bigger-bore carburettors, while the 350 also got a new-profile inlet cam; in 1958, a new AMC four-speed gearbox was fitted, which might have been derived from that used on Norton street bikes, but boasted stronger materials and ball bearings for both mainshaft and layshaft.

By now Doug Hele, who would find fame as the architect of BSA-Triumph's 1970s racing programme, had joined the company to work alongside Polish engineer Leo Kuzmicki in refining the Manx engines. Meanwhile, a heightened appetite for revs and ever-increasing power output caused a spate of reliability problems. Cam-drive bevels were failing in increasing numbers, and Hele's solution was to fit a redesigned and much stronger bevel shaft he'd developed for Norton's experimental desmodromic engine. Solid nickel-alloy valves replaced the sodium-filled designs, increased in size for the 350. With the 30M engine's compression ratio boosted to a stellar 10.7:1, its power output likewise improved – to 50.5bhp. Finally, the clutch friction plates got inserts of a new material to improve heat dissipation.

In the first year of the 1960s, the Manx Norton was nearing the peak of its development. Now there came one or two modest changes to the cycle parts that included a new fibreglass seat pan, new handlebars, and new rubber mountings for the oil tank. Internally, Hele tackled increasing numbers of big-end failures by widening the big-end. Modified pistons increased the compression ratio of both engines to 11:1, while changes to gudgeon pins, piston rings and tappets all extended their service life. In an attempt to improve low-engine-speed acceleration, the pistons were modified again, this time to reduce weight, and the 350 received a modified inlet cam profile that opened the valve earlier. The Oldham couplings on the cam driveshaft by now had been replaced by splined bevels. There was more ignition advance, and both engines were given longer, larger-diameter inlet tracts to improve cylinder filling.

A shortened, two-ring piston, and hence a shorter barrel, headed the changes for '61. A revised Amal GP carburettor gave better starting, the oil tank was reshaped, and a larger-capacity oil pump fitted.

The final changes to the cycle parts of the Manx included a redesigned megaphone mounting bracket in an effort to stop fractures; a double-sided, seven-inch twin-leading shoe front brake that some found better than the old single-sided eight-incher, but which needed careful setting up just the same; and, as Dunlop ceased manufacture of its alloy rims, Borranis began to appear.

In January 1963 the last handful of Manx Nortons left Bracebridge Street as the race shop closed for good and Norton manufacture moved to London. Yet the end of factory production was merely the opening of a new chapter for the Manx. It had been the backbone of British racing for more than a decade and wasn't finished yet.

Red shift

When it came, the G50 Matchless stumbled into being as if an afterthought, yielded unmemorable performances for a season, then flourished briefly, declined, and was gone from the factory's books. After four years, factory production totalled 180 bikes (compared with four times as many AJS 7Rs between 1948 and 1962); but as with the Manx, its official end was also a new beginning. If the declining AMC had lost interest in its racers, others hadn't, and the G50 would become a doughty competitor during the final eight or so years of its competitive life.

The bike made its first headlines at the 1958 TT, where Australian Jack Ahearn rode the prototype. The bike was a lash-up, using a 7R chassis and an engine based on 7R crankcase halves that were built up with weld to take the larger cylinder and a 7R cylinder head, complete with 7R valves, machined to accommodate a larger bore. The engine shared the 78mm stroke of the AJS, but was bored to 90mm for a capacity of 496cc.

Variation on a theme: this is Ray Petty's reverse-head 350 Manx. Better breathing added significantly to performance, though the cylinder fins had to be trimmed to coax the engine up to working temperature. (Courtesy Adrian Sellars)

24

Claimed power output was 47bhp, but pundits thought the engine's stifled breathing meant this figure had more to do with hope than expectation. Ahearn duly completed the event, dogged by gearbox problems, to finish 29th at an average speed of 88.71mph, a poor showing compared even with the unloved G45.

The following year the G50 took its place in AMC's catalogue, now with larger valves, a 1½in Amal GP carburettor, and a compression ratio of 10.6:1. The newcomer was rated to develop an even 50bhp at 7200rpm (compared with 39bhp at 7600rpm for the 7R). It attracted few customers to begin with. Just four bikes were entered for the 1959 TT (run in memorably unpleasant weather), and although three of them finished in the top ten – Derek Powell leading the way in fourth place – the TT would prove the G50's high-water mark for 1959.

For 1960 still larger valves were fitted – the inlet measuring 1⅞in diameter – and power output rose to 51.5bhp at 7200rpm. Alan Shepherd, riding Geoff Monty's bikes in his low-key role as AMC development rider, gave the G50 its best grand prix finish of the season with third place in the Ulster Grand Prix.

The 1961 season marked a new production peak for AMC's thumpers, with a grand total of about a hundred G50s and 7Rs built. The following year, its last in production, the G50 was built to order, with yet larger valves and a claimed peak power output of 52bhp. Compression ratio was boosted to 11.6:1. A forged piston replaced the earlier cast unit, and the gudgeon pin was increased in diameter. Dry weight of the bikes as delivered was 284lb (129kg) for the 7R, 290lb (131.5kg) for the G50.

The 1962 engine included a forged light-alloy big-end cage running in the rod eye rather than on the crankpin, under-barrel shims for adjusting squish volume, and two-inch valves – and was never a match for its immediate predecessor, lacking torque at low engine speeds and proving prone to mechanical problems that tarnished the bike's reputation for reliability. Cracked pistons and broken crankpins (a 60% failure rate caused by poor hardening, according to some critics) saw the bike disappear from the AMC range on a low note.

In its final years the 7R underwent a series of detail improvements. Changes to carburation and the inlet port pump claimed power in excess of 40bhp for 1959, while the exhaust was tucked in further to increase cornering clearance. Fork trail was lengthened and damping altered to improve handling.

Cornering clearance was improved again for 1960 when Jack Williams altered the run of the nearside frame tube, and narrowed the swinging arm to tuck the exhaust in a little tighter. Further changes to the chassis came in 1961. Both the 7R and G50 received new fork springs and seals while the Girling rear units were given improved damping. Minor changes to the front brake on both bikes included a bigger air scoop. Finally, the gearbox was mounted in alloy plates to help counter the damaging effects of vibration, and given a 22-tooth output sprocket.

Then, in 1966, entered Colin Seeley: as AMC trimmed down its operations, the British sidecar champion secured the immediate future of all four of the bikes chronicled in this chapter, 30M and 40M Manx Nortons, 7R AJS and G50 Matchless, by buying tools, patterns, blueprints, and component parts, setting up production of engines, and then his own bikes, in his Belvedere, Kent factory.

What was old was new again.

You pays your money...

Factory development of the British single-cylinder racing motorcycle during the 1950s had been a story in several parts. During the early years of the decade, the stress-bearing elements of both the 7R and Manx Nortons were beefed up to exploit the more energy-rich fuels made available by oil companies released from the constraints of wartime production. Conrods, crankshaft assemblies, main and big-end bearings, clutches and gearboxes were strengthened as compression ratios rose and power outputs increased. At the same time crankcases and flywheels were lightened. Major developments in chassis design came through improved suspension, particularly at the rear end with the continued evolution of the swinging arm. Meanwhile each factory's teams experimented with engine dimensions, and increasing engine speeds. In the years that followed more work was done to maximise cylinder filling, generating as much energy as possible from each power stroke instead of boosting engine speeds further into the danger zone. Exhausts, cam profiles, valve trains, inlet tracts and carburettors were all modified to coax more charge into the combustion chamber and out again as efficiently as possible to dissipate heat and raise pressure on the piston crown at the right time and so increase power. Finally, progressive refinement of design and materials brought about further weight savings and increased cornering clearance to help the rider exploit extra grip offered by improving tyres, first from Avon and later Dunlop. Exhaust pipes were raised or tucked in, frame rails squeezed together. The law of diminishing returns had been invoked, and every fraction counted.

Now the story of the singles was almost complete, at least so far as the parent factories were concerned. *Motor Cycling* announced the coming of the 1960 Manx Nortons, AJS 7R and Matchless G50 in its 11 February issue, duly recording the improvements to all four bikes for the coming season. The Manx Nortons were each priced at £496 19s 6d including purchase tax, while the 7R was pegged at £422 3s 9d and the G50 at £434 5s. At the time, the average British annual income was £950, a modest house cost £2500 and £500 would bag one of the newly released 850cc Austin/Morris Minis.

The investment bought a bike capable of reliable race-winning performance at sub-GP level. Each of the 500s would deliver 50-52bhp, a 7R some 40bhp and a 350 Manx about the same – enough to give the 500s a maximum road speed of 130-135mph and the 350s 115-120. All those figures could be improved for the rider fortunate enough and/or rich enough to gain their mounts the sympathetic attention of engineers and tuners such as Steve Lancefield, Tom Arter, Ray Petty or Geoff Monty.

Unlike modern owners' manuals, which contain little of use beyond the supplying dealer's details, the paperwork accompanying the bikes was of real practical value. The manual for the 1960 7R AJS contains, in addition to detailed specifications and a dyno chart for the engine of the bike it accompanied, notes on ignition and valve timing, camchain adjustment, gearing, and optimum tyre pressures.

The mainstream press was likewise helpful. In April 1957 *Motor Cycling* ran a two-part feature on servicing the 7R, penned by Bruce Main-Smith "with the assistance of Jack Williams and racing mechanics of Associated Motor Cycles Ltd."

With or without the help of the press, most riders prepared their own bikes. Men in cold sheds and workshops up and down the land spent damp winter evenings putting dreams of fame and fortune on hold while carefully organising circlips and collets, gaskets and seals during the first engine overhaul of the new season.

The overhaul would typically include a new piston, big-end bearing and perhaps main bearings; clutch plates as required. Valve guides, and the exhaust valve in particular, would be scrutinised and springs replaced at the first hint of power loss. Primary and final drive chains would probably be replaced; perhaps, too, the 7R and G50's cam chain. Steering head bearings and the swinging arm would be checked and adjusted or replaced as required. And then the routine check, front to back, of every nut and bolt likely to be worked loose by the hostile vibrations of a large-capacity, high-performances single-cylinder engine run at near constant redline rpm: one Australian rider explained the demanding nature of the job by pointing out that two bottles of beer were needed to complete it.

While the 7R AJS quickly gained

"I'm just a holiday racer." Yorkshireman Rob Fitton was a local government engineer, and typical of the self-reliant breed who rode Manx Nortons throughout the 1950s and '60s. (Courtesy Paul McElvie)

widespread acceptance among legions of would-be champions almost from its 1948 release, the G50 didn't really get going until 1961, quite late in its production life, and it would be longer still before it became a leading force in 500cc single-cylinder racing.

The Manx Norton's position at the top of the pecking order during the '50s and early 1960s was assured by the advent of the Featherbed frame in 1951 and the short-stroke engines three years later. Derek Minter set the first single-cylinder 100mph lap of the Isle of Man in 1960 on a Steve Lancefield Norton, and he would remain loyal to the marque – with two extended interruptions, for Gilera in 1963 and Colin Seeley in 1966 – until the end of his career in 1967. Bob McIntyre (Mac) and Mike Hailwood both fielded Nortons for years, but later tended towards a 7R and 30M Manx combination. Mac, searching for an edge in what would be his final season, rode a lightweight Matchless G50-powered special to a number of wins, but wheeled out a 500 Manx for his last race on 6 August 1962. John Cooper too was a Norton man, ploughing his own largely self-reliant furrow until discovering Colin Seeley's AMC-powered bikes after winning the 350 and 500cc British championships on his Nortons in 1966.

For the crimson team, Alan Shepherd finished second to Hailwood's MV Agusta on a G50 in the 1962 (for Geoff Monty) and 1963 (for Tom Kirby) world championships, while Mike Duff started life on a Manx Norton, but found the G50 lighter and easier to ride, and took particular delight in his '61 7R. He would later strike up a solid and rewarding relationship with Tom Arter, and together they would, among other things, try to revive one of the more exotic beasts from AMC's menagerie, the AJS Porcupine.

Most riders who sampled all the leading contenders found the Nortons a little faster and to be better handling, particularly in quicker going when the Manx would feel planted whereas the opposition was perhaps a little skittish. The AMC bikes tended to be quicker off the mark, were lighter and handled tolerably well, give or take the occasional headshake. They were also easier to maintain and to tune, and generally simpler to get along with. They were cleaner too: the Nortons' open valve gear tended to coat bike and rider with a fine oil mist that could collect in the rear wheel rim, sometimes with alarming results. Of course, dedicated Norton riders found ways of solving the problem, using coil springs or judiciously placed foam rubber.

Regardless of the emblems on the tanks of their bikes, the men in the sheds worked on until the first weekend of the season, usually in March, and then began their year's competition with a chilly early morning drive to race around a private park or airfield, usually in the midlands, sometimes along the A20 at Brands Hatch. The 1960 season, which began the final decade of the British single's supremacy, opened a little later than most, in April with the British Motorcycle Racing Club's Hutchinson 100 meeting. The Hutch had found somewhere to call home again – although getting there had been a trial.

Chapter 3

Blank Canvas

Motor Cycling – 'the Green 'un' – broke the story in its issue of 3 January 1946: Brooklands, it appeared, would be "no longer available as a test or sporting venue" following a vote by its shareholders approving the sale of the circuit to engineering and armaments manufacturer Vickers Armstrong for £330,000. Elsewhere in the same issue was news that Donington Park was to be "retained by the War Department for the foreseeable future," the War House no doubt wanting the best possible return on the £264,000 it had spent upgrading the facility during hostilities. Which facility now, at the beginning of the first calendar year of peace, acted as a repository – dump, possibly – for some 80,000 assorted war surplus vehicles. The news was as big as it was unpalatable, a double announcement that had the immediate effect of reducing motorcycle racing to near-homelessness.

True, there remained the three-quarters of a mile of dusty concrete at Cadwell Park. This had been constructed, opened and relaid before the war for the sole purpose of attracting motorcycle competition and had not been requisitioned by anybody during hostilities. Louth & District MCC, driven by the Wilkinson family, had already planned a meeting there for Easter 1946, which was oversubscribed by February and had to be extended to two days to meet the needs of a racing-hungry nation. Understandably, the press was anxious. Responsibility for the country's racing future clearly could not be met exclusively by the enthusiasm of Chas Wilkinson and his tribe. Happily, others had suggestions to put forward. As early as 1942, grand prix veteran Ted Mellors had floated the idea of turning over disused bomber airfields to the pursuit of racing, come the cessation of hostilities, a suggestion that quickly gained the support of the press. Meanwhile, Graham Walker of *Motor Cycling*, thinking along different lines, took a bold and lengthy stride further by advocating the establishment of a 'National Road Racing Park.' His opposite number at *The Motor Cycle*, Arthur Bourne, agreed that action was needed, and foretold a grim future for the British racing community unless vigorous measures were taken to put the nation on a par with Germany and France, both of which appeared to have escaped the recent holocaust with at least some of their racing facilities intact.

Whitehall responded in measured tones. "The Government," it said, "is shortly to make an announcement on how it is to deal with airfield runways that are no longer needed." There was more: in one statement, which suggested the presence of sympathetic views within the corridors of power and bemusement at the laggardly performance of the sporting fraternity, John Charles Wilmot, aka Lord Wilmot of Selmeston and Minister of Supply in the first Attlee administration, lifted his head above the parapet to observe that "the motor industry has not approached my department for assistance in obtaining racing tracks."

Routes out of the wilderness were being found, with or without the help of the Ministry of Supply. On the Isle of Man, the Mountain Course was being resurfaced in anticipation of the 1946 Manx GP, while Cambridge University Aero Club tweaked the tail of the Air Ministry by proposing race meetings at Gransden Lodge and North Weald aerodromes – with proceeds to go to RAF charities. In July the North Wilts Motor Cycle & Light Car Club clearly had similar ideas, making plans for a meeting at Cerney Aerodrome, with its 16-yard-wide runways.

The Motor Cycle, commenting on the emerging phenomenon of 'Runway Racing,' confessed its reservations about the bumpy nature of runways and perimeter tracks alike, and about the width of runways (some of them much wider than Cerney's), proposing that circuits "be tailored for racing, lest vastness dwarfs the speed. The time for exploratory action," it noted, "is now."

Yet neither the Air Ministry nor the RAF was yet wedded to the idea of surrendering their disused facilities to racing: as June became July, two planned meetings at unspecified aerodromes were summarily cancelled by their base commanders. Fortunately parks, private and otherwise, were also providing fruitful exploration. In August 1946 the rumour mill had it that Scarborough & District MCC was working with Yorkshire Centre ACU and Scarborough Borough Council to establish a 2.41-mile circuit around a local landmark, Oliver's Mount. The word became the deed, and the first meeting was held just weeks later, in September, with Dennis Parkinson and Syd Barnett (Nortons both) posting wins.

From further south came news that the Brands Racing Committee, which was formed from an alliance of local clubs to plot the future of a one-mile kidney-shaped grass track at Brands Hatch in Kent, was proposing to give its circuit a tarred surface. Meanwhile the Leatherhead club, scaling the heights of ambition, noted the successful running of bicycle races at Battersea Park, in the heart of London, and wanted a slice of the action for motorcycles. The local council, after a little perfunctory chin-stroking, said no; but racing at Battersea had seemed at least as likely as a return to Donington Park, despite persistent whispers of the army pulling out and the number of vehicles in its resident motor pool declining.

The Air Ministry, now admitting to having "no firm policy" concerning racing on its airfields, had at least invited the RAC to screen all such applications. Among the first of these came from the Blackburn club, staking a claim to Brough aerodrome in East Yorkshire, while in Hampshire it seemed the Ringwood club had found an airfield not far from Andover that had been home to RAF Whitleys and Albemarles before being turned over to the P-47 Thunderbolts of the USAF's 366th Fighter Group in the months before D-Day; a place called Thruxton.

Not far away, in Dorset, Blackmore Vale MCC advanced plans for a new circuit "inspired by Scarborough" near Bryanston School that offered one-, two- and three-mile variants and had an enthusiastic *Motor Cycling* talking about a Dorset Grand Prix. The plan collapsed at the eleventh hour but then the club was offered a nearby alternative by Viscount Portman and a Captain H G F Brown. This substitute 1½-mile circuit ran near Bryanston House, the viscount's 19th century family seat, through its home farm and Bryanston village. Some were sceptical, particularly those who didn't want to risk overturning their precious racing machinery on the half-mile of gravel road integral to the planned circuit, but racing went ahead all the same, disrupting the serene charm of its rural setting deep in Hardy country, as Tommy Wood (348 Velocette) and Johnny Lockett (490 Norton) set about earning their corn.

Airfield circuits continued to come and go. There were meetings at Stapleford Tawney (proceeds to the Army Benevolent Fund), Ansty and then Dunholme Lodge in Lincolnshire, where the Hutchinson 100 re-entered the calendar and record books in October 1947 after an eight-year break. The Hutch dated back to Brooklands in 1925 and was the signature event of the world's oldest motorcycle racing club, the British Motor Cycle Racing Club – 'Bemsee.' This was big news. The future of the club had been in jeopardy from the moment Brooklands, its historic home, had been sold, and at the beginning of 1947 it seemed likely to go under. But the reappearance of the meeting and subsequent revitalisation of the club helped to give an air of stability to a hitherto largely nomadic racing community. The first post-war TT was run in June 1947, the Hutch in October; and if it weren't for the coming withdrawal of the petrol ration, Britain's long-standing love affair with the motorcycle might even have recovered a semblance of normality.

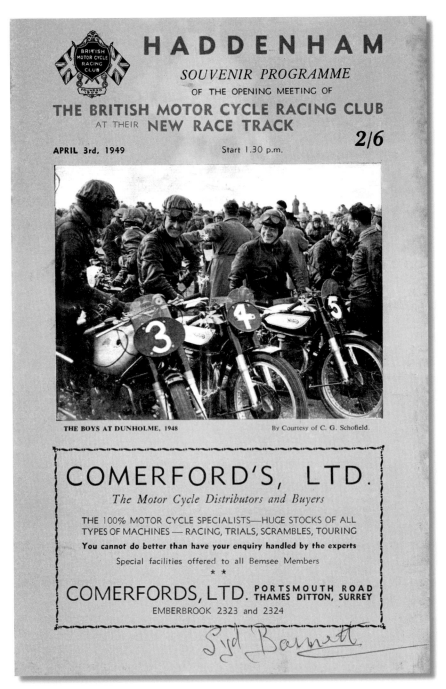

Open for business: programme of the first meeting at Haddenham on 3 April 1949, complete with Syd Barnett's autograph. George Brown (499 Vincent) won the big race of the day. (Courtesy haddenhamairfieldhistory.co.uk)

On the road

A petition bearing a million signatures didn't help, and neither did lobbying from the AA and RAC. The basic fuel ration would be stopped from the end of November 1947, and thereafter no private vehicle would be allowed on the road "except for special purposes in accordance with the provisions of the Control of Motor Fuel Order, 1947." Fortunately, and with superb timing, the government over the Christmas holidays decided to make available supplies of fuel for 'reliability trials.' Racing could continue, though just how spectators might travel to see it – and where they might go – remained ticklish issues.

The problem of finding venues persisted despite a brisk trade in promising starts. Regular meetings at Cadwell Park and Scarborough were all very fine, but did little for racing in the southern half of the country. Yet if the RAF seemed periodically miserly in granting access to its disused stations, the army would from time to time come to the rescue. Races were held at a camp near Warminster in Wiltshire and, from halfway through the 1948 season, over a fast three-mile track (officially pegged at 3 miles, 247 yards, 6¾ inches) round a camp occupied variously by the RASC and REME at a place called Blandford in Dorset. Bob Foster was the first master of the camp track's challenging array of fast curves, winning both 350 and 500cc events and posting a lap record at 85mph.

The season ended with the Hutchinson 100 returning to Dunholme, but the year closed with reports of a new and important venue being made available by the RAF at an airfield in Northamptonshire called Silverstone. The RAF handed responsibility for the track to the RAC, which formulated an access and usage policy for the new circuit and then refused to grant further access to Dunholme, rendering the BMCRC homeless again. With Silverstone open for business, the RAC explained crisply, "no other aerodrome under the control of the Air Ministry is to be used."

Aerodromes not under the control of the Air Ministry were another matter, however, and Bemsee gathered up its flags and moved south, this time setting up shop at Haddenham airfield, not far from Thame in Buckinghamshire, which had been bought after the war by a private hire company. The track, 2.2 miles of largely unrelieved rectangle, opened at the beginning of April 1949 with George Brown (499 Vincent) winning the big race and Geoff Duke (Norton) claiming 350 honours from Les Graham (AJS). But just as the club had found a home – "after wandering like bombed-out evacuees," according to *Motor Cycling*, it moved again, and Haddenham's moment of glory proved brief indeed. BMCRC was given the job of organising motorcycle race meetings at Silverstone, beginning with the 1949 Hutchinson 100 that October, and the club had no choice but to abandon the Thame venue to its fate as a commercial airfield and future gliding centre.

Meanwhile, Blandford seemed to go from strength to strength, holding the first post-war international meetings on the mainland and attracting hefty crowds, in early 1949, to see factory AJS rider Les Graham do the double, winning the 350 race from Geoff Duke (Norton) and the 500cc event from Bob Foster (Triumph).

During the 1949-50 close season, Brands Racing Committee finally got its one-mile grass-tracking circuit transformed into a road-racing track, with the first meeting pegged for April 1950. BMCRC, meanwhile, announced its second major meeting for the calendar – Silverstone Saturday, reviving and adapting the pre-war Donington fixture. Fine weather and a stellar entry drew a crowd of 45,000 to see Duke take a 350/1000cc double for Norton, and Graham claim the remaining 350cc event for AJS.

Duke backed up a fortnight later to win the 500cc event at the Blandford spring international – giving both the Featherbed Norton and one-piece leathers their debut – but the day lost its lustre with the deaths of two riders, beginning an unhappy catalogue of safety problems that would cloud and disrupt the 13-year history of the circuit. "I don't think there was much feeling shown," the coroner observed frostily of this grim episode. "One would almost have thought that when a poor man had been done to death, racing would have been stopped. But not a bit of it, it still goes on. People must be amused."

Racing was suspended at Blandford after the August Bank Holiday meeting ('Blandford Farewell'), when 30,000 came to see Duke continue his winning ways in the 500cc class, with Dickie Dale turning the tables to claim the 350cc race for AJS. Southampton & District MCC now thoughtfully provided an alternative venue for the south-west, with the first of several Thruxton iterations, this one a 1.89-mile journey along part of its perimeter track, and over three of its mighty 52-yard-wide runways.

More familiar names began to appear: the Aberaman club brokered a deal to run the races around the improbably short (three-quarters of a mile) and narrow drive at the picturesque Aberdare Park, in South Wales, staging its first meeting in September 1950, two more in 1951 – attracting more than 100 entries for each – and claiming dates each Whitsun and August Bank Holiday Monday thereafter until the middle 1960s.

An aerodrome at Goodwood, in Sussex, ran a motorcycle meeting in April 1951 but didn't repeat the experiment. Meanwhile, the Bristol MC & LCC discovered an airfield of unusual charm at Castle Combe, in Wiltshire. The 1.84-mile diamond-shaped perimeter track, which had been in business since 1950 for the car crowd, ran its first bike meeting in July 1951 and remained on the calendar, in spite of running conflicts with organising clubs, local residents and developers.

Two steps forward ...

Redundant airfields continued to be tried, tested, and in most cases forgotten, throughout the early 1950s: as Ansty closed, meetings were held at Boreham, Ibsley and Snetterton, and at Altcar Rifle Range. Boreham, in Essex, looked especially promising. Using the three-mile perimeter road, the track traced an irregular hexagon that combined the sweeping, broad-radius bends of Silverstone with the straights of Snetterton, and offered

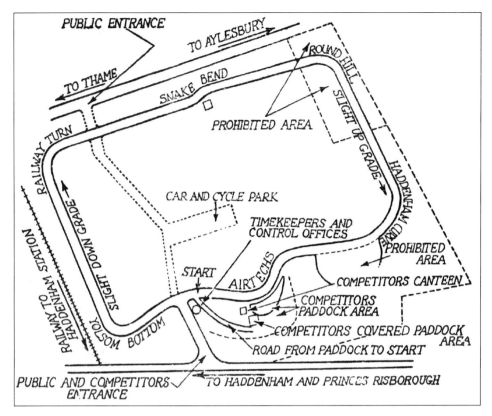

The war-surplus British airfield: fast curves, faster straights. This is the 2.2 miles of the
former RAF Thame – Haddenham – used by the BMCRC during 1949.
(Courtesy haddenhamairfieldhistory.co.uk)

good, fast racing. Meetings held there attracted attention, crowds, and sponsorship from
the *Daily Mail*. True, the surface posed problems, with the number of cracks and ripples –
even local subsidence – warranting a complete resurface, which took place in time for the
big events of the 1953 season. The operator, Motor Racing Co Ltd, clearly had ambitions:
grandstands went up, as did a scoreboard and a better PA system. The company's plan "to
make Boreham one of Europe's premier race circuits" was obviously no hollow boast. But
there was trouble in paradise. A spate of wet meetings added weight to persistent rumours
that the circuit was losing money, and then came the announcement that Ford had bought
the place for use as a testing facility, and that, sadly, was that.

No such problems befell Brands Hatch, which continued to gain momentum: the track
was resurfaced in the 1951-52 close season, and in a bid to reduce the number of crashes
on the uphill route through the challenging Paddock Hill Bend, the direction of racing was
switched from anticlockwise to clockwise – and that's how it stayed.

Even better for residents of London and the south-east, racing returned to the pre-war venue at Crystal Palace in June 1953. The park and its circuit were reclaimed from its wartime occupants (who were, among other things, engaged in the hush-hush manufacture of radar equipment) by the London County Council, and the track trimmed to a 1.39-mile version of the slow and snaking pre-war two-miler. Now clear of "the debris of its wartime function" – and, no doubt, of the damage from the occasional stick of bombs bestowed upon it by the Luftwaffe – AJS- and Norton-mounted Bob Keeler added his name to the record books by taking a 350/1000cc double at the first post-war meeting, setting a lap record for the new circuit at 71.49mph.

Later plans to double the length of the track were quietly dropped.

Further north, in the grounds of Alton Towers, the former seat of the Earl of Shrewsbury now being slowly developed by a group of local businessmen into a tourist attraction, racing was staged over a 0.85-mile triangle of access roads during which Peter Ferbrache began to establish his Ariel hegemony. There was news too from the east. After serving a two-year apprenticeship as a car track, Snetterton, in the familiar 2.71-mile form that would remain in use for decades, opened for motorcycles with two meetings in 1953: in May, when 19-year-old John Surtees claimed both 350 and 500cc races for Norton; and in September, when Bob McIntyre launched one of his many successful southern incursions to relieve Surtees of the 350cc trophy, and then miss the 500cc final with engine problems after winning his heat. Further north, Cadwell Park was being extended by half a mile to 1.25 miles with a loop extending from the end of the start/finish straight left over Coppice Hill, through sharp right-handers at Coppice and Mansfield and so back to the foot of the Mountain.

North of the border, Scottish fans claimed their own airfield circuit at Charterhall, with a 1.3-mile track that incorporated the main runway in a rough triangle. Bob McIntyre staked a strong claim to supremacy here just as he had done at the 1.4-mile woodland circuit of Beveridge Park, Kirkcaldy, which had been open for racing since 1948.

Park life

Now the north-west of England found its own parkland circuit, with a track "in the grounds of Sir Philip Grey-Edgerton's private estate" at an idyllic Cheshire spot named Oulton Park. The 1.5-mile track, then roughly rectangular, was "designed specifically for road racing," reported *The Motor Cycle*, "and features three sweeping right-handers, a right-hand hairpin and a shallow S-bend" – the "hairpin" being an ambitious description of Lodge Corner. The first meeting, shared with cars, came in October 1953 with Dennis Parkinson (Norton), winning the big race of the day and posting the first lap record at 74.39mph.

The track was an immediate success, with most riders professing a liking for its fast curves and undulations that continues to today's generation. "The green folds of the park environment were a delightful change from the grey bleakness of disused airfields," ran one press comment, and *The Motor Cycle* said the new venue was "regarded by some enthusiasts as a possible successor to pre-war Donington." Work on the first of two extensions began straight away, with the first meeting on an interim 2.23-mile circuit, extended as far as the present Island Bend, in May 1954, with John Surtees claiming a 350/ Unlimited double for Norton. The full-strength, 2.76-mile circuit was in business by May the following year, when Surtees returned, though now on factory Nortons, to win every race he entered.

There were improvements at Scarborough, with Quarry Bend resculpted, fencing added on Memorial Road and hard standing for the competitors' enclosure. Brands Hatch, meanwhile, was being realigned and extended from an even mile to 1.24, the track now running further up the opposite side of the valley from Paddock Hill Bend to take in the current Druids hairpin.

And by way of local competition for Oulton Park, 150 men were working each day and 40 through the night to finish a new three-mile circuit at Aintree, near Liverpool, the home of the Grand National steeplechase. The first meeting was held there in September 1954, and despite a glittering entry, spectators proved thin on the ground to see John Surtees' Norton split the factory Gileras of Geoff Duke and Reg Armstrong in the 500cc race, and Bob McIntyre take the 350 laurels from AJS team-mate Rod Coleman. A combination of poor attendance and persistent bad weather on race days would hasten Aintree's end as a circuit of international standing.

Thruxton Mark 2 came into being in 1954. It was 2.75 miles long, taking in the western half of the perimeter track at the expense of the east-west runway that had started to show signs of impassable deterioration. Geoff Monty (GMS) led the celebrations in the 350 class, with Derek Powell's Norton running home first among the 500s.

Donington continued to make headlines, even when any immediate prospect of its further use was the stuff of fantasy. Late in 1955, *The Motor Cycle* said it expected the circuit to be "freed of its military installations by the end of 1956," and that "plans for its revival were going ahead." Alas, the words were 20 years and one visionary building magnate short of any real action.

More useful at the time were stories of a new circuit opening for business 20 miles to the south of Donington, in the grounds of the long-demolished Mallory Park House. Clive Wormleighton had bought the Leicestershire estate in 1955 and laid plans to tarmac its one-mile grass track circuit, which had been in use throughout the early 1950s, adding a loop for a hairpin – Shaw's – and taking the total circuit length to 1.35 miles. Mallory Park was opened in April 1956, with the first bike meeting in May. Bernard Codd (Norton) won the 350 race, with Terry Shepherd (Norton) claiming the 500cc event in front of an encouraging tally of 20,000 spectators. Repeated hefty attendances would lend credence to Mallory's claim of being "the finest viewing circuit."

In its issue of 19 December 1957, *The Motor Cycle* published the ACU's competition calendar for the season ahead. It included dates for 32 national and home international road race meetings at 13 major circuits. Blandford was still among them, despite its mounting tally of fatalities (two car drivers had been killed at separate meetings) and injuries; otherwise the circuit list looks, give or take a couple of names, much as it might in the second decade of the 21st century, given a similarly busy calendar. Airfield circuits would continue to appear in the years ahead, running for a season or two like pop-up shops in the high street, then disappearing just as quickly: Biggin Hill, former home of 610 and 92 Spitfire squadrons during the Battle of Britain, flourished briefly in 1959; Ouston and Catterick – army camp and aerodrome – Wroughton, Staverton, Little Rissington in the 1960s and '70s, Gaydon and a dozen more. Croft, a former bomber station in the north-east not far from Darlington, was unusually busy, opening for racing as early as 1949 to serve as a club circuit for a year or two, then closing when the RAF decided further use might be made of the base, opening once more for racing as Croft Autodrome in the 1960s – and this time acquiring national importance.

The exceptions proved the rule: the terrain for national and international-level motorcycle racing in Britain for the 1960s and beyond was growing more certain. There were still changes to come, though fewer than before, and the next of these was the advent of Thruxton Mk 3, forced into being by the increasingly dilapidated state of the airfield's roads and runways. The new track, which eliminated now crumbling elements of the western perimeter road and one of the runways for a rather shorter new lap distance of 2.275 miles, was used by the Southampton club from 1958, the highlight of its first season being the August gathering for the British championships when Derek Minter, in indomitable form, bagged four from four, which included the 350 and 500cc events for the national titles.

As the 1950s drew to a close there came one last major news item: that Brands Hatch was soon to undergo a second extension, this time out into the country from Kidney Bend and back to Clearways, taking the anticipated track length to more than double its 1954 lap of 1.24 miles. Work started in January 1960, and the first meeting for motorcycles was held on a soggy weekend in July, just as Cadwell Park management revealed plans to extend its circuit by a mile into a field west of Mansfield Corner.

The stage was set, and the last decade of the single-cylinder catalogue racer's supremacy in British domestic competition would begin on a dull, blustery day at the former airfield near Silverstone, Northamptonshire. It had opened in 1943 to house an RAF training unit for bomber pilots, but on 8 April 1960 was occupied by the British Motor Cycle Racing Club for the running of the 28th Hutchinson 100.

Chapter 4

1960: Mercury

"I'm sure I could have done it"

By the summer of 1957 Bob McIntyre was reaching his peak. He had taken Gilera's dustbin-faired fire engines to unqualified success in the Golden Jubilee TT, where his two wins, impressive enough in the Junior event, and downright magisterial in the marathon eight-lap Senior, were surely just the first step on the road to the world championships that were his due. But a damaging fall at the Dutch TT delayed the apparently inevitable, and then, at the end of the season, the Gileras disappeared, wheeled away into a quiet corner of the Arcore factory. There they stayed until six years later, when it fell to others to continue the struggle.

Still under contract to Gilera but left to his own devices, Mac renewed his relationship with Glasgow tuner Joe Potts. At first there was talk of reviving the AJS Porcupine Mac had last ridden in 1954 as a member of the Woolwich factory's unhappy team, but the first practical result of their collaboration was a pair of short-stroke Manx Nortons in lightweight frames – the famous 'Razorblades.' These proved fast but troublesome, taking Mac to lap records in the early months of the 1958 season, but keeping him out of the results with ailments ranging from uncooperative suspension to a dropped valve, and even a broken clutch cable.

Come the TT, Mac was back on Nortons with Featherbed frames, but the change of hardware did little to improve his fortunes. He was fast enough in both 350cc and 500cc races to harass the all-conquering MV Agustas ridden by John Surtees and new signing John Hartle, but a lap at 99.89mph in the Senior race, the fastest yet by a single-cylinder

BOB McINTYRE   "MOTOR CYCLING"

Determination in every line: Bob McIntyre was a life member of Glasgow's Mercury MCC – the club's emblem on his helmet was as familiar as the famous McIntyre jutting jaw. (Courtesy Elwyn Roberts Collection)

bike, was as good as it got. In the Junior, Mac's engine tightened and in the Senior, perhaps in response to that lap, his Norton stripped a bevel gear in its cam drive.

His luck had to change. Back in the Isle of Man a month later for the Southern 100, Mac and Terry Shepherd went toe to toe and settled the 350 and 500cc events by inches, McIntyre taking the flag in the 350 race, Shepherd in the 500. More wins came at Charterhall, then at Oulton Park, where Mac claimed the silverware not only in the 350 and 500 races, but in the Les Graham Memorial Trophy too. This from an entry which included six-time world champion Geoff Duke, Bob Anderson and Australian hard man Bob Brown – though not Derek Minter, who was at Thruxton claiming the 350 and 500cc British Championships.

At the Ulster Grand Prix, Mac finished what he started at the TT, splitting the MV Agustas in the 500 race and leaving Hartle behind by almost a minute as he pursued the fading howl of Surtees' MV through the rolling farmland of County Antrim.

If his Dundrod performance was an impressive candidate for the ride of the season, more were to follow. At Silverstone for the Hutchinson 100 meeting he used his new 7R AJS to impressive effect in the 350 race to see off Derek Minter. He repeated the prescription in the 500cc event, this time winning by a bike's length after he and Minter had staged the kind of race that makes reputations and gives spectators something to talk about on winter's nights in licensed premises.

The season ended with Mac chasing Surtees' MV home again, this time at Oulton Park. McIntyre liked the Cheshire circuit in the way he liked Dundrod, which the newly crowned double world champion came to understand as he edged home a bare second ahead of the Scot's Norton.

Mac began 1959, the third year of his Gilera contract, as he'd started the second: hoping in vain for a summons to Italy for tests while helping the Potts equipe with its preparations for a packed domestic season – which got going on a wet March Sunday at Mallory Park. For reasons that would soon become clear, Mac was back on a Norton in the 350cc class, and did well enough, finishing sixth in a race won by a kid named Hailwood, from Oxford. But the 500 race belonged to the Scot. Starting from the back of the grid, he took half a dozen laps to get moving, but then proved unstoppable, passing Hailwood, Bob Anderson, Bob Brown and, with two laps to go, his own Potts team-mate, Alistair King, to take the flag.

Yet by Easter, the gremlins that stalked him throughout 1958 seemed to be back. Mac beat Derek Minter in his own back yard at Brands Hatch, but then retired from both feature races at Oulton Park: in the 350 race with lubrication difficulties, in the bigger class with a seized motor after scything through the pack to lead at the end of the opening lap.

Special brew

At Silverstone a fortnight later, Mac was back on his 7R AJS, which bore the latest in a series of modifications that included a narrower frame for increased cornering clearance, Norton forks, and work on the steering head that altered the rake and trail in a bid to cure the occasional headshake. Mac took the evolving bike into second spot behind John Surtees' MV in the 350 race and held it until his engine went flat on the final lap, letting Bob Anderson and Alistair King through to complete the podium.

In the 500 event, Surtees made a rare mistake and slid from his MV at Club Corner, throwing the race open to the pack, led by McIntyre, King, Anderson and Hailwood, all Norton-mounted. All four took a hand at the lead, Mac leading on seven laps and King four. With three laps remaining it was Anderson's turn and he edged away, towing Mac along but fending off the Scot's last-lap lunge to claim a memorable win. At least Mac got the lap record, setting a new outright mark at 98.26mph.

At Mallory Park the following day Mac gave his tweaked 7R its maiden win from King and Anderson before the Potts team-mates headed back north, first to Beveridge Park and Charterhall, then to the North West 200 (Mac won the 500cc class, King the 350), and Oulton Park, where King won the Les Graham Memorial Trophy and Mac the 500cc race. The Potts men then launched a raid south to Blandford, the fast but narrow three-mile ribbon of tarmac around the perimeter of the Dorset army base. Here Derek Minter bolstered southern pride by winning the 500cc race from Mac, while King took 350cc laurels and Mac claimed his second runner-up spot of the day.

The 1959 TT would become memorable for its foul weather, but it began brightly enough and Mac opened his account by winning the short-lived Formula 1 TT on a stock Manx Norton. For the Junior race he practised on both a 350 Manx and his 7R, deciding on the AJS as the better all-round bike. It seemed the right choice. After three laps Mac was running second to the Surtees MV, but then vibration struck and he retired a lap later with a broken fairing mount. In the Senior race Alistair King claimed runner-up spot behind Surtees, after Mac spent half a lap in the pits fixing a slipping clutch.

Mac followed his TT campaign with a double win at Mallory Park and backed that up with an emphatic display in the 350cc class at the Southern 100. He was on track to complete the double there too, until his 500cc Manx was halted by a broken valve spring. Bill Smith won, claiming an early victory for the new G50 Matchless; the big Manx Norton's doughtiest challenger had arrived. Mac now headed for home to undertake his traditional pre-Ulster GP rebuilds, finding new big-end bearings and pistons for his mounts. Again he missed the British championship meeting, now switched to Oulton Park, where Mike Hailwood claimed the 500cc title while Derek Minter fought the effects of concussion from a fall in the 250cc race.

A handful of major meetings remained before the end of the season. At the Ulster GP, Mac, back on his favourite circuit, harried John Surtees in both Junior and Senior events. He was stopped in the Junior when this time his 7R broke a valve spring, but chased the World Champion all the way in the Senior race. Double wins followed at Silverstone for the Hutchinson 100 and at Oulton Park, each time showing Mike Hailwood, now 19 and learning fast, the way home.

A fall at Scarborough ended a run of seven straight wins but Mac was back on top with a double win at Aintree and three more the following weekend at Mallory Park for the Race of the Year. Added to the calendar in 1958, the £300 first prize – the largest sum ever offered for a single race in the UK – immediately made it the Leicestershire circuit's premier two-wheeler event.

From the flag Mike Hailwood took the lead, making an early break from Bob Anderson and Bob Brown, all three Norton-mounted. Anderson set about closing on Hailwood, while Mac, working his way up from sixth, laid siege to Brown and got past him on the fifth lap, just as Anderson passed Hailwood for the lead. Anderson's advantage was short-lived. Three laps later Mac eased underneath him at the hairpin, gunned the Manx on the exit and put his head down. The race was his. Mac added the Race of the Year cheque to his winnings from the 350 and 500cc finals earlier in the day.

Discomfort from his Scarborough fall prevented Mac from playing a starring role in the final meeting of the year, at Brands Hatch, but it was a minor blemish on what had been by any measure a successful season.

Mac entered a new decade and his 32nd year at the top of his form. The 1950s might not have brought him the international success his talent merited, but he had placed himself among the dominant forces of a smaller, busier empire. He was pre-eminent on street tracks in Britain and Ireland, and a regular winner on short circuits, particularly in the north but making successful raids into the south to mix it with Derek Minter and Bob Anderson.

Yet things were changing. John Surtees and Anderson would shortly be gone, lured into the bigger world of car racing as younger, more precocious talents matured to take their place. Mike Hailwood had already made an impression, and would soon develop his transcendent ability to the full; a newcomer from Cumberland named Alan Shepherd would set himself to perform the impossible and very nearly succeed; a Rhodesian, Gary Hocking, would burn brilliantly but briefly, and two lads from London's satellite towns, one from Luton, the other from Maidstone, would take the first steps on a shared journey that would end in a unique combination of triumph and tragedy.

Mac would do battle with most of them as he rode through the last year of his moribund Gilera contract on Joe Potts' bikes at home circuits. Then, perhaps, he would be free at last to pursue the world championship that had so far eluded him.

The Canterbury Rocket

If, at the turn of the decade, Mac had a rival for the crown of British road racing, that rival was surely Derek Minter. Turning 28 in 1960, Minter already had two British championships to his name, been called 'King of Brands' by Murray Walker, and become

Bob McIntyre finished third in the 1960 Junior TT on his Potts 7R, two minutes behind winner John Hartle's MV, but less than half a minute adrift of Surtees' ailing four. Mac rarely failed to impress on the Island. (Courtesy Elwyn Roberts Collection)

the man to beat at other southern tracks such as Thruxton and Castle Combe. Wincheap Garage, one of Minter's earliest sponsors, dubbed him the 'Canterbury Rocket.'

Although physically dissimilar, Mac and Minter brought many of the same characteristics to their racing: each was determined, dogged, prepared and able to go it alone; each had a shrewd racing brain and was equally adept at grand prix racing and short-circuit sprints; each had talent in abundance; and if Minter was occasionally let down by his tendency to make leisurely starts, Mac had a reputation for sometimes asking more from his mounts than they could deliver. They each had one more ace: while Minter's Nortons were prepared by Steve Lancefield, Mac had privileged access to the services of Joe Potts.

In March 1960, Minter's Manx Nortons were not his immediate concern. He had been flown to Italy to test Bianchi's fast but fragile twins at Monza, where an engine seizure brought proceedings to a halt and sent Minter home nursing a broken collarbone that forced him out of his first scheduled rides of the British year, at Silverstone for the Hutchinson 100, on 8 April.

Mac, on the other hand, was fit and still enjoying the winning form that had carried him through the latter half of the 1959 season. At Silverstone, his bikes – a 7R for the 350 class and 30M Manx for the 500 – now had almost identical chassis designed and built at Joe Potts' Bellshill workshop on the south-eastern fringe of Glasgow. These, according to Mac, had been devised for two reasons: "The first was to decrease vibration and the second was to have two identical bikes to ride – I dislike swapping from one type of frame to another."

They worked. In the 350cc race Mac got away behind Mike Hailwood with Ulsterman Tommy Robb (AJS), ahead of another newcomer, 21-year-old Phil Read (Norton). The 15-lapper proved another Silverstone classic, with the leading pair riding "brilliantly," according to *Motor Cycle News*. Mac closed remorselessly on Hailwood, passed him on lap six but was unable to get away. Hailwood hung on like a limpet but Mac got to the flag with half a second to spare, with Read third and Alan Shepherd working his way through the field to finish fourth on Geoff Monty's 7R. "There's nothing much wrong with his new frames," one paddock wag noted of McIntyre's win.

The 500cc race was McIntyre's. By the end of the 15 laps distance, he had a ten-second lead over Hailwood (Norton) and Canadian Frank Perris (Norton). Bill Smith brought home his G50 Matchless in fourth.

Less than a week later, the circus convened at Brands Hatch for the Good Friday opener of Easter's three-meeting dash. Here they were without Mac, who had returned to Scotland. But Minter, recovered from his Monza fall, took up the running and, with some help from the young Hailwood, dominated the meeting. Indeed, the pattern of the 350 race must have seemed disconcertingly familiar to Hailwood. He got into Paddock Hill Bend first and led the run up to Druids from Phil Read, Bob Anderson and Minter, but then found himself hunted down by Minter, who took the lead on the fourth lap of the 1.24-mile circuit. The pair swapped the lead for the next 11 laps, but with five remaining Minter repassed Hailwoood and edged away. "As the end drew near," reported *Motor Cycle News*, "he pulled out all the stops, and riding absolutely on the limit, beat Hailwood by 30 yards." Read again finished third. For Minter came the added satisfaction of breaking the existing lap record (his) to leave the new mark at 75.41mph. At gusty Silverstone, neither Mac nor Hailwood had been able to better Alistair King's 350 record of 94.04mph.

Minter repeated the dose in the 500cc event, leading Hailwood home by a slightly extended margin with Ron Langston (Matchless) completing the podium. Minter was unstoppable. In the main race of the day, the 1000cc Invitation, Hailwood again led from the line; again Minter caught and passed him. This time, however, Minter put his head down and went, winning by half a lap and equalling his own outright lap record at 76.97mph. Hailwood collected another second place, this time from Tom Thorp's Norton.

The boys were back in action on Easter Sunday at Snetterton in Norfolk. Relatively new to the calendar, Snetterton, like Silverstone, Castle Combe and Thruxton, was an airfield circuit, bestowed upon the racing community by the Air Ministry, whose wartime tenant had been the 96th Bombardment Group of the 8th US Air Force, which had used it as a home for their B17s.

This was one of the fastest circuits in the country, and Minter relished it. Mac hadn't entered, and with Hailwood sidelined after a fall in the 250cc race Read (Norton) provided the opposition, leading for the first two-thirds of the 10-lap 350cc final before the inevitable happened and Minter eased clear to lead the run home from Read and Langston (AJS), setting a new class lap record at 89.83mph into the bargain.

Minter's sluggish start in the 500 race allowed Tom Thorp (Norton) into the lead, but by lap three the King of Brands was in control and pulling away from the skirmish developing between Thorp and Read (Norton). Tommy Robb, on Geoff Monty's G50, joined the party and got past Thorp into third place, and that was pretty well that. Minter had now starred in two meetings with a string of five feature race wins and a couple of lap records to his name.

Honours shared

The big confrontation came the following day, Easter Monday, at Oulton Park. The place was packed, with more than 50,000 spectators lining the fences to see the first round of the season's major struggle.

Minter took first blood. The 500cc event produced a race-long dice between McIntyrre and Minter that was eventually decided when Mac missed a gear, giving Minter enough of a break to beat him to the flag. Bob Anderson (Norton) claimed the last step on the podium from Ron Langston (Matchless). But the race of the day was the 350cc event. Minter and Mac again went at it, with Minter holding a precarious lead for most of the

John Hartle was one of the few to have a factory ride in the late '50s, though his unfortunate record at the Isle of Man was established long before his MV burnt out at Governor's Bridge in the 1958 Senior TT. (Courtesy Mortons Archive)

journey – but Mac had sized up his man to perfection and this time made no mistake. He took the lead on the last lap to beat Minter over the line from Alan Shepherd (AJS) and Phil Read's Norton. The lap record fell in both classes, with Minter claiming the 500cc mark at 88.75mph and sharing it with Mac in the 350 class at 86.43mph.

The two rivals went their separate ways for meetings the following weekend, Mac to take a 350/500 double at Charterhall, Minter to face a rejuvenated Mike Hailwood around the sweeping, if bumpy, bends of Castle Combe in Wiltshire. Mint duly won the 500 final, beating home Read and Hailwood, both Norton-mounted, and setting a new outright lap record for the 1.84-mile circuit at 88.31mph. Hailwood, however, saved his best effort for the last race of the day, the 350 final. After Minter had led for much of the race, Hailwood squeezed his AJS past the Norton man at the last right-hander of the final lap to win the dash for the line by half a length, setting a new class lap record, at 85.79mph.

Hailwood extended his winning streak the following weekend at Mallory Park by beating Mac into second place in the Senior race while the Scot won the Junior event from Read's Norton. Then, after Mac had travelled back to Scotland – "Bob's Day at Beveridge Park" – came the first of the year's major open-road events, the North West 200, on 14 May.

Mechanical ailments kept the two favourites apart. Minter was running second in the 350 race when his engine expired, leaving Mac to head for an apparently comfortable win. Alan Shepherd however had other ideas and, after seven laps of the 11-mile course, squeezed his 7R into the lead, rounding Quarry Hill for the last time to snatch a last-gasp win. Before long, Shepherd's accomplishment on street circuits would become the stuff of legend.

Minter did better in the 500 race, winning comfortably from Geoff Monty's runners, Tommy Robb and Shepherd, both riding G50 Matchlesses. Mac had retired after a brisk start. He thundered into the pits with his Norton coated in oil, wheeled it straight into the van and headed for the ferry terminal.

Minter, too, left Northern Ireland promptly, to ride at Brands Hatch the following day. There, with his 350 Norton hors de combat, he contented himself with two wins on his 500, beating Hailwood home each time.

The next confrontation between Mac and Minter came at Silverstone on 27 May, and proved doubly disappointing for the Scot. In the 350 race he was handily placed in the early laps, but then retired when his 7R's engine began to tighten. Later in the day Mac's 500 Norton seized in Stowe Corner, putting him down and out of the Senior race. He was "lucky to walk away with bruises and a skinned nose," according to *Motor Cycle News*.

While Mac struggled, Minter was triumphant. In the 350 race John Hartle (Norton) made the best start and pulled away from the pack, leaving Minter to work his way past Mac, Read and Hailwood. Hartle eventually got 10 seconds clear of his pursuers, but Minter closed and dropped underneath him at Stowe Corner, to the audible approval of a crowd warmed by an unseasonably hot sun. During his pursuit of Hartle Minter posted a new class lap record at 98.48mph, which sat neatly alongside his practice best for the 500cc race of 100.93mph, the first three-figure lap speed set by a motorcycle at the Northamptonshire airfield.

In the bigger race Hailwood got away first, with Minter again working his way through the pack after a poor start. This time, however, he could go no higher than second, and Hailwood took some revenge for his double defeat at Brands Hatch the week before.

The annual migration to the Isle of Man for the TT began a week later. Mac had entered just two races, Junior and Senior, fielding his 7R special for Wednesday's Junior and, after damaging his Manx special during his Silverstone fall, a stock Norton for the climax of the week, Saturday's Senior race. Mac's failure to shine at the 1959 TT had been a low spot in an otherwise successful season, and he was widely tipped to redress the balance by leading home the privateer pack after the MV team – John Surtees in his valedictory season, and John Hartle – had taken the flag.

And so it proved, at least for the first act. Hartle won the Junior race, with team-mate and five-time world champion John Surtees coming home in an unfamiliar second place after suffering gearbox ailments. Mac, using a five-speed gearbox in his 7R special, was right behind Surtees, with Minter fourth, riding a "steady and beautifully judged race," noted *Motor Cycle News*.

Mac and Minter pushed off together in the Senior race, but neither enjoyed much success. Mac's stock Manx was dogged by a worsening misfire from the opening lap, and Minter retired with a split oil tank on the third lap – but at least he had the satisfaction of posting the first 100mph lap of the Mountain by a British single, at 101.05mph.

"Thinking back," Minter reflected, years later, "I should have gone harder from the start and perhaps set the 100 on the first lap. I'm sure I could have done it."

Meanwhile, Mike Hailwood took his turn in the limelight, posting a 100mph lap and taking his Bill Lacey-turned Norton into third behind Surtees and Hartle.

Mac's next appearance came at Mallory Park for the Leicestershire circuit's Post-TT meeting. Fielding a brace of Nortons, he got away fourth in the 350 final behind Mike Hailwood (AJS), Read (Norton) and Bruce Daniels (Norton). He got past Daniels and Read, but was unable to challenge Hailwood and had to settle for second place. In the

500cc final Hailwood again led off the line with Read (Norton) and Mac tucked in close behind. Mac eased into the lead as early as the second lap, but Hailwood was in no mood to give up and a scrap developed from which Mac emerged the victor, easing into a narrow lead by the flag. Hailwood came home second from Ron Langston (Matchless), Read, South African Paddy Driver (Norton) and Dickie Dale (Norton).

While Mac began July by heading back to the Isle of Man for the Southern 100, Minter stayed at home for the first meeting on the newly opened Brands Hatch long circuit, reaching out 2.65 miles into fields south of the familiar 1.24-mile kidney bowl and giving London its own grand prix track. The weather didn't co-operate and heavy rain fell to accompany the start of the 350 race. Hailwood got away first but Minter was soon past him and leading according to script until, proving even the mighty are human, he fell at Paddock Hill Bend, damaging an ankle and, it was later discovered, chipping a vertebra in his neck. Mike Hailwood collected the kudos and the prize money, winning all four solo events.

Meanwhile, Mac had been making headlines in the Isle of Man, finishing second to Ron Langston's AJS in the 350 race at the Southern 100 and then finding himself disqualified from the 500 results after a stellar performance that included new lap and race records, for refuelling during the event. "I should have read the regulations," said Mac, ever the sportsman.

Shep

Minter was still out of action at the beginning of August when the 1960 British championships came around at Oulton Park. Back on his AJS and Norton specials for the occasion, Mac took home both 350 and 500 titles after vigorous disputes for possession. Mike Hailwood, the reigning champion, chased the Scot home in both the 500cc title event and the Les Graham Memorial Trophy, but Alan Shepherd also starred, finishing second to Mac in the Junior event and taking third place in the Senior.

Shepherd's finest hour was approaching. John Surtees, completing his last full season on motorcycles with two more world titles for MV Agusta, had perhaps the toughest weekend of his career at Dundrod for the Ulster GP. In the 500cc GP Mac took his Norton to an impressive lead after Surtees was forced to pit and change a broken gearlever. But it wasn't to be the Scot's day, and he retired at half distance with his Norton special vibrating badly. John Hartle, riding his own Norton, managed to hold off his sometime MV team-mate to win, while Alan Shepherd claimed the third step of the podium with a fast and fuss-free ride on Geoff Monty's G50 Matchless. Ralph Rensen, Rhodesian Jim Redman and Australian Tom Phillis, all riding Nortons, completed the top six.

While Mac retired early from the 350 race, Alan Shepherd smelt blood. He thought he'd spotted a chance to do the impossible during practice. He saw that while Surtees would was faster through the open sections of the 7.4-mile circuit, his lightweight, agile

Shep: Cumbrian Alan Shepherd made a speciality of getting the best from AMC hardware on open-road circuits. This is Tom Kirby's 7R AJS. (Courtesy Elwyn Roberts Collection)

AJS single could stay with the bigger, heavier MV through the bends. He thought that if he geared up the 7R and could get a tow from the MV along the straights, he might have a chance to slip past Surtees on the twisty last section of the course before the finish line.

The plan almost worked. Shep stalked Surtees' heavy MV relentlessly, getting past him at one point. But the AJS couldn't maintain the pace, and its timing chain broke at half distance, leaving Shepherd with the slender consolation of a new lap record at 95.41mph, and a demand from an indignant MV team that his engine be stripped and measured. Its displacement was found to be 349.209cc – dead stock.

Then just 24 years old, Shepherd would become one of the most accomplished of Matchless G50 riders, chasing home Mike Hailwood to finish second in both the 1962 and 1963 world championships.

Back on the mainland, while Mac took a break to marry fiancée Joyce Campbell, Minter shrugged off the last lingering effects of his July fall, and returned to the Brands Hatch short circuit on 21 August to do battle with Mike Hailwood, narrowly losing out to the Oxford Ixion man in the 350cc race, but getting his own back in the 1000cc event, setting a new lap record at 79.15mph.

At Snetterton a fortnight later Minter won both 350 and 500cc finals. Hailwood, de-tuned after falling in the 350cc final and leaving Tom Thorp (AJS) to chase Minter, finished third in the Senior race behind Minter and Tony Godfrey (Norton).

Minter's last major journey of the year was a return trip to Monza to ride for Bianchi in the Italian Grand Prix, with much the same result as last time – he fell at high speed after an engine seizure. A broken nose, cuts and bruises kept him out of the running almost until the end of the season, which left Hailwood and Read to divide the spoils at Brands on 18 September, with the Oxford Ixion club man taking three wins and Read following him home each time.

Hailwood didn't have it quite as easily at Aintree the following Saturday, where he found John Hartle in indomitable form and had to be content with third behind the Derbyshire rider and a rested Mac (AJS) in the 350 race. Hartle won again in the 500cc event, but this time Hailwood beat Mac home for second. The Scot spent much of the meeting struggling with unco-operative forks on his 500 Manx, but managed to mix it with Hartle for the lead of the big race, the Aintree Century, with Thorp (G50) and Shepherd (G50) harrying the leading pair after Hailwood retired with an oil leak from the Norton's cam drive. With three laps to go Mac and his Norton parted company and as Hartle took evasive action, Thorp nipped through to take the lead – and hold it to the flag.

A day later the circus reconvened at Mallory Park for the Race of the Year, where speculation about Mac signing for Honda was suspended while he added two more wins to the ledger, in the 350 and 500 races. The smart money was riding on Mac for the Race of the Year, now worth a cool £1000 to the winner, but Bob Anderson (Matchless) led early and Hailwood dropped in behind him with Hartle in tow. Mac made a mediocre start but thundered through the field and gate-crashed the party developing between S M B Hailwood and R H F Anderson, bringing with him Terry Shepherd on Francis Beart's Norton. Mac, Hailwood and Shepherd were ten seconds clear of the field when the Scot's engine died, and Hailwood set about building a five-second lead over Shepherd. The money was his.

A subdued Derek Minter appeared at a gloomy Brands Hatch for the final national of the year, finishing fourth in the 1000cc race, well adrift of winner John Hartle's Norton, to bring the curtain down on a patchy season. Minter soon announced that he would be racing at home in the year ahead, again riding Nortons tuned by Steve Lancefield and sponsored by Hallets' Garage. Mac, on the other hand, had had his name linked with an assortment of factory teams but made no announcement about the season to come. The champion was biding his time.

Chapter 5

1961: Out of the Shadows

"The best rider I'd come across"

There was plenty of news to digest either side of the 1960 Christmas turkey, and precious little of it welcome. December opened with the formal announcement of John Surtees' retirement – and so his defection to car racing – with Surtees himself saying that MV's team planning left a little to be desired, and that with the 'autocratic' Count Agusta's strict control over all his riding (grand prix and major internationals only, exceptions at the Count's say so), he just wasn't getting enough track time.

There was more: in its 15 December issue, *The Motor Cycle* told its readers Blandford wouldn't be available for racing in 1961 because its current tenant, the Royal Signals, was extending its interest in the camp, so "for the next year or so extensive building operations will be under way" – and racing shelved. Jim Rendell of Blackmore Vale MCC released the news with the best possible spin, but with car racing already gone from the Dorset circuit, prospects of a return seemed slender at best.

At least the Hailwood family had cause for celebration. For the second year in a row, Mike had made a clean sweep of the ACU's Road Racing Stars. The Stars were decided on the basis of points awarded at national meetings throughout the season, the best eight results per class counting – and Hailwood had posted near maxima in the 350 and 500cc classes during 1959 and 1960. The Stars weren't the British championships; these, for the next five years anyway, would continue to be settled by a single race per class at Oulton Park in August. Both awards offered the prospect of some attractive tinware to add to the trophy cabinet, but the championship had the incentives of a cash prize – and the title.

The ACU Stars had little immediate benefit on a rider's balance of payments, and the more mature names were often under-represented in the final points count: in the 1960 500cc tally, Hailwood got home on 60 points from Minter on 51, while Mac languished on 28 for having teased himself away from key nationals to ride in higher-profile meetings. The two half-heartedly-pursued awards finally became an important one, and would in time deliver a credible financial reward. But not yet.

Before January 1961 was out international racing took a body blow with MV Agusta announcing its immediate withdrawal from grand prix, citing the insupportable expense of competition now the 500cc world championship had increased from eight rounds to ten, with one of those now outside Europe (Argentina). Gary Hocking, who'd put in yeoman service supporting Surtees in the 1960 350cc World Championship,

John Hartle was nothing if not versatile, proving his accomplishments on a wide range of machinery and terrain. The '63 Gilera was more memorable than successful. (Courtesy Elwyn Roberts Collection)

winning in France and Italy, shrugged and said, "they told me I am still under contract."

The day of the *Privat* MV was about to dawn and John Hartle, after three years' intermittent service to the cause, would be having no part of it. Following three seasons on Nortons – two for the factory team, one for Comerfords – he'd joined MV Agusta in 1958 at the suggestion of Surtees, who thought Hartle "the best rider I'd come across." He'd repaid Surtees's faith in him with a hatful of second places that season – five in the 350cc class, two from fewer rides on the 500 – taking runner-up spots in both championships and giving his team leader a leg up to the first of his three pairs of titles on MV's fire engines. The Count rewarded Hartle by keeping him on in the 350 class for 1959 but giving his 500 ride to Remo Venturi, repeating that arrangement informally in 1960 when, given even fewer rides, Hartle broke through for his first TT win, beating Surtees in the Junior. He also won the Senior event at the Ulster GP that year on his Norton after Surtees had to pit and replace the MV's broken gearlever. Revenge is a dish best eaten cold, they say, and the County Antrim weather did its best to co-operate.

After MV's official withdrawal, Hartle didn't need to be told which way the wind blew. He parted company from the Gallarate outfit and looked forward to a season when he'd at least be his own boss. Aged 27 at the beginning of the 1961 season, Hartle, from Chapel-en-le-Frith, Derbyshire, was a noted wet-weather rider and a fine hand over true road circuits despite a truly horrible record at the Isle of Man, where he'd run out of juice only minutes from a Senior Manx GP win in 1954, suffered the same fate while running fourth on a factory Norton in the 1955 Senior TT, had his MV catch fire at Governor's Bridge in the 1958 Senior and fell in the corresponding race a year later at Glen Vine in filthy weather. Now he was back on his Manx Nortons under the Comerfords banner and seeking better fortune. In February 1961, Bill Lacey was busy preparing 14 Norton engines for the coming season; four of them were Hartle's.

Lacey was busier than ever, going his fastidious way with the preparation of customer engines while working on his hefty, flanged drive-side main bearing for the Manx in a bid to stop crankcases cracking. Ray Petty was finding his own remedy to the problem. He told *The Motor Cycle* the weak point was a misplaced oilway at the rear of the housing, and so was working on a new crankcase half that shifted the oilway forward and replaced the external crankcase webs with solid metal. Meanwhile, Allen Dudley-Ward's workshop was busy working up a one-piece crankshaft for Mike Hailwood's 500 Manx that would be more rigid than a built-up unit and give big-end bearings an easier time.

In Glasgow meanwhile, Joe Potts, mechanic Pim Fleming and Bob McIntyre were slotting Mac's 7R engine into a new, lightweight frame – marking, indirectly, the birth of the famous McIntyre Matchless – while experimenting with twin-plug heads and inlet ports, and trimming piston crowns for his 500 Manx. And then Mac was gone, exchanging the cold of Glasgow for the cold of Modena at the invitation of Bianchi, to test its light and lithe 47bhp 350 twin. The session was inconclusive because of the tight nature of the track, and tests couldn't be held up the road at Monza as there was ice on the circuit. So Mac made a second trip, this time testing at Monza and returning with a signed Bianchi contract to ride selected GPs in the 350 class that also allowed him to ride his own bikes "when time permits." Would he be riding the Bianchi at British events? "I don't believe in bringing foreign works bikes to race against the lads," he told scribe Mick Woollett.

'Who's King of Brands now?'

The racing year began at Brands Hatch on Good Friday. With Mac giving the meeting a miss altogether and Derek Minter making one of his habitually poor starts, Mike Hailwood declared the season open by running away with the 350 race on the twin-plug 7R he'd been spotted testing at Silverstone a few weeks earlier. Hartle got home third after being passed by Read and seemed set to do better in the Over-350 race, catching leaders Minter – who'd made a good start for a change – and Hailwood. The Derbyshire man got past Hailwood for second, and had begun to challenge for the lead when Minter slowed to avoid a fallen rider: Hartle and Hailwood touched in the ensuing melee and both went down and sat out the rest of the race, while Minter collected a comfortable win with Phil Read a remote second from Paddy Driver and Banbury Dan Shorey, all Norton-propelled. The rest of the meeting was Hailwood's, setting a lap record in the Over 350s and in the Over 250 finale to leave the outright mark for the months-old GP circuit at 89.15mph, again showing Minter the way home and logging a claim for local supremacy.

Battle resumed at Snetterton on Easter Sunday, but not before Tony Godfrey had upstaged everybody by presenting Hailwood with a giant cardboard key to mark his 21st birthday. Hailwood continued the celebrations by winning the 350 race, tailing Minter for most of the way, and then having the presumption to pull out and pass him on the last corner and win the drag to the line. Mint turned the tables in the 500cc event, leading from Hailwood early and breaking his own lap record (leaving it at 94.9mph) to stay in front. Hailwood's Manx lost its edge later in the race but he hung onto second from Shorey.

Easter Monday, typically the most congested day of many a crowded season, in 1961 included three national meetings (at Thruxton, Cadwell Park and Crystal Palace) as well as the Oulton Park international – where most of the big names lined up, including Bob Mac for his first meeting of the year. Fans looked forward to a resumption of the unending struggle between Mac and Minter, but it wasn't about to happen. The Scot retired from the 500cc race after five laps with his Manx engine off song, leaving Minter in front from Hartle, who again looked a man at the top of his form until an ailing gearbox slowed him. Phil Read broke clear of Fred Neville (Matchless) to take second place at the flag. The 350cc race, which came typically for Oulton Park at the close of the programme, didn't offer any Mac-Minter action either. In a small masterpiece of administrative ineptitude, British Railways had contrived to lose Mac's 7R somewhere between Glasgow and Chester, reducing the Scot to spectator status while Minter did it again, easing smoothly past first-lap leader Read (Norton) to win as he pleased, while Hartle bagged third. Hailwood, meanwhile, had returned south to take two wins at Thruxton, beating New Zealander Hugh Anderson in the 350 race, and Dickie Dale in the 500.

They gathered from the four winds the following Saturday at Silverstone for the BMCRC's 29th Hutchinson 100, and for all the routine groaning about the grey, featureless expanse of airfield circuits, for once the sun shone, albeit patchily, and the Northants track provided some of the best racing ever seen there, with Minter and Hartle again in the thick of it. The action began with the 350 BMCRC Championship event, Kent and Derbyshire again swapping the lead, sliding and diving past one another trying to cut a lead of "a yard rather than inches," according to *The Motor Cycle*, until Hartle slid off at Copse, leaving Minter to ease home well ahead of Read's Norton, with Alan Shepherd (AJS) third.

Still looking for that first big win of the season, Hartle resumed the struggle with Minter in the 500 BMCRC Championship race, this time with Mac's help. The three

Mechanical failure dogged Bob Mac's career. During the 1961 season, Bianchi's 350 twin proved fast but fragile, and he sat out much of the Junior TT after its gearbox failed. (Courtesy FoTTofinder Bikesport Photo Archives)

55

ran nose to tail, swapping positions until lap four when Hailwood joined in, his Manx now running the Dudley-Ward one-piece crank. At Stowe, Minter called on his new Oldani front brake to pull a hair-raising move, outbraking Mac and Hartle for the lead; at Woodcote Hartle returned the compliment, riding round the outside of Minter and McIntyre to get back in front. It couldn't last. On lap nine Hailwood's engine tightened, while Hartle and Minter drew away from Mac, whose motor had lost its edge. Two laps later Minter toured in when his engine cut, leaving Hartle out on his own to bring his Comerfords Norton home by 10 seconds from Mac, the trophy and a share of the new lap record, at 100.74mph, in the bag.

Minter went home while Hailwood, Mac and most of the others journeyed north for Mallory Park on the Sunday. Here Mac and Hailwood mounted a furious scrap in the 350 final with Read and Fred Neville, Read finally getting the upper hand as Mac led Hailwood home and Neville slid off at the Esses. In the 500 race Hailwood disappeared into the distance, posting a new lap record at 89.33mph as Mac came home a relatively subdued third behind Terry Shepherd on Francis Beart's Norton.

Exit

Entering the second month of the season, Hailwood had won seven major events to Minter's five, with Hartle in promising form behind them. It seemed the momentum was clearly with the Oxford star. He was also compiling an impressive tally of 250 class wins on his loaned RC162 Honda four. Back at Brands come the end of April he did it again on the 250 Honda, and tried to make a claim on the 350 race with the usual suspects, Minter on Lancefield's Norton and Hartle on Bill Lacey's, making up the balance of an epic three-way dice. It ended badly. Hailwood lost the front end at Stirling's, taking Hartle down with him. Phil Read (Norton), recovering from a poor start, passed Fred Neville's 7R for second and took the scrap to Minter, the pair sharing a new lap record for the class at 86.41mph. The race was red-flagged after 18 of its scheduled 20 laps to get help to Hartle, who was diagnosed with a broken arm. Hailwood fared little better in the 500 race, falling at Paddock while Minter took the lead from Neville. Read, in third, became the second headline faller of the day at Stirling's with a punctured rear tyre. Minter got home comfortably, his slipping crown firmly back in place.

A week later Mac was back in the headlines after bagging a double win at the North West 200, clearing off from the start in the 350 race but having to work his way up after a sluggish start in the 500. Read took both runner-up spots. Optimistic forecasts were meanwhile coming from Hartle, whose injury tally was thought to be no more serious than a fractured humerus and some bruising – wounds that would, it was felt, keep him out of action for weeks rather than months. Less welcome news came from Germany, with the death of Dickie Dale at the Nürburgring.

With the big beasts at Hockenheim for the West German GP, Read made hay at

Mallory on the 14 May national, bagging two wins on his Nortons. In Germany, Mac was becoming acquainted with his Bianchi's fragility as it holed a piston. "As one bother is remedied, another crops up," he said, prophetically.

Back on his own bikes the following weekend the Scot took three from four at Beveridge Park and Charterhall, missing the Whit Monday excitement south of the border. For once Derek Minter left his Brands Hatch home turf to head west for the Blackmore Vale Club's traditional Whitsun meeting, now at Thruxton instead of Blandford. While the Mint kept a clean sheet in Hampshire, winning the 350 and 500 finals from Read, Neville was winning over the short circuit at Brands Hatch, taking the 350 race from Ron Langston (AJS) and the 500 from Joe Dunphy (Norton), who claimed the 1000cc race from Ron Grant (Norton). Completing a weekend of doubles, Dennis Pratt (Nortons) again claimed the lion's share of silverware at Cadwell Park.

There was just one more major stop before the TT, at Castle Combe in Wiltshire, where Hailwood warmed up nicely for his June fortnight with wins in the 250 and 500 races, while Ginger Payne (Norton) claimed the 350 prize.

John Hartle wasn't doing quite so well. A month on from his fall, with his arm

For the love of the sport: Mike Hailwood won three TTs in 1961, in Friday's Senior at an unprecedented average, for a single, of 100.60mph. The front brake is one of the Oldani's popular instruments. (Courtesy Elwyn Roberts Collection)

recovering but still in splints, the Comerfords man now fell ill from a chest infection caused by an undiagnosed cracked rib. It seemed he wouldn't be under starter's orders at the TT after all, and would miss the ride he'd been offered on a factory 250 Honda. Fortunately Mike Hailwood was available to take up the slack, and won the 125 and 250 races for the marque during the week that did so much to make his name. As every then schoolboy knew, 'Michael the Bicycle' was perfectly placed to win the Senior TT at a hitherto unimaginable average (for a single) of 100.60mph on his Bill Lacey-tuned Norton after Hocking's MV went out of the running with a sticking throttle. He might have won the Junior too, when Hocking's smaller MV went off song, but while leading well his 7R stopped with a broken gudgeon pin – an AMC affliction in 1961, particularly among G50s – and Phil Read took the win for Norton.

Mac had finished second in the Senior yet had a poor week, retiring from the 250 race with a win in sight after setting a class lap record at 99.58mph on his Honda four, and spending at least part of the Junior sitting on a doorstep between Sulby and Ginger Hall, after the Bianchi continued its 100% failure record by breaking its (hollow) layshaft on the first lap. Minter fared no better, finishing fourth in the Junior, behind Ralph Rensen, on a Norton short of revs. In the Senior he had to push in after running out of juice, and in the exchange of views that followed, Minter and engineer Steve Lancefield dissolved their five-year partnership.

Two days later, Rensen succumbed to injuries he suffered when falling heavily from his Norton at the 11th Milestone on the fifth lap of the Senior.

Action on the mainland resumed on 18 June with Mac cleaning up at Mallory Park, beating home Potts team-mate Alistair King (Norton) in the 500 race and Hailwood in the 350. Word in the paddock had it that Hartle might be back in action as early as the Belgian GP in three weeks, and though he'd never been the luckiest of riders there he was, right enough, running as high as fourth in the 500cc grand prix behind Hocking, Hailwood and Mac before his weakened arm gave up and he could no longer brake effectively.

Low boy

Derek Minter was back in business at Brands Hatch on 9 July, riding a stock 500cc Manx Norton and, from the factory, an experimental short-stroke 350 using a low-boy chassis. The bike ran coil ignition and 18-in wheels, while the engine was slung low between the bottom frame tubes; and it didn't handle too well. Minter said he felt "slightly off-colour" after manhandling his new instrument into third spot in the 350 race behind winner Read and runner-up Fred Neville's AJS. He fared better on the stock 500, taking wins in both the Over 350 and Over 250 events from Read, with Hartle – stronger, faster and better – running third in the Over 350s while Hailwood crashed after leading early, grounding his fairing at Dingle Dell, splitting a finger and gashing a leg.

The problem with Mint's new 350 was traced to its rear suspension, and the bike was clearly a better proposition at a wet Castle Combe the following Saturday, where he

Derek Minter had a quiet TT in 1961 by his own exacting standards. While Mike Hailwood grabbed the headlines, the Mint ride took a modest fourth place in the Junior and retired from the Senior after running dry. (Courtesy Elwyn Roberts Collection)

bagged the 350 race from early leader Tony Godfrey (Norton) and Louis Carr (AJS). For once, Minter got no trouble from Hailwood, who had his hands full with a poor-handling and misfiring Ducati. Godfrey led again for the opening three circuits of the 500 race before Hailwood got past, and then, as the track began to dry, Minter; but then Hailwood was gone and the Mint had to be content with second.

The following weekend Hailwood disappeared again, this time to East Germany to maintain his dogged pursuit of Hocking's MV in the 500cc World Championship and collect his fourth second place of the season. Mac, meanwhile, claimed third in the 350 race to add to his hard-fought second at the Dutch TT, at last giving Bianchi's 1961 title campaign a welcome sheen of plausibility.

Oulton Park, 7 August 1961: John Hartle was close to full fitness again, but his oil contract with Mobil now seemed more likely than anything else to prevent him becoming a full member of the Castrol-backed Honda team. Yet he was able to put in the occasional ride on the RC162, and at the Cheshire circuit seemed to have the race for the 250cc British Championship won until Hailwood, on a similar bike, got out of Lodge Corner faster on the last lap to drive past his Honda rival through Deer Leap and claim the big ticket. The day held better luck for the Derbyshire rider. In the 350 race Minter planted his experimental Norton at the front after deposing Read while Hartle got through to second and stayed with Minter as Fred Neville (AJS) came up to close on Read. Now Mac and Hailwood steamed through the field to join the leading pairs and the immediate future looked intriguing – but little further business was conducted. Hailwood's Norton ran out of sparks, and then Minter's engine seized with two laps to go. Hartle, in the right place for the first time since the 500 race at the Hutch, went on to win and become 350cc British Champion, leading home McIntyre, who'd got his Norton past Read's in the closing stages to finish just seven seconds in arrears.

The 350 race marked high water for Hartle and Mac alike, the Derbyshire man's early lead from Hailwood in the 500cc event notwithstanding. Mac, third from Minter at the end of the first lap, slid off at Esso Bend. Then Ginger Payne's Norton caught fire at Clay Hill, laying a thickening cloud of smoke across the track, but not even that could stop Minter, who passed Hailwood to win, with Neville then relegating Hailwood to third after Hartle, on the larger Comerfords Norton, retired with brake problems. Champion Minter was the man of the hour, and though he finished well adrift of winner Alistair King in the Les Graham Memorial Trophy race, he used the occasion to post a lap record at 90.03mph.

August Bank Holiday weekend was the third busy weekend of the season together with Easter and Whitsun, and there were three more major meetings on the Monday, at Crystal Palace (Ned Minihan double), Thruxton (Tony Godfrey double) and at the newly extended 2.25-mile Cadwell Park, where Dennis Pratt took the honours in the 350 and Coronation Trophy races. Meanwhile the heavyweights packed up shop and headed west across the Irish Sea for the Ulster Grand Prix. Hocking had just about wrapped up the 350 and 500 world titles but Hailwood once again gave chase in the 500cc race, taking second place in filthy weather after Hartle had retired with unspecified "machine trouble." Meanwhile Mac's Bianchi again expired in the 350 event, with the very particular ailment of a broken layshaft – but at least he'd had the consolation of winning the 250 grand prix from Hailwood.

Minter returned to his home patch at Brands Hatch on 20 August to suffer the indignity of falling at South Bank on the second lap of the 350 race. Hailwood meanwhile built on an early lead to pull away from a scrap between Read and Neville. In the 500 race Minter and Read went at it for the full 12 laps, Read getting the verdict by two lengths, while Neville's turn for a convincing win came in the 1000cc race, taking the flag from Tom Thorp and Canadian Mike Duff (Matchlesses), on a 597cc Norton 99-powered Domiracer built for him by Erith scooter dealer Paul Dunstall.

The following weekend, newcomer John Herbert Cooper "twinkled brightly" at Aberdare, according to *The Motor Cycle*. While Hailwood set new lap records as he stole away with the 350 and 500cc races, lifting the 500cc average for the serene parkland circuit to a dizzying 59mph, Cooper brought his 350 Norton into fourth in the 1000cc race, which was won by Godfrey on his 500 Manx.

Fred

Hailwood was winning overseas, as well as across the Severn. Taking his first rides for MV
Agusta at the Grand Prix des Nations at Monza on the first weekend of September, the
Oxford youth won the 500cc event after Hocking retired, and ran a dutiful second to the
Welsh-Rhodesian in the 350 race. For Mac, the Italian classic was memorable for different
reasons. His was one of five Bianchis to start the 350 race, and one of four to retire, the
survivor being ridden by Alan Shepherd into fourth place. Then, in the 250 event, Mac fell
from his Honda while disputing the lead, breaking his collarbone and ending his season.
On the same day, Minter fell at Snetterton in the wet. He won the 350 race after Read had
slithered off, then, in the 500 race became one of the casualties in a five-bike pile-up resulting
from mud on the track, leaving Godfrey to win from Lewis Young (both on Nortons).
Minter was unhurt, but within a week the sport had received another brutal reminder of the
severe penalty occasionally levied when things go awry: Fred Neville died from head injuries
sustained in a crash at Appledene, on the last lap of the Junior Manx Grand Prix. Riding
Tom Arter's 7R, he'd built a two-minute lead in horrible weather, mile by sodden mile
revealing, if only in outline, an impressive future. And then, aged 26, he was gone.

Minter made the journey to Cadwell Park the following weekend, but seemed
reluctant to be there, posting a best result of eighth in the 350 final. Hartle, on the other
hand, revelled in the tight nature of the woodland track, chalking up two wins on his

**Lost champion: Fred Neville was leading the 1961 Junior Manx Grand Prix by two
minutes on Tom Arter's AJS when he crashed at Appledene on the last lap, suffering
head injuries that proved fatal. (Courtesy FoTTofinder Bikesport Photo Archives)**

Comerfords Nortons, and new lap records for both classes (71.54 and 72.84mph). In the 350 race he swapped the lead with the precocious John Cooper for half a dozen laps, but in the 500 race he had no company at all, waltzing away to win by more than 20 seconds from Alan Shepherd (Matchless) and Dennis Pratt (Norton).

Cooper broke through for one of his first major wins at a wet Scarborough the following weekend, winning the 350 race from local ace Peter Middleton (Norton), but Hartle's encouraging run of good form ended abruptly when he locked the front wheel of his Norton on the descent to Mountside Hairpin, falling and breaking his arm for the second time in four months. Pratt won the 500cc race from Shorey and Middleton but Hartle's poor luck made the headlines.

Minter returned to Brands Hatch to bag three from three at the September national but didn't journey north the following weekend for the biggest meeting of the domestic year, the Mallory Park Race of the Year. An impressive £1000 first prize was offered for the name event, but Minter would have none of it, thinking the circuit too dangerous. Gary Hocking did attend, however, and some 60,000 turned up to see his fire engine. The Rhodesian duly cleared off with both the 500cc race and the name event, with Norton-mounted Hailwood following him home each time. Yet Hailwood could make no impression on the double world champion, who broke away at the rate of a second a lap in the name race, lifting the lap record to 89.66mph – having had the MV's megaphones raised for the meeting – while Alan Shepherd brought Geoff Monty's G50 home in third.

Hailwood journeyed north to Aintree for the following Saturday, taking a clean sweep of 250, 350 and 500cc races, together with the main event, the 100km Aintree Century. Yet at Oulton Park on the final weekend of the season, he had to be content with a win in the 500cc race, Read chasing him all the way. Minter, riding Paul Dunstall's Domiracer, started from the back of the grid and battled his way through to fourth, behind Alan Shepherd's G50. It was, said *The Motor Cycle*, "a tame affair." Shepherd's turn to post a win came in the 350 race after Minter retired with electrical problems and Hailwood missed the start.

The curtain came down on the season at Brands the following day. Minter was back on form, bagging wins in the 350 and 500cc events from Read, who'd taken over Tom Arter's 7R and G50 for the day and used the Matchless to beat Minter's 597cc Domiracer home in the 1000cc race. Hailwood, sidelined with electrical problems in the 350 race and being baulked by a slower rider while making a last-ditch bid to win the 500cc event, had a modest weekend. On the other hand, he was 250cc World Champion, runner-up in the 500cc title and had – just – retained his 500cc ACU Star, if losing the 350 title to Phil Read.

In November, John Hartle was admitted to Chester Royal Infirmary for bone grafts. The humerus he'd fractured at Scarborough wasn't knitting properly so surgeons pinned the bone and grafted part of his left thigh onto the break. Now the arm was in plaster and fixed in position to a body cast. He would, he said, be out of action for some time.

Chapter 6

1962: The Best of Us

"Racing has lost its last real personality"

Mac was busy. During the closing weeks of the old year he was testing at Oulton Park, and subsequently buying a G50 Matchless. After the Christmas break he was on his way south again, this time for tyre tests with Dunlop at Mallory Park, where no-one was saying precisely what was going on. "We're trying different mixes and so on," Dunlop's Dickie Davies said airily to *The Motor Cycle*. "We like Mallory because Gerard's Bend can tell us things we can't find out at any other convenient circuit." Mac, ever serious about his craft, was spotted during a break in the action pushing a broom round the racing line at Gerard's.

The Scot was uncertain about his season: "It's too early for plans," he said. "And as for Bianchi, they haven't even been in touch with me yet." Alistair King was also at Mallory, but still receiving treatment for injuries received in a fall during the Race of the Year, and wasn't ready to decide anything. Positive noises were coming from John Hartle, however, whose casts had been replaced by a simple sling. He hoped, he said, to be fit for the start of the season, and reunited with his Bill Lacey-fettled Comerfords Nortons.

Soon Mac was on the move again, this time heading for Tokyo.

Work was under way at Brands Hatch and Mallory. While the Kent circuit received, among other things, two new restaurants, a new control tower and resurfacing work on Paddock Hill Bend, Mallory was being resurfaced over a third of its length, and having a new spectator bank built at the Esses. Important work, too, was being done at Devil's Elbow. This most exacting of bends was being widened by four feet (1.2 metres), with a new crash barrier being erected round the curve as far as the foot of the control tower. There was still criticism from Mick Woollett, sports editor of *Motor Cycling*, who pointed out the possible danger posed by the thick concrete post near the racing line at the Devil's Elbow end of the pit barrier. Derek Minter, however, who hadn't raced at the Leicestershire track for two years, inspected the changes during tyre tests and declared himself ready "to have a go."

Minter too was busy. In the season ahead he'd be riding 350 and 500 Manx Nortons for Hallets, his long-standing Canterbury sponsors, had a deal to ride the 600 Dominator Paul Dunstall had built for the late Fred Neville and, like Mac, he'd lined up a berth with Honda. But where the Mint had agreed to ride an RC162 1961-spec 250 Honda in British internationals, the TT and the Ulster GP, Mac returned from Japan with a full deal to contest the 250 and 350cc world championships.

Mac's other secret weapon for the season was revealed in *The Motor Cycle*: his new G50, now extensively altered and said to weigh just 260lb (118kg), some 40lb lighter than stock. Its frame, made by Alex Crummie, was similar to that he'd planned for his 7R in 1961. Cycle parts included shortened Norton forks, 18in wheels, a Norton swinging arm and Norton hubs. The engine was angled forward six degrees to reduce height, and mounted a full inch (25mm) lower than a stock 7R's. With no frame tubes running beneath the engine, the exhaust was tucked in so tight that it couldn't ground, it was said. The engine made 51bhp, compared with 53 of the JP7 engine in Mac's 500 Manx. But the story, said Mac, was about "adding more lightness." There was a light alloy fuel tank, a fibreglass oil tank, and plenty of Duralumin.

In Surrey, Francis Beart also had his hands full. He was backing Ellis Boyce on a 7R and 500 Manx for the TT, the Manx to be equipped with a twin-spark magneto and the requisite number of plugs, while the 7R reputedly weighed just 259lb (117.5kg) dry. He was also preparing 7R and G50 engines for Roy Mayhew. Allen Dudley-Ward meanwhile was working on Tony Godfrey's Nortons, and across the border in Hampshire, Derek Minter was getting to know his new tuner, Ray Petty.

Bill Lacey too had his usual shedful of Manx engines waiting for attention. These were for Mike Hailwood (together with 7Rs), Phil Read and John Hartle, and were, unfortunately, in line behind a batch of Coventry-Climax Formula 1 engines requiring the Lacey touch. Hailwood, currently tearing out his thinning hair over the difficulties of working for MV Agusta, probably didn't mind too much. "I've never been so disorganised in my life," he growled to the man from *Motor Cycling*. Apart from anything else, it seemed there'd be no 350 MVs for the first half of the season. The congenial Mike had almost had enough. Almost.

John Hartle was fed up too. His arm wasn't healing as quickly as he'd hoped and he'd be out until the TT. He was selling the Nortons he'd raced in 1961 but clearly was in no great hurry to collect his fresh engines from Lacey. As for Joe Potts, he'd just about put up the shutters. With Mac's move to Honda, Potts decided it was time to close his race shop, leaving the lightweight G50 as the sole example of the shop's craftsmanship in Mac's charge.

"These things happen"

The first of the year's 40+ nationals and home internationals was held at Mallory Park on April Fool's Day, but nobody was laughing at Minter, who marked his return to the Leicestershire track with a win in the 350 race and a big effort in the 500. Hailwood, back on his British hardware for the day, retired from his 350 heat with ignition failure, and Mac bent his newly acquired RC170 285 Honda in practice when, unsighted on a full-noise exit from Shaw's Hairpin, he struck Tom Thorp's fallen G50, bruising himself into the bargain. Two senior Honda employees witnessed the aftermath, one of them heard to say "these things happen."

Star absentees notwithstanding, Minter made hard work of the 350cc final when he stumbled on the start line and got away 24th and last. Alan Shepherd, riding Geoff Monty's 7R, worked on his getaway at the front of the field, taking Alistair King (Norton) with him after they'd deposed first-lap leader Read (now back on his Nortons). While Shepherd and King scrapped, Minter quietly made progress, taking King for second on the tenth lap of 20. After that the question was when rather than if and, sure enough, Minter claimed the lead with seven laps remaining and led the field home.

The 500 final began in a shower of rain with celebrated waterbabies Hailwood and Read leading the field away. On lap three Shepherd (Matchless) joined the party, as Read slipped past Hailwood to take point. Eight laps later and Hailwood was in charge again, with Read slowing as his exhaust worked loose. Minter, uncomfortable in the wet on a track he still had misgivings about, nonetheless managed to dislodge Read from third at Gerard's on the last lap.

The pattern was similar a week later at Silverstone for the Hutchinson 100. Mac was without a ride for the 350 race, with his 285 Honda still bent and 7R unprepared. Hailwood's 7R meanwhile had been cured of its ignition problems but spat back on the grid, leaving the Oxford rider pushing frantically while the field, led by Peter Middleton's Norton, headed for Copse. By the end of the second lap Minter had assumed control, leading from Hugh Anderson (who'd taken over Tom Arter's bikes with Read's return to the Norton fold), Read and Shepherd. Hailwood sliced his way through the field and by the tenth of 15 laps he'd fought his way into second from Shepherd and Anderson, but by then Minter was gone and seven seconds clear of Hailwood at the flag.

It was Minter's turn for a poor start in the 500cc event and Hailwood's to head for the horizon. Mac, in his shakedown ride on his lightweight G50, got the better of a dice with Shepherd (Matchless) to take a fine second while Minter laboured through the field, getting up to tenth before his Norton expired with ignition problems.

Minter's week improved, however: first with the arrival of his 250 Honda – though its precious box of spares and range of sprockets had gone astray – and then with good news from Bracebridge Street.

Norton development chief Doug Hele was looking forward to a good season. After four years of experimenting, his Domiracer was coming along well and looked likely to develop into the hoped-for low-cost, more powerful alternative to the Manx. Its frame was both lighter and lower than the thoroughbred's, and the OHV engine, derived from the 88SS roadster, was lighter than the Manx even without resorting to exotic alloys. At the 1961 TT, when Tom Phillis did so much for the project by riding the Domiracer into third place in the Senior with a best lap of 100.36mph, it was making 52bhp at 7200rpm. Hele had anchored the bottom end with main and big-end bearings sturdier than the roadster's, and the two engines he'd had available for the TT showed a range of tuning through different inlet designs, compression ratios, camshafts and carburation.

Now, more was coming. Development would continue on the 497cc Domiracer, and with the release of the high-visibility 650cc Norton Manxman in the USA in 1960 and the

Tom Phillis established Doug Hele's Norton 88-based Domiracer with third place in the 1961 Senior TT. Through Paul Dunstall, the concept would make an impact long after Bracebridge Street had closed and Hele had left Norton.
(Courtesy FoTTofinder Bikesport Photo Archives)

650SS in Britain the following year, a 647cc engine became available. But with Phillis now riding for Honda in four GP classes, Ron Langston was recruited to replace him as Norton development rider for the immediate future. Meanwhile, two new 650 Domiracers were under development at the Norton factory. One for Langston, and one, Derek Minter now learnt, for him.

Minter's Domi was a going concern by Easter and firmly in the spotlight. But first it was Hailwood's turn, arriving at Brands Hatch on Good Friday in no mood to take prisoners. He'd finished a mediocre fifth to MV team-mate Gary Hocking at Imola's season-opening Gold Cup international, and now the MVs he'd been promised for the home Easter meetings hadn't arrived. He made amends by running away with the 350 race on his 7R, passing early leader Phil Read's Norton on lap four and clearing off while Minter struggled up to fifth after one of his trademark starts, then putting in a crowd-pleaser to pass Alan Shepherd, Anderson and Read in the closing laps to finish second. Minter turned the tables in the opening round of the new, Brands-only 500cc Redex Trophy series, to win going away, albeit after Hailwood had led for four laps and then been slowed when he grounded his Norton's gearlever, bending it, and limping home in fifth.

The damage repaired, Hailwood led the first four laps of the Over 250 race until Minter shot past on his new 650 Domiracer, to "win as he pleased," said *Motor Cycling*. The big twin (aided by one of Minter's favoured Oldani brakes) was just too fast for Hailwood's Manx, even with help from a Michael Schafleitner six-speed gearbox. Hailwood hung on for second, from the G50s of Shepherd and Roy Mayhew.

If Easter Saturday was about Peter Middleton riding his Nortons to a 350/500 double at Scarborough, Hailwood was back in the headlines the following day, this time at Snetterton and with both fire engines present and correct. With untroubled wins in prospect, he took on the lap records, streaking away to post new marks for the Norfolk circuit at 92.55mph (350) and 96.21mph (500).

The hectic round of Easter racing came to a climax on the Monday, and while Mayhew starred at Cadwell Park and Joe Dunphy at Crystal Palace, Hailwood gave his MVs an outing at Thruxton, winning going away in both events from Anderson and Godfrey. Mac, who rarely travelled south of Oulton Park and then usually no further than Mallory or Silverstone, spent Easter Monday at the Cheshire circuit giving his lightweight G50 its maiden win in the 500 race, beating home Alan Shepherd and Minter's 497 Domiracer, and posting a new lap record at 90.36mph. A further episode in Mac's troubled career with Honda closed the programme. He jumped away from the start of the 350 race, but, by the second lap, Alistair King (Norton) led from Read and Shepherd, with Mac back in tenth. A lap later, the leading three had reversed spots, with Mac now fifth – an intermittent misfire had cured itself and the 285 Honda had chimed in on all four again. By the 13th lap of 19 he was running second, tight behind Shepherd's AJS, but that was as much as he managed. Shepherd went through to win while Mac rolled to a stop at Old Hall Corner – with a puncture. Minter, who'd finished the 350 race an innocuous fourth, fared better in the 250 race, taking his Honda to a win from Shepherd, who rode one of those odd little Aermacchis Bill Webster had imported after seeing some impressive high-speed tests at Monza.

Broken

Mac finally broke his duck on the 285 Honda in the 350 race at Mallory Park the following Sunday, its fourth scheduled appearance; at the chequered flag he was 400 yards clear of Alan Shepherd (AJS), with Minter third, arriving late again but in time to depose early leader Mayhew (AJS). The formula was repeated in the 500 race, with Mac giving his G50 a second win. There were two fallers at Devil's Elbow: Mayhew, late in the 500 race, breaking his collarbone; and one M J Stevens, who fell without injury to see his 350 Norton destroy itself against the concrete post at the end of the pit barrier.

The Mint was back on top a week later at Castle Combe, beating Godfrey in the 350 race, and then giving a masterclass in wet-weather riding in the 500cc event, tailed home again by Godfrey and localish (Newbury) new boy Tom Phillips. Then he was back on his home turf at Brands, winning another 350 race from Godfrey, and giving his 497 and 647 Domiracers an outing each to collect the 500 Redex Trophy and come through the field in the 15-lap 1000cc race to lead home Joe Dunphy. Roy Mayhew crashed at Paddock Hill Bend on the final lap of the big race, "with tragic consequences," reported *The Motor Cycle*. Mayhew was 30 and a dock

foreman, and was survived by his wife, Molly and their two daughters.

The Minter-Godfrey show reconvened at Snetterton a week later with similar results, while Mac won both major events in his back yard at Beveridge Park, but was making bigger news with the results of Dunlop's pre-season tests at Mallory Park – enter the Dunlop 'triangular' racing tyre, the RMT1. The bottom line of the Mallory tests, said Dunlop, was an increase in

Mac was regularly the fastest member of the Honda team led by Jim Redman in 1962, but mechanical failure often kept him out of the results. This is the TT, where he posted two retirements; mechanic Pim Fleming stands by. (Courtesy Elwyn Roberts Collection)

cornering speeds of up to 8.5% with the new tyre, thanks to its larger full-cant contact patch, while the narrower upright contact area reduced rolling resistance but didn't affect braking performance. "Forget all previous tyre developments," asserted Mac, "this new one is it."

Now the Island beckoned, with or without Dunlop triangulars, and certainly without John Hartle, whose arm still wasn't up to the demands of racing. The talk now was of his return in September for the Italian Grand Prix. TT week opened with Mac's record-shattering opening lap in the 250 race, hustling his Honda round at 99.06mph from a standing start and taking 30 seconds out of Derek Minter to lead on the road. It didn't last: the lubrication problems of '61 became electrical gremlins in '62 and Mac stopped at Barregarrow on the second lap with an engine firing on only two. Minter took up the running, his privately entered 1961 RC162 fitted with a 1962-spec engine for the occasion, and led home team-mates Jim Redman and Tom Phillis in a 1-2-3 for Honda – except they weren't quite his team-mates, and that was a problem. Before the race, Honda team manager Reg Armstrong advised Minter to keep out of the way of the factory Honda men as they came past, which got Minter's back up and made him more determined to win in defiance of team orders, with unfortunate repercussions for him later on.

Hailwood won the Junior from Hocking, who was on his spare MV after a practice crash saw his race bike immolated. Mac's 285 Honda was tucked into a promising third behind the MVs when his engine died at Keppel Gate, while Minter retired with the rear of his Norton covered in oil. But the story of the 1962 Junior TT was the story of Tom Phillis, who died after crashing his 285 Honda at Laurel Bank on lap two. Few were as often tipped for big things as former Sydney motor mechanic Thomas Edward Phillis, and few as popular. Hocking, who was a particular friend to the Australian and shattered by his death, took a start-to-finish win in the Senior TT (Hailwood retired with a fried clutch after losing first gear), with Ellis Boyce a fine second on Francis Beart's Manx in spite of a loose exhaust. It seemed there wasn't much to celebrate, though.

Minter had fallen at Quarry Bends in the Senior and taken some bruising, so wasn't a starter at Mallory Park's Post-TT meeting on the Sunday. Mac was, and led Hailwood's MV for seven laps of the 350 race, and then coasted in, his Honda's engine dead, while Alistair King (Norton) claimed second from Paddy Driver. Hocking, whose 350 MV had holed a piston, cleared off at the start of the 500 race, with Mac, Matchless-mounted, in second. Hailwood, however, recovered from a bad start to pass them both, posting a new lap record at 91.69mph.

At Brands on Monday, with Minter still out of action and in front of 50,000 fans, Hailwood crashed his smaller MV at Druids late in the 350 race while well in front. He restarted in the lead but then lost it to Phil Read's Norton on the last lap after the fire engine's gearlever fell off, leaving it stuck in third. Hailwood's performance on the 500 was more impressive, tailing early leader Read for four laps, then giving the bigger MV its head and clearing out while Read fended off Anderson.

Elsewhere on this congested Whitsun weekend, Canadian Mike Duff and Tony Godfrey shared the spoils at Thruxton, Godfrey posting a new lap record at 88mph. At Cadwell Park, it was Dennis Pratt and Lewis Young. Hocking, meanwhile, flew home and announced his retirement from the sport, effective immediately.

Clay Hill

Doug Hele had had an informative TT. The titanium conrods tried in Fred Stevens' 500 Manx and Roy Ingram's 350 had been a qualified success in the stated aim of "lessening the inertia loading on big-end bearings." Difficulty had come with the lightweight metal's tendency to stretch when hot, so requiring very close, power-sapping bearing clearances at low temperatures.

For the 497 Dominator, the team had tried new cam profiles, valve springs and porting. Maximum power was up to 57bhp at 8000+rpm, but torque was way down, and the engine wouldn't pull its 1961 gearing. The Mint had practised for the Senior on the bike but chose his Manx on race day.

Now recovered from his fall in the Senior, Minter was back for the Dutch TT, running a fine second to Hailwood's MV in the 500cc race. Mac was again out of luck – his 285 Honda was clearly faster than the 350 MVs, but expired early in the 350 race after ejecting its oil. He fared better among the 250s, running second to Redman, and went one better at the Belgian GP for just his fifth career grand prix win. Minter, by then back on his home turf, took five from five at Brands, beating home Read's Nortons in all three major finals.

During the heat of July, when the frequency of meetings diminished just a little, there came other news: of a proposed merger between the companies that ran Brands Hatch and Mallory Park; of a Hornchurch dealer named Tom Kirby, who would be sponsoring Robin Dawson on a 7R and a G50 at the Manx Grand Prix; and of Bob and Joyce McIntyre, who had, on 18 July, been blessed with a daughter, Eleanor.

The action resumed at Castle Combe on the Saturday following the young McIntyre's arrival, with Minter still in the groove. In the 350 race he struggled from mid-pack to catch Hailwood, whose 7R then abruptly slowed with a misfire. Minter swept into the lead, with Godfrey second from Tom Phillips. Hailwood's AJS chimed in again, but too late; the world champion-elect had to settle for third. The 500 race was likewise Minter's; he got home from Hailwood and Godfrey (both Norton), posting a new lap record at 89.99mph.

The last stop before the British championships came at Snetterton, where Minter suffered a rare failure in the 350 race, leading after Hailwood went out with a seized engine, but then retiring himself when his Norton's ignition failed, leaving Read a winner from the 7Rs of Lewis Young and Peter Darvill. Minter fared better in the rain-shortened 500 race, leading comfortably after Hailwood's challenge had faded, Young and Darvill again in line astern.

Oulton Park, 6 August: the 30-lap race for the 350cc British Championship got going in patchy sunshine, with Bob Mac making good use of his 285 Honda's 53bhp to take the lead from Minter (Norton) and Hailwood (AJS). Mac built on his advantage, setting a new lap record at 88.59mph, until lap eight when, he later said, "the engine just stopped." Mint and Hailwood took over the running, swapping the lead until the last lap when Minter put his head down to get home in front of Hailwood, with Read third.

The heavens opened for the 500 championship race. Read led from the line with Hugh Anderson on Tom Arter's G50 following him into the rain. Minter was third away and into the lead by the second lap, while Mac and Hailwood – on a borrowed Reg Dearden Norton – recovered from poor starts. By lap 16 of 30 Mac, reunited with his Norton for the event, had passed Read for second and began to close on Minter, with Hailwood up to fourth. Three laps later the Scot crashed heavily on the uphill left-hand kink at Clay Hill and was taken to Chester Royal Infirmary with, said *The Motor Cycle*, "serious head, arm and other injuries." The Mint went on to win the race from Read and Hailwood, ending the day as British Champion in 250, 350 and 500cc classes.

Mac's friend and team-mate, Alistair King, inspected the site of his crash, finding a long skid mark which he thought indicated a gearbox seizure. Others said the mark was not made by Mac's Norton, that at an estimated 100+mph he had simply aquaplaned off the circuit. Some said he'd then hit a tree; others an advertising hoarding. What was certain was that Bob McIntyre was critically ill. In its 14 August issue *Motor Cycle News* said his condition had deteriorated; that he was "fighting for his life."

Bob Mac looked a winner in the race for the 1962 350cc British Championship at Oulton Park, but the engine of his 285 Honda "just stopped" after eight laps. Here, he leads Phil Read, winner Derek Minter, and runner-up Mike Hailwood. (Courtesy Elwyn Roberts Collection)

Mac died on 15 August and the motorcycle world faltered at the shock of his passing. It was almost inconceivable: Mac had embodied so much that made the sport great, he seemed immortal; we knew and saw his courage, strength, determination in abundance, his clear-sighted professionalism. Mac was a lion of a man who'd chosen to make his life among us, who'd made motorcycling the greater for his part in it. For many of us, he was the big brother we never had. "Racing," said Geoff Duke, "has lost its last real personality."

The stars regrouped at the Ulster GP, where Redman demonstrated the pace of his new 339cc RC171 Honda to win the 350 race. Hailwood, back on his MV, lapped the field up to fourth place in winning the 500cc event. Of Minter there was little sign. He'd fallen during the 125 race, sustaining a cut to the head and a broken finger that put him out of action for six weeks.

Man of the Year

Domestic action resumed at the 19 August Brands national, where Phil Read, Lewis Young and David Downer, riding Paul Dunstall's 650 Domiracer, posted a win each. Good news meanwhile came from Oulton Park. John Hartle, who'd been threading his way over selected bits of countryside on his trials Velocette, now went to the Cheshire circuit for a canter on his 500 Manx, pending a return to racing – if not quite yet. "My doctor's not keen," he said, "and as I can't race until he signs my form, I may have to wait till next year."

Back in the Island for the Manx Grand Prix, Robin Dawson recorded a win in the Junior on Tom Kirby's 7R, with Dunphy claiming victory in the Senior on Francis Beart's Norton – the Surrey tuner for the second time in a season claiming an Island triumph overshadowed by tragedy.

Phil Read's double win and flurry of record-breaking laps at the Cadwell Park autumn international was pushed out of the headlines by the news that Norton would at the end of the year leave its Birmingham ancestral seat to move into AMC's Woolwich, London works. Held in some quarters to be on par with the ravens fleeing from the Tower, the news was serious enough, carrying with it the announcement that the race shop would be closed and all development work stopped. Doug Hele was leaving to take up a job with Triumph.

Minter, restored to fitness, took a clean sweep at Brands on 23 September, beating Read home in the 350 and 500 races, and winning the battle of the Domiracers in the 1000cc event after being pushed hard by Downer on the Dunstall bike. Meanwhile at Scarborough, Dan Shorey rode Tom Arter's 7R to a win in the 350 race while Peter Middleton cleaned up in the 500.

The last internationals of the season came the following weekend. At Aintree, Minter got his eye in with wins in the 500cc event and the Aintree Century, but had to concede defeat in the 350 race to Dan Shorey after another of his poor starts. The following day at Mallory Park for the Race of the Year there was no stopping this Man of Kent. Hailwood was absent after falling at the Finnish GP, damaging an arm and a leg, and Minter's opposition in the name event came from Read until he dropped his Norton at the hairpin

Joe Dunphy and entrant Francis Beart achieved big things in the '62 Manx GP, though not immediately. Dunphy retired the Beart 7R (pictured) on the first lap of the Junior – then won the Senior two days later. (Courtesy Elwyn Roberts Collection)

on lap 14 of 40. After that Minter was on his own, leading home Alan Shepherd and John Cooper, who ousted Jim Redman's 250 Honda from the top three on the run to the flag. Minter also won the 500cc race and finished fourth in the 350 on Geoff Monty's lightweight Norton, while Read claimed the laurels.

A last journey north: everyone who could, spectator and competitor alike, turned out for the Bob McIntyre Remembrance meeting the following weekend at Oulton Park. Minter won both 350 and 500 races, in the smaller class putting on a memorable burn from the stern to beat home Fred Stevens (Norton) and Shorey. Jim Redman won the Bob McIntyre Handicap, but Geoff Duke stole the show by running a few demonstration laps on Mac's 1957 TT-winning Gilera; and Alistair King, who'd announced his retirement immediately following Mac's death, pulled on his leathers one last time to ride Mac's lightweight G50.

The season ended at Brands Hatch, where Minter won the 350 race, then crashed his 125 and spent the rest of the day spectating, while Paddy Driver won the 500cc race and Tony Godfrey, on Minter's Domiracer, the 1000cc event. The crash changed nothing: Minter was British Champion in three classes, had won the 350 and 500 ACU Stars and the Redex Trophy. In November, *Motor Cycle News* readers voted him 'Man of the Year.' But after all that, the season to come was full of uncertainty: "I don't know what I'll be riding," he told *Motor Cycling*.

Chapter 7

1963: The Mint

"Out of this world"

Charlie Rous, veteran sports reporter at *Motor Cycle News*, had it right: at the beginning of 1963 Derek Minter was the best in the business. He might have lacked the cavalier charm of Mike Hailwood or the raw charisma of the late Bob Mac, but he knew his craft inside out; could ride anything and beat anyone. He wasn't at his best at narrow woodland tracks such as Cadwell Park or Scarborough, and had a hearty dislike for road circuits like Dundrod, but he knew how to make a living while putting on a show for his fans; he was thoroughly professional about his craft and easy on his mounts.

Minter was canny, and his own man. During the closing months of 1962 he was approached by Honda to ride in Japan, but the two parties couldn't agree terms and, incredibly after an impressive season on his RC162, Minter never rode another Honda. There were no immediate difficulties, though, when Geoff Duke invited him to ride Bob Mac's demothballed 1957 Gilera while at Mallory Park for tyre tests with Avon, and on which he lapped within a second of Hailwood's lap record.

John Hartle, who'd ridden the Gilly at Oulton Park and pronounced it "marvellous," was looking forward to the coming season. His arm was improving. He'd received physiotherapy, and had signed with John Surtees to ride the seven-time world champion's Reynolds-framed 500 Norton as well as his 250 and 350 JSDs – John Surtees Ducatis – in the world championships.

Meanwhile, AMC development chief Jack Williams and Tom Kirby had been having a chat. AMC had approached the Hornchurch dealer (and AMC shareholder) as far back as November 1961 about his helping to develop its race bikes, and now it seemed the Kirby team would become one of the twin conduits (Tom Arter's would be the other) through which Jack Williams would channel AMC's experimental work on the 7R and G50. South African Paddy Driver was signed to ride the bikes on short circuits and at the TT, with Lewis Young in support. A second team would be made up of Roger Hunter, Johnny Jacques and Ron Chandler. The rapidly-expanded Kirby team went to Snetterton in December to test the latest bikes from AMC's rapidly-diminishing production of racing hardware, complete with special tweaks from Williams. The riders declared themselves impressed, especially with low-rev power pulling out of the Hairpin, some saying they were pulling a higher gear there than ever before.

Meanwhile, the contents of the Norton race shop had been sold. Manchester dealer Reg Dearden bought three truckloads of tools, experimental parts and components – six tons in all – to bring the total number of Manx Nortons in his custody up to 46. Paul Dunstall was another snapper-up of Norton's unwanted trifles.

Ray Petty told *Motor Cycling* he'd be sponsoring Tom Phillips in the season to come, while Francis Beart aimed to continue his run of success at the Isle of Man with Joe Dunphy at the TT, riding a 7R and a 500 Manx. He'd also be preparing Dunphy's Nortons for short-circuit work, bikes for Peter Darvill at the Manx GP, and the usual queue of customer engines.

There was news from Gallarate. MV Agusta would be back with a full factory team in 1963, and had signed a second rider – Alan Shepherd would be aboard the team's fire engines alongside Mike Hailwood. Shepherd, who'd also been courted by Honda, signed for the Italian team after tests at Monza. "It was very, very good," the Cumbrian said of the bigger MV. "It almost seems silly now that I've ever bothered to chase them on my Matchless."

Minter, however, seemed reluctant to confirm his plans for the coming season. Ray Petty would again be fettling his Hallets Nortons, and he'd turned down an offer from MZ to ride in 125 and 250 GPs; that much was known at the end of January. Yet the stories tying him to Gilera just wouldn't go away. MV, already concerned about the performance of its 350s after being robustly handled by Honda in 1962, was no doubt delighted when *Motor Cycling* ran a stirring piece about how much better Gilera's bikes had been the last time the two marques had done battle, in 1957 – no doubt trying to encourage the Arcore factory from afar.

The worst-kept secret in motorcycle racing was finally out in the open during the first week of March, when the Mint, John Hartle – fit again, at last – and Geoff Duke flew to Milan for tests with Gilera at Monza. "Despite near-freezing temperatures, Minter lapped within one second of the 500 lap record," said *Motor Cycling*. Hartle wasn't far behind, and Duke was particularly impressed with the 350: "much better than expected," he said. Yet MV wasn't the only team haunted by the spectre of those Hondas, fast enough in 285cc guise and now running a full 350.

By the second week of March, Gilera's plans seemed finalised, with eight engines in preparation for Minter and Hartle. Interestingly, *Motor Cycling* ran a piece saying Hailwood had been approached by the Arcore concern to ride its wares, but that he'd decided to stay put as his MV contract allowed him to ride his own bikes, should time permit. "But I don't know whether I'll bother with them," he said.

Far away from Monza, Erith scooter dealer Paul Dunstall was making his own preparations for the season. He'd bought a sizeable percentage of the hardware from Doug Hele's recently deceased Domiracer project at Norton's Bracebridge Street sale, including engines and the complete 497cc factory bike. This would be ridden during 1963 by David Downer, and with 11.5:1 pistons Dunstall was hoping the bike could be coaxed to develop 54bhp. He was also working on a 647cc engine, to go into a second frame.

Phil Read, meanwhile, whose star rose so sharply in 1962, explained to *Motor Cycling* that his ambition was to become 'King of Brands.' To help achieve that he would be riding Steve Lancefield's Nortons in 1963. "All the main points have been thrashed out," said the Norwood, Surrey engineer. "It only remains for a contract to be signed."

Sentence deferred

Everybody was ready. A test day at Brands Hatch on a cold Wednesday towards the end of March found plenty of runners working up to race pace, including David Downer on Dunstall's 497 Domi (fastest man of the day), Joe Dunphy on Francis Beart's Manx, and Tom Arter's new recruit Mike Duff, who was taking over the team's 7R and G50 from former Waikato rugby league player Hugh Anderson, who was now riding for Suzuki. All eyes were on Derek Minter, however, who was sampling Ray Petty's Nortons, both with high-level exhausts, and the 500 a twin-plug head.

It all came back to Minter, a likely lad since the middle 1950s when he'd completed his national service and began picking off highly fancied scalps on his BSA Gold Star. Since then he'd won six British championships, plenty of ACU Stars and put in mesmerising performances at circuits everywhere. In 1962 he'd taken more than 50 wins on Ray Petty's bikes alone. If Minter was in form, even Hailwood was hard-pressed to stop him.

Yet the Mint liked to sleep in his own bed, and knew how to make a good living without going 'foreign.' He had reached his prime when factory rides were in critically short supply, and his forays into international racing had been, at least until Honda, on unproven machinery with limited backing. Perhaps things would be different with Gilera.

The season opened at Mallory Park on the last day of March without a four-cylinder Italian motorcycle in sight, but with Minter in the same invincible run of form he'd enjoyed through much of 1962. Hailwood, who'd sold his 7R and 500 Manx to Syd Mularney, would ride the Reg Dearden 500 Manx he'd been fettling till midnight the night before, and had his old 7R on loan, which made him first off the line in the 350 final – and

Wide-open spaces: The 1963 Gileras were far from sorted for the Hutch, the first major meeting of the year, but Phil Read (Norton) did well to keep in touch with Hartle around the fast curves of Silverstone. (Courtesy Elwyn Roberts Collection)

stationary again within the opening lap thanks to a blocked jet. John Cooper took over from Peter Middleton (Norton), and then Mike Duff (AJS) led for four laps, but, sure enough, Minter reeled him in and led home the field with Duff a good second from Chris Conn's Norton. For once, the Mint made a good start in the 500 race but was content to sit in second while Hailwood led for four laps; he then passed and pulled away to win in his own time with Hailwood second by a length from Read's Norton and Matchless-mounted Duff.

Minter made the headlines again the following Saturday at Silverstone for Bemsee's Hutchinson 100, but not before Hailwood had put in a classic ride in the 350 race. With his borrowed 7R arriving at the circuit scant minutes before the off, he started from the back of the grid yet led by the end of the first lap, and drew away to leave Duff, Read (on his own Nortons for the meeting, fettled by Allen Dudley-Ward), Driver and Minter haggling over second. Minter retired on lap seven with a split exhaust and Driver faded, but Hailwood forged on, his 7R pulling 8700rpm down Hangar Straight, he said. Jack Williams "puffed a little harder on his pipe" at the news, and calculated Hailwood's speed to have been a thoroughly implausible 147mph.

Excitement of a different kind came in the 500cc event when Minter and Hartle, in their first competitive ride on Gileras, returned a one-two for Scuderia Duke. Minter posted the fastest lap, though a full second shy of the outright lap record he shared with his current team-mate. *Motor Cycling* knocked a little gilt from the gingerbread by reporting that Minter's bike was "snaking terrifyingly" as he passed Read for the lead on the second lap, but the win was emphatic enough, with the Mint getting home from

Hartle by 13 seconds, who was himself four seconds clear of the gaggle of Nortons behind, headed by a tenacious Read and Hailwood.

Minter was in record-breaking mood for Brands on Good Friday, and winning plenty. In the 350 event which, shouted *Motor Cycling*, was "one of the most exciting races ever seen at Brands Hatch," Hailwood and Read broke early, but were soon caught by Duff and Minter. Hailwood hung on and led into Clearways on the last lap, only to fall when a full-lock, 100mph slide became a high side, cracking a wrist as Minter came through to win.

The Mint followed that up by taking control of the Redex Trophy race from Gilera team-mate Hartle with Driver, his Matchless resplendent in Tom Kirby Racing's new red and white, and Read (Norton) giving chase. Hartle had to make two pit stops for plugs, putting Read clear in second while Driver fended off a late-charging Downer on the smaller of Dunstall's Domiracers. If he was efficient in the Redex, Minter was imperious in the 1000cc race, passing Read on lap two and clearing off in a manner, said *Motor Cycling*, "which underlined the power and improved handling of the Gilera." In the process Minter set a new lap record at 90.34mph. Read held off Hartle's Gilera for two laps, then bowed to the inevitable and settled for a good third from Duff.

High tide

Some 60,000 had gone to Brands on Good Friday, and 60,000 turned up at Oulton Park on Easter Monday to see the main event resumed. There was no Hailwood now, but Minter and Hartle's two Gileras were there, and Phil Read – now on Lancefield's Nortons – to chase them home. Or better: Read put a smart pass on Minter early in the 350 race and after four laps had a handy four-second break at the front. The Mint had other ideas and by lap ten the two were side by side and swapping the lead. Then Minter did what he'd so often done, putting his nose in front and keeping it there, while Read squeezed home from Hartle.

Read led the 500 race too, pulling out a similar lead. He was passed on lap five by Minter and a lap later by Hartle. Again Read held on impressively but eventually lost touch, though held third from a rampaging Downer on the Dunstall Domiracer. Bill Smith and Derek Woodman, running fifth and sixth, were lapped by Minter, who set a scorcher of a lap record at 91.86mph.

Elsewhere on Easter Monday, John Cooper continued his apprenticeship at Cadwell Park with wins in the 350 class from Billie Nelson, and from Derek Phillips' Norton in the 500 race. Joe Dunphy had a good day at Crystal Palace where he collected the laurels in the 350 class, and just failed to catch Griff Jenkins' Charles Mortimer-sponsored Norton in the 1000cc event. Completing a day of doubles, Mike Duff cleaned up at Thruxton. On Tom Arter's hardware he saw off a persistent Tony Godfrey, Kiwi Ginger Molloy and Dave Williams on Syd Mularney's ex-Hailwood AJS in the 350 race, then in the Commonwealth Trophy got his G50 home first, chased hard by Williams (Norton).

Scuderia Duke was enjoying its extended period in the sun. Talking to *Motor Cycle News* back in March, Minter described both Gileras as "fabulous," praising their engine performance and brakes and saying he'd never ridden a bike "so fast, that handles so magnificently." Certainly the Gileras looked the goods in their British-designed, Bill Jakeman fairings. *Motor Cycling*, comparing some characteristics of the Gallarate and Arcore products, reckoned the Gilly slimmer, lower and lighter; but judged the MV a better handler.

To be fair, Gilera's handling woes at Silverstone were in part due to rock-hard front suspension, set up for the aluminium dustbin fairings of the 1950s that were heavier and offered more downforce than Jakeman's dolphins. Minter had suggested a longer swinging arm to get more weight on the front wheel, but with little sponsorship there was no money for such work.

Minter, who was due at Imola on 24 April for the first clash of the year with Hailwood's MV, didn't enter for Castle Combe the Saturday before, leaving Selwyn Griffiths (AJS) to win a sodden 350 race by 20 seconds from a scrap between the Nortons of Downer and Ray Watmore, while Tom Phillips splashed his way to victory in the 500 race.

Alan Shepherd was a non-starter at the Imola Shell Gold Cup clash. His MV had expired with valve trouble at an earlier meeting and there was no bike available for him. Hailwood played a lone hand for MV therefore, and got out to a good lead in the 500 race despite trouble from the wrist he'd injured at Brands just 12 days before. Yet Minter chased him down and took the lead at half distance. Hartle later passed the weakening Hailwood and even had the brass to pop past Minter on the penultimate lap, but this was Minter's race. It wasn't all roses in the Gilera camp, however. Minter had suggested the bikes needed their footpegs raised and received a polite rebuff for his pains. It would be "impossible to lay the bike over so far," said Gilera. Minter demonstrated the force of his argument by sliding off in the 350 race, grounding the smaller Gilly's brake pedal while dicing with Remo Venturi's Bianchi.

Hailwood's post-Imola problems seemed more serious. *Motor Cycling* described him as "despondent." "The way Minter's riding at the moment," reckoned Hailwood, "I wouldn't attempt to stay with him. He's out of this world." The odds on Minter winning the 1963 500cc World Championship shortened dramatically.

Minter, home in time for the Brands national meeting on 12 May, caught up with the work Ray Petty had been doing on his Nortons, which included a new twin-plug head for the 350. Yet the Junior race didn't quite go his way. He'd chased down early leader Read to take the front by lap four, but then found oil on his left foot and slowed, allowing Read to close up again; and when the Mint missed a gear at Stirlings, Read needed no second invitation.

Minter turned the tables on Read in the Redex Trophy race with Downer coming in third, and then prepared for the headline event of the day, the 1000cc race, which pitted Downer on Dunstall's 647 Domiracer with its factory lowboy frame against Minter on his twin-plug 500 Petty Manx. Much was expected from the event and much delivered; but, said *Motor Cycling*, "the most exciting race ever seen at Brands ended in tragedy." After a race-long scrap, Downer led as the pair crossed the line to begin the last of 15 laps. Minter outbraked him going into Druids, knowing he had to get past, as Downer could outdrive him from Clearways to the line. But when Minter, with oil on the rear of his bike, went into a high-speed slide at Dingle Dell and crashed heavily, Downer could do nothing to avoid him and went down as well. It was a bad one: Minter damaged vertebrae – crushing one – and was taken to West Hill Hospital in Dartford, where he was described as "comfortable." Downer died in the ambulance from a punctured lung. Dave Degens, running close to the leading pair, went on to collect the win from Joe Dunphy and Ron Chandler.

Read the news

A week later *Motor Cycling* suggested that Minter might be out for the season, with injuries "more serious than at first thought." Duke meanwhile confirmed that the Mint's place in the Gilera team would be taken by Phil Read. Alan Shepherd didn't know nearly as much about his own future. The supply of MVs seemed to have dried up, even for the TT, but for the Junior he'd at least been offered the John Surtees Ducati that Hartle was to have ridden before his Gilera call-up, and would be test-riding one of MZ's 250 two-strokes at the West German GP.

Meanwhile, from Southampton Syd Lawton, bike dealer, entrant, sponsor and all-round good guy suggested that he might have a few of those odd little Aermacchi four-stroke singles, in 350cc guise, for the 1964 season.

Within the week, Minter had walked back into his own house and Shep had received confirmation that there would be no MV for him at the TT, the factory saying it would have no time "to prepare the machine you broke." Shep, bristling, said: "One valve broke and there was no other damage, so I can't be accused of over-revving." So that, it appeared, was that for Shep. At least Tom Kirby had offered him a G50 for the Senior TT; there would be life after MV Agusta.

Yet the TT was surely an anticlimactic affair after the promise of April. The 350 Gileras were outclassed by Redman's Honda, who won the Junior by seven minutes after Hailwood retired; Hartle limped into second on a Gilera running on three cylinders. The Senior was emphatically Hailwood's, getting his MV home with more than a minute to spare from Hartle, who had four minutes on Read. Mike Duff, meanwhile, put in the ride of his life to bring Tom Arter's G50 into fourth at 99.29mph. Tony Godfrey fractured his skull after crashing his new 250 Yamaha at Milntown, becoming the first TT casualty to be airlifted from the scene of his crash by the new Shell-backed rescue helicopter.

Phil Read got a place in the Gilera team after Derek Minter's Brands Hatch crash. At the Senior TT he started with Alan Shepherd, who was riding Tom Kirby's G50 after his MV deal collapsed. (Courtesy Elwyn Roberts Collection)

With Hailwood and Minter absent, Read, back on his Lancefield Nortons for Mallory Park's Post-TT fixture, looked likely to make more hay in the 350 race until a coming together with Cooper at Shaw's had them both out of the running, allowing Dan Shorey (Norton) through to win from Joe Dunphy's Norton. The Luton rider fared better in a wet 500cc race, beating Dunphy home after both had shared the fastest lap. Cooper had recovered by the following weekend and journeyed north to Scarborough, where he won the 350 race and was well placed to take the 500 from Rob Fitton (Norton), until slowed by a lapped rider. His form fell away a touch at Cadwell a fortnight later, where he took a flag-to-flag win in the Invitation race from Roger Hunter's Kirby Matchless; fell in the 350 while Lewis Young claimed victory for the Kirby team, and finished fifth, a long way behind winner Tom Phillips, in the 500 race. The talent was clear: the racecraft maturing slowly.

Minter, by now almost fully mobile, put in an appearance at a Brands open test day, and suggested he might be back for the Ulster Grand Prix. Tony Godfrey was on the mend, too, walking unaided but still very weak. There was good news as well for Gilera, with Hartle taking what would be Scuderia Duke's only classic win at the Senior Dutch TT after Hailwood retired with suspected piston failure.

Read was back in the spotlight when the circus reconvened at Brands in mid July, where he took three from three on Lancefield's Nortons. Chased home by Joe Dunphy's Nortons in the 350 and Redex Trophy races, he rounded off an impressive day with a win in the 15-lap Alan Trow Memorial, again leading from start to finish, again towing along Dunphy on his Beart-fettled Norton. He extended his run of good form at Mallory a week later, taking a comfortable win from Cooper in the 350 class but working harder in the 500 race. After getting out to an early lead, Read was challenged first by Cooper, then by Dunphy. Alan Shepherd joined the party on Tom Kirby's five-speed G50 but Read reclaimed the lead in the closing laps, and stayed there with Shepherd hard on his back wheel.

Lone wolf

Astonishingly, before July was out, the Mint was flying to Monza for tests with Gilera, where he broke the lap record before the excitement almost came to a premature end when a loose pinch bolt jammed the 500's steering. Still, he stayed aboard and completed the day, after which, said Charlie Rous in *Motor Cycle News*, "he was in perfect physical condition." Gilera, said Rous, was "delighted with his performance."

There was still the chance of his challenging Hailwood for the world title, and a shakedown ride at Oulton Park for the British championships might be just the thing.

Minter had just two rides at Oulton Park, both on his 500 Gilera, but they were enough to make sage observers wonder whether he had really broken his back just ten weeks earlier. In the Les Graham Memorial Trophy race Minter settled into second behind John Hartle, but when the Derbyshire man dropped his Gilera at Esso Bend he won as he

Derek Minter broke his back in May 1963 yet, by August, was riding again, winning the 500cc British championship (his third in a row) at Oulton Park, and breaking his own lap record. (Courtesy Elwyn Roberts Collection)

pleased. Read was a non-starter, his Lancefield Norton receiving some last-second tweaks, but Dan Shorey, having a canter on one of Tom Arter's G50s, ran in a game second from his team-mate du jour, Mike Duff.

Hartle's day didn't improve. In the race for the 350cc British Championship he led early on the smaller of his lightweight Lacey-tuned Nortons, but ran off at Cascades on lap two, handing the lead to Read, who'd been busy seeing off Alan Shepherd's 7R. Read made good his escape from Shepherd as Shorey did the same to Ray Petty's new protégé Dennis Ainsworth. It was Read's title, and modest enough reward for the entertainment he'd offered in months past.

Which just left Minter's ride of the day, in the 30-lapper for the 500cc British Championship. "Minter all the way," asserted *Motor Cycling*, after the Gilera team leader cleared out to lift his own lap record to 92.03mph while Hartle retired with a slipping clutch, thought to have been caused by oil leaking onto the plates in his earlier fall. The scrap of the race was between Read and Shepherd, who fought all the way for second with Read getting the nod. Australian Jack Findlay was fourth on the lightweight G50 Bob Mac had developed and campaigned during 1962.

For all his dominance at Oulton Park, the fragility of Minter's recovery soon became clear. At the Ulster Grand Prix, just a week later, *Motor Cycling* told of "lone wolf" Hailwood and of "strangely subdued" Minter, who was making his first appearance at Dundrod in five years. Early in the 500 race, while Hailwood built on a steady lead, Minter could run no higher than fourth behind Gilera team-mates Hartle and Read, and coming under increasing pressure from Kirby Matchless-mounted Shepherd. By lap six Hailwood was half a mile clear of Hartle, Read had fallen at Leathemstown, and Minter was being passed by Shepherd in corners, but using the Gilera's power to squirt past him on the straights. And so it finished, with Hailwood bagging his third grand prix win of the year and Minter securing third place only after Shepherd had to pit for fuel.

Read was taken to hospital with back injuries but was soon on the mend, while Minter made his first trip to the behind the Iron Curtain to take second behind Hailwood in the East German GP – Hartle retiring from the same event with a jammed mudguard.

The world got its first real glimpse of John Cooper's transcendent talent the same weekend at Aberdare, where he took apart the opposition to notch six wins from as many starts on his Wraggs Nortons, claiming victory in his heats and the finals of the 350, 500 and 1000cc races, with Selwyn Griffiths running second in all three. Cooper was in action again in the wet at Snetterton as the season began its final month, but the day was Dunphy's, who splashed through the rain to win both 350 and 500 races.

On the Island for the Manx Grand Prix, Francis Beart enjoyed another successful week on his chosen ground as first Peter Darvill (7R, Junior) and then Griff Jenkins (Mortimer Manx, Senior) claimed wins on bikes he'd prepared.

Fine tuning

Tom Kirby's plans for 1964 were already well advanced. He would enter four runners –
Lewis Young, Paddy Driver, Australian Jack Findlay and Roger Hunter – on stock bikes to
begin with, but with the prototype of a new 350 to be available for testing by the start of
the season.

Yet it seemed the music was about to stop for Scuderia Duke. At Monza for the
Grand Prix des Nations, the team fell apart in front of a deeply critical home crowd:
Hartle jettisoned his Gilera at 130mph in the Curva Grande during practice, injuring
a hand and scratching himself from the meeting, and during the 500 race, first Read
and then Minter retired, as Hailwood cleared off to win by two laps from Jack Findlay's
McIntyre Matchless.

Scuderia Duke's swansong began at Scarborough. Minter, Norton-mounted for the 350
race and finishing third behind the Nortons of Cooper and Tom Phillips, fell from his Gilera
at Mere Hairpin on the first lap of the big race "on a lot of broken and loose gravel," reported
The Motor Cycle. At least Read was on hand to take an easy win for the team from Cooper
and Phillips. Minter fared better back on his home turf at Brands, though retired from
the 350 race on his own Norton while Mike Duff won on Tom Arter's AJS. In the 500 and
1000cc races, the Mint was untouchable, passing team-mate Read early in each event to win.

**In 1963 Ray Petty cut a dashing figure in his fishing hat, and built his experimental
reverse-head 350 Manx. It was first raced by Derek Minter the following Easter,
proving fast but troublesome. (Courtesy Adrian Sellars)**

Successful at home or not, however, Duke said he "expected Gilera to throw in the towel." The effort, so great by some, now seemed flawed from the outset by Gilera's apparent ambivalence, and by the obduracy of key figures. Much had been said, but it seemed less had been heard, and very little understood.

While Hartle flew home from Milan to have the plaster removed from his damaged hand, Minter's last race against Hailwood's MV came at the Mallory Park Race of the Year. He opened his account quietly enough, running fourth in the 350 race behind Alan Shepherd and Dennis Ainsworth, with Redman's Honda far in the distance taking the win. In the wet 500cc preliminary, Shepherd tucked himself into second place behind Hailwood's MV and stayed there to the finish, fending off the Gileras of Minter and Read. The pattern was set, with Hailwood indomitable and Shepherd riding out of his skin. In the Race of the Year Hailwood and Redman got away first from Read, Minter and Shepherd. The two Gileras soon overhauled Redman, but Shepherd came too, and on the tenth lap he put himself alongside Minter's Gilera at Gerard's, then passed him at the hairpin. Minter eventually repaid the compliment, but Shepherd stuck close until a lurid slide encouraged him to settle for third. By race end, Hailwood had lapped all but Minter and Shepherd.

The last meetings of the season belonged to Read. Back on his Nortons, he twice beat Minter in a fair fight at Oulton Park, repeating the dose in the 350 and Redex Trophy races at the Brands Hatch curtain call in mid October. Minter regained a little pride in the 1000cc race, beating home Dennis Ainsworth, while Read and Hartle were both non-starters because the bikes they'd entered – 650 Domiracers – weren't available. Read, not surprisingly, took both 350 and 500 ACU Stars, albeit with Joe Dunphy a strong second in both.

At the end of the season Gilera folded up its tents and stole quietly away, having tarnished its reputation with an under-resourced effort that had achieved little. Avon, meanwhile, announced its withdrawal from racing, citing "steeply rising costs of competition," together with the "downward trend of the motorcycle market."

In late October, as Geoff Duke flew to the Gilera factory to see if anything might be salvaged from a ruinous season, Phil Read boarded a plane bound for Japan and talks with Yamaha to discuss what might be; while Minter reflected, and perhaps not for the first time, on what might have been.

Chapter 8

1964: Empire of Speed

"It's high time something was done"

Some came for a season on a shoestring effort, sustained by baked beans and optimism, a sleeping bag sharing the back of an ancient van with a well-worn Manx; some came with two new bikes and a three-season strategy, a string of home wins already behind them. Some travelled the 3000 miles from the forests of Canada, others from Australia, New Zealand, the sunburnt cities of southern Africa. They sounded odd, these visitors from the far corners of the world, and had strange ways of making tea; but they were family and could ride a bit, most of them, and as like as not could work miracles with pliers and fencing wire.

Jack Ahearn, Tom Phillis, Jack Findlay, Kel Carruthers; Hugh Anderson, Ginger Molloy; Mike Duff, Frank Perris; Jim Redman, Gary Hocking, Bruce Beale, Paddy Driver. All were winners – champions, some – who made an impact beyond their numbers in a decade of challenge and change.

Canadian Mike Duff began his journey in 1955, when he was 15 and started racing a sprung-hub Triumph at Edenvale, a former RCAF airfield north of Toronto, his home town. Two years later, he was winning on a new Manx Norton, and by the turn of the decade, he and his Manx were under starting orders in Britain.

Next came the shift to AMC machinery: "I hated oil constantly being spewed from the cam followers of the Norton," wrote Mike, now Michelle, many years later. "The Canadian agent offered me a new G50 and 7R at distributor cost – I accepted, and it was a decision I never regretted." He found the AMC bikes fast and reliable. "Barring major engine blowups or serious crashes, the 7R would usually do a season without having to split the cases, though the G50 would need a new big-end bearing and probably a timing-side main."

Sponsorship was a little easier to find back then: "At the 1960 North West 200, Brian Heath from Avon gave me two sets of racing tyres without asking any questions; Lew Ellis from Shell gave me oil and petrol – and money to sign a contract, again without asking any questions or even seeing me ride. A few months later I agreed to use Renolds chains and Girling shocks, with free product as needed."

Within a couple of seasons, Duff's name was becoming a regular inclusion at the top of results sheets. Then: "thanks to Hugh Anderson's recommendation, Tom Arter asked if I'd like to ride the AMC development bikes at the TT and Ulster Grand Prix, while riding my own bikes on the Continent. The following year Hughie was under contract to Suzuki so I became Tom's number one rider."

In 1964, Duff was one of a handful of riders receiving assistance, albeit indirectly, from British factories. Alan Shepherd had been another, but in December 1963 decided to give up riding homegrown hardware and pursue opportunities from elsewhere – including Yamaha, which had offered him rides in a number of 250cc classics. Among the private runners Derek Minter, though still listening hard for any encouraging word from Arcore, expected to make his living in Britain on Ray Petty's Nortons, which included, from November 1963, a new bike – the reverse-head 350, or 'back-to-front' Norton. Petty believed the arrangement offered a number of advantages, among them superior cooling, a constant supply of cold air for the carburettor, and a straight-run exhaust, albeit with the disadvantages of an awkward entry to the inlet tract and difficulty in coaxing the engine to run hot enough. The bike first ran at a Brands Hatch test day, with encouraging, free-revving, results.

Despite a heavy mid-season crash, Canadian Mike Duff (40) became 350cc British Champion in 1964. He's pictured at Brands Hatch – for once without his trademark Bell 'space' helmet – dicing with Norton-mounted Tony Godfrey (Courtesy Elwyn Roberts Collection)

John Hartle, disillusioned with Gilera's apparent decision to put its bikes back in the shed, had considered retirement but then thought better of it and came out, all guns blazing, with two Norton engines in Reynolds frames, a 500 "breathed up" by Bill Lacey, but both with Swedish Torsten Aargard five-speed gearboxes and Bill Jakeman fairings. He also renewed his tie-up with Comerfords.

The opening weeks of the year brought news from Southampton, whence Syd Lawton was preparing to fly south and attend Aermacchi's tests of its new 350. This, unsurprisingly, would boast a number of modifications from the 250, including a forged rod, new camshaft, new cases and improved oiling. Should the tests prove successful, said Syd, he'd place an immediate order.

Running light

The classic season got going unusually early, with the US GP run in Florida's particular brand of February sunshine. Alan Shepherd, having turned down the Yamaha offer, won the 250 race for MZ, while Gilera chose to enter a 500 with Argentine ace Benedicto Caldarella doing the steering. His run was short-lived, however; after leading a curious Hailwood for a time, Caldarella retired with gearbox failure, allowing Read to claim second on one of Tom Kirby's G50s after he'd won a grapple with Norton-mounted Hartle. Mike Duff ran unobtrusively into fourth on his 1957 Manx.

Things were beginning to happen for the Canadian. At Phil Read's prompting, Yamaha had asked Duff to ride its factory 250 two-stroke twins at a handful of early grands prix, including the TT, while Tom Arter worked on a plan to rework the largely forgotten AJS Porcupine for racing in a new decade.

With the start of the season proper just weeks away, Lawton returned from Italy apparently delighted with everything he'd seen. The new 350 Aermacchi would rev to 9000rpm with peak power (35+bhp) at 8500; dry, it weighed just 225lb (102kg), and almost 100lb lighter than a 350 Manx Norton. Best of all, perhaps, it had clocked 128mph on the back straight at Monza. Lawton ordered half a dozen bikes on the spot, which he expected to sell for £500 apiece.

By March Phil Read was back in the headlines. Although adamant up to now he'd be riding Steve Lancefield's Nortons when not about Yamaha's business, *Motor Cycling* now reported otherwise: Read would campaign Tom Kirby's G50 and aim for second place in the 500cc World Championship, behind the then inevitable Hailwood MV. Steve Lancefield declared himself "bitterly disappointed" to be left with no rider so close to the start of the season.

Enter John Hartle who, announced *Motor Cycling*, would ride Lancefield's bikes in Britain. "I'd like people to know I haven't fallen out with Comerfords or Bill Lacey, whose bikes I'll still be riding on the Continent," said Hartle. "I'm very happy to have fixed things up with John," chipped in Lancefield. "I'm working day and night to get the bikes ready for Oulton Park on Easter Monday."

A week before that, on 22 March, came the season opener at Mallory Park. A crowd of 20,000 braved the cold and damp to witness the resumption of hostilities, and were rewarded with a minor classic in the 350cc department. John Cooper, finding Mallory ever more to his liking, leapt away from the start. Minter and Hartle caught him, with Hartle sweeping past both to lead. Minter made a grab for second but Cooper, fastest of the three through the Esses, inched away. The Mint wasn't quite finished. He made a last-ditch challenge with two laps to go, passing Cooper and closing on Hartle. "But Hartle's bike appeared to have the edge and he drew away to win by a couple of lengths," said *Motor Cycling*.

There was more of the same in the 500 race, this time with Hartle skipping away from the start with Read and Cooper giving chase. Cooper grabbed the lead in the Esses but Read was soon back in charge – until Minter, scything through the field, got in front and pulled away to win by 600 yards with Read, Hartle and Duff, reunited with his Arter G50 and the cold of Britain, following him home from Cooper in fifth.

The pattern was set, and the opening weeks of the season showed that Minter was approaching his best again after the difficulties of 1963. By the end of Easter the Mint had won the 500cc and 1000cc races at Brands, the 500s at Mallory Park and Snetterton, and was prevented from taking a clean sweep in the class only by a fall at Oulton Park on the Monday. He hadn't fared so well in the 350 class. Ray Petty's reverse-head special was a sluggish performer at Brands and Snetterton, and a non-starter at Oulton Park; but at least Minter's comparative failures gave others a glimpse of the gold: Read took 350 honours at Brands, Hartle at Snetterton, with Read popping up again to take a double at Oulton Park.

Duff chose to spend Easter Monday at Thruxton for the Commonwealth Trophy meeting, scrapping in the name race with Paddy Driver and Peter Darvill (Norton) until the South African retired with an off-song engine and Darvill faded to let through Tom Phillips (Norton). Dave Williams won the 350 race, running away to win from Londoner Ray Pickrell and Ray Watmore (AJSs) after Duff and Phillips had both retired.

Wild card

Though yet to be sighted in open combat (the latest forecast was Brands Hatch on 18 May), a steady trickle of details about Tom Kirby's new short-stroke 350 AJS appeared in the press. According to *Motor Cycling*, it would first run in a stock frame while Bill Jakeman built a copy of Bob McIntyre's frame – and then Ken Sprayson of Reynolds would build an even lighter frame in consultation with Kirby and Jack Williams, giving the bike an all-up weight of about 240lb (110kg). Finally, there was to come a new, Williams-designed cylinder head.

More tangible was Tom Arter's heavily modified AJS Porcupine, raced by Duff at the Hutchinson 100. In Silverstone trim the 498cc twin made a claimed 54bhp at 7500rpm,

Tom Kirby's team became a conduit for Jack Williams' 7R and G50 development early in the sixties. South African Paddy Driver, pictured during the 1964 Senior TT, gave the team three seasons of loyal service. (Courtesy Elwyn Roberts Collection)

but the bike was far from easy to ride. A sizeable gravity-feed tank sat above steeply angled carburettors, giving the top-heavy bike an awkward riding position.

The meeting was cold and wet, keeping spectator numbers down but not MV-mounted Hailwood, who diced with Read's Kirby G50 for a time in the 500cc BMCRC Championship race, then went about his business. Minter made one of his trademark leisurely starts but battled up through the field to catch and pass Read on lap 12 of 25, then hit a patch of oil and slid off without injury, handing second place to Read with Tom Phillips' Norton third. Duff brought the Porcupine into seventh after a long dice with Yorkshireman Carl Ward and Chris Conn.

In the 350 championship race Phillips offered a glimpse of the future. While Jim Redman ran away, lapping the field up to and including fifth spot in an effortless win for Honda, Kirby AJS-mounted Read and Aermacchi-propelled Phillips waged a furious dice that reached a late settlement when Phillips slipped in front to claim second by a length and a half.

Phillips was on a roll. A fortnight later at the newly resurfaced Castle Combe he won the 500 race on his Norton, setting a new lap record at 90.75mph. Minter had retired with a seized motor but managed to beat Phillips the following day in the 350 race at a wet Brands Hatch, though the Berkshire rider again cornered the bulk of the tinware. With the track flooded in places, Phillips took an early race-winning lead in the Redex Trophy race. Minter ran second from a lad named William David Ivy, who'd graduated from lightweight classes to ride Geoff Monty's 500 Triumph-engined Monard. Ivy's race ended prematurely when his tank ran dry, but Phillips forged on from Minter, with G50-mounted Dave Degens taking third. Phillips repeated the dose in the 1000cc race while

John Cooper stuck with him to half distance and Minter trickled home a subdued third.

The Mint journeyed to Snetterton intent on ending Tom Phillips' run of success, but didn't quite manage it in the 350 race. Phillips got past him on the last lap to bring his Aermacchi home first, giving the Italian marque its first major 350 class win in Britain. Minter was having none of it in the 1000cc Senior Service Trophy, cleaning up by some 300 yards from Phillips' Norton and, in third, Ivy on Geoff Monty's 650 Monard. After the meeting, Lawton said his 350 Aermacchi was running low compression – 9.6:1 compared with 11:1 for the British singles, and that there was another 600 safe rpm to be had. The announcement wasn't everywhere met with spontaneous outpourings of joy.

At the start of May Mike Duff sidelined himself for a month at the Nürburgring. Running his 7R wide while in pursuit of Heiner Butz' Norton, he plunged down a bank and fell heavily, breaking a collarbone and suffering concussion. He took up light duties in Tom Arter's workshop.

Meanwhile, Minter sought to defuse rapidly escalating speculation that he might appear on a Gilera at the TT. "I'm just not interested," he told *Motor Cycling*. "I don't think [Gilera] has much chance of winning because the MV handles so much better. I'd rather finish second on my Norton – there's some prestige in that."

John Hartle, who journeyed to Imola for the Shell Gold Cup and then fell, cracking a forearm and sustaining a hairline fracture of the skull, didn't share Minter's views. He hoped to be back in action at Whitsun, and was keeping his fingers crossed that Gilera might yet come to the Island party.

Cooper

John Cooper was working himself into form nicely, cleaning up at Mallory Park on 3 May with near start-to-finish wins in both 350 and 500 races instead of "tiring as he has so many times in the past," observed *Motor Cycling*. Griff Jenkins bagged both runner-up spots while the Mint, never in the hunt, fell at Shaw's in the 500 race and watched forlornly as his Norton caught fire.

The following Saturday at Aberdare, Cooper rode Francis Beart's Nortons to wins in all three major classes with newcomer Malcolm Uphill following him home each time. It looked for a time too as though Cooper had won the 350 race at Snetterton next day, but race organisers said he hadn't because he'd turned out on a Norton instead of the AJS listed in the programme, and they gave the trophy to Dennis Ainsworth. Nothing daunted, Cooper was in the thick of it again in the 500 race, scrapping furiously with Joe Dunphy, Rex Butcher and Degens for the lead until Minter swept past with all the fluency of old and pushed on to win.

Minter was on top at Brands on Whit Monday too, fighting off Paddy Driver's G50 in the 500 race while Rex Butcher claimed third. Phil Read, fresh from victory for Yamaha in the 250 French Grand Prix, didn't figure in the 500 race at Brands – his Kirby G50 had magneto trouble – but had taken the 7R to an impressive 400-yard lead in the 350 race before its five-speed gearbox started playing up. The pack surged up to join him, Minter, Driver and Dave Williams leading. Minter slipped into the lead at Paddock and promptly retired with a broken oil line. Read's gearbox righted itself and away he went, posting his second win for the day (with the 250 race), while Driver took Williams for second.

While *Motor Cycle News* revealed Jack Williams was leaving AMC after ten years as development engineer and race manager, the Kirby short-stroke 7R underwent "secret testing" at Brands, where Read posted a 350 class record for the short circuit at 57 seconds even (78.32mph) before an ill-fitting gudgeon pin brought the day to a premature end. Come the Junior TT the bike was still out of action for want of spares, making it one of several notable non-starters. John Hartle, still suffering headaches, was told that his skull fracture was more serious than first thought while Hailwood, who was fighting a combination of laryngitis and tonsillitis, also missed the race. Meanwhile, Tom Phillips crashed Syd Lawton's now fuel-injected 350 Aermacchi in practice at Greeba Bridge, suffering spinal injuries. He later developed something the medics diagnosed as shock-induced pneumonia, rendering him comatose and very poorly indeed.

There was no sign of the Arter Porcupine after TT practice. The bike had run well and over-revved on gearing as high as Arter could fit but, chasing a 100mph lap, Duff got as far as Sulby Bridge when he discovered oil on his foot. Thinking it came from a blown seal, he slowed and completed the lap (94.5mph). Alas, Arter soon discovered a crack in the magnesium cases and Duff returned to his G50.

With Jim Redman winning by seven minutes, the story of the Junior TT was the scrap between Read, Minter and Duff for second, with Read getting the nod by 11.8 seconds from the Canadian while Minter slowed with a broken valve spring. Hailwood rose from his sick bed for the Senior and won by more than three minutes from Minter, while Read retired on the opening lap with a dropped valve and Duff, having led the event for a time, went out at Appledene when his G50's motor seized.

Making his first visit to the Island, Cooper suffered mixed fortunes, retiring with a seized engine in the Junior but finishing a creditable ninth in the Senior. Even so, he relished being back at Mallory Park for the Post TT meeting, leading home Read in the 350 race and Dave Williams' Norton in the 500. Minter, who'd done altogether better at the TT with second in the Senior and fourth in the Junior, ran home eighth in the 350 race at Mallory and retired with an absence of sparks in the 500.

There was no doubt Cooper was the coming man, but for all his success at northern circuits he still hadn't cracked it at Brands, and at the 21 June national Minter took three from three with Cooper running second each time. Still riding Beart's Nortons, Cooper next headed north and swept aside all opposition at Scarborough to win the title 'Cock o' the North'. A fortnight later he was underlining the point at Mallory Park, again collecting the tinware in both 350 and 500cc events. Minter didn't attend the Mallory meeting, one of several stars to stay home in response to the circuit management's decision to make "severe cuts" to start money – as much as 90%, according to some.

There was good news from the north east. A new circuit at Croft Airfield, five miles south of Darlington, was nearing completion. A 1.75-mile triangle traced around the perimeter track of the old RAF bomber base, it was to be known as Croft Autodrome, with the first meeting pegged for August. Sadly, however, it seemed Aintree's days were numbered, at least in three-mile form. Never a successful venue, it had slipped off the national calendar after the 1962 Aintree Century meeting, and now it seemed part of the circuit complex was destined to be redeveloped for housing.

Five

Hartle was out for the season. His skull fracture was mending well, but he prudently shelved plans for an early comeback. Steve Lancefield, having to look for yet another replacement rider, had agreed terms with Griff Jenkins, but conflicting oil contracts sank the deal, so Rex Butcher agreed to ride his bikes till the end of the season. Meanwhile Dave Degens would ride Paul Dunstall's Domiracers for the immediate future, covering for Sid Mizen, who was recovering from a TT crash. At least Tom Phillips was up and about.

Minter was back in action at Castle Combe in late July after a month's break, taking a comprehensive double win with Chris Conn chasing him home each time. The following day he and Cooper again went head to head, this time at Snetterton. In the 500 race Minter slipstreamed Cooper for most of the journey, pulling out to pass on lap nine of ten and winning by 150 yards. To be fair Cooper was running a new and very tight engine, having made a hasty swap when his five-speed gearbox jammed in top during his heat. Minter's run in the 350 race was more difficult. He was hounded all the way by Cooper, Dave Williams and Butcher on Lancefield's device, with "Derek's experience carrying him through," said *Motor Cycle News*.

Phil Read was Minter's next challenge, having returned from another successful European odyssey for the British championships at Oulton Park, but the Mint was in no mood to entertain rivals and cleared off for his fifth 500 title, leaving a seven-bike scrap for second place to provide the entertainment with Duff to the fore, restored to his G50 again after a patchy time on the continent

Banbury Dan. The tighter the going, the better Dan Shorey liked it. He excelled at Scarborough, but was no slouch around faster hairpins, such as Esso Bend at Oulton Park. (Courtesy Elwyn Roberts Collection)

with the quick but unreliable Porcupine. Gyula Marsovszky, Fred Stevens, Derek Woodman, Read and Cooper were all in the mix, but Cooper retired with a seized engine and Read with a misbehaving gearbox; Stevens then slid off to leave Woodman claiming second from Duff. The Canadian emerged top from a similar last-man-standing battle for the 350 title. Cooper led, but was slowed by carburation troubles; Jim Redman's Honda expired, as did Minter's Norton (with a holed piston); Bruce Beale led for a couple of laps on his factory 305 Honda but went out with a broken gearbox; so up came Mike Duff, sweeping past an ailing Cooper in the closing stages to win. "There was no way I should have been first," wrote Michelle in her excellent autobiography, *Make Haste Slowly*, "but it's the last lap that counts." As for Cooper, at least he'd won the Les Graham Memorial Trophy event earlier in the day, chased home by Read in his last full race on Tom Kirby's G50.

At Thruxton, the visitors from former colonies, provinces and protectorates were on top as usual. Paddy Driver controlled the 500 race followed by Norton-mounted Brits Dave Williams and Ray Pickrell. The South African almost did the double, leading nine laps of ten in the 350 race when a holed piston stopped him, leaving Rhodesian Alan Harris (Norton) to take his first major win in Britain.

The weather closed in a week later for the Ulster Grand Prix but Read took it in his stride, winning the 250 race from Redman's Honda to put Yamaha and himself within sight of their first world title; and with no Mike Hailwood MV in the 500 race (he'd already clinched the title), Read won that too – on a Reg Dearden Norton. The bike was the result of a chat between Dearden and Read at Oulton Park, when Read had parked his Kirby Matchless after the latest in a run of gearbox problems and despite a trip to Kirby's Hornchurch HQ for attention. Dearden there and then agreed to supply him a Norton for the Ulster. Tom Kirby, who'd been told by Jack Findlay that Read was riding Dearden's bike, was unimpressed. "I'm at a loss to know why [Read] didn't ring me for a replacement G50," the Hornchurch entrant told *Motor Cycling*. "All I know is he's under contract to ride my machines in the 500 class."

Minter, who'd gone home after Oulton Park and missed all the excitement, generated his own at Brands Hatch on 16 August, collecting wins in the 250, 350 and 500cc events, with Driver chasing him home in the 350 class and Redex Trophy race.

Motor Cycling meanwhile carried a small piece announcing that Phil Read was to quit the 500cc class for the foreseeable future.

Cooper, who'd stopped three times to change goggles in the Ulster GP and had finally retired for the excellent reason that he couldn't see where he was going, missed the Brands Hatch August national because his entries arrived too late. He resumed the struggle at Aberdare where he won the 350 final but then collided with a fallen rider in his 500 heat. Though in pain at Mallory Park the following weekend, he won the 350 and 500 races while Ivy took the 125 and 250cc. Nobody was about to stop him at Castle Combe

Phil Read rode a Kirby G50 to second place in the 1964 500cc US Grand Prix, and, for much of the season, juggled rides on Kirby's bikes with his Yamaha commitments. He's pictured at Brands Hatch on a Kirby 7R. (Courtesy Elwyn Roberts Collection)

either, where he collected another double with Conn second in both 350 and 500cc races. Cooper's run was finally halted at Snetterton the following day where the Mint kept another clean sheet, beating Reg Everett in the 250 race, passing Cooper at half distance to win the 350, and holding off Conn's Norton in the 500cc event.

With the onset of autumn John Hartle, who was spectating at Monza for the Grand Prix des Nations, said he hoped to be back on his Nortons in '65; while Tony Godfrey, who'd collapsed at Snetterton, was still struggling with the after-effects of injuries suffered at the Hutch way back in April; Ray Pickrell was out of action, too, having broken a leg at Brands in early September. In the racing at Monza, Hailwood had seen off Caldarella for the last time, and his employer took the opportunity to unveil its new 350 triple – which was upstaged by the first appearance of Honda's new 250 six, the RC164.

The British season entered its final phase with Cooper faltering unexpectedly. At Cadwell Park he stopped in the 350 race with a fouled plug, leaving Conn to win and new boy Rodney Gould (Norton) to chase him home. In the 500cc, race Cooper led again and stopped, this time with a sticking throttle, while Conn again came up to win from Ivy's 498 Monard. At Scarborough the following weekend he did better. While Read cleaned up in the 350 race on an overbored RD56 250 Yamaha, Cooper held second throughout, and looked likely to win the 500 race until his rear brake cable broke. Blackpool native Derek Woodman went on to win after Conn fell at Drury's Hairpin.

New territory

Cooper's Brands breakthrough came at the 20 September national, when he broke free of Paddy Driver's challenge early in the 350 race to take his first win at the Kent circuit. Driver fought off the Mint for second, and was in the thick of the melee again when the tribe reconvened for the Redex Trophy race. For the opening laps Minter had the South African's Kirby G50 for company, along with Dunphy and Conn, but then he cleared off leaving Dunphy to better Driver. The 1000cc event was a better spectacle, with six bikes angling for first. None got the better of Minter, but Degens, Driver, Dunphy, Cooper and Conn did glorious battle, with Degens, on Dunstall's 647 Domiracer, finishing best to beat Cooper for second.

That rarest of sightings in Britain for 1964, Mike Hailwood and his MV, looked in to scoop the pool at the Mallory Park Race of the Year, winning the title event and the 500 race from John Cooper's Norton while Phil Read showed Jim Redman the speed of his 251 Yamaha in the 350 race. Yet there was mutiny in the background. Earlier mutterings about cuts to start money almost became open rebellion when it became clear that prize money for the Race of the Year only paid down to sixth place, and that just £10. "It's high time something was done," growled Mick Woollett in *Motor Cycling* – and so it was, with organisers pledging a minimum of £10 for every finisher in the 1965 race.

Meanwhile the caravan rolled on to Oulton Park, where Cooper won the 350 race, fighting off Dan Shorey while Minter struggled through from 12th, caught his man and pulled out to pass at Deer Leap on the last lap – but failed by inches. Minter's turn came in the Bob McIntyre Memorial, leading from the start, and going away while Cooper fended off fast-improving Dave Croxford for second. Duff, taking what would be his last ride on the Porcupine, retired with an ailing gearbox.

The season ended with the final struggle for possession of the ACU Star in the 500 class. Cooper had already won the 350 Star and, going into the final 500 national race of the year, he and Minter had ten wins apiece, while Cooper had three seconds to Minter's one. Cooper led early from Minter, but on the second lap his bike began to misfire and the Star's destination was settled. Cooper won the 350 race, while Minter, on the reverse-head Manx, was slow getting away and had to settle for third behind Duff, who posted his second runner-up spot of the day. It was Minter, though, who brought the curtain down on seven months of racing with a win in the 1000cc event, dicing hard with Dave Degens' Dunstall Dominator, but always in control.

Casualties: Chris Conn, who'd fallen doing 90mph at Gerard's Bend during the Race of the Year meeting, was up and about, but the year ended badly for Alan Shepherd who'd fallen heavily testing a 350 Honda at Suzuka, only regaining consciousness four days after the crash. Meanwhile, Hailwood offered the strongest indication yet he might go car racing, saying he was fed up at the few rides he was allowed by MV. John Hartle, perhaps more severely tested by Lady Luck than anyone, was "disillusioned" and again talking about retirement; and Mike Duff ended the year in hospital, having remedial surgery on the hand injured in a fall at the season-ending Japanese GP.

Minter, meanwhile, flew to Milan to ask the good and the great at Arcore if he might have a bike for the 1965 500cc World Championship.

Chapter 9

1965: The Kirby Boys

"Some people think you make a lot of money racing"

Tom Kirby's fastidious grooming, his camelhair coat and neatly trimmed moustache, no doubt looked incongruous to some in the rough and tumble of a motorcycle racing paddock, but not so his team's gleaming machinery. From 1963, Kirby's bikes were an increasingly purposeful adornment to racetracks across the land, and the team a forcing house of British riding talent: Phil Read, Bill Ivy and Mike Hailwood all did stints on Kirby's bikes, and even such fierce individualists as Derek Minter and John Cooper came close.

Kirby's interest in things mechanical came about through wartime service with the RAF, and an engineering apprenticeship. His association with motorcycle sport began through a 1950s partnership with the grass-track ace Alf Hagon, and by the early 1960s Kirby was a successful motorcycle dealer who had sampled racing sponsorship through Ernie Wooder and the late Peter Ferbrache. Soon, with the endorsement of AMC boss Bill Smith and development engineer Jack Williams, Kirby Racing – and Tom Arter's smaller set-up – was becoming the unofficial AMC development team.

Kirby was a fan of AMC's racing hardware and understood its engines. "There was great scope for improvement. I designed a forged slipper piston for the G50 that allowed bigger valves," he explained. "But although this increased performance, the higher inertia loading meant that crankpin breakage became a problem. So we designed a new one and increased maximum safe engine speed by 300rpm.

"We wanted more rpm but the crankcase became prone to fracture. A heavier aluminium alloy case cured the trouble and the extra weight helped handling. The next step was to design titanium conrods."

Kirby attributed his team's reputation for fielding fast, reliable bikes to a simple formula. "They are completely stripped every 800 racing miles and if I spot something only slightly worn I replace it immediately."

His riders kept all their start and prize money and the team attracted plenty of famous names. By 1965, Read, Alan Shepherd, Ron Chandler, Paddy Driver and Lewis Young had all won for Kirby, with more stars to come; and the team's secret weapon, the final refinement of the 7R Jack Williams had done so much to develop, was nearing completion.

There had been whispers about the bike for more than a year, but few had so far seen it. "We've been doing extensive bench tests," Kirby explained to *Motor Cycling*. "We're using so many new materials we're bound to run into problems."

There was also the matter of cost. Finding titanium for conrods and valve gear was expensive, and further expense came when Kirby found the components had to go to France for machining. The piston was made in Italy and contained beryllium, an exotic and very lightweight metal typically used in aircraft and rocketry. Durability proved a problem and more prosaic materials were a better bet, but making the discovery proved costly.

The benefits of such experimentation ran downstream and riders of private 7Rs and G50s enjoyed stronger gudgeon pins, crankpins, conrods and pistons as a result of Kirby/Arter development – and now an announcement from Woolwich had it that the G50 conrod was to be beefed up for '65 with a sturdier, reshaped small-end eye.

Meanwhile Paul Dunstall, now with bigger premises in Eltham, was experimenting with the 745cc Norton Atlas engine, building one each for Dave Degens and sidecar champion Colin Seeley. His 650s were giving 62bhp at the crank, and Dunstall was hoping for 70 from the bigger unit.

The season grew ever longer and busier: for 1965 more than 50 national and home international meetings were scheduled, starting at Mallory Park on 7 March. The meeting attracted a staggering 800 enquiries from prospective entrants. Elsewhere, however, there were problems. Thruxton's surface had now crumbled to the point where questions were being asked about its viability. The Easter national could go ahead, it was decided; but after that, all bets were off. There was no uncertainty about Aberdare's status: the tiny parkland track was unavailable for 1965, ending 15 years on the calendar. "Council horticulturalist Mr Peter Ellis is turning what used to be the paddock and most of the spectator area into a flower garden," explained *Motor Cycling*. Where Manx Nortons once stood, Mr Ellis had plans for 100,000 crocuses, daffodils and snowdrops.

Mike Hailwood re-signed with MV, but only for one season, along with new signing 250cc Italian Champion Giacomo Agostini. Up the Via Lecco at Arcore, Gilera first

The twins are coming: Dave Degens pictured on Paul Dunstall's 497cc Domiracer at the Mallory Park Post-TT meeting in 1965. (Courtesy Elwyn Roberts Collection)

announced it would back Calderella for the world championship on 1964-spec bikes, and then said it was withdrawing altogether.

Derek Minter, whose winter trip to Milan had yielded nothing, seemed unlikely to lament Gilera's absence. "The people in charge wouldn't take any notice of what the riders said about the handling of the machines," he said of the failed 1963 campaign to *Motor Cycling*. "There was no adhesion at the front end," he said of the 500. "You could turn the bars lock to lock at Monza and keep going in a straight line."

In any case, he had Petty's bikes to help with. Testing the reverse-head 350 at Silverstone, he reported that "it accelerates like a rocket." Bill Ivy was also testing a 350 Norton, this one belonging to Geoff Monty and equipped with Wal Phillips fuel-injection. "Starting was better," said Monty, "and pick-up was excellent."

Meanwhile, Syd Lawton told of improvements to the year's output of 350 Aermacchis. The '65 bikes would include a lighter clutch, stiffer frame and a new oil pump – though the new gearbox would have just four speeds. Price £550 each; one size only.

Two for the show

John Cooper began the new season at Mallory Park in fine form, winning the 350 and 500 races, while a slow-starting Minter working up to second in the 500 race and fourth in the 350. The coming generation looked likely to offer stronger opposition, particularly from Dave Degens on Dunstall's Domiracers and his own Aermacchi, but also from Rex Butcher on Charles Mortimer's Nortons and Dave Croxford on a G50 and 7R backed by Charlie Oakley. Bill Ivy, who for the moment still rode Geoff Monty's bikes, looked most promising of all.

At Brands for the second meeting of the season the youngsters were certainly trouble. In the wet 350 race, Degens' Aermacchi appeared behind Cooper and Minter, passed both and had enough steam to pip Minter on the line. Minter won the Redex Trophy race but Degens had the last word in the 1000cc event. Riding Dunstall's 647 Domiracer, he stalked Minter relentlessly, passing him on the last lap to "win easily," while Ivy secured third on the 649 Monard. At Snetterton, the last meeting of the March shakedown, it was Shorey's turn to win the 350 race from Minter, while the Mint showed Banbury Dan the way home in the 500 event.

April opened with news of the first meeting at a new circuit in the Kent countryside at Lydden, running to seven-tenths of a mile and obviously to the liking of Charlie Sanby, who ran away with the 1000cc event on his 500 Manx and established a lap record at 61.2mph, recorded in a whisker over 41 seconds. In Surrey, Francis Beart was now on the point of retirement. He sold his Ladymead premises and moved, with a much smaller workload, to a house in Brook.

Alan Shepherd too seemed destined to retire. Recovered from his Suzuka injuries, he'd undertaken private tests at Oulton Park on an old 250 Honda four, but seemed to have lost his edge and told Honda he'd had enough. It was a sad, subdued end for a rider whose talents included an uncommon kind of probing, self-reliant intelligence.

John Cooper and Dan Shorey journeyed north to Scarborough on the last weekend before Easter to divide up the tinware, Shorey – "I like hairpins" – leading Cooper home in the 350 race, Cooper returning the favour in the 500cc event. And then it was on, the vortex of Easter competition this year pulling in Hailwood, who neatly sidestepped Count Agusta's ban on the use of his bikes for the carnival by borrowing a Tom Kirby 7R AJS and a 500 Norton from Syd Mularney.

The champion's Easter got off to a poor start at Brands on Good Friday, however. The Kirby 7R's five-speed 'box gave trouble and he found Mularney's Norton was apparently fitted with old tyres. But to begin with all looked well: Hailwood led early in the 350 race from Kirby team-mate Paddy Driver until Minter and then Read on the '254cc' version of Yamaha's grand prix twin passed and was set to win – before the Yamaha fouled a plug, allowing Minter home from Mike Duff – with Hailwood a lowly 11th. With Cooper "off form" and Hailwood struggling on his borrowed Norton, Minter had Ivy's Monards

Newbury rider Tom Phillips did much to establish Syd Lawton's lightweight Aermacchi singles in Britain, but he was a fine hand on a 500 Manx, too. (Courtesy Elwyn Roberts Collection)

and Degens' Domiracers for company for the Redex Trophy race and the inaugural 1000cc King of Brands, yet Minter was in vintage form and won both. In the King of Brands, Ivy fell at Druids while Yamaha-mounted Read got past Degens for second, but he couldn't close the four-second gap to Minter, who duly collected his crown from pop singer Lulu.

The circus moved to cold, blustery Snetterton where Hailwood again struggled on his Kirby 7R, leaving Read to turn it on in the 350 class after seeing off early leader Cooper. Hailwood looked better in the 500 race, deposing Shorey after five laps to win comfortably. Then it was Cooper's turn, returning to form at Oulton Park on Easter Monday, where he won the 500 race after Minter had led for 15 of the 19 laps, and then discovered his left boot soaked in oil and began missing gears. In the 350 race Minter and Shorey put on an 11-lap show before Minter eased away to win easily from Duff on Tom Arter's 7R. The party came to an end at Mallory Park on something known in the English Midlands as Easter Tuesday. Minter had gone home but Cooper carried on, bagging both the 350 and 500 races, with Rod Gould (Norton) getting home second in the 350 class and Joe Dunphy in the 500.

The weekend was plagued by filthy weather. According to *Motor Cycling*, the 500 race at Cadwell Park on the Monday "went to the man who could see best in the snow," which was Norton-propelled Billie Nelson, echoing similar heroics from a revitalised Tom Phillips (Aermacchi) in the 350 race. Things were no better at Thruxton, where Dave Williams braved the wind and hail to take a double from Ray Watmore; nor at Crystal Palace where John Blanchard (Aermacchi) won the 350 race and Matchless-mounted Ron Chandler the 500 – from 20-year-old Peter Williams, son of Jack, on a Manx Norton.

Nemesis

Reports of an ACU plan to combine its Star awards with the British championships were overshadowed by news from Geoff Monty, who'd received a call from Bill Ivy to say he was leaving the team – and joining Kirby Racing. "I don't like upsetting anyone," Ivy told *Motor Cycling*. "But I want to race an AJS and a Matchless and I want to do the TT." Monty, who'd told Ivy he couldn't afford to let him do the Junior or Senior TTs, was aggrieved at being left without a rider at short notice.

Ivy, explained his biographer Alan Peck in *No Time to Lose*, had been talking to Kirby since the start of the year about riding his bikes; but Kirby repeatedly refused him, saying he didn't want to come between Ivy and Monty. When Ivy then said he was going to leave the team regardless, Kirby relented to the extent of allowing him a test session at Brands on the Wednesday before Easter, where he had Hailwood for company and the pair whooped it up, running close to the lap record on Kirby's G50s. Hailwood then had a word with Kirby about the scale of Ivy's talent and the deal was soon done.

Now a few months short of his 23rd birthday, Ivy was winning the affection of his contemporaries with an engaging, cheeky demeanour which, allied to an abundance of natural riding talent, helped him appear much taller than his 5ft 3in. He was from Maidstone, was devoted to his mum and a committed tearaway from his school days. Ivy had been racing since 1959 and had won regularly during the early '60s on a CR93 Honda backed by Chisholms, the local bike dealer where he worked. In 1963 he met Twickenham dealer Geoff Monty, who gave him a 350 Manx Norton for a couple of shakedown rides, and then offered him a gentleman's agreement to ride the Norton and Monty's Triumph-engined Monards during 1964. Now Ivy was finding a place in the big league.

Minter and Cooper had both gone down with flu early in the season and Cooper missed the May junket at Castle Combe as a result, but the Mint had to work for his prize money just the same. He won the 350 race comfortably, but fluffed the start of the 500 and worked hard to get past Peter Williams' Norton, who hung onto second from an in-form Dave Croxford. Down at Aberdare, meanwhile, sheep had apparently strayed into the park and laid waste to 100,000 newly planted flowers.

"Minter still reigns" said *Motor Cycling* after the Brands national on 12 May, but there was room for dispute after Ivy had taken a win in his first race on a Kirby G50 – the Redex Trophy event. He chased Minter through the field in pursuit of Cooper, the early leader. Driver took a turn up front, then Ivy, who'd had the cheek to dive past Cooper and then Driver at Clearways of all places, and then hang on to win. Minter, meanwhile, wobbled home sixth with shot rear wheel bearings. The 350 race was Minter's, working forward to pick off Shorey, Driver and then Ivy, as was the 1000cc race. With a back wheel borrowed from John Cooper, he shoved his 500 Petty Manx in front on lap three and stayed there, beating off challenges from Cooper, who retired with a loose exhaust, and Driver.

Ivy was clearly the man to beat, taking on the usual suspects the following weekend at Snetterton, and thumping them in the 500 race after a tight scrap that saw even Minter shoved back to fourth in the dash for the line. There was more argy-bargy in the 350 race, though without Ivy, who retired after having his face splashed with petrol, or Minter, who fell in his heat. In the end Ray Watmore (AJS) took the glory, from Dunphy and Shorey.

Final call before the TT for most of the stars was Mallory Park, where William David Ivy continued both his triumphal run on Kirby's G50 and his dubious relationship with the short-stroke (81 × 68mm) 7R, which was said to rev to a stellar 8600rpm. He started well in the 350 race but first Cooper got past, then Minter, and it became their race, with Minter's Norton proving the faster. Cooper was the brisk starter in the 500 race, leading by 100 yards at half distance; but Ivy pegged him back, taking the lead with three laps left and fending him off to win. Degens was third from Peter Williams, with Minter a modest sixth. Three from three for Ivy.

Patchy weather persisted into June, though it behaved while Honda star Jim Redman completed his TT double hat-trick with another emphatic win in the Junior, beating home Read's Yamaha by almost two minutes. Hailwood had led for three laps on the new MV triple but retired with a sick engine while Agostini ran third in his first race over the Mountain. Cooper (oil leak), Minter (engine) and Ivy (broken chain) all retired, leaving Griff Jenkins to lead the singles home on Steve Lancefield's Norton.

The weather closed in on Friday but, after falling at Sarah's Cottage on the third lap and kicking the bike straight, Hailwood limped home to win the slowest Senior since 1959. Ivy retired at Ballaugh, Cooper fell on the Mountain and Minter went out with magneto problems while Joe Dunphy steeled himself to continue Francis Beart's run of Island success and took second place, almost four minutes clear of Duff's G50.

Back on the mainland, Minter went home rather than head for the Mallory Post-TT meeting where Redman collected the gong for the 350 race, and Hailwood gave his MV a rare short-circuit outing to win the 500, ousting early leader Ivy, who chased the champion home with Cooper third. Making a sleepless, overnight dash to Brands Hatch from an unsuccessful Saturday at the Dutch TT didn't help Minter draw the teeth of his latest challenger the following weekend. He did well in the 350 race, borrowing a 7R from Tom Arter and getting home from Ivy and Ron Chandler (AJS). But in the 500cc event Ivy was at his rampant best, leading from the off with Minter finishing second from Jenkins.

Minter found some respite at one of his favourite stamping grounds, Castle Combe, where he collected wins in his 250, 350 and 500cc races at the July national meeting, losing out only in the Avon Trophy when his Norton abruptly began running rich, dropping him to fourth behind winner Ray Watmore (Matchless). At least Minter had a new lap record at 91.75mph.

By August, the game was almost up for Thruxton. The surface was too poor to withstand the 500-mile production race, which had been a part of the Hampshire circuit's schedule since 1955. The event was shifted to Castle Combe – but with misgivings

Billie Nelson campaigned Manx Nortons successfully for many years on the Continent and at northern tracks such as Cadwell Park. He was recruited to ride Bill Hannah's Patons when Fred Stevens retired. (Courtesy Elwyn Roberts Collection)

about its future after this temporary Wiltshire lodgement. Thruxton's August national went ahead and proved to be the last gasp for the Hampshire track in its Mk 3 guise; Ivy damaged a hand when falling in the 350 race after his 7R's rear brake was jammed by a flying stone. Pickrell (Norton) went on to win and then take second to Driver's Kirby Matchless in the Wills Trophy. The big story was of the circuit itself, however, and the writing, if not on the wall, was certainly in its potholes.

The poacher

Bemsee had moved the Hutch to August to avoid the unalloyed misery of Silverstone in the cold of April, which had the knock-on effect of shifting the Oulton Park British championship meeting to the end of the month. And if the Silverstone weather didn't quite cooperate, the racing made up for it. In the 350 event Read (254 Yamaha), cleared off with Bruce Beale (305 Honda) hanging on as best he could. The excitement lay in the dice for third, where Hailwood (Kirby AJS) swapped paint with the Nortons of Minter and Cooper. Read and Beale then bowed out, each with a broken crankshaft, and Hailwood squeezed home from Cooper while Minter equalled his own lap record at 98.48mph.

The wet Production race offered the unfamiliar spectacle of grand prix stars doing battle on an approximation of catalogue road bikes. BSA development rider Tony Smith led away but overshot at Stowe, handing the lead to Percy Tait's Triumph Bonneville. Phil Read, also on a Bonnie, then had a go; but with eight laps left Hailwood took point on his BSA Lightning and stayed there. Later, back on his fire engine, Mike the Bike also cleared off with the 500 race, while Yamaha-mounted Read did battle with Ivy's Matchless, Read getting ahead until the Yamaha's engine lost its edge; the scrap for second then became the business of Ivy and Minter, with another round going to Ivy when Minter's Norton went out with a broken oil line, allowing Cooper into third.

A week later, at Brands for the first major meeting on the short circuit since 1961, Ivy again took the 500 race from Minter, but finished third behind Minter and Cooper in the 350cc event. There was more of the same at Oulton Park for the British titles. "Minter rode one of the greatest races of his career," reported *Motor Cycling*, but the race for the 500 title was beyond even the Mint after he'd started badly, being left on the line juggling the twistgrip while the field streamed round Old Hall Corner and down The Avenue. A masterclass in aggressive riding followed, as he stormed through the field to catch the leader, Ivy, and pass him with four laps to go; but Minter had given his all and Ivy repassed to win by a length.

The 350 championship looked like becoming Read's second in the class after he'd run away to an early lead, but the 254 Yamaha again oiled a plug, leaving Shorey, Minter and Mike Duff haggling over the spoils. The length of a picnic rug covered the three of them, with Shorey motoring home two lengths clear of Duff, Minter and Ivy. The Mint's consolation success of the day came in the Les Graham Memorial Trophy, which he won from Driver and Shorey.

Dan Shorey had enjoyed a successful August, kicking off the month with a win at Cadwell Park and ending it with the 350cc British Championship. Not so however John Cooper who, despite having picked up the other big ticket at the Cadwell meeting, now faced hefty bills after both his 500 Nortons had blown up, one in the Ulster Grand Prix, the other at Oulton Park. "Last time I wrecked a Manx engine it cost £217 to repair," Cooper told *Motor Cycling*. "Since then spares have gone up and are harder to get. Some people think you can make a lot of money racing – they don't realise the expense." At least prize money was up. After the mutterings of discontent at Mallory Park in 1964, Grovewood Securities, owner not only of Mallory but of Brands and Snetterton, was posting a record £50,000 in start and prize money for 1965. But the battle wasn't quite over.

After the Mint had journeyed west again to take another hatful of wins at Castle Combe, the circus regrouped at Snetterton on the first Sunday of September, and again Ivy and the Mint ended the day with a win each. In the 350 race Minter deposed South African Martin Watson to lead by half distance, with Watson finishing second after fighting off Chris Conn. Ivy was fourth on a Kirby AJS "that just wouldn't go." Not so his G50: Ivy got a cracking start in the 500 race, and although Dave Degens put Tom

In 1964 Derek Minter began using a Mitchenall fairing featuring a transparent nose cone. The ACU didn't like it, saying reflected light made the racing number tricky to read – but it didn't stop him winning. (Courtesy Elwyn Roberts Collection)

Arter's Matchless into the lead, Ivy turned up the wick to win comfortably. Watson was third after slowing with oil on his back tyre, and Minter a remote fourth after coming together with Watson in the new kink on the start/finish straight – called Russell's – and running wide.

Read and Cooper divided the spoils at the Cadwell international a week later. Read enjoyed a rare clean run on his 254 Yam in the 350 race, but the gremlins struck in the wet Invitation race and the Yamaha slowed with a misfire. Cooper gunned his 500 Manx into the lead and collected a useful £500 to add to his depleted coffers. He did it again at Scarborough, beating home Read's Yamaha in a wet 350 race as fog swirled about, reducing visibility to 50 yards. The Derby man just made the start of the 500cc race, having put in some hasty remedial work after discovering a loose clutch centre in his heat. Still he led from the start of the final, surrendered it to Shorey and then took it back again, recording the circuit's first 70mph lap to resume point while Shorey fell, allowing Peter Williams into second.

At Brands Hatch the following day, Ivy and Minter each did what they'd hitherto found beyond them: Ivy won a 350 race – albeit on a factory Yamaha – after seeing off early leader Cooper, who was slowed by a loose gearlever; and Minter won the Redex Trophy event after passing Cooper and hanging on grimly from Ivy by a wheel. The Mint had an easier time in the 1000cc race, galloping away from Driver and Griff Jenkins.

One for the money

Mike Hailwood was there, riding a hack bike in what proved his last outing on a 500cc MV; Phil Read was there too, again to do battle with his unruly 254 Yamaha; but neither could prevent John Cooper from collecting the 1000-guinea cheque that came with first place at the Mallory Park Race of the Year. A shower of rain before the start and a Norton engine newly rebuilt by Ray Petty were all he needed.

Degens drew first blood in the streaming wet 350 race. After Read had galloped off into an early lead and his Yamaha had then gone about its habitual plug-oiling, Degens and Peter Williams, both riding Tom Arter 7Rs, staged a grand dice for the lead with Cooper, Degens pipping his temporary team-mate for the win and Cooper settling for third. Hailwood cleared off with the 500 race with Ivy and Cooper struggling for second. Minter got as far as fourth after a poor start, and then fell at Gerard's doing 90, cutting a hand and damaging a wrist. Ivy and Cooper got home unscathed, Ivy leading by a length at the flag.

Hailwood and Read led away in the big race, but were first passed by an audacious Driver, and then by Cooper at his favourite spot, the Esses. Read took the lead after a couple of laps, but Hailwood was by then going in the other direction, slipping to fifth on an MV proving unaccountably wobbly. Meanwhile, Cooper managed to keep Read in sight on the wet track, and at half distance passed him again as the Yamaha lost 1000rpm and began to slow. With four laps to go, Cooper's clutch failed, but by then he was far enough ahead to lead home Read, Ivy, Driver and Hailwood.

Derek Minter was spectating at Oulton Park a week later, reporting no broken bones but a season-ending skin graft to his knuckles. He saw Cooper continue his fine run by winning the 350 race from Stuart Graham, with Ivy fourth behind Degens. The Derby man didn't fare so well in the 500 race, featuring in a first-lap collision with Joe Dunphy that gave Cooper a broken collarbone, scattered the field, and left Matchless-propelled Fred Stevens with a 200-yard lead. Ivy passed Stevens to win, with Malcolm Uphill putting his Norton into third.

At Brands Hatch a day later, Tom Kirby had Mike Hailwood back as a temporary recruit, though the world champion didn't immediately prove his worth, struggling with a slipping clutch while Dave Degens won the 350 race for Tom Arter. Then came the race

**Bill Ivy enjoyed a successful 1965 season on Tom Kirby's G50 but cracked cases put
him out of the Senior TT on the second lap. This is Quarter Bridge.
(Courtesy FoTTofinder Bikesport Photo Archives)**

Kirby had been waiting long seasons to see, with his boys filling the podium after the
20-lap 500cc Evening News Trophy. Hailwood won from Ivy and Driver, after Ivy had
tried everything he could to pass the champion on the last lap, squeezing into the lead
at Paddock and then seeing Hailwood pull out and pass at Clearways to win by a wheel.
Degens, who'd led from the line, rode the Arter Porcupine into seventh, struggling to
match the best Nortons and G50s, said Tom, because the bike had a four-speed gearbox.

Hailwood completed his day's toil by easing into the lead on the third lap of the Redex
Trophy event and falling off at Druids. Ivy was on hand to take up the challenge and
stormed home for the win from Driver, with Jenkins third on Lancefield's Norton.

The season ended on the last day of October where it had begun almost eight months
before, at Mallory Park. At the Japanese GP, Hailwood had won his last 350 grand prix for
MV and his first in the 250 class on the Honda six. Ivy had finished third in the 250 grand
prix for Yamaha before dashing back to Leicestershire, again to heighten the intensity

of 500cc racing, and splashing to victory by three lengths from Chris Conn, while Peter Williams completed a good day for AMC by winning the 350 race on Tom Arter's 7R.

The AMC lobby had had a good year. Ivy had performed prodigies of excellence on the Kirby G50, while Degens and Williams had put in fine rides on Tom Arter's bikes late in the season. In December came confirmation that Chris Conn was to join Kirby Racing with the retirement of Ernest Gould – Paddy – Driver, and there was something else – a persistent rumour that Derek Minter was about to switch camps. Before the year was out he had been offered bikes by Tom Kirby and Colin Seeley, who was in the process of building a batch of AMC-powered bikes in chassis of his own manufacture.

Minter was unsure what lay ahead. He reckoned Kirby's G50 would "compare favourably" with his Nortons, but, he said, "I'm worried about Tom's 7R. His 350s aren't nearly so impressive, and I must have two good bikes."

Bill Ivy, about to disappear into the Yamaha fold, had the 500cc British Championship and ACU Star for the 500cc class to his credit (Minter won the 350cc Star), but confessed himself foxed about the 7R: "I don't know whether it's the bike or me," he said, "but it's true I can't match my G50 performances." Whatever the reality, it was soon about to be revealed. "I'm going to try Kirby's bikes soon after Christmas," explained the Mint.

Ray Petty, who was working on another special 350 Manx, seemed resigned. "I'll just have to wait and see what Derek decides," he said wearily.

Finally, with Christmas, came the unwelcome news that Silverstone was now unavailable for major motorcycle meetings. Persistent poor weather and a lack of sponsorship were both blamed, though a BMCRC spokesman told *Motor Cycling*: "The type of promotion necessary for the Hutchinson 100 was better suited to the Brands Hatch grand prix circuit." Whatever that meant, there would be no further top-level motorcycle action on the Silverstone calendar for six long years.

Chapter 10

1966: Eyes Front

"Funny old place, Brands"

The beginning of the story is familiar enough for its period – commonplace, even. It began in the mid-1950s, with trials riding on a 197 James, then a tentative road race on the same bike and an unexpected win. The disruption of two years' national service with the army would have stopped most of us, but back in civvy street, a chance meeting led to a chat with a garage manager, who offered a ride on his 500 Gold Star – and John Herbert Cooper, the son of a Derby tailor, was on his way.

The garage manager was Russ Warren, the garage Wraggs of Sheffield; and after the 500 Gold Star came a 350 Goldie in a Manx frame, then a 350 Manx Norton; and by then the alliance between Warren and Cooper was developing into one of the most enduring in the sport. Cooper looks back on those early days fondly. "I used to do quite well at Mallory, Cadwell, Oulton Park … Aberdare suited me: it was narrow, bumpy, a bit dangerous. I held the lap record there for 13 years. Then somebody said I should ride at Scarborough, and I broke Geoff Duke's Gilera lap record there …"

By 1963, equipped with a brace of Manx Nortons and the distinctive cartoon-character mooneyes he'd adopted for his red helmet, Cooper was a winner everywhere north of Watford, and particularly Mallory Park, where he knew the fast way through Gerard's and the Esses, and understood you couldn't go rushing up the inside at Shaw's and expect to get round quickly.

Elsewhere, he was still learning the ropes. At Brands Hatch: "Londoners used to run up the right-hand side of the track to Druids and baulk you. You couldn't take a nice line because you'd get halfway round and there they were, stuck in the middle of the road. It was a funny old place, Brands." Discovering who went where at Silverstone also needed work: "I was in a dice with Hailwood and Minter there one year [350 race, 1965 Hutch] and worked out I was faster through Abbey Curve than Hailwood and could beat him on the run into Woodcote. So I slowed down a little bit to get good drive through Abbey but Minter came past and baulked my run. I managed to get past Minter again but Hailwood won."

At different points of a clean, largely crash-free, good-humoured and highly successful career, Cooper would ride bikes prepared by Francis Beart and Ray Petty, yet did the bulk of his own preparation. "Ray first did me an engine in 1965 for the Race of the Year [Cooper's first win of three in the big-money Mallory race], but it was a confidence thing; it was never any quicker when he'd done it." He found Francis Beart impressive in a different way: "I took an engine to him in Guildford once, when Phil Kettle was there. The place was immaculate, the way the bikes were laid out. When you went for your chips at lunchtime you'd to have to eat outside because Beart didn't like the smell in the workshop. I thought to myself then, that's the way to be: really nice and clean and tidy; smart.

"He didn't like doing jobs in the paddock. I remember once at Mallory Park Terry Shepherd fell off at the hairpin, broke the front brake lever and bent a 'bar. I told Beart I had spare handlebars in the van, but he said 'Oh no, that's not a paddock job'. So he loaded up the bikes and went home."

At the beginning of 1966, it looked as though Cooper might benefit from Derek Minter's imminent change of marque. Minter hadn't yet decided between offers from Kirby and Seeley, but he'd handed over his Nortons to Ray Petty for sale, and the Farnborough tuner said he might hang onto the better of the 500s for Cooper's use.

Others on the engineering side rumbled with exasperation, if for very different reasons. Steve Lancefield said he was having trouble finding a rider. "The position is grim," he said. "It cost me more than £1000 to go racing last year [when the average wage was £23 a week] and I can't afford to continue unless I can regain some of that." Tom Kirby declared himself foxed by Derek Minter's wish to test the team's bikes. "Minter wouldn't ask to try out the Hondas if they offered him a contract," he said to *Motor Cycling*. Colin Seeley saw things differently: "I certainly wouldn't expect Derek to ride for me until he'd tried my bikes," he explained. "In fact, he's already ridden a 500 and I hope to have a 350 ready soon."

By the end of the month, Minter had tested Seeley's wares at Silverstone and made his decision. "I've been very impressed by Colin's bikes," he said. "I think we'll make a very good team." Kirby was fatalistic. "We just couldn't reach an agreement," he reflected. "Perhaps it's all for the best."

Cooper was happy too. "I'm pleased Minter's going to switch to AJS and Matchless," he said. "He should be a bit easier to beat; he's a bit old to start learning new tricks."

111

With Minter's destination confirmed, Tom Kirby announced he would stick with Bill Ivy and Chris Conn for the season ahead, with Lewis Young on the continent. "I don't want to pinch a rider from anyone else," he said, "but later on I may pick an up-and-coming lad to join the team." Meanwhile, Tom's brother Reg was about to enter the fray. Having opened a bike shop at Stanford le Hope in Essex, Reg had decided to sponsor Ron Chandler on a 7R and G50.

Syd Lawton, although struggling to provide Aermacchis in numbers since America had started clamouring for the Varese factory's products, said he'd be offering half a dozen 250s for sale and a similar number of 350s, all with works-type five-speed gearboxes. He was also to become agent for Daniele Fontana's trick-looking twin-leading-shoe brakes.

All change

Back in December, word had come that motocrossing brothers Don and Derek Rickman were to build a road racing frame for Tom Kirby, drawing from the experience gained when making a frame for their scrambles bikes, which they'd called the Métisse (French for mongrel). The project received the blessing of AMC chief Bill Smith, and by February had advanced to prototype stage. The racing Métisse frame would, it was reported, carry

Mike Hailwood on his new gadget for domestic races, an RC173 350 Honda, at Brands, Easter 1966. He won the 350 race and took third in the 1000cc King of Brands. (Courtesy Elwyn Roberts Collection)

oil in the frame tubes, allow removal of the cylinder head with the engine in situ, and include eccentrics for chain adjustment. There was also a small matter of a Rickman-Lockheed disc brake; a variation was coming, at Syd Lawton's request, for the 350 Aermacchi. The bike could, he thought, "do with a more robust frame."

Meanwhile, Dave Degens had agreed to ride Lancefield's Nortons in a deal brokered by Syd, who would himself supply Degens with a 250 Aermacchi, together with a Triumph Bonneville for Production races. All of which left Tom Arter with an empty berth, which he seemed in no rush to fill. "I'll be quite happy to start the season with Peter Williams and see what happens," he said.

In February, the ACU said it was considering holding the Hutchinson 100 – homeless since the loss of Silverstone – at Brands Hatch, but running the races anti-clockwise to negate the locals' track knowledge. The ACU Star/British championship competition was also being overhauled. Henceforth, the Star competition would become the British championships and the August meeting at Oulton Park would lose its title. Points for the titles would be awarded on a sliding scale – eight for a win, down to one point for sixth place – at every British national meeting, a rider's eight best performances to count.

Alas, there would be no national meetings – nor anything else very much – at Thruxton in 1966, as the track surface was now too poor to use; nor was there any likelihood of resurfacing in the foreseeable future. The news from Aberdare was different, however, where it seemed neither the council nor the residents were very happy with the way their park had turned out, and were wondering if racing might one day be restored to their verdant patch of South Wales.

The season got under way at Mallory Park on 6 March, with Minter settling in quickly on his new Seeleys by winning his 350 heat, and starting the final tucked in behind Reg Everett's Yamaha. Both retired, Minter's bike with a loose exhaust while Everett's ran a big-end, leaving Cooper in the lead until Degens whistled past to win, with Shorey third and Kirby AJS-mounted Ivy fourth.

For the 500 final Degens rode his third-choice bike: the bigger Lancefield Norton wasn't ready, and the Norton he'd borrowed from Syd Lawton suffered oil pump failure, so he began the race on one of Tom Kirby's G50s. After leading early, Degens missed a gear, letting Ivy and Chandler through. Degens repassed Chandler, and though unable to catch Ivy's new G50 Métisse, the Kirby team took a 1-2 from slow-starting Minter.

The settling-in process continued at Brands a week later. Ivy won the 350 race on his new AJS Métisse but in the Redex Trophy race could do no better than fifth on the G50-powered version. Minter started well on the 350 Seeley but dropped to eighth with a front tyre that was sliding badly, then took his revenge by winning the Redex Trophy race on the 500. He limped home fourth in the 1000cc race on the same bike after replacing a split exhaust with a pipe from a 7R while Rex Butcher, now managing Paul Dunstall's shop and

Derek Minter joined Colin Seeley for 1966, but had returned to his Nortons by mid-season after a run of problems. (Courtesy Elwyn Roberts Collection)

riding his boss's Domiracers alongside Griff Jenkins, claimed the win from early leader Cooper and Ivy's G50 Métisse.

Jenkins didn't fare too well on Dunstall's poor-handling 745cc Atlas-powered Domiracer at Brands, so the Eltham dealer called the Rickman brothers at their increasingly busy Hampshire premises and tried to organise a Métisse frame for the 68bhp engine in time to take on Mike Hailwood's 64bhp 350 Honda over Easter.

At Snetterton the following weekend it was Ivy's turn to strike trouble, damaging ligaments in a fall from his 350 Métisse when the bike suddenly began venting its oil, coating the rear tyre in the process. Butcher fell too, spraining an ankle while testing a 350 Aermacchi, which he nonetheless described as "a fantastic little tool. I went down Norwich Straight with Dave Degens' G50 and he couldn't get away." He said he was revving to 8600rpm, which gave 130mph on Snetterton gearing.

Minter took up the running in Norfolk, winning the 350 race from Dave Degens' Lawton Aermacchi and going away with the 500 race until he holed a megaphone, taking the edge off the G50 engine and allowing Cooper in for the win – his first at the Norfolk circuit in three seasons of trying.

Tanks for the memory

After Ivy's Snetterton tumble, Tom Kirby, foxed by his bike's sudden oil loss, asked that his team's Métisse frames be fitted with fibreglass oil tanks. Paul Dunstall too wanted an oil tank for his Atlas frame. "I'm not keen on having oil in the frame," explained Dunstall. "I'm not convinced all of it is circulating." Others said that such frames might prove difficult to clean out following mechanical trouble such as a big-end failure.

With the imminent collapse of AMC rumbling in the background, the teams prepared for Easter. For the Rickman brothers this meant making oil filters to their own design, and persuading Kirby and Ivy to give the oil-in-frame system another shot. Then came the news that Manxman Sid Mizen had been killed at Le Mans in a collision with another bike halfway down the Sarthe Circuit's four-mile Mulsanne Straight.

John Cooper missed most of the Easter excitement. He felt off-colour at Brands Hatch and skipped Snetterton on the Sunday. Not so Mike Hailwood, at Brands revealing his new domestic-race gadget, an RC173 350 four-cylinder Honda. In the 350 race Hailwood passed early leader Ivy "then whipped away," reported *Motor Cycling*, "to win as he pleased". Dave Degens too was in fine form. United at last with his Lancefield Nortons, he ran third in the 350 race then scraped home by a length to win the Redex Trophy from Jenkins (497 Dunstall Domiracer) and Minter.

Ivy's turn came in the 1000cc King of Brands. Hailwood led early but the Honda was down on speed and the race became the business of Ivy and Degens, swapping the lead continually, though with Ivy ahead by a few lengths at the flag and Hailwood third. Degens, meanwhile, collected his second win of the day in the supporting 1000cc bash.

Minter did some rain dancing at Snetterton, but retired early in the 350 race as a protest against the slippery nature of the track, particularly at the new stretch around Russell's. Without him, Hailwood took point until Peter Williams had the cheek to pass him. Hailwood then fell, as did others, and the race was stopped after four laps with Williams still in front from Ivy. Degens, back on Tom Kirby's Matchless while his Nortons went north, splashed his way to a win in the 500cc Race of Aces, with Ivy bagging another second.

The rain abated for Easter Monday, when Selwyn Griffiths took a double at Cadwell Park, Ron Chandler (500) and John Blanchard (350) one each at Crystal Palace while the big guns attracted a crowd of 50,000 to Oulton Park. There Jenkins and Minter did battle, vying for the lead in the 500 race after Degens dropped the Lancefield Norton at Old Hall Corner on the opening lap. Cooper came through the field to muscle aside Jenkins (struggling with a loose megaphone) for second, while Minter cleared off. The Mint led early in the 350 race too, but there was no arguing with Hailwood's 350 Honda, and he had to be content with second after Degens ended a bad day by crashing the smaller Lancefield Norton at Cascades, as Cooper slipped into third.

The weekend wrapped up back at Mallory Park on 'Easter Tuesday' with a limited turn-out – no Hailwood, no Minter, no mobile Degens. Cooper asserted himself on his home turf, leading home Dave Simmonds' 305 Honda in the 350 race. Jenkins was again in the thick of it in the 500cc event against Dave Croxford's G50, and narrowly failed to pip the Londoner. Ivy had a dismal meeting; his G50 Métisse's rear suspension collapsed in the 500 final and the 7R version ran a big end, making four such burnt bearings in a weekend for the team. Nothing would now stop Tom Kirby from having oil tanks restored to all his bikes. "The oil wasn't circulating properly," he said. Rickmans' works manager, Ron Baines, held an opposing view. "We're sure the oil-in-frame idea could work," he mused, "but if everyone wants oil tanks, we'll supply them."

Meanwhile, Colin Seeley was receiving orders for his wares on the back of Minter's early-season successes, among them a request for a frame from Paul Dunstall. The resulting bike, powered by an Atlas motor, performed creditably at Imola. Dunstall said he'd also try the 650 engine in a Seeley frame, and another new motor he was preparing – a 180-degree crank 500.

April ended at Castle Combe, where Griffiths pipped Minter in the 350 race and Croxford beat Griffiths in the 500. The following day at Brands short track, Degens was mobile again, starring in the 350 race on his Aermacchi and in the Redex Trophy event on Tom Kirby's G50, winning from Minter and Croxford. But the afternoon ended badly for the Londoner. While Cooper, riding Rex Butcher's 500 Manx (his own had been damaged when he'd been run off the road in the Redex Trophy race), claimed the 1000cc event after Butcher (647 Domiracer) and Minter had each taken turns in the lead, Degens fell at Paddock while third, hitting the trackside banking heavily. He was badly shaken up, and sponsor Syd Lawton packed him off to Devon for a no-argument rest cure.

High and dry

Both Lancefield Nortons were in dry dock after Degens' falls at Oulton Park, and Lancefield doubted whether he'd have them repaired in time for the TT. If he were fit, Degens would instead ride Lawton's 250 and 350 Aermacchis and a Kirby G50 Métisse. As things turned out, everyone had plenty of time to complete their preparations. In May, the National Union of Seamen launched a national strike, forcing the postponement of the TT until September and a run on the pound.

Whitsun opened at Scarborough where Dan Shorey won the 350 event and ran in second to Peter Williams in the 500, before joining the migration south to Snetterton the following day. The Norfolk circuit was redrawn for the meeting to eliminate Russell's, the

(Continued on page 125)

Picture Gallery

An exercise in composure: Mike Hailwood takes his favourite Honda, the 297cc
RC174, to a record-breaking win in the 1967 Junior TT.
(Courtesy FoTTofinder Bikesport Photo Archives)

A demonstration from the master:
Derek Minter rounds Druids at Brands
Hatch, where he'd won so often. He was
back on his Petty Nortons for 1967, his
final season, when this photo was taken.
(Courtesy Mortons Archive)

Route one: Alan Sellars' 499cc 30M Manx Norton dates from 1961, and is a fine example of the bike that dominated British racing for so long. "The engine was built from Norton original items and others, including Bosch twin-spark ignition, supplied by Ray Petty," explained Adrian. "The crankcases, from a Bill Boddice engine, are stamped FB – Francis Beart – who fettled Bill's engines." (Courtesy Adrian Sellars)

Above: During 1968 and the first half
of 1969, Ray Pickrell was irresistible on
Paul Dunstall's Nortons. Here, he rounds
Ramsey Hairpin during to the first of his
four TT wins, the 1968 Production race.
(Courtesy FoTTofinder Bikesport
Photo Archives)

Right: Local advantage: at times John
Cooper exerted the same dominance
at Mallory Park as Derek Minter did at
Brands. Here, he exits Shaw's Hairpin,
early in the 1967 season, on his
Wraggs-backed 500 Manx.
(Courtesy Mortons Archive)

The embodiment of style: Alan Barnett
on Tom Kirby's G50 Métisse during his
ride to second place in the 1969 Senior
TT behind Ago's MV.
(Courtesy FoTTofinder Bikesport
Photo Archives)

Twilight: In battered Norton leathers,
Peter Williams gives 'Wagon Wheels' a
last ride, into second place behind Jack
Findlay's TR500 Suzuki in the 1973
Senior TT.
(Courtesy FoTTofinder
Bikesport Photo Archives)

A last flash of Ludlow Green. Clive Brown rides Francis Beart's 350 Aermacchi to victory in the 1970 Junior Manx Grand Prix – Beart's 12th and final Island win. (Courtesy FoTTofinder Bikesport Photo Archives)

notch on the start/finish straight where most of the Easter tumbles had come. Williams almost stole the show here too, and led the 350 race until overhauled by Simmonds' 305 Honda, then hung on to get the best of a five-way scrap for second, after Minter (puncture) and Degens (forks) had retired. Williams was helping with Tom Arter's latest project, a lightweight G50 inspired by the 7R-powered special developed by John Surtees half a decade before. He used the bike well in the 500 race, jumping out to a good lead until the rubber retaining strap from the oil tank was sucked into the carburettor; still, he kept going, and quickly enough to land fourth after Cooper had won from Croxford and Butcher.

On Whit Monday the stars came out for the Brands Hatch Evening News International, where Hailwood won the feature race on his battle-stained 'private' 350 RC173, coming from the back of the grid to win as he liked. The star of the race, however, was surely Griff Jenkins. Riding Dunstall's Atlas-engined Domiracer, he hared through the field and set off in pursuit of Hailwood, looking the goods until the bike's fairing shook loose, jammed the rear wheel and threw him off at South Bank, letting Williams through to claim second place from Croxford and Ivy. Williams finally got his win in the Redex Trophy race, while Yamaha-mounted Phil Read claimed the 350 laurels. Of Derek Minter, however, little was to be seen. A bad day at Snetterton ended when his 500 Seeley had broken its primary chain on the start line, and now he had a lacklustre Brands, bagging a modest fourth and a fifth.

The final meeting for the Whitsun weekend, at Cadwell, saw John Cooper away home with the bulk of the spoils, winning the 500 race and running third in the 350 behind Rod Gould (Norton) and Selwyn Griffiths (AJS). Then came an unusually quiet June – though the stars might have welcomed the unscheduled break. So far, the season had proven as competitive as any, with the usual suspects each hitting form, but then struggling with injury or mechanical failure. Degens and Cooper had won five major races each, Minter, Ivy, and Peter Williams three. There was plenty to settle. Just as well, perhaps, the TT had been postponed.

Racing resumed again at Mallory Park for the post-non-TT meeting. Hailwood was back and riding strongly, clearing off with the 350 race while Phil Read struggled to fend off Cooper. Ivy stopped with his AJS Métisse coated in oil. The 500 race, perhaps the best of the day, lacked the services of either world champion, but Cooper did his best, an early lead dwindling as he came under pressure from Williams and then Croxford. Williams faded with a slipping clutch, but Croxford swept into the lead, triggering a race-long argument with Cooper that finally went the Derby rider's way through knowing a faster way round Gerard's and the hairpin.

By July, many dream teams were no more. Chris Conn, still serving with the RAF but now in Germany, had parted ways with Tom Kirby, while Steve Lancefield told *Motor Cycling* he was "no longer backing" Degens as a result of his costly falls at Oulton Park;

The hat, the cravat, the aquiline profile: Francis Beart warms up his 500 Norton for Joe Dunphy at the delayed 1966 TT. Behind him, Mike Hailwood has a moment's quiet reflection. (Courtesy Elwyn Roberts Collection)

and Minter was clearly having problems with his Seeleys, being thrown from the 500 at Mallory Park and breaking a small bone in his ankle. Ivy too was struggling: the oil-loss problem with his 350 Kirby Métisse was unsolved, and he retired from the Mallory 500 race with braking problems.

As Jim Redman flew home from the Belgian GP nursing an arm broken when crashing his 500 Honda while aquaplaning over ankle-deep water, Colin Seeley announced that Derek Minter had left the team. "Derek came to see me and we agreed to part," Seeley told *Motor Cycling*. "I'm in no particular rush to replace him." Minter retrieved his 350 Norton from Seeley's showroom, where it had stood for some time wearing a 'for sale' sign, went to Castle Combe and rode it to his first major win since April. At the same meeting he ran second to Peter Williams in the 500 race in what proved to be his last race for the Seeley team. Within a week, Minter's Nortons were getting the once-over at Ray Petty's Farnborough workshop, while Colin Seeley confirmed that John Blanchard would be joining his team. "I'm going to give him a chance and see how he goes," explained Seeley.

Old story

While Tom Kirby tried to salvage something from a bad season by running a series of tests for up-and-coming riders at Snetterton, Derek Minter was on the phone to Gilera, hoping to tease a bike out of the Arcore factory for the postponed TT. He didn't think Gilera was interested in a full comeback, but, after taking a couple of toe-in-the-water rides in Italy earlier in the year, he thought the bike might be a useful performer at the Island. "Hartle lapped at 105mph in 1963," he explained to *Motor Cycling*. "If I can get round at the same speed – and keep it up – I'll be happy."

Before that, however, there was the small matter of BMCRC's Hutchinson 100 meeting, which would go ahead as planned, anti-clockwise at Brands Hatch. The arrangement didn't suit everyone. "You can't see the apex or exit of a lot of corners," said Hailwood, "particularly Clearways, where you're going a bit quick." Minter too had reservations: "I think Paddock is very treacherous taken uphill," he said. "The camber is all wrong." Not so John Cooper, however: "Coming up Paddock and Clearways, getting the power on there … super," he said.

There were early casualties. Peter Williams, after getting his eye in with a win at Cadwell Park a week earlier, tore off a fingernail while getting his bikes into his van and rode with his right hand swathed in bandages. Minter fell when his 250 Cotton seized in practice, spraining a wrist; and Bill Ivy brought his 350 Métisse to an abrupt halt in practice after Rex Butcher had come alongside waving frantically: Ivy's bike was on fire, caused by oil leaking from a broken union and ignited by the exhaust.

There was racing too, and although Phil Read's 254 Yamaha was no match for Hailwood's 350 Honda, he managed to hold second place in the Junior race until, with two laps to go, he stopped for a plug change and then fell at Paddock a lap later. Minter limped into second, struggling with his damaged wrist, while Blanchard claimed third from a melee that had included Ivy, until the Métisse slid out from under him at South Bank, the 70mph crash giving Ivy severe concussion and deep lacerations. Another oil line had let go, making a sad and frustrating end to the Kirby-Ivy partnership, as Ivy's services were now exclusively Yamaha's. Capping a bad weekend for Team Kirby, Degens had fallen from his G50 Métisse in practice with oil coating his back tyre, and it couldn't be rebuilt in time to race.

Cooper meanwhile started the Production race on a BSA Spitfire that proved memorable for the wrong reasons. During Saturday practice, Cooper recalls, "it was wobbling all over the place going round Bottom Bend and up towards Druids. Apparently the people in the paddock were frightened to death the bike was going to chuck me off.

"That night in the hotel, Alan Shepherd, the team manager, said: 'it's that bad at steering, if you ride it tomorrow we'll give you £100.' I told him I never had any intention of not riding it. Anyway, I won the race." After a slow start, Cooper deposed early leader Percy Tait (who had trouble with his front brake cable adjuster), and new boy Mick Andrew, then wobbled his way to the flag and the money. And he hadn't finished making headlines. Mike Hailwood rocketed into the lead at the start of the 500cc BMCRC Championship race and stayed there for 17 of 25 laps, when the 350 Honda blew a gearbox oil seal. Williams and Cooper then staged a three-lap scrap for the lead, and, when Williams ran out of fuel, Cooper rolled home comfortably from Dan Shorey and Swiss-Hungarian Gyula Marsovszky.

With Ivy in hospital and at least two of the team's bikes immobile, Tom Kirby was near the end of his tether. Not knowing what else to do, he sent for analysis a sample of the plastic tube he'd been using to make his 7Rs' oil lines, bought new from AMC. The tests revealed the tube was three years old and made from material that typically began to deteriorate after 12 months. Mystery solved.

Now it was Cooper's turn to suffer, stepping off his 350 Norton at 100mph in practice for the Ulster GP and "bouncing up the road for 200 yards." While Hailwood bagged a 350/500 double, Cooper started the 350 race on a scruffy Norton borrowed from Irish tuner Joe Ryan, but retired, then pulled out of the 500 race feeling unwell. Yet he was back at Mallory Park a week later, winning the 350 race, and retiring from the 750cc event with a blown engine while Croxford went on to win. At Oulton Park (the former British title meeting), the final stop before the delayed TT, Cooper did it again, leading the 350 race from start to finish and finishing third in the 500cc event on his spare bike behind the Nortons of Jack Ahearn and Malcolm Uphill. All was far from well, however, and after just a couple of laps' practice for the Senior TT, Cooper packed up and went home, declaring himself sore and fed up at having a vanful of broken bikes and not being able to find spares for them.

Cooper at least had a choice in the matter; not so Derek Minter. Having acquired a

Gilera for the Senior TT (and the GP des Nations a week later), he fell heavily at Brandish during practice, breaking a wrist that meant the end of his season, and would still be giving him problems at the end of the year.

Road closed

September opened with Ago's first TT win, the Junior, and the first of Peter Williams' five runner-up spots, which came two days before Hailwood revealed his hitherto unexampled skill at all-in wrestling, by taking Honda's fearsome 490cc RC181 to victory in the Senior TT. By the middle of the month AMC had been saved from going under by Manganese Bronze Holdings, owner of two-stroke specialist Villiers. Norton, AJS and Matchless were still a going concern for the time being therefore, though the news was small comfort for regiments of lads across the land clamouring for the marques' racing products. There had been no new bikes since 1963, and now there were precious few spares. Britain's well-tried make-do-and-mend ethos prevailed in the larger classes of motorcycle racing. There were Aermacchis for the 350 class and a variety of production-engined twins available in larger displacements, but as yet there was no clear route forward.

The singles soldiered on. At Castle Combe in mid-month, Dave Croxford claimed the race of the day on his Oakley Matchless, fending off Norton-mounted pursuers Rod Gould and Tom Phillips. Finishing 12th with a dragging clutch was Percy Tait, riding a smart Triumph Daytona that was destined, apparently, for more serious use in the USA. In the 350 race the twins held sway, with Dave Simmonds' Honda proving a better bet round the Wiltshire airfield than Reg Everett's Yamaha.

The big names were back for Cadwell's autumn international a week later. Here, for the first time, mainland racegoers heard the banshee wail of Honda's six-cylinder 250, the RC166, as Hailwood went to work in the Experts Invitation, thumping the field and leading home Cooper, who'd been dicing energetically with Peter Williams until the Arter man went down. Dan Shorey, who ran third after Phil Read's Yamaha was slowed by another fouling plug, won the 350 race after a wet track had claimed Cooper, Conn and Simmonds, and then went north to add a 350/500 double win at Scarborough to his autumnal prize haul.

Giacomo Agostini took his mainland bow at the Mallory Park Race of the Year, cleaning up with flag-to-flag wins in the 350 and 500 races, and then taking the feature event after Honda six-mounted Hailwood had retired. Yet Ago's route to the 1000 guineas was hardly straightforward. He started hemmed in by a barging, jostling pack, only passing Ivy's Yamaha for second near half distance. By then Hailwood was ten seconds clear, and in control of everything bar a deflating rear tyre, which left Ago to win from Ivy and Mike Duff with a sore Williams fourth from Cooper. Ago equalled Hailwood's lap record at 91.69mph, while Hailwood took the consolation of a win in the 250 race.

The following Saturday Cooper was back to his best, staking a strong claim for both 350 and 500cc British championships at the Oulton Park Bob McIntyre Memorial meeting. The name race was excitement itself. Williams led early, stalked relentlessly by Cooper and Shorey with Croxford a close fourth. Cooper and then Shorey passed Williams, but at the end of the six-lap journey the leading three were so close the timekeepers couldn't separate them – yet somehow gave Cooper the win. There was more of the same in the 350 race, with Cooper again scraping home from Shorey and Williams.

For the last international of the year, the Race of the South at Brands, Hailwood only took one bike, the 250 six, which broke its crankshaft on the start line of the main event, so, for the second time in a fortnight, Ago ran out winner of the 350, 500 and name races. His strongest competition came from Croxford, who chased him home in the 500cc event and the Race of the South, with Duff back on a Yamaha to claim second in the 350 race. Alas, the two 500 Gileras entered, ridden by Frank Perris and Remo Venturi, contributed little. Perris, who'd retired his after missing a gear, offered a sorry epitaph for the whole sad Gilera venture, describing the bike as "about as fast as a 350 Benelli – but the Gilera doesn't handle as well."

Man of the hour

In October, Colin Seeley made the headline of the year with the announcement that he'd bought all race rights from AMC – "lock, stock and barrel." Seeley was the new owner of all "drawings, jigs, castings and spares – the lot," and would soon, he said, restart production of both Manx Nortons, the 7R AJS and G50 Matchless. "They laughed at me," he said of an earlier attempt to buy the race shop, "but I was ready when they finally folded."

Two national meetings remained of the season, but Cooper needed just one to take both championships. Borrowing Dave Degens' Lawton Aermacchi at Snetterton, Cooper ran home fourth in a depleted 350 field – Williams had fallen in practice and new Kirby recruit Pat Mahoney retired when his Métisse oil pump failed. The race was Shorey's from start to finish, while Cooper maintained station in a seven-bike dice for second. Martin Watson led the bunch home from John Blanchard's Seeley, but fourth was enough for Cooper. The 500cc race was just as tough, with Cooper fighting his way through from a poor start to catch Gould and Degens at the head of the field. Cooper slipped into the lead; twice Degens passed him; twice Cooper came back; and he led across the line while Gould made a successful last-ditch bid to relegate Degens to third. Cooper was a double British Champion and rubbed it in at Mallory Park for the last meeting of the year. He and Shorey put on a show in the 350 race with Banbury Dan claiming the win. Shorey tried in the 500 race too, but slowed with oil on his back tyre, later traced to a cracked gearbox, and Cooper swept past. Croxford took Shorey's place, passing Cooper and easing away; but Cooper got in front again when Croxford nearly fell at the hairpin. The Londoner staked everything on a last-lap pass at Shaw's and this time he did fall; while Cooper, as he did so often in a clean, largely crash-free and highly successful career, took the fast way round.

Chapter 11

1967: Mike

"Start money is a necessity"

If, at the start of 1963, Derek Minter was the best we had, by 1967 the mantle had long since passed to Mike Hailwood. As he began his second year with Honda, Hailwood had chalked up seven world championships and 60 grand prix wins, putting in virtuoso performances everywhere, on everything. He often saved his best for the Island, of course: winning three TTs in 1961, battling the weather in the 1965 Senior, his unruly Honda and Agostini's MV in the 1966 Senior, and there had been stirring performances elsewhere, such as his riding masterclass at the 1966 French 250cc GP and the '65 Hutch, where he'd won three features races, each on a different bike, in rain and shine.

In March 1967, Hailwood flew to Japan to test the season's new bikes. There was a 250 six with a new engine and new frame, a 297cc six (the RC174) for the 350 class, and a tweaked version of the world's most powerful 500, the RC181. He discovered that Honda wanted him to pursue three world championships, and that two of the three new bikes still needed work to be reliably competitive, but he'd still find time to race at home.

Tom Kirby's plans for the season centred on team leader Dave Degens, who would also ride his own 650 Dresda Triumph. Kirby would be keeping Pat Mahoney, too, along with evergreen Lewis Young, and decided to offer support to a young aircraft instrument technician from Iver, a successful club racer named Alan Barnett.

With the disastrous oiling problems that dogged Kirby Racing's 7Rs in 1966 now history, the team's Métisses would achieve something of the success they deserved and be an impressive form of advertising for the Rickmans' products. The first Métisse chassis available had been offered for private sale as early as the middle of 1966, and in the closing weeks of the year *Motor Cycling* ran the magnifying glass over a G50-powered example and discovered a bike that weighed 290lb, a little lighter than a stock G50, had a nickel-plated twin-cradle frame, a fairing designed by Doug Mitchenall, and a Rickman-Lockheed hydraulic disc front brake (complete with cooling ring). The bike was, declared tester Bruce Main-Smith, "exceptionally good handling, with steering much better than a standard G50's, and a fractional improvement on that of a Manx." Every little helped.

John Hartle, making a comeback after another two years out of racing, sampled one of Syd Lawton's 350 Aermacchis and decided to slot the engine into a Métisse frame – as he would Triumph engines of 490 and 649cc capacity that were being prepared by drag-racing star Fred Cooper; he was soon appointed Rickman 'factory' rider.

Others preferred things as they were. Dave Croxford would again run his 7R and G50 backed by Newark butcher Charlie Oakley, while Rex Butcher would rely on his 350 and 500 Manxes – and something else Paul Dunstall was putting together. Elsewhere among the traditionalists, Derek Minter was still struggling. The wrist he'd broken in his

John Cooper bade farewell to his Wraggs Nortons in 1967, taking to Seeleys after one or two test rides. He's pictured early in his last season on the 500 Norton, leading Dave Croxford and Ron Chandler. (Courtesy Elwyn Roberts Collection)

fall during practice for the '66 TT still wasn't flexing properly; but at the end of January Brands Hatch arranged a special test session for him. "The wrist was tired afterwards," he said, "but I'm confident I'll be fit by the start of the season." A couple of weeks later he was back again, turning in an impressive 40 laps of the short circuit.

As the melancholy announcement came from Francis Beart that he was building his last Manx – "I've no more bits left" – Colin Seeley signed John Blanchard for the season, while over in Eltham, Paul Dunstall was preparing for what many expected to be a watershed season for big, street production-based machines. He was building bikes for Butcher and Griff Jenkins using Norton frames, which were 2lb lighter than the Métisse. Each would receive a 68bhp 745cc Atlas engine, mounted as far forward as possible. They'd each keep their stock primary chaincase, which held its oil better than the alternatives, and so eased the task of the increasingly stressed primary chain. He'd hold onto the Métisse frames too, he said – just in case.

Big twins were the hot topic of 1967. A three-lap Production TT was planned, and the Production race at the Hutch would run for the third year in a row. The factories recognised the importance of the Production TT, with some big names promising bikes for the occasion and contracting high-profile riders to steer them. A persistent rumour had John Hartle riding a Triumph Bonneville, and Paul Dunstall was also taking an interest. "I'll definitely enter two bikes," he said. Percy Tait too was to receive new hardware, but for open-class racing. The Triumph factory was building seven 'Daytona'-style racers based on the 490cc T100, weighing a trim 290bhp and reputedly making 51bhp at 8000rpm. Six were for use in America, and the seventh was for Tait to ride in Britain.

New deal

Meanwhile Hailwood was doing his own deal in Britain, agreeing to ride eight meetings at MCD circuits – Mallory, Brands, Oulton, Snetterton – in 250, 350 and Unlimited classes.

The season opener at Mallory Park on 5 March wasn't on Hailwood's list but the old firm was there in force, and while Peter Williams ran out a winner in the 350 race from Degens and a fresh-faced kid named Paul Smart on an Aermacchi, Cooper retired when a footpeg fell off then dropped his bigger Norton at the Esses while running second on the last lap of the 500 race. Chandler escaped to a comfortable win from Barnett while Cooper picked himself up and began to think about Brands Hatch.

Hailwood too was thinking about Brands, getting word to the circuit that he couldn't make the Good Friday meeting. He'd be at Mallory on the Sunday and Oulton Park at Easter Monday, he said, but the Honda tests weren't exactly plain sailing. It's part of the Hailwood legend that during his first test on the 250 six he told Honda's men it was "bloody awful" and underlined the point by unbolting its rear suspension units, chucking them into a nearby pond and demanding Girlings. Now he had two new bikes to contend with and the reworked 500, which had had its power boosted from 85bhp to somewhere on the high side of 90, while its horrible handling remained just that.

Mick Woollett criticised MCD's decision to pay Hailwood handsomely for his appearances, when guys further down the food chain plainly struggled to make ends meet. He cited the experience of Paul Smart who, after taking third places in the 250 and 350 finals at the Mallory Park season-opener, left the circuit with £18 (the average weekly wage was £26.55). "Let's encourage the people who make the racing possible by cutting the big money paid to the works riders and using it to increase the prize fund substantially," thundered 'Scoop' from the pages of *Motor Cycling*.

Among the beneficiaries of such a plan was Ron Chandler, who had derived much of his income from working as a Thames lighterman, piloting barges and supervising the handling of their cargoes around the waterways of London. He was now on the point of turning professional, and becoming King of Brands on Good Friday simplified the decision. It helped that Williams, Cooper and Minter all retired; but Blanchard had already won the 350 and 500 races and took an early lead in the main event. Chandler caught and passed him as did Rex Butcher (Dunstall Dominator), but Blanchard got going again, repassing the Dunstall man. A big slide at Paddock persuaded him to ease off, leaving Chandler the winner. He made it two by taking the 750 race from Croxford, Butcher and Williams, and the lately unfamiliar sight of John Hartle, on his new 650 Triumph Métisse.

Somehow, Hailwood found the time to test his RC173 Honda at Brands before Mallory Park, particularly its newly acquired Ceriani forks and twin front discs supplied by Colin Lyster. Not that it did him much good, because the seven-time world champion suffered the indignity of being lapped during the headline event, the 30-lap Master of Mallory. Chandler led from the flag with Cooper in pursuit and, for a couple of laps anyway, Hailwood too; but while Cooper passed Chandler and pulled away into a race-winning lead, Hailwood slowed with the Honda handling "atrociously," as he later said. First Alan Barnett came past him, then Pat Mahoney, and then, were the day not proving dramatic enough, snow began to fall. Mahoney passed Chandler and gained on Cooper, and by two-thirds distance the leaders were lapping Hailwood. Blanchard, up to fifth after a sluggish start, fell at the hairpin, breaking a collarbone. Then the snow stopped and Chandler repassed Mahoney, but the Master of Mallory was clearly John Cooper. Hailwood later traced the Honda's problem to suspension that had unaccountably lost all its damping fluid. The meeting would be remembered, however, for sidecar world champion Fritz Scheidegger, who died in a high-speed crash at Shaw's.

Hailwood had his RC173 fixed for the 350 race at Oulton Park, and after dicing with Cooper and Minter for a time, gave its 64bhp free rein and cleared off in search of the chequered flag, leaving Minter to get the better of Cooper. Minter was in good form for the 500cc Race of the North too. An early squabble between Peter Williams and Percy

His name became synonymous with Yamahas, but Rod Gould put in plenty of successful rides on Nortons before the arrival of the TR2. Here, he leads Rex Butcher at Mallory Park. (Courtesy Elwyn Roberts Collection)

Tait saw the Arter man in control – the Triumph broke a primary chain – but he was soon joined by Cooper and Minter. Breaking from the field, the leading three became two as Williams dropped back, and then Minter was alone after Cooper fell trying to pass at Esso Bend. Williams cruised into second from Steve Spencer on Steve Lancefield's Norton. The Mint was back.

Yaw, pitch and roll

Elsewhere in the nation, Rod Gould brought his Easter to a close with a double win at Cadwell, as did Chandler at Crystal Palace. Meanwhile, Hailwood had a quiet word with Ken Sprayson, celebrated frame designer at Reynolds Tubes, in Birmingham, to ask if he might make a frame for his troublesome RC181 Honda. Sprayson said yes, but "I told him that to do the job properly it would take about three months," he recalls in his autobiography, *The Frame Man*. Not having the luxury of time, Hailwood took his problem to Colin Lyster, who put together a design and had it made by a Signor Belletti in Milan, in just over a fortnight. Hailwood then used the Lyster-framed Honda to beat Ago's lithe MV three at the Rimini international, although Honda took a dim view of his breaching the party line and demanded he abandon the project and ride the bike as provided.

While Gould (350) and Croxford (500) shared the spoils at Castle Combe for the Wiltshire circuit's April national, Hailwood was testing the Lyster Honda at Hockenheim. He reverted to the stocker for the West German GP, as required – and retired with a broken crankshaft, while Peter Williams got Tom Arter's lightweight G50 home in second, behind Agostini. Chandler fell heavily from his 7R in the 350 race, collecting severe concussion, but was back in action three weeks later at Mallory Park, winning the 350 race from Mahoney on Uncle Tom's short-stroke 7R Métisse. Williams, who'd faded in the Mallory 350 event with carburation problems, forced his way to a fine win in the 500 race, chased home by Cooper and Tait's rapidly improving Triumph. In the 750 race it was Williams again from Cooper, who'd been under heavy pressure from Croxford until his gearbox seized at the hairpin, with Tait again completing the rostrum.

Hailwood, by now doing a passable impression of being permanently frustrated, had entered two bikes for the Brands Whit Monday international, the 250 six and the Lyster-framed 500 – which at least meant the locals had the run of the place in the 350 race – or almost. By the second lap 7R-mounted Peter Williams had passed Chandler and Croxford for the lead, but the growling little twin moving into second was Fred Stevens' Paton, making a rare appearance north of the English Channel. The Italian bike lost its edge, however, letting Mahoney (Kirby Métisse) and Paul Smart (Aermacchi) surge through to challenge Williams, Mahoney grabbing the lead with two laps to go and Smart taking second on the dash to the line.

The Redex Trophy 500 race belonged to Hailwood and his Lyster Honda. Its 90+bhp was more than enough to win, but its poor handling prompted speculation about just how hard Hailwood had to work with the stock frame. All in all, it was no surprise Hailwood chose his 250 six for the Evening News 750cc International, and still less remarkable that he ran away with it. For once, Peter Williams had his own handling problems, but still managed to get his Arter Matchless home second, after Degens' Métisse developed a cruel last-lap misfire.

At the close of May, Dave Degens made headlines with the news that he was leaving Kirby Racing to ride his own bikes, a 250 Aermacchi and his 650 Dresda-Triumph, but with the approach of TT week the spotlight swung back towards Hailwood. After crisply dismissing the handling of his Italian-framed RC181 at Brands as "too bad to talk about," he discovered he'd been excluded from the results of the meeting because he'd turned up with 250 and 500 Hondas instead of the 350 he'd entered (which wasn't ready), and because he'd ridden Ralph Bryans' 1966-spec 250 six in the 20-lap Evening News International, which was open to bikes with a minimum capacity of 251cc, not the 175cc Hailwood had understood. The organisers offered financial compensation to those who'd finished behind him but the argument persisted and, however reluctantly, Hailwood's name was removed from the results altogether. Now he faced the prospect of climbing back aboard his stock RC181 for six laps of the TT course, albeit with the new forks the factory had sent him to try.

Better news came from Colin Seeley, who had built a Mk 2 version of the Seeley frame, two inches lower than its predecessor, stiffer around the steering head and made from smaller-diameter, heavier-gauge tube. It would be mated to a rectangular-section swinging arm, shorter forks and 18-in wheels.

Meanwhile, in a deal brokered by Lew Ellis of Shell, Australian Jack Findlay was to have ridden Francis Beart's last TT Nortons, but the plan came undone when Findlay was thrown from his 250 Bultaco in practice, injuring a foot. Malcolm Uphill took his place but retired from both races, with ignition failure in the Junior and with a broken exhaust valve while lying third on the last lap of the Senior. Beart's rival Steve Lancefield fared better, with his rider Steve Spencer finishing eighth in the Junior and third in his first Senior – behind Peter Williams in another superb ride on his Arter G50.

John Hartle, too, had a good week, winning the inaugural Production TT on a factory Triumph Bonnie, averaging 97mph and getting home by almost two minutes from Paul Smart's Dunstall Dominator and Tony Smith's factory BSA – and then taking sixth in the Senior TT aboard the Kirby G50 Métisse Degens had vacated. Yet the story of the 1967 Diamond Jubilee TT was of Mike Hailwood taking three wins in a week for the second time, and riding a Senior race worthy of the occasion, with the lead swinging back and forth between him and Ago, Honda and MV, until Agostini's drive chain broke when he seemed poised for victory.

Size matters

Hands blistered from the Senior TT, Hailwood was at Mallory Park the following Sunday to do battle with Ago but posted his only win of the day in the 250 race, retiring early in

the 750cc event with his old 350 suffering valve trouble. Ago picked up the slack, winning the big race from Degens' 650 Dresda Triumph and Hartle, who was clearly enjoying life aboard Tom Kirby's G50 Métisse, and the 500cc event from Hartle again after Cooper tangled with Joe Dunphy at Shaw's. Pat Mahoney completed a good day for the Kirby équipe by winning the 350 race on the short-stroke 7R Métisse.

In Kent, the lights were burning late into the night at Colin Seeley's Belvedere workshop. German sidecar ace Helmut Fath was keen to see the four-cylinder DOHC engine he'd developed for his sidecar outfit in a solo frame, and wanted it racing at the Hutch on 13 August. Seeley completed the frame in just six days.

Trouble was brewing elsewhere, however. In the first of a series of unhappy developments that would cloud the rest of the year, Steve Lancefield used the press to

A sore Ron Chandler on his Reg Kirby-backed G50 at Governor's Bridge in the 1967 Senior TT. He finished ninth but ended the season a champion. (Courtesy Paul McElvie)

137

claim that oversized engines were being used and called for the ACU to introduce spot checks. "I know these engines are in existence," he said, "and I've a good idea that riders are using them."

Hailwood and Agostini were going win for win in the 500cc World Championship, Hailwood taking the Dutch, Ago winning in Belgium and now East Germany, where Hailwood retired with a broken gearbox. Cooper crashed in the 500 race, but while he was unhurt, Peter Williams' fall in the 350 GP resulted in a broken arm and ankle that would keep him out for the rest of the season. Hartle had a better meeting, running second to Ago in the 500 race on a G50 borrowed from Ray Cowles – it was the start of a beautiful friendship.

Domestic competition resumed at Snetterton, where the rain held off for once and Derek Minter showed a glimpse of his best form to win the 500cc race. It was just like old times: Cooper led from the start, Shorey got past him at Russell's kink, Minter caught them on the third lap, tucked himself in and waited. Sure enough, he slipped past with half a mile to go, and beat Cooper across the line. Tom Phillips was also back in form, adding a fourth place in the 500 race to his second in the 350 race behind Dave Simmonds' Kawasaki rotary-valve two-stroke twin, but it was Ray Pickrell who would share the headlines with Minter. Newly recruited by Paul Dunstall, Pickrell took to the big Domiracer like a fish to water and showed Phillips (748 Norton Métisse) the way home in the 750 race, with Cooper's Manx and Shorey, cutting an unfamiliar figure on a Cowles G50, giving chase. Times, they were a-changing.

Hailwood won in Czechoslovakia and Ago in Finland, and as Ron Chandler declared himself fully recovered from his fall in the West German GP, he discovered to his surprise that he held a two-point lead over Dave Croxford in the 500cc British title chase. Croxford, as well as being handily placed in the 500 title, led the 350 championship by four points from Rod Gould.

On the eve of the Hutch, Motor

Mike Duff suffered a massive accident in Japan at the end of 1965, returning to racing briefly two years later on Tom Arter's bikes before returning to Canada for good. He's pictured in the 1967 Senior TT, from which he retired with a seized engine. (Courtesy Paul McElvie)

Circuit Developments managed to shock everyone by announcing a plan that would address the contentious issue of start money at national meetings, and do something to solve the developing problem of falling attendances. Next season, explained spokesman John Webb, MCD would do away with start money at nationals altogether and pay prize cash further down the finishing order. A typical 1967 national, *Motor Cycle* explained helpfully, paid £850 in start money and £650 in prize money (when the average wage was £27 per week). Under the new scheme, all £1500 would be paid in prize money, getting it, said Mr Webb, "to riders who really earn it."

The plan drew a mixed response. Rising stars Paul Smart and Ray Pickrell thought it a grand idea: "We'll all start with the same chance," said Pickrell. Entrants Tom Arter, Charles Mortimer and Tom Kirby also approved of the scheme. Not so the established stars. "Start money is a necessity," said Dan Shorey. "What happens if you get knocked off at the first corner?" Derek Minter was also unhappy. "This has made up my mind for me," he declared. "I'm going to retire."

Hail and farewell

For the Hutch, again at Brands, the main race would this year be run for hardware up to 750cc, and over two 15-lap legs. Hailwood entered his favourite Honda, the 297cc six – the RC174 – and cleared off to win both races, with Ray Pickrell (750 Domiracer) holding off Dan Shorey's Manx for second, again in both races. Cooper, appearing on a 'factory' 500 Seeley, took fourth after waging war with Croxford's Oakley G50, while Hailwood established an open-class lap record for the 'new' circuit at 88.17mph. Norton-mounted Shorey bagged the 350 race after Kel Carruthers had apparently run away with it, only to have the gear linkage of his Aermacchi Métisse break. In the race of the day, the 20-lapper for Production bikes, Paul Smart (Dunstall Atlas), Mick Andrew, Rod Gould and John Hartle (all on Bonnevilles), broke clear of the field and looked winners. They were joined by Pickrell, Smart's Dunstall team-mate, at half-distance and it looked while the pair ran first and second as if capacity might tell, but then Pickrell's gearbox began playing up. Hartle and Gould passed Smart, whose gearbox also became a problem, and Hartle kept his nose in front for another solid Production win in a class he was making his own.

Blanchard did well enough on the Seeley-Fath Four (URS) in its debut event, finishing ninth in the second leg of the big race after oiling a plug in the first; but the tension in the Seeley camp glimpsed during TT week boiled over at Brands. Blanchard had crashed the bike during practice when circulating with Pickrell's Domiracer. "He was going too quickly too soon," Seeley told *Motor Cycle*, "I only wanted him to get the feel of the bike." Blanchard told Mick Woollett the crash was caused by a grounding footrest, but the bottom line was that the Seeley crew had to work long and late repairing the damage and, so far as the boss was concerned, enough was enough: Blanchard might be seen on the URS in the future (his fluent German was an asset), but not the team's singles.

John Hartle took his second and last TT win in the 1967 Production race, bringing home his factory Triumph Bonneville almost two minutes clear of Paul Smart's Norton. (Courtesy Paul McElvie)

Hailwood boosted his 500cc World Championship campaign with a win at the Ulster as Ago struggled with clutch troubles, and Blanchard brought the Seeley-Fath Four into fourth – behind Hartle (Cowles G50) and Jack Findlay (McIntyre Matchless) – with a badly adjusted front brake.

While Cooper next appeared at Mallory Park to win the 500 final from Midlander Barry Randle and Chandler, who led but shut off a lap early, and Gould the 350, the Seeley-Fath Four was next on view at Scarborough the following Saturday. Blanchard made a bad start in the 500cc Gold Cup on the Anglo-German multi, now equipped with a Rickman-Lockheed disc front stopper, but bellowed off in pursuit of leader Cooper, setting the fastest lap and getting into fifth before falling at Mere Hairpin. Cooper, meanwhile, took the win with Shorey getting the better of Hartle's Cowles Matchless for second.

The storm broke anew. Helmut Fath had acquired and fitted the Rickman-Lockheed disc without consulting Seeley, it appeared. "I was amazed," wrote Seeley in his autobiography, *Racer and the Rest.* "I'd had no communication whatsoever from Fath or Blanchard, let alone the opportunity to discuss a front brake problem." The bike was withdrawn from competition and the team disbanded.

At Snetterton the following day Hailwood and Phil Read were back in action. Read, recovered from a recent foot infection, got to grips with Hailwood in the 250 race, though the champion won, setting a lap record for the Russell's-inclusive circuit at 94.35mph. Hailwood was expected to star in the 350 race, too, and made short work of early leader Kel Carruthers, but his ageing RC173 developed a misfire and he retired, leaving Carruthers to claim his win from Shorey and Tom Phillips' Aermacchi.

Neither Read nor Hailwood featured in the Race of Aces because Read's RD56 and Hailwood's RC166 were both below the minimum capacity limit. Entertainment, and plenty of it, came instead from a six-way dice for the lead between Cooper, Shorey, Gould, Randle, Chandler and Croxford. After eight laps of elbow-to-elbow argument, Shorey was in front and inched away to win from second-placed Croxford; Chandler finishing third by a wheel from Cooper.

Hailwood was setting lap records again on the Monday, this time at Oulton Park, where he was timed at an astonishing 97.07mph in his only race of the day, the 250. Meanwhile, Carruthers led early in the 350 race, putting his Aermacchi Métisse in front of Hartle's, while Norton runners Minter, Spencer and Shorey closed up to make it a five-way dice won by Carruthers from Minter.

Gone

Minter got another second place after a wobbly start, this time behind his old sparring partner, John Cooper, in the Les Graham Memorial Trophy. It was exhibition stuff, with Minter going from fourth to second in one classic move on the run down into Knicker Brook; by then Cooper was an unassailable ten seconds clear. The Derby man also won the main race of the day, the Avon Gold Cup, clearing off from Hartle's Cowles Matchless, while Shorey provided the sparks by fighting his way up from 12th to third.

Down south Chandler gave his British title aspirations a nudge at Crystal Palace, winning the 1000cc event from Joe Dunphy, with Charlie Sanby (AJS) collecting the 350cc honours while Chandler battled his way through the field to finish fourth.

From the rainswept opening 1000cc race to the end of the day's card, the Brands

John Cooper's best place at the TT was fourth in the 1967 Senior. Here, he leads Chris Conn's Norton across the Mountain. (Courtesy Elwyn Roberts Collection)

September national belonged almost exclusively to two riders: Croxford chased and harried Cooper through Druids and Clearways, Westfield and Paddock; but Cooper won both 350 and 1000cc races from the Ruislip star. Chandler picked up third places in the 350 race and the second 1000cc, and Dave Degens won the 250cc scrap, but it almost seemed as if Cooper and Croxford were the only blokes on view. Almost.

Derek Minter was hit by another bike on the start line for the first 1000cc race, injuring a leg. He spent the rest of the day starting from the back of the grid, and for the 500cc Redex Trophy race made a poor start, taking four laps to catch the leaders – Cooper and Croxford. Then the three swung around the circuit in tight formation for six laps, each taking turns to put his nose in front until the Mint made his move, passing first Cooper, then Croxford, to lead at the flag.

On the same day, Mike Hailwood limped into second place in the 500cc Italian GP, the Honda's gearbox failing while Ago posted another win. The Italian now had only to finish in Canada to become champion. Hailwood was still a champion on a credible bike, making short work of the 350 world title and standing poised to win the 250 class in spite of a tired RC166 and a chronic shortage of spares. At home in September he proved the point at Cadwell's Autumn International by taking a start-to-finish win in the 350 race and walking away with the 750cc Invitation, being content to sit behind Rod Gould's 500 Norton for ten laps before passing to set a new lap record at 78.79mph, the 297 Honda's trademark wail echoing across the fields and woodlands of East Lindsey.

At Mallory Park for the Race of the Year Hailwood went toe to toe with Ago, who rode an old 420cc MV triple, and Phil Read's Yamaha. First blood went to Hailwood, who led the 350 race from flag to flag with Ago second and Read third, while Paul Smart won the battle of the singles on Tom Arter's Aermacchi Métisse. Ago accounted for the 1000cc race after being led by Cooper (Seeley) for four laps. Cooper ran home second with Ray

Pickrell (Dunstall Domiracer) getting the best of an elbow-to-elbow barging match

Bill Hannah's Patons were a rare sight in Britain. Fred Stevens gave the 350 an airing at the '67 Brands Hatch Whitsun International. (Courtesy Elwyn Roberts Collection)

John Blanchard rounds Drury's Hairpin during his scorching ride at Scarborough on the Seeley-Fath four, complete with controversial Rickman-Lockheed front disc brake, in August 1967. (Courtesy Paul McElvie)

for third, heading Croxford and Tait to the flag – with the additional news that John Hartle had fallen at Gerard's, this time breaking his left arm in three places. The Race of the Year ran to form with Hailwood leading home Ago and Read (on his Yamaha RD05 V-four), with Cooper's Seeley the best of the singles in fourth place. MCD had been as good as its word, posting £2215 in prize money for the first nine finishers and a tenner for everybody else.

A week later, Tom Kirby revealed that he'd sacked Pat Mahoney. "He had become an expensive luxury," Kirby told *Motor Cycle*. "He's crashed nine times on my bikes and the repair bills are no joke." Mahoney bit back a week later: "Of my nine so-called crashes," he said, "four were caused by engine or gearbox seizures and I came off once to avoid a fallen rider. Even in the worst cases, the damage was never more than a broken screen or fairing."

There was some good news. The British Automobile Racing Club had, it seemed, lost the use of Goodwood, and was now engaged in promising discussions with the owner of

Thruxton about racing on its perimeter track. "I understand it is to be entirely resurfaced," reported Neville Goss of the Southampton & District MCC.

Francis Beart had sold his last pair of Nortons. Ridden by Keith Heckles, they'd led the Junior and Senior Manx Grand Prix, but had both retired. Yet there was life still at the workshop, where FB had apparently turned his attention to 250 and 350 Aermacchis for Jack Findlay to ride in 1968.

Pre-race tension: Mike Hailwood at the 1967 Ulster GP, where he won the 250 and 500cc races, keeping his world championship hopes alive in the bigger class. (Courtesy Elwyn Roberts Collection)

Curtain call

Hailwood won the 500cc Canadian Grand Prix, but Ago's second place ensured the title remained in Italy. Furious, Hailwood said he would not sign any further contract with Honda until he was satisfied its bikes were competitive. His last domestic appearance came at the Brands Hatch Race of the South in October. He led the 350 race from flag to flag, shaving half a second from the class lap record, which had, incredibly, been unsullied since 1961. Ago came in a polite second, but behind him battle raged. No fewer than eight riders diced for third, with Degens' Aermacchi gaining the upper hand until a "wet clunk" left him a spectator and let Shorey win an unseemly scramble for the line from Minter. Ago fell – an event in itself – at Paddock in the Redex Trophy race, leaving Shorey in charge and keeping the throttle pinned through a hair-raising slide at Clearways on the last lap. Minter took evasive action and his planned last-ditch challenge was hastily shelved in favour of a safe second from Croxford. With no Ago in pursuit, Hailwood was clean away in the Race of the South, while Read slotted his Yamaha into a comfortable second from the men in form, Minter and Shorey; all a bit anti-climactic, really, compared with what had gone before.

The last three meetings of the season got Croxford to his 350cc British championship, with a second to Shorey at Snetterton, a third behind Minter and Shorey at Brands, and a second to Padgetts Yamaha-mounted Cooper at Mallory Park; Chandler, a shade more comfortable at the top of the 500 table, took his title with a second, a fourth and a fifth. Derek Minter's retirement overshadowed everything, though. He'd mentioned it during the start money episode back in August and, with the Mint as firm-minded as ever, one of the great careers of the decade was drawing rapidly to a close. "I'll be at Brands on 22 October and that will be that," he said.

For the last ride on his 350 Norton, Minter made a fair start, and by the second lap was fighting his way past Jenkins and Shorey to close on leader Croxford. He got past a lap later, and that was that – business as usual. Things didn't quite run to the script in the Redex Trophy race. Minter led most of the way, but less than half a second covered himself, Shorey, Croxford, Chandler (sampling a Seeley) and Cooper. The group "rang every change in the book," said *Motor Cycle*, "but Minter always led" – until the penultimate lap, that is, when Shorey took over. Minter repassed him but Shorey got back again to end a breathless eight-lapper ahead by a length.

Minter's last ride was, curiously, not on his 500 Petty Manx but on a 650 Curtis Domiracer. He made good use of it, dicing in the 1000cc race with Pickrell's Domiracer, Croxford's G50 and Degens' Dresda Métisse, picking them off one by one and then catching and passing John Cooper (Seeley) for the lead. There would be no mistake now. Minter took the flag to a roar from the crowd, and then rode slowly back through the tunnel to the paddock in the fading light of an autumn evening. It was over.

The world kept turning. Rex Butcher left Paul Dunstall's shop to turn pro, Peter

Derek Minter's last rides at Snetterton came in October 1967, when he held off champion-elect Ron Chandler (500 Seeley) to win the 500cc race (Courtesy Elwyn Roberts Collection)

Williams' arm was still in plaster from his East German GP fall, and while BP had pulled out of racing altogether, partly in response to the Six-Day War between Israel and its oil-producing Arab neighbours, Shell and Castrol said they were cutting back and shifting their support to off-road competition. Meanwhile, the argument about oversize engines rumbled on with no clear likelihood of resolution.

At least the resurfacing of Thruxton was going ahead, and Colin Seeley said he hoped to cut the price of some AMC spares. Before the year was out Hartle had started light training. He would be riding Ray Cowles' G50 again in 1968, while Peter Williams would be back with Tom Arter, and Shorey would again have his engines done by Ray Petty. John Cooper had bought himself a 500 Seeley but was undecided about the 350 class, and Paul Dunstall, who was working on an alloy block for his Atlas Domiracers, would again have Ray Pickrell as his star turn.

Gradually, the rumours that Weslake, the car engine firm, might be building a grand prix motorcycle engine were gaining strength. With financial backing from super-dealer Reads of Leytonstone, it seemed the engine would be a DOHC parallel twin based in part on the V12 the firm had built for F1 star Dan Gurney. A prototype was expected to be running by February.

Towards the end of the year, Mike Hailwood and Ken Sprayson had another conversation about a frame for the 500 Honda, and this time agreed terms. The parts arrived at Reynolds and Sprayson began measuring and drawing, bearing in mind that the world's best rider could fling his bikes into corners at an angle of lean said to have been measured by Dunlop at 59 degrees. Almost 50 years on, MotoGP stars manage 64 and World Superbike riders 61, and to much larger headlines.

Chapter 12

1968: All the Way from Middlesex

"If people say it's bad sportsmanship, that's all right with me"

Dave Croxford was three times British Champion before the end of the 1960s – and well on the way to his infamous total of 180+ crashes and zero broken bones. He was a dedicated short-circuit man who excelled in the cut and thrust of Brands and Mallory, and enjoyed putting last-lap moves on people. He had little interest in chasing glory on the grand prix trail, and the TT bored him. "I tried for a fast lap in Senior practice last year, did 98 and lost interest," he told *Motor Cycle* in May 1968. "I prefer scratching around short circuits with a couple of blokes beside me – it's more fun."

For David Lawrence Croxford, the embodiment of the irrepressible Londoner, pleasure in racing was essential, despite confessing to being "a bundle of nerves" on race day. "I can't stand blokes who take life too seriously; blokes who have long faces if the motor's off-song or the track's wet."

Croxford found his way into racing in 1961 after being booked for speeding and losing his licence for a year. He tried a Manx Norton for a time, then part-exchanged it on an ex-Roy Mayhew G50, which proved more to his liking. He found his long-standing sponsor, Nottinghamshire butcher Charlie Oakley, by advertising for support in the specialist press. In due course a letter with a cheque arrived in the post. "If it wasn't for Charlie I'd have packed it in long ago," he said. "I owe him a lot."

Although establishing his name and taking his first national title on AMC hardware, Croxford was equipped with Seeleys in 1968, and was full of admiration for the service

Seeley offered – and for the bikes themselves, saying after early tests he was lapping Brands up to four seconds quicker on the new 500.

Nor was Croxford alone in making the change. Ron Chandler switched to Seeleys after sampling them towards the end of the 1967 season, together with Norton defector John Cooper – and all three would have their engines prepared by Wally Rawlings, now Seeley's right-hand man after spending years on his left, in the sidecar of their Matchless and BMW outfits.

Gradually, the pool of talent available for preparing Manx Norton engines was dwindling: Bill Lacey was gone; Francis Beart, although in semi-retirement, was still devoting at least a part of his time to Aermacchi's lightweight singles, as was Allen Dudley-Ward; Syd Mularney – and his rider, Dave Williams – had missed all of 1967 to work on a new four-cylinder engine, and looked set to do the same in 1968; Geoff Monty declared he was to concentrate on Production racing engines during the season ahead; and Steve Lancefield said: "I've sunk all the money I can afford into racing" – and was himself looking for a sponsor.

Of the great names, only Ray Petty seemed to be working as hard as ever, and would be looking after Dan Shorey while working on his outside-flywheel 350.

At Weslake, the crankshaft for the new 75bhp DOHC racing twin was being machined before Christmas, but the project was now behind schedule because the company had decided to make its own internals for the five-speed gearbox rather than use AMC components, as originally planned. The prototype would be complete, Weslake now estimated, in March. Meanwhile, Colin Lyster had declared his intention to build a new 500cc engine based on two cylinders of the Hillman Imp rally engine. The water-cooled, twin-cylinder DOHC powerplant would make 60bhp at 10,000rpm, he reckoned, and go on sale in March.

At Kirby Racing, Alan Barnett would be the main man for the coming season and would ride, as well as the team's 7R and G50-powered hardware, a 654cc BSA-powered Métisse. Meanwhile, Jack Williams had been appointed development engineer at BSA where the race shop was working on a couple of lightweight 350 and 500cc singles, based on the Victor engines, to be ridden by Tony Smith and Paul Smart.

Finally, in the last of the awkward questions remaining from 1967, the issue of big engines fizzled out in January with news that the ACU would institute random capacity checks at the bigger meetings.

Down on the farm

With opinion in racing circles already polarised over the decision to stop paying start money at its 1968 nationals, MCD now added fuel to the fire with a plan to introduce longer-distance races with a compulsory pit stop. These would feature in the early meetings of the year, albeit on the say-so of the Ministry of Agriculture, which had been

Brands' 1968 season opened in the leafless grey of winter with the 40-lap Redex Grand National. Winner John Hartle (Matchless Métisse, 3) is tucked in and following Rex Butcher (Norton, 5) off the line. (Courtesy Elwyn Roberts Collection)

battling since autumn to contain an epidemic of foot and mouth disease and had imposed strict movement controls in critical rural areas. In the event racing gained more than it lost. While the 9 March Oulton Park national was postponed, tobacco giant Player's came knocking with a big chest of cash, intended for a winter scrambles series that was now a casualty of the outbreak. In its place a six-round road racing series – the Player's No 6 Championship – was organised for up to 1000cc bikes at Cadwell, Croft, Crystal Palace, Scarborough, Silloth and the new (Mk4) Thruxton.

Castrol came to the party too with a nine-event series for 350s at MCD circuits – the Castrol Challenge. The first round was logged for the King of Brands meeting in April, which would itself be changing. Now, the King of Brands and Master of Mallory titles would be decided on the basis of points awarded in the 250, 350 and 500cc races.

Meanwhile, Syd Lawton reported he'd have eight 1968-spec 350 Aermacchis for sale, together with five engines. These offered 2bhp more than their immediate predecessors, thanks to a new inlet cam and reshaped port. Chassis improvements included Ceriani forks and brakes. The price: £610. Never one to give up without a fight, Colin Seeley cut the prices of his bikes, dropping a four-speed G50-powered Mk 2 to £740 and offering a similar-spec 350 at the same price as the Aermacchi. "I'm determined to give foreign-made bikes a run for their money in the 350 class," he said. By way of comparison, Joe Public could wander into Elite Motors of Tooting and pick up a new Triumph T120 Bonneville for £309.

One more major announcement was to come before the start of the season. In mid-February Honda told the world it would be withdrawing from grand prix racing, effective forthwith. Motorcycle racing was still blinking uncomprehendingly at that one when the first flag of the season fell at Mallory Park, on 3 March. There was no start money, but the stars turned up rather than stay at home. In the 350 race, the latest shifts in the evolution of motive power became clear from the start, with John Cooper clearing off on the Padgett's TD1C Yamaha from Hartle's Aermacchi Métisse with Rex Butcher, on one of Kawasaki's disc-valve two-strokes, running third from Chandler's new Seeley. When Cooper retired with an off-song motor, Hartle motored home from Butcher.

Cooper led the Unlimited 30-lapper as well, with Shorey (545 Norton) and Ray Pickrell's 750cc Dunstall Dominator hard on his tail. It was Pickrell who lasted longest, taking the flag after Cooper had faded with a loose tank, a strong-running Tait dropped his Triumph and Hartle retired, still feeling the effects of his '67 Race of the Year injuries.

Cooper and Croxford headed for Cadwell Park the following Sunday, where Chas Wilkinson was still paying start money, rather than take part in the Brands prize-money-only meeting and its 40-lap marathon, the Redex Grand National. Cooper believed he'd struggle under the new MCD regime to recoup the £2000 he'd spent on his three new Seeleys and besides, he said, he suffered from the cold.

Sure enough, in Lincolnshire Yamaha-mounted Cooper and Croxford (AJS) were in the thick of things in the 350 race, at least until the third lap when Cooper slid off at the foot of the Mountain and brought Croxford down with him. Tom Armstrong, a 26-year-old welding lecturer from Sunderland, managed to thread his Norton through the litter and take the win. Cooper did better on the 500 race, beating home Steve Spencer's Norton by a length, while Steve Jolly (G50) held off Croxford. At Brands meanwhile, Hartle rode Ray Cowles' Matchless Métisse to victory in the Redex Grand National, though professed reservations about the long-race format. "I kept thinking about what a bind the race must be for those watching," he said. "It was far too long." After almost 80 minutes' racing on a cold, dull day, Hartle got home from Martyn Ashwood (Matchless) and Pat Mahoney (Matchless Métisse). Alan Barnett picked up the consolation of a win in the 350 race on Kirby's 7R-powered Métisse, and Pickrell continued his good form on the 750 Dunstall Dominator, proving victorious in the 1300cc race.

In the balance

MCD's series of long races continued with a 20-lapper at Snetterton. After Croxford (gearbox) and Pickrell (misfire) bowed out, Cooper, Shorey (back on his 499 Manx) and Tait – whose 490cc Triumph now used Doug Hele's Daytona cams, making it a match for the bigger twins on speed – took up the running. Tait's Triumph led into the last lap but Cooper, in the unfamiliar saddle of a Curtis Domiracer, got past him coming out of Russell's and won the squirt to the line. Shorey took a double in the 350 and 500cc seven-lap support races, in the bigger class beating Tait on the dash from Russell's on the last lap.

Snetterton retirement or not, Croxford had emerged as the man to beat by the end of Easter. A series of solid performances had made him King of Brands and Master of Mallory, and if he hadn't been quite so unsuccessful at Oulton Park, where Tait hit form, he wasn't out of the headlines for long. Before April was out, he and Barnett were winning and establishing records at the new Thruxton circuit. Croxford claimed the 500cc race after a race-long three-way dice with Uphill and early leader Barnett. The new circuit, fast and obviously conducive to tight racing, proved to Croxford's liking. He swept past last-lap leader Uphill to win by a length and establish a lap record for the revised Hampshire track at 90.81mph. The Londoner might have figured in the 350 final as well, had not a pulled nipple deprived him of a front brake. Barnett took over, leading from start to finish, and posting a class record at 86.55mph.

Castle Combe, which had been under siege since Calne & Chippenham Rural District Council responded to residents' complaints about noise by rejecting circuit promoter AFN's 1967 application for renewed planning permission, suddenly looked a little safer with the village parish council deciding to support AFN's appeal. Mother Nature, indifferent to such trifles, provided rain for the 350 and 500 races at the April national and Croxford, riding one of Syd Lawton's Aermacchis in the 350 race, was one of several fallers

Sydneysider Kel Carruthers had a good season in 1968, winning the Castrol 350cc Challenge, and putting Aermacchi-powered bikes among more fancied machinery. In the Junior TT (pictured) he ran as high as fourth before a seized crankpin stopped him. (Courtesy FoTTofinder Bikesport Photo Archives)

at Camp Corner, allowing Tony Rutter (Norton) to canter away with the win. In the 500 race, Tait put his Triumph into the lead from the flag, and although caught and passed by Croxford, licked his rival and the weather by repassing on the outside through Camp and going on to win by 20 yards.

Out of the box

At the end of April, a clipped statement from Weslake Technical Director Mike Daniels said the current task was to redesign the new engine's gearbox internals, responding with "no comment" to a question about the bike's readiness for the TT. Syd Lawton had news, however, with the impending arrival of Varese's latest, a 382cc Aermacchi to be ridden by Paul Smart. "Fingers crossed," said Syd.

Croxford was back on top at Mallory Park's Derby Cup meeting, accounting for Barry Randle (Norton) and Tait in the 500 race, while Jim Curry led Randle home in the 350cc event. Cooper was overseas, winning the 250, 350 and 500cc races at Tilburg in Holland, and Tait soon put himself out of action at the Brands 500-mile Production race with a fractured forearm. He fell from the factory Bonneville he shared with Rod Gould when a footpeg dug in at Hawthorns. The Ray Pickrell/Dave Croxford 750 Dunstall Norton also went out after leading (broken primary chain), as did the BSA Spitfire shared by Paul Smart and Pat Mahoney (broken swinging arm). At the end of the journey Production specialists Dave Nixon and Peter Butler were winners for Triumph on their 490cc T100.

The end of May brought a spate of high-profile casualties. Cooper crossed the Irish Sea and won the 500cc class of the North West 200, while Peter Williams retired with a headache and double vision, and Ron Chandler crashed, breaking the collarbone he'd already fractured in a fall while testing a 350 Seeley. Alan Barnett, meanwhile, was clearly out of sorts at the Cadwell Park May international, and was diagnosed with a grumbling appendix.

Mike Hailwood, who'd warned of the consequences for his racing should MCD extend its abolition of start money to internationals, obligingly entered for Cadwell, where it was paid as a matter of course, bringing with him his RC174 and the Sprayson-framed, RC181-engined HRS – Hailwood Reynolds Special. Now running a building business in South Africa with Frank Perris, and having been paid by Honda, it was said, a cool £50,000 not to ride in grands prix for anyone else, Hailwood might have been rusty, but wasn't. He beat Read's Yamaha home in the 350 race, posting a new lap record at 78.64mph, but found his HRS too much of a handful on a damp track for the Invitation race, slithering home in fifth while Read slipped past Cooper's Seeley on the last lap to win. Pickrell, meanwhile, kept his eye in with a win in the Production race.

Dave Degens seemed destined not to get his eye in for some time. Back in November he'd been charged with receiving stolen engines, and now an ACU court decided to suspend his competition licence until March 1970. He would, he said, appeal. Yet there was better news from elsewhere. The Lyster engine – dubbed the Lynton – was ready for testing at the TT, while the new Norton Commando was being readied for Peter Williams; John Hartle had been offered MVs – a 350 triple and an old, 1966-spec 500 four – for the Island, and so passed on his Ray Cowles Matchless Métisse to Selwyn Griffiths.

Whitsun saw the next of MCD's long races, at Mallory Park. This one was for Production bikes; required a Le Mans start and a compulsory co-rider to help complete its 40.5 miles. Pickrell and Croxford shared a 750 Dunstall Norton and got home comfortably. Croxford won the 500 race, too, with Peter Williams second and Shorey third. Banbury Dan did better in a hotly-disputed 350 race, with up to five bikes running abreast down the Kirby Straight until Shorey eased away to win from Curry and Carruthers.

Before Mallory, Banbury Dan had spent the Saturday of Whitsun weekend cleaning up at Scarborough in both the 350 and 1000cc races; now he headed for the Brands international on the Monday where the Evening News-backed feature event was cut from 30 laps to 20 and the proposed pit stop scrapped. Pickrell celebrated by leading from the second lap to the flag, steadily pulling away from Croxford, who was passed in the closing laps by Griff Jenkins on one of Reg Curley's 650 Nortons. Shorey had been running well

Knees and elbows became more apparent as adjuncts of effective cornering in the late '60s, but Tom Kirby runner Alan Barnett reversed the trend, keeping it tidy. (Courtesy Elwyn Roberts Collection)

but fell with a locked front wheel, breaking a collarbone. Otherwise, the meeting ran to the form book. While Pickrell won the 1000cc event, Croxford notched another 500cc win in the Redex Trophy, while Carruthers extended his unbeaten run in the 350 class. Cooper, who might have caused them trouble, was at Cadwell Park's second meeting in a fortnight, winning the second round of the Player's title, together with the 500cc race, while Aermacchi-mounted Tom Phillips took the winner's tin of biscuits from the 350 event.

Mutiny

Without Hailwood's Hondas to trouble him, Giacomo Agostini had the Junior and Senior TTs to himself. He ran home more than two minutes clear of Renzo Pasolini's Benelli in the Junior race, and beat Brian Ball's Seeley by a staggering nine minutes in the Senior. But domestic interest there was. For a few glorious minutes Hartle seemed destined to repeat his '67 Production TT

By 1968 – its second year – the Production TT was rapidly gaining popularity. This is the scrap for second, with Billie Nelson (Norton) leading Rod Gould (Triumph) and the BSAs of Paul Smart and Tony Smith. (Courtesy Elwyn Roberts Collection)

win, but stepped off his Triumph Bonneville at Windy Corner, putting Pickrell (Dunstall Norton) into a winning lead, with Billie Nelson (Norton Atlas) and Tony Smith (BSA) following him home. Hartle's scrapes kept him out of the Junior, but Ago managed just the same; and while the Derbyshire rider did start the Senior on his '66 MV four, he soon slowed with gearbox troubles and then fell at Cronk-ny-Mona after finding a neutral he didn't want. Meanwhile Cooper came storming through the field into second, but stopped on the last lap at Ginger Hall, adding to the G50's tally of notable crankpin failures and allowing Ball into second from Barry Randle's Norton.

Hailwood was in action at Mallory Park for the following Sunday's Post-TT meeting, but must have wondered whether he'd get to ride at all in the 1000cc feature race when half the qualifiers refused to take their places on the grid. The action was taken in protest against MCD's policy of paying the big stars start money when many regulars went without. MCD countered, saying start money for the world champions – principally Hailwood, Ago, Read and Ivy – was paid in addition to the prize fund, but the rebels then pointed out that there wasn't much of that left either when the blokes on factory bikes had won everything. MCD capitulated – the decision no doubt hastened by a slow hand-clap from the crowd – and agreed to reinstate start money in full for the 1969 season.

Sure enough, Hailwood and Ago helped themselves in the bigger-capacity races. Hailwood cleared out from Read's 251 Yamaha in the 350 race after Ago's smaller MV failed to proceed, thanks to a flat battery. Jim Curry's Aermacchi was the pick of the singles, coming in third ahead of Brian Ball's TD1C Yamaha. In the 500 race it was Ago's turn, and with Hailwood having no suitable bike, he took a comfortable win from Alan Barnett's Kirby Métisse and Cooper's Seeley. When the 1000cc race did come under starter's orders, it was Hailwood again from Ago and Read, with Barnett fourth. Tom Phillips was the loser of the day, breaking his right thigh when falling from his Domiracer Métisse at Gerard's. A conrod broke, it was said, as he shut off for the corner.

Percy Tait had retired from the Senior TT when a bolt securing the Triumph's flywheel jumped out and broke the cases, but the bike was in fine fettle for the Snetterton 150 on 23 June, and now had matching Fontana brakes front and rear. The Triumph man didn't immediately figure though, as Pickrell put his Dunstall Domiracer into a full minute's lead after 20 laps of the scheduled 50; three laps later, however, the Dunstall man was pushing in with a failed magneto, allowing Cooper, short-shifting to preserve his engine, into the lead. Behind him Tony Smith (Daytona BSA), Butcher (648 Francis Domiracer) and Gould (on Tom Phillips' Domiracer Métisse) were hard at it until Butcher retired with an oil leak, Gould lost seven laps fixing a jammed clutch, and Smith retired with a broken clutch arm. Up came Tait, one of the last away, into third and ultimately to second from Carruthers' 500 Manx. Carruthers' turn came when he cemented his place at the top of the Castrol 350cc Challenge, beating home Cooper, Williams and Smith's Beesa.

In Hampshire on the same day, Alan Barnett waved the Kirby Racing flag vigorously at Thruxton, cleaning up the day's three feature races and breaking his own 350 lap record. All was not well among the private constructors, however. Work on the Lynton had been dogged with problems, first with finding subcontractors willing and able to supply components, later when Colin Lyster suffered a recurrence of a kidney problem that had its origins in a crash at the East German GP some years earlier. Two bikes were "virtually" complete by late June, however, after suffering camchain and gearbox problems in testing. At the same time Weslake was working on castings for more than 20 engines, and hoped to have two ready for testing "in a few days."

After Thruxton, Alan Barnett led the 350cc British Championship with 49 points from Dan Shorey's 36. Croxford led the 500cc chase from Barnett, 44 points to 25. Alas, with Charlie Oakley now withdrawing from sponsorship, Croxford had just one bike left; fortunately, it was his 500 Seeley.

Despite the sunshine, the Brands Hatch fences were sparsely populated for its fourth major meeting of the year. Here, Croxford pipped Barnett in the Redex Trophy, while

Percy Tait's 1968 GP 500 Triumph made 53bhp at 8700rpm, and weighed a trim 290lb (132kg). The double front-mounted oil tanks were added to combat the Daytona heat. Front brake is a nine-inch Fontana. (Courtesy FoT Tofinder Bikesport Photo Archives)

Curry notched another 350 win for Aermacchi. The 1300cc race honours went yet again to Pickrell, who brought home his Dunstall Domiracer in front of Mahoney's thundering Curley Norton – and then made it two in the Production race by reeling in early leader Peter Butler (Triumph) at the staggering rate of four seconds per lap.

Rumours

The rumours came, multiplied and strengthened. Some came from Europe, others from America, but all said the same thing: that Yamaha was building twin-cylinder two-stroke racers for private sale. There was word of a 250 and of a 350, based on the TR1 Canadian Yvon Duhamel had ridden into second place behind Cal Rayborn's Harley at the '68 Daytona 200 – a 150mph projectile concocted from the YR1 350 road bike and the old RD56 grand prix 250.

For the moment, though, it was business as usual. John Cooper, whose latest continental outing included four rounds of the world championships, spent the first weekend of August climbing back to the top of the domestic heap at Snetterton, winning the 250 race on one of Padgett's older Yamahas, leading the 350 race from start to finish on his smaller Seeley, and taking the 1000cc event on his 500 Seeley after Alan Barnett crashed Kirby's BSA Métisse at the Esses. The 500's engine, said Cooper, had been a winner despite having no attention since his last visit to Snetterton in June, but now its magneto cried enough and Cooper didn't come to the line for the 500 race. Percy Tait did, however, and got the best of a seven-way dice to win from Percy May's Norton.

The international names were back for the Hutch, but not so some of the local stars. Alan Barnett, feeling the effects of his Snetterton crash, was a non-starter; Paul Smart hit a patch of oil in practice and likewise withdrew from the meeting. Chandler seemed likely to miss out for want of a bike, but borrowed Croxford's Seeley from Hailwood, who found he didn't need it. His RC174 he certainly did need, and made use of it to win the three events he'd entered. He tidied up the Castrol 350cc Challenge and both 15-lap legs of the feature race, in the first leading home 350 Benelli-mounted Renzo Pasolini, who was making his Brands debut, and the Yamahas of Read and Ivy. Pickrell had been up to fourth but retired with loose carbs, so Cooper came home best of the locals. Mick Andrew, a fresh face but no novice, gave the new Norton Commando its first international result with seventh in the opening leg while Peter Williams retired the Arter Commando with a flat battery.

Read and Ivy followed Hailwood home in the second leg – Pasolini's 350 Benelli had blown up in the Castrol Challenge – after Ivy had fought his way clear of Pickrell's Domiracer. The Dunstall man starred in the best race of the day, the 20-lap Production event, which he led from the start, fending off the Triumphs of Gould and Uphill, and Tony Smith's BSA.

By mid-August there was more news from Lynton Racing. Colin Lyster was fit again and, said he: "We've just about completed the first racing engine … we should be out testing next week." Weslake too was back on track. "Everything fits and goes round," asserted Mike Daniels. "The engine is a reality."

Ray Petty and Steve Lancefield were meanwhile fielding complaints about a lack of Manx Norton spares. Petty gave lie to the problem. "I've got 40 engines on my books," he said, "and not one of them stuck for spares. What Colin Seeley can't supply, I'm making for myself." Lancefield agreed. "I have enough Bracebridge Street spares to make five complete engines and one complete bike," he said. "Stories like this … do a lot of harm to the Norton name."

Manx-mounted Barry Randle did his best to repair the damage at Mallory Park. In the 30-lap 350 marathon Barnett and Jim Curry moved out early, swapping the lead by the lap until Randle came steaming through, passing Rod Gould for third at half distance. On the last lap, Barnett and Curry closed on a backmarker at Shaw's. Barnett went outside, Curry took the inside – and both fell, letting Randle through to win while they scrambled to their feet and remounted, Curry getting home second from Barnett. A win in the 500 race was some recompense for Barnett, though Croxford's second place did his British title ambitions no harm.

Sundown

For all the financial problems now besetting the Scarborough club – largely caused by falling attendances – the August international went ahead at Oliver's Mount.

Welsh sponsor Ray Cowles offered John Hartle a G50 when he was without a competitive ride for the 1967 East German GP and kept the 500s coming until Hartle's death at Scarborough in August 1968. (Courtesy Elwyn Roberts Collection)

It did not go as planned, however: John Hartle had made a bad start to his 500cc heat, but by the last lap had pulled through to fourth and was trying to pass John Blanchard for third. Accelerating out of Mere Hairpin, the two collided, and Hartle's Matchless Métisse struck a support of the pedestrian bridge that spanned the track on its steep ascent of Quarry Hill. He died of his injuries. In Hartle's 15-year racing career, opportunity had routinely been outweighed by cruel misfortune; even so, he had won at national, TT and grand prix level and left a legacy of rare accomplishment at the most challenging of circuits, often in impossible weather. On his helmet he wore the crest of his Derbyshire hometown, Chapel-en-le-Frith: *Cave et spera,* read its motto; in English, Beware and hope. He was 34. The meeting ended quietly, with Curry a winner in the 350 race from Billie Nelson – Norton-mounted for the meeting – who won the 500cc race, deposing early leader Croxford and a subdued Shorey.

The following day at Snetterton, Mike Hailwood was back in action for the Race of Aces, bringing two bikes, his 297 six and the 500cc HRS. He won everything, beating home Carruthers in the 350 race again, then Phil Read's Yamaha and the ubiquitous Ray Pickrell in the Race of Aces, posting a new lap record for the Norfolk circuit at 95.65mph. He won the 500 race almost as comfortably, while Barnett and Croxford fought their way clear of a "hair-raising" seven-bike dice for second, with Barnett winning the dash for the line. As for the HRS, Hailwood was still unhappy with it and now talked of fitting a longer swinging arm to improve handling.

On Bank Holiday Monday, the circus went its separate ways. Hailwood journeyed to Oulton Park, where, in the Castrol 350cc Challenge, he trailed Carruthers and Ginger Molloy for most of the race, before sweeping past to win, posting a new lap record at 92.20mph. Carruthers took second, which left him just two points shy of winning the Castrol-backed series. For the 500cc Avon Trophy, Hailwood rode a Seeley with an engine borrowed from Bill Smith, after the original broke a crankpin in practice. He won just the same, scrapping with Read on a borrowed G50 and Cooper's Seeley until Read's tank ran dry. Cooper ran in second from Percy Tait, who also won the eight-lap Les Graham Memorial Trophy on a 490 Triumph that now ran 18-inch rims and fatter tyres.

The weekend wrapped up with Steve Jolly (350 Higley Aermacchi) and Tony Smith (654 BSA) on top at Cadwell and Ray Pickrell dominant at Crystal Palace, winning the penultimate round of the Player's Championship.

As September drew to a close Mike Hailwood won his fifth Mallory Park Race of the Year in nine attempts, and Bill Ivy had just about had enough. Without consistent, credible opposition, he and Yamaha team-mate Read had sliced up the grand prix season as they chose. Yamaha had told its riders it wanted Read to take the 125 world title and Ivy the 250, but after securing the 125 crown, Read decided to go for the 250 as well. After each man had claimed five wins and two second places, Read became champion on the basis of time elapsed in the four races where they'd both been placed, his total time being two minutes shorter than Ivy's. Ivy lodged desperate protests after Read's crucial Italian GP win but these were overruled. Little Bill, the clown of the paddock, was incensed. "If people say it's bad sportsmanship, that's all right with me, I'm a bad sportsman," Ivy rumbled. "Being a good one didn't do me any good."

Meanwhile, Colin Seeley unveiled the latest development in his running battle with Aermacchi – the Mk 3 Seeley frame for the 7R engine. This lacked front downtubes and anchored the engine with plates from the top tubes and rubber-mounted lugs to the rocker box. The result was a 25lb (11kg) weight reduction over the Mk 2, with a further 10lb (4.5kg) still to come off. Cooper rode the prototype at the Race of the Year meeting in the Castrol 350cc Challenge. He slid off at the Esses but declared himself delighted with the development. "It's a really beautiful little job," he told *Motor Cycle*. "We've been waiting ten years for this and it's a joy to ride." Hailwood won the race with Ago second and Curry third from Carruthers, whose fourth spot was still enough to give him the series overall.

Hailwood decided not to ride the HRS in the 1000cc race and as the RC174 was below the minimum capacity limit for the event Ago cleared off alone, leaving Tait, Barnett (G50 Kirby Métisse) and Tony Smith (654 BSA) to haggle over second, which went Barnett's way after Smith fell at Shaw's and Tait retired with an ailing clutch. There was no holding Hailwood in the Race of the Year, however. The race began with a shower, and Hailwood bolted while Ivy overhauled Ago with Croxford, Williams and Randle hustling up astern; but as the track began to dry, Ago got going, moving into a clear second after Ivy fell at Gerard's, and Randle claimed third. Barnett, meanwhile, held off Croxford's Seeley and Tait's experimental 749 Triumph – an overbored Bonnie engine in a Rob North twin-downtube frame. "We've got to think about development for higher speeds," said Doug Hele of the bike, "now we've got the three-cylinder 750 roadster."

Hailwood was beset with a similar problem, if with very different results. "I've more or less given up hope of ever getting it right," he said of his decision to park the Sprayson-framed HRS after practice. "It was leaping all over the place." Even so, he seemed in a far better frame of mind than Ivy who flew to Italy after the Mallory meeting. "I'm fed up with everything and everybody," he declared.

Surprise packet

A week later at the new Croft circuit Rob Fitton pulled start-to-finish wins in the 350 and 1000cc races, beating home rising Teesside star Ken Redfern in the 1000cc race. Redfern, described by *Motor Cycle* as "the surprise packet of the race," rode a 650 Domiracer whose engine was the product of brother Derek's labour and fitted into a

Steve Spencer gave Steve Lancefield his last great Isle of Man result with third place in the 1967 Senior TT. Here Spencer, from Birmingham, is pictured at Memorial Corner, Scarborough. (Courtesy Paul McElvie)

Manx frame bought from John Hartle. Malcolm Uphill fell heavily in the same event when the drive chain of his Seeley jumped its sprocket and jammed the wheel, but was still on the grid – though battered and now Norton-mounted – for the final round of the Player's Championship the following day at Cadwell. Needing just a top-eight finish to win the title, he happily ran sixth while Barnett (Kirby Métisse) won from title runner-up Barry Scully (Norton).

The final international on the calendar, the Brands Hatch Race of the South, brought few surprises: Ago won the 500 Redex Trophy race with Barnett in another good second from Croxford. The 350 race was Hailwood's with Ago second from a melee for third that went to Carruthers from Barnett and Croxford. Hailwood had to work harder in the title event, posting a new lap record at 90.86mph, but was ultimately a comfortable winner from Ago, Read and, emerging from the ravening pack to Read's rear, that man Pickrell on Dunstall's 750 Domiracer.

Three national meetings were left to run, and it came down to this: Croxford now led the 500cc British Championship by 62 points from Barnett's 51 and Tait on 34; in the 350 title Jim Curry led on 52 points with Barnett on 50 and Shorey 37. At Snetterton for the first of the three, Pickrell stole headlines by winning the newly instituted 1000cc Squire of Snetterton, blasting past early leader Derek Chatterton's 250 Yamaha and staying in front to the flag, while Tait got the better of Barnett and Randle for second. Tait was in the mood for the 500 race too, leading from half-distance and fending off Barnett's last-lap bid to pass at Coram. Jim Curry, now the proud owner of Kel Carruthers' Castrol

Challenge-winning Aermacchi Métisse, led early in the 350 race but was soon passed by Gould's Aermacchi Métisse, which lost power on the last lap, letting Barnett through to consolidate his title lead.

A week later at Mallory Park, Cooper won both races while Barnett languished in fifth in the 350 race. Still, he did better than Croxford, whose engine broke a crankpin in the 500cc event while Tait finished second and Barnett third. Everything would be settled on the short circuit at Brands.

Curry knew what was at stake. He set a scorching pace in the 350 race, albeit with Barnett close behind. Dave Simmonds sailed past them both and went on to win, but Barnett had only to beat Curry, and squeezed past to finish second from Pat Mahoney's Aermacchi Métisse while Curry faded. Barnett, the aircraft instrument technician from Iver, had his title.

Croxford took the direct route to his first 500cc crown. He took the lead from the start and stayed there, despite having Pickrell snap at his heels on Dunstall's smallest Domiracer. Barnett finished third from Brian Hunter's Coleshill Matchless and deposed champion Ron Chandler. Pickrell went one better in the 1300cc race to bring Dunstall's 750 Domiracer home to yet another win, this time from Croxford's 750 Curley Norton and Mick Andrew on one of the new Norton Commandos, entered by Gus Kuhn.

The year ended as it had begun, with news of the Weslake engine still causing a stir. Mike Daniels reported it had undergone six weeks of bench testing without problems, and had been run up to 9500 and then 11,500rpm. Come the dawn, Tom Kirby would take one of the first engines for testing in a Métisse frame by Alan Barnett and Tom Arter another, this one for a Reynolds frame and Peter Williams. At Lynton, meanwhile, progress had slowed again. Colin Lyster was suffering a recurrence of his illness, and could manage just two hours' work a day.

The last word on the Weslake issue went to Phil Read. A week before Christmas he offered his services free of charge to help with development. "I want to see an all-British machine back on top," he said, "and I'm willing to do all the test riding and race the bike."

Chapter 13

1969: Nemesis

"You again"

Yamaha had been developing its racing two-stroke twins for more than a decade. The Iwata company took its first tentative steps into Japanese racing as early as 1957, heading to Europe for the first time in 1961 and offering the TD1 for sale in the USA during 1962.

The factory made less than 60 examples of the original 246cc TD1, and its buyers acquired a motorcycle very different to anything then available from Europe. The 31bhp from the torquey twin-cylinder air-cooled engine might have been enough for about 120mph, but performance was compromised by critical shortcomings. The fork seals would blow after a handful of races and the rear suspension units were damped only on the rebound stroke; the clutch was fragile, the three-port aluminium anodised cylinders were prone to wear and there were ignition problems.

Still, it was a start; and by 1967 the last of the line, the TD1C, enjoyed a solid reputation on both sides of the Atlantic. Yamaha built around 320 TD1Cs, which became acknowledged as the marque's fastest and most reliable production racing 250 yet. It was rated at 40bhp and made good power from 8500rpm to the engine's 11,000rpm redline, if at the expense of regular small-end bearing replacement. Handling was much improved from the first TD1s; even the brakes, carried over from earlier models, were considered adequate.

Factory racers of the time were faster and more powerful – and more difficult to ride. Michelle Duff recalls having to keep the engine speed of the early RD56 twin-cylinder 250s above 9000rpm to avoid the usually terminal problem of plug fouling. Phil Read's world-championship-winning bike of 1964 developed 48bhp; his '65 mount 55bhp. The RD05 and RD05A water-cooled V-fours, designed to counter Honda's RC164 six-cylinder 250 and its successors, were formidably powerful at 70+bhp, but suffered wayward handling – and became a developmental blind alley from the moment the FIM decreed that 250cc grand prix racers would be limited to two cylinders and six gears from 1970. The fours were mothballed after the 1968 season, but Yamaha had already done much work to develop new bikes in America, using the frame of the old RD56 and modified piston-ported road bike engines.

Duff, who'd ridden one of the hybrid 350s at Daytona in 1968, alongside Yvon Duhamel, said the bike had the potential for a 104mph lap of the Isle of Man and was faster than the old rotary-valve RD56 250 factory bike, offering performance comparable to the 1965 MV 350 triple. The bike weighed about 280lb, he said – a little less than a British single, but appreciably heavier than a 350 Aermacchi – offering good power from 7500rpm and revving to 10,500rpm.

New bikes were coming, but the drip-feed of information, official or otherwise, offered nothing about specification, price or delivery dates – though *Motor Cycle* reported that four British dealers would be among the first to receive them: Ted Broad, Mick Chatterton, Hector Dugdale and the Padgett Brothers. The new bikes were designated the ITD2 (250) and ITR2 (350).

Meanwhile, Phil Read, Yamaha's newly minted double world champion, spent the early weeks of 1969 in talks with Weslake. His enthusiasm was clear: "with a 500cc bike weighing only 250lb and giving 70bhp you couldn't help but win," he said; but reservations were being aired about the resources that might be needed to complete the project. Read said he hoped for support from accessory manufacturers; even so, before the month was out, Read (Phil) had bought Reads' (Leytonstone) stake in the scheme.

More tangible evidence of Weslake's workmanship was shortly to become available. The Rye concern had developed, at the request of Rickmans, a bolt-on, eight-valve conversion for the 649cc Triumph Bonneville engine, that also took capacity to 683cc. While Allen Dudley-Ward and Doug Hele disagreed in print about whether the stock Bonnie two-bearing crank could cope with the extra stress, Alan Barnett prepared to test the revised engine under the Kirby banner.

Barnett would remain team leader for the Kirby outfit in 1969, though there was plenty of movement elsewhere. 500cc British Champion Dave Croxford, who'd been out on a limb since Charlie Oakley withdrew his sponsorship, would ride for Gus Kuhn Motors. Kuhn boss Vincent Davey wanted to sign Malcolm Uphill, but when that plan fell through, he and Croxford had a chat, and two Seeleys and a Norton Commando Production racer were the result for the Ruislip rider, who would be backed up by Mick Andrew. "I'm very happy," said Croxford. "It's a right handsome set-up."

Peter Williams became King of Brands in 1969. He's pictured during the 350 race on Tom Arter's 7R. "You have to work so hard among all the TR2s that it just isn't worthwhile," he would soon say of the AJS. (Courtesy Elwyn Roberts Collection)

Split

The ACU's latest reorganisation of the British championships met with criticism. Under the new scheme each class would be run over seven rounds with the classes to be split into two groups – 125, 250 and sidecar in one, 350 and 500 in the other – each with its own meetings; but some of these clashed with internationals, said the riders, and the plan would in any case make life tricky for those wishing to compete in, say, the 250 and 350 championships. Yet having the titles concentrated at a small number of meetings, rather than at every national in the season, had its advantages, not least in tallying points. Meanwhile the 350cc Castrol Challenge had gone, and the oil company would instead channel its sponsorship cash into the British titles, giving £200 to the winner of each class.

In mid February, Weslake's GP prototype underwent low-speed tests at Thruxton. Read said he expected to ride the bike at Easter, shortly after which, he hoped, his four new Yamahas, two 250s and two 350s (now known as the TD2 and TR2) would arrive. These, it was said, would have the massive Fontana-style double twin-leading-shoe front brake used on the works RD05, and Ceriani-type forks. Rod Gould decided not to wait, and went to America to buy one of each and race them at the Daytona 200 meeting.

With a dusting of frost on the grass and an air temperature close to freezing, the season's racing got under way at Brands Hatch short circuit on 2 March. A sparse entry revealed the incompleteness of many would-be champions' plans, but the racing was gratifyingly close, with Pat Mahoney's Henderson Aermacchi having just enough extra puff in the 350 race to beat Alan Barnett's Kirby Métisse, and Croxford taking a debut win on his Kuhn Seeley in the 500cc encounter – harried all the way by Ray Pickrell's 497 Dunstall Domiracer. Pickrell, too, was back in charge of the big boys, leading the 1300cc race all the way and fending off a late challenge from Tony Smith's BSA.

The first pictures of the new Yamahas appeared in the following week's papers, together with a few facts and figures. The 61 × 59.6mm 348cc TR2 would give 54bhp at 9500rpm, have a duplex frame Yamaha had hitherto reserved for its works bikes, 18-in wheels and that front brake. Dry weight was given as 253lb (115kg).

The British championships got going the following weekend, at Oulton Park on the Saturday for the 350s and 500s, and Snetterton on the Sunday for the smaller classes. At Oulton the writing again appeared on the wall in the 350 race; in smallish letters as yet, but getting larger by the season: Alan Barnett, on Kirby's short-stroke 7R Métisse, cleared off from the start, but was passed by two Aermacchis (Tommy Robb and Mahoney). The Kirby rider kept his third place from Croxford – first time out on his 350 Kuhn Seeley – and another Varese lightweight, ridden by Irish star Brian Steenson. Barnett fared better among the 500s, winning from Croxford and Andrew in a race punctuated by falls on oil dropped in the sidecar race.

At Snetterton the following day Pickrell was again in indomitable form, though not immediately. Along with Croxford (oil leak), Smart (loose flywheel) and Barnett (split oil tank), the Londoner was a non-starter in the 350 final after falling in his heat, leaving the scrap between Jim Curry (Aermacchi) and Peter Williams (Arter AJS) as the major source of action. Curry collected the win, but Williams was centre stage again in the 500 race, chasing Pickrell home for his second runner-up spot of the day, with Croxford third. Pickrell also won in the 1000cc event, this time beating home Croxford's Seeley and Williams' Arter-Matchless.

A week later at Mallory Park for the last of the March meetings, Barnett managed to beat Mahoney's Aermacchi in the 350 race, but in the 1000cc event could do no better than third after a furious dice with Tony Smith (654 BSA), Percy Tait (490 Triumph) and Croxford (496 Seeley), whose Seeley led into the back straight on the last lap, but ran out of sparks while Smith and Tait streamed past.

At least one of Phil Read's wishes was about to come true: Castrol decided to back the Weslake project, make a "substantial cash payment." Read rode the bike at Lydden, declaring himself impressed with the torque of the twin, and with the diaphragm clutch; though the five-speed gearbox was not so good: "It jumped out of gear a few times," he said. Yet if progress was being made on the Weslake, it wasn't on the Lynton. Colin Lyster had now been discharged from hospital after his latest bout of kidney trouble, but still couldn't work at full capacity.

All change

As the first long weekend of the year approached, word came from Eltham that Pickrell was shortly to give its debut a new, lightweight Eddie Robinson frame for the Domiracer that dispensed with front down tubes and anchored the motor from the three-inch-diameter top tube. The frame located the engine low and well forward and, packing a 745cc Norton motor, the new bike's dry weight was estimated at 306lb (139kg).

The struggle for the 350 and 500cc British championships resumed at Brands Hatch on Good Friday with the King of Brands meeting. This year Peter Williams became part of Brands royalty after strong finishes in all three qualifying races. Even so, in the 350 race on Tom Arter's 7R, Williams could do no better than seventh, while Barnett and Mahoney resumed their battle for supremacy – this time with an added ingredient. Rod Gould was back from America with the Yamahas he'd ridden to good finishes at Daytona, and used them to win the Brands 250 and 350 races as he pleased. Barnett eased past Mahoney's Aermacchi to claim second in the 350 race, but Gould's performance was a clear indication of what lay ahead.

In the 500 championship race Williams got ahead but Barnett and Croxford went with him, with Barnett leading them home on the last lap to consolidate his title lead. In the 1300 race Williams (Arter Commando) again looked a likely winner after early leader Tony Smith stopped with a bent gearlever; but up came Pickrell, sweeping past to win as Williams slowed with a loose fairing. Still, Willliams had done enough to earn his title. Barnett, who'd had one hand on the Brands crown going into the 1300cc race, fell from his BSA Métisse and so excluded himself from the overall accountancy.

At Mallory Park on Easter Saturday Gould again won the 250 and 350 races and acquired a title of his own – Master of Mallory. While Mahoney tailed Gould home in the 350 race, the meeting's principal display of four-stroke merit came in the 750s. Smith and Croxford were non-starters after falling in their heat but Barnett turned it on, with help from Percy Tait (on his now Sprayson-framed, five-speed 490 Triumph), Brian Kemp's 750 Curley Norton and Ray Pickrell, breaking in his new lightweight Dunstall. Tait came out on top after Pickrell, who'd been stalking the Triumph man remorselessly, missed a gear at Shaw's and dropped to third, behind Barnett.

Pickrell then doubled back to London to star at Crystal Palace on the Sunday, putting his Aermacchi into second behind Mick Andrew's Seeley in the 350 race, and leading the field home in the 1000cc race on the lightweight 750 Dunstall, as well as adding a new lap record at 81.90mph

If there were any doubts left about the might of the new Yamahas, Gould dispelled them

**Alan Barnett (AJS Métisse) and Giacomo Agostini (MV) start the 1969 Junior TT.
Ago won, Barnett retired – but finished second to Ago in Friday's Senior.
(Courtesy Elwyn Roberts Collection)**

before close of business at Oulton Park on Easter Monday. Again he won the 250 and 350 races, in the 350cc event pulling away from Mahoney's Aermacchi at a scarcely credible five seconds a lap. The 500 and 750 races were more competitive, with Derek Woodman (Seeley) getting home in the 500 race after a long scrap from Dan Shorey in one of his last rides before retiring. Meanwhile, Brian Kemp (Curley Norton) took 750 honours from Gould's Norton Métisse. The fastest lap of the day went to Gould – on his 350 Yamaha.

A week later the Lynton dream was officially put on hold. "My backers simply can't raise the cash needed for production," said Lyster, who'd already sacked his two full-time mechanics to cut costs. He still hoped, he told *Motor Cycle*, to race the prototype and raise cash that way. The market was real, and growing. Mick Woollett had already mooted the end of the British single as a competitive ride. He now suggested anyone interested in remaining competitive in the 350 class needed a Yamaha – and, "a sobering thought is that a slightly overbored version would be a very competitive mount in the 500 class." A week later, Britain's first full consignment of TD2s and TR2s arrived.

Spreading the word

While Phil Read was calling for the Weslake prototype's Métisse frame to be ditched in favour of the much lighter unit Ken Sprayson had designed for the Tom Arter version, the third round of the British championships unfolded at Castle Combe. With no TR2s entered, the 350 race proved to be a classic, with up to five riders vying for the lead until Malcolm Uphill's Bridgestone-powered Altair seized, bringing down Barry Randle (Norton), and Dave Croxford's rear wheel began to collapse. That left Andrew (Seeley) pulling away from Barnett's Métisse while Mahoney, who'd been left on the grid, steamed through the field to snatch second from the Kirby man. The 500 race was as hard fought. Barnett led early from Croxford, Tait, Andrew and Robin Duffty on a Petty Norton. The lead changed at almost every corner; but as Andrew fell back Croxford began to gain the upper hand, leading throughout the final lap to run home a winner from Tait and Barnett.

The future, at least at sub-750cc level, was two-stroke; and the growing Yamaha clan gathered on Whit Monday for the Brands short-track international. Read now had his new twins and, after a poor start in the 350 race, pulled out all the stops to catch and pass Gould. Bill Ivy might have made it a 1-2-3 for Yamaha had not his new bike stopped with ignition failure, letting Croxford's Seeley in to spoil the party. Surprisingly, all three of the fancied Yamahas failed in the Evening News International, Ivy with ignition problems, Gould and Read with oil on their tyres – though Read first managed a new lap record for the circuit at 79.43mph. There was no stopping Pickrell anyway, the bark of Dunstall's mighty Norton filling the Brands amphitheatre as he eased away to win both legs from Croxford, with Barnett third in the first leg and Chandler in the second after Barnett fell at Clearways. The 500 race was the pick of the day: the usual suspects got away, Croxford leading. Barnett passed him at half distance but Croxford got back in front to set up a last-lap dash that saw Barnett baulked by a slower rider and Croxford home by half a wheel. And then it was TT time.

Notable absentees included Peter Williams, who was in a London hospital receiving treatment for his asthma, and the Weslake team. "We can't afford any more adverse publicity," said Read. Under a new schedule, Weslake hoped its bike would be running at the Hutch in August. John Cooper was also out of action after crashing his new TR2 Yamaha at Cadwell, breaking a collarbone.

The Production TT went ahead with Rod Gould riding Cooper's Bonnie, but without Alan Barnett, who said he had enough to do with the Junior and Senior races, or Percy Tait, who'd fallen during practice at Sulby, breaking a collarbone, when his Senior Triumph's gearbox locked; Ray Pickrell too was absent with a broken shoulder after taking over Tait's Senior ride and falling at Quarter Bridge in practice when an oil line let go.

The Norton team, meanwhile, was engaged in a barney over the eligibility of its disc brakes for the Production TT, but Malcolm Uphill led from start to finish on his factory Triumph anyway, posting the first Production ton lap at 100.09mph. Paul Smart's Norton came in second, half a minute adrift, with Darryl Pendlebury third on another Triumph after Gould stopped at Crosby. Star retirements or not, the Production TT was becoming a highlight of the Island programme.

TR2 Yamahas notwithstanding, Ago enjoyed fuss-free runs in both the Junior and Senior TTs. Eight of the Yamahas started the Junior and two finished; Gould's holed a piston and Read's ran a big end after each had held second, and at the flag Brian Steenson (Aermacchi) was runner-up, ten minutes adrift of Ago's MV and a minute clear of Jack Findlay (Aermacchi Métisse). Alan Barnett retired in the Junior but fared better in Friday's Senior, taking second place to Ago on the opening lap and hanging on tenaciously. Derek Woodman (Seeley) closed on him but then slowed with brake problems, allowing Tom Dickie (on Croxford's Seeley) into third. Jack Findlay, driven to distraction by his Italian Linto's catalogue of mechanical failure that now extended to cracked cases, rode instead Syd Lawton's 382 Aermacchi and got up to fourth before the gearbox failed. Ago was oblivious to it all, finishing nine minutes clear of Barnett's new G50 Métisse, now with the motor more than an inch lower and angled forward, and Elektron (magnesium alloy) fork yokes a whopping 11.5lb (5.5kg) lighter than stock.

Foreign fields

Ago and Gould turned it on at the Mallory Park Post-TT meeting, taking one win apiece before meeting in the 1000cc final, where Ago was boxed in from the start. Despite

equalling Hailwood's outright lap record at 93.46mph, Ago never got on terms with the Yamaha man and had to be content with second, well clear of Croxford's Seeley.

The news of Ago's defeat at the hands of a private runner was quickly eclipsed. John Cooper was, it seemed, on the point of following Dan Shorey into mid-season retirement. He'd sold all his bikes except his 1968 Seeley, and was clearly brassed off with his medics' news that his collarbone would take another five

With scant opposition, Ago won the first ten rounds of the 1969 500cc World Championship. At the Ulster GP – win number ten – he beat home Brian Steenson's Seeley by three minutes. (Courtesy Elwyn Roberts Collection)

weeks to heal. He wasn't alone in his frustration. Pat Mahoney lost his lead in the 350cc British Championship at Thruxton a week later when his Aermacchi failed to fire on the start line. Fortunately his principal threat, Barnett, got his Kirby Métisse no higher than fourth behind the TR2s of Derek Chatterton and Cliff Carr and Martin Carney's Kawasaki A7R, but it was enough for Mahoney to start asking loudly for a TR2 of his own. Barnett, meanwhile, looked better all the time. At Thruxton he took his G50 Métisse to its third win from four starts in 500cc British championship races, while Andrew's Seeley broke a crankpin and Croxford held second from Tait, who was still feeling the effects of his TT crash. If that wasn't enough, Barnett gave the Rickman-Weslake eight-valve Triumph a winning debut in his heat. He was well placed in the final, too, until a loose sparkplug dropped him to fifth, behind a four-way scrap for the lead won by Brian Kemp (750 Curley Norton) from Paul Smart (750 Francis Norton).

Barnett continued his good work the following Saturday – but at Assen for the Dutch TT rather than the sixth round of the British titles at Croft; so while the Kirby man took third in the 500cc Dutch, behind Ago and a revitalised Peter Williams (having his first ride since being discharged from hospital), the Kuhn Seeley boys were amassing valuable points, most of them going to Mick Andrew, who took a good 500 class win from Redfern. In the 350 race TR2-mounted Chatterton walked away with it while Mahoney hustled his Aermacchi into third, behind Martin Carney, now Yamaha-mounted. While Mahoney still led the 350 title, Barnett was now second behind Croxford in the 500 points tally, 59 to 55.

July closed with a national at Castle Combe, where Croxford scraped home in the 500 race from a fully fit Tait, while Mahoney, who now had his Yamaha, ran home second to Tony Rutter's TR2 in the 350 race. There was also the news of Bill Ivy's death at the East German GP. Since flying to Italy, livid, at the end of the 1968 season, Ivy had been Formula 2 car racing and agreed to ride Jawa's two-stroke V-four in the 350cc World Championship as an extra source of revenue for his four-wheeler plans. As the season progressed he bagged a couple of second places behind Ago's MV, and then went out one wet morning at Sachsenring for practice. The Jawa seized on a fast left-hand bend – some suggested a shattered big-end cage as the culprit – and struck an unprotected wall. Ivy suffered massive head injuries and died in hospital. He was 27.

The Weslake wouldn't be at the Brands Hutchinson 100 after all. "We're having trouble with the gearbox," reported Technical Director Mike Daniels, "and it's gone back for modification." Meanwhile the Lynton was now reported "dead and buried," with Colin Lyster apparently developing a racing engine based on the Honda CB450 – the 'Black Bomber.'

His TT injuries mending, Ray Pickrell returned cautiously to the fray for the Hutchinson 100, although the story of the meeting was of Rod Gould and his 348cc TR2 Yamaha. In the first 15-lap leg of the Evening News Trophy Andrew took his Kuhn Commando into an early lead, but by the second round Gould was at the front and pulling away. Read, also TR2-mounted, caught him and they circulated together for a while; but while Read's race ended with a broken piston ring, Gould got away to an easy win from Andrew. Smart (750 Francis Norton) beat the fragile Pickrell (750 Domiracer) for third from Rex Butcher's Weslake Triumph.

Read, resorting to his 247cc TD2 for the 350 race, did what he could to check Gould until his engine went off song. Gould then built a colossal lead over Andrew's 350 Seeley, but fell on oil with two laps to go, breaking a clutch lever and giving Andrew the win from Barnett, Williams and Cliff Carr's Yamaha. It was a temporary hiatus. Gould and Read were back at it in the second leg of the Evening News Trophy until Read's retirement, this time after wearing a hole in an expansion chamber. Gould cleared off again while Andrew and Barnett had a dust-up for second with Smart, finishing in that order. Relief from the two-stroke onslaught came only in the Production race, won by Andrew's Kuhn Commando after Smith had hounded him all the way. Gould was the best of the Bonnevilles in third, ahead of Williams' Commando and Percy Tait – on a Triumph Trident.

"You couldn't keep it in a ten-acre field"

Pat Mahoney would, it appeared, be without bikes for the British championship finale at Crystal Palace on August Bank Holiday Monday, following a difference of opinion with his sponsor. His task of securing the 350cc championship was eased, however, with the news that Derek Chatterton wouldn't be at the Palace – and then came word that Alan Barnett too would be out of contention after breaking an arm in a testing crash at Snetterton. Barnett had been riding the team's eight-valve Triumph Métisse when oil from the gearbox leaked onto the rear tyre and Barnett went down in the Esses at 70mph. "This bike is not ready to be raced," an angry Tom Kirby told *Motor Cycle*. There was even talk of the team disbanding.

Ray Pickrell was in difficulties too. Still troubled by his TT injury, he was about to go back into hospital for another operation. "I thought it was a simple collarbone fracture," he told *Motor Cycle*. "But it turns out I had broken just about everything in my shoulder except the collarbone."

John Cooper was coming back, however. His plans of retirement now on hold, he rang Mike Hailwood and got his approval to ride the Sprayson-framed HRS at Snetterton. Gould continued his winning ways there, adding the 1000cc Race of Aces silverware to his trophy cabinet, and equalling the lap record he'd set in his 350 heat – 95.83mph – without being pushed. Some 20 seconds to his rear came a ding-dong scrap that included the 750 Nortons of Smart and Kemp, the 500 Seeleys of Croxford and Steenson, Rutter's TR2, Williams' Arter Matchless, Percy Tait's Production 650 Triumph (with Lockheed discs) and Cooper on the weaving HRS. One second covered the lot until the penultimate lap when Rutter and Croxford broke clear, with Rutter inches ahead. Cooper somehow fended off the rest, perhaps because the HRS effectively blocked the track.

Another eight-way dust-up involving the usual culprits distinguished the 500 race, at least until the drizzle began. Cooper wobbled into an early lead on the HRS until Steenson summoned the courage to pass him; Degens, reunited with his racing licence early and firmly back in business on his Dresda Triumph, then had a go at Cooper, as did Tait on his 490 Triumph and Seeley-mounted Smart. Metal fatigue set in, stopping Steenson with a broken primary chain, while Williams struggled with a loose fairing. Cooper ended the frolics with a giant slide that scared people as far away as Norwich, and came in a subdued fourth while Tait got his nose in front to claim the win.

Afterwards Joe Ryan, he of the famously untidy but impressively quick Fireplace Nortons, came over to inspect the HRS, shook his head and said to Cooper "you couldn't keep it in a ten-acre field." Cooper was entered on the bike at Oulton Park the following day, but a problem with the cush drive made it a non-starter. Thus did the mighty Honda RC181 pass into history. "I don't know whether it was because the engine ran backwards that it handled so badly," reflected Cooper, years later. "It was so bad to ride and yet Hailwood won on it; I don't know how."

The Oulton 350 race went the way of Carr's Yamaha after Gould's stopped with ignition failure and Read's seized in his heat, while a "dashing young" Barry Sheene, then just 18, took second on his Bultaco from Mike Hatherill's Aermacchi. Croxford crashed his 350 Seeley at Snetterton and did the same at Crystal Palace the following day, while Mahoney became 350cc British Champion after borrowing a bike from the Gus Kuhn team – Mick Andrew's, who'd fallen in a support race – and finishing fourth behind Ron Chandler (Seeley), Charlie Sanby (7R) and Graham Sharp (Aermacchi). Croxford took his second 500 title with a third place behind the Seeleys of winner Chandler and runner-up Paul Smart. Barnett, of course, was in plaster.

Internationals at Oulton and Cadwell ended August, the principal question at both being whether the Yamaha boys could beat Ago's MVs. Read did in the Cadwell 350 race, but with the aid of the wet weather. On the slick Lincolnshire track

The team most likely. Tom Kirby does a plug chop on Alan Barnett's AJS Métisse during practice for the 1969 Ulster Grand Prix. (Courtesy Elwyn Roberts Collection)

Under pressure: Ago renews his acquaintanceship with Yamaha's TR2, here ridden by Phil Read and Rod Gould, in the 350 race at the 1969 Mallory Park Race of the Year meeting. Ago won. (Courtesy Elwyn Roberts Collection)

Ago could use only five of the MV's seven gears, and then at half throttle; he got home second, with Redfern's Aermacchi behind him. He did better in the 1000cc Wills Trophy but didn't have it all his own way even on the 500 MV. Redfern thundered along behind him, putting his 750 Domiracer into second, a bare eight seconds down on the champion at the flag.

Journey's end

The season wound down. Ago, now 500cc World Champion for the fourth year in a row, didn't enter the Yugoslavian Grand Prix and the race looked likely to go to one of the factory 382 Aermacchis. Gradually, however, the more fancied runners fell away, leaving bearded Londoner Godfrey Nash to cross the line first on his 1960 Manx Norton, a bike he'd owned for eight years. It was the 41st and final solo grand prix win for the Manx in the 21 seasons since the world titles were instituted.

At Mallory Park, the atmosphere at the Race of the Year meeting crackled in expectation of another exercise in giant-killing as the private Yamahas prepared to take on the Agostini MV. It was a task beyond Mike Hailwood for once. With his Hondas unavailable, Mike arranged to borrow Derek Woodman's Seeley. The walking wounded were on hand to spectate. Tom Dickie, who'd fallen heavily in the Ulster GP and broken an arm, said he expected to be back in action for 1970 – as did Alan Barnett. Although a long way from being fit, Barnett had undergone surgery on his right elbow and he too looked forward to a new season.

Ago warmed up with a comfortable win in the 1000cc race, but the interest lay in the battle for second. Whether on a winning bike or not, Mike Hailwood invariably heightened the intensity of any event he took part in, and Seeley-mounted Mike scrapped hard with Redfern (750 Domiracer), Croxford's 750 Kuhn Norton, and Percy Tait on a Rickman Triumph Métisse. In the end Croxford retired with a broken primary chain and Redfern ran out of fuel, leaving Tait to get the better of Hailwood for second.

The Yamahas got their first crack at Ago in the 350 race, but while Gould and Read both took turns to lead, the Italian came home a good winner after Read's TR2 had stopped with a broken exhaust. Read's fortunes didn't improve. Unable to get his Yamaha going at the start of the feature event, he was struck from behind by Brian Kemp's Norton. Gould did get going, until his Yamaha seized at the Esses and Gould damaged a knee in the fall. Now behind the sight and sound of Ago's roaring MV came the spectacle of another elbow-to-elbow dice for second between Hailwood, Tait, Croxford and Redfern, this time with Malcolm Uphill's Rickman Triumph Métisse in the mix. Tait retired and Hailwood's Seeley was, naturally, the first single home; but Redfern was a clear second. After the race, Ago turned to him and said "you again."

Gould was diagnosed with a chipped kneecap and went under the knife in Oxford to have the fragment screwed back into place. His American mechanic, Randy Hall, helped on Phil Read's bikes a fortnight later at Brands Hatch for the Race of the South – and saw Read turn the tables on Ago in the 350 race, winning by ten seconds after the MV lost its edge. Ago made up for it in the Redex Trophy and then got straight down to business in the Race of the South, building a solid lead while Read, in second, was caught by Kuhn Commando-mounted Andrew. The pair "disputed every corner," and on the last lap Read sat in Andrew's slipstream and waited. The Kuhn teamster was equal to the task, however, and blocked Read's every move to run home second.

The season ended with the final Mallory meeting of the year being cancelled due to fog, leaving only the bone-chilling prospect of the Christmas meeting at Brands. Yet there was no let-up in the pace of Colin Seeley's activities. In August he'd announced Colin Seeley Racing Developments would drop the manufacture of Manx Norton spares. "I don't want to see the Manx die but I've got to streamline the business," he told *Motor Cycle*. Enter John Tickle. In November came the announcement that the former sidecar racer had bought production rights, spares and jigs for the Manx, and looked forward to resuming manufacture at an early date.

Meanwhile Seeley was moving to a new factory, allowing more room for manufacture

No substitute for displacement: at the end of 1969, Gus Kuhn boss Vincent Davey asked Colin Seeley for a new bike, marrying a lightweight Seeley frame with the Norton's 745cc engine. This is the result. (Courtesy Elwyn Roberts Collection)

and development. There were new brakes and new forks coming from Eddie Robinson – and an entirely new bike, using a 750 Norton engine in a modified Mk 3 Seeley frame. The bike had been ordered by Vincent Davey of Gus Kuhn, who wanted to see a British bike capable of beating Agostini's MV.

At Rye, Weslake reported it had pinpointed the current trouble with its engine as "excessive friction." The company expected to cure the problems during the winter, perhaps by changing the bottom end from plain bearings to rollers, but the project no longer had Phil Read's full support. After winning the 250 and 350 classes at the Italian GP in September, he found himself in demand again and wanted to return to racing on a permanent basis.

Dave Croxford, meanwhile, decided to leave the Gus Kuhn team and go freelance once more. In October, he bought Rod Gould's phenomenally successful TR2 Yamaha, and was now looking for a 500. "I'm not interested in being second," he said. Ray Pickrell, restored to fitness, stayed where he was. He re-signed with Paul Dunstall and returned to racing at the Brands Yuletide meeting, on 28 December where, "teeth chattering, frozen to the marrow" he won the ten-lap final, giving his 750 Dunstall Domiracer its first win since May.

The year ended with the closure of the Ace Café on the North Circular Road. After 30 years the doors were shut, the jukebox turned off a last time, and its sad transition into a tyre centre begun. Graham Forsdyke, clearly no fan, gave it a drab epitaph in *Motor Cycle*: "Clients who remained began to notice cracks in the cups, the weak taste of the coffee and grease on the chips," he wrote. "In its last days, a handful at the Ace was a crowd."

Fortunately, Mark Wilsmore was of a different view.

Chapter 14

1970: Eclipse

"The bike just shot out from under him"

Yamaha's withdrawal from grand prix racing had lasted a single season. In the first days of 1970, the factory announced plans to support Rod Gould and Swede Kent Andersson in the 1970 250 and 350 world championships on TD2s and TR2s much improved over the catalogue offerings, with electronic ignition and re-ported barrels. There was talk too of longer swinging arms and six-speed gear clusters; it all added up to easier-starting, more potent, more flexible, better-handling bikes that would soon be available to the privateer.

At the other end of the capacity scale, an increasing number of races for bikes of 750cc or more, whether Production machines or street hardware modified for racing, made clear the growing prestige of open-class racing. Engines such as the Rickman-Weslake eight-valve Triumph, Domiracer, and BSA, in Rickman, Manx or modified Mk 3 Seeley frames were appearing in increasing numbers. Adding to the appeal, if through a limited number of bikes as yet (principally Percy Tait's factory Triumphs), the vivid colour of American racing was coming to Britain. The American Motorcyclist Association was opening its racing to 750cc four-strokes and 500cc two-strokes from the 1970 season, and British promoters seemed keen to establish something comparable.

Occupying an increasingly uncomfortable position between the 350 Yamahas and the 750s was the blue-riband class of motorcycle racing, for racing machines of up to 500cc. While secure at grand prix level thanks to tradition, to MV Agusta and to a handful of smaller Italian manufacturers, the class in Britain was beginning to look vulnerable despite the best efforts of Colin Seeley and others. In *Motor Cycle*, Mick Woollett wrote of the "sad plight of 500s" as star riders began to shift their efforts to other classes for want of more flexible machinery. Aermacchi saw the future and announced it would be switching production of racing engines from single-cylinder four-strokes to twin-cylinder two-strokes. However you looked at it, the Manx Norton didn't seem quite as indispensable nor so invincible as in years past.

But life yet remained in the kennel. Shell launched a new 500cc championship to be shared among MCD circuits, which would replace the Brands-only Redex Trophy; and the 500cc class still sat firmly atop the British championships, which for 1970 would be run over eight meetings embracing all five classes, five best results to count, avoiding the problems of the split system used in 1969.

Croxford said he wanted a real crack at both the 350 and 500 titles and would, it appeared, be parking a Ray Petty 500 Norton alongside his ex-Gould TR2 Yamaha. Alan Barnett was expected back on Kirby's bikes once his elbow – giving 90% movement at the start of the year – was fully recovered. Uncle Tom had a full programme planned for Barnett, comprising both grand prix and home racing, with newcomer Jim Harvey in support. The bikes, said Kirby, would not be entered under the name Métisse, though they'd keep their existing frames.

BSA told the press its 500 single and 650 twin would be ridden by Bob Heath rather than Tony Smith in the season ahead, and John Tickle announced details of the first run of Nortons he'd produce – 500s that would be identical to the final Bracebridge Street models of 1963 but for the addition of a six-speed gearbox and Gardner carburettor. Price was expected to be £895, compared with a new Yamaha TR2 at £738 plus £262 for a spares kit.

There was more big news: Ken Redfern was to join Ray Pickrell in the Paul Dunstall team to ride a replica of the bike Pickrell used to take five wins from seven starts in the opening months of the '69 season, which featured the Eddie Robinson-designed spine frame, and would now receive a twin-disc front brake. Each man would take half the country, with Pickrell riding at southern circuits and Redfern in the north.

Showstoppers

John Cooper, who'd spent much of 1969 in a quandary about his future rides, had come to a decision. "In 1969 I asked speedway star Barry Briggs to send me a 350 Yamaha from America because the Seeley 7R wasn't fast enough," recalled Cooper. "The Seeley was a beautiful motorbike, very light, but just not quick enough. I took the two bikes to Cadwell and practised on them both. The Yamaha went like stink but you couldn't steer it. I decided to ride it in the race, went round a long right-hander, flicked left to go down the hill and it pitched me off; I couldn't get on with it at all.

"I went to bed that night and thought the best thing I could do would be to put the Yamaha engine into the Seeley. So Ron Herring designed some tubes, Colin Seeley bent them, Ron welded them in and I went home and built the Yamsel."

The grid for the 350 race at the 1970 Hutch reveals the decline of four-stroke power in the class. Kel Carruthers (30) and Kent Andersson (27) have Yamaha TR2s, Alan Barnett (37) a Lawton Aermacchi and John Williams (16) an AJS Métisse. John Cooper (1, Yamsel) won. (Courtesy Elwyn Roberts Collection)

Cooper's new bike was 25lb (11kg) lighter than a stock TR2 and 2in (50mm) lower. He still had his 500 Seeley too.

Peter Williams was also back in business. After a patchy couple of years with illness and the after-effects of heavy crashes, his stated ambition for 1970 was to stay at home and have a tilt at the 500cc British title on his Arter Matchless – the Mk 3 version with another lightweight frame and six-spoke magnesium alloy wheels. He had, however, parked the Arter AJS. "You have to work so hard among all the TR2s that it just isn't worthwhile," he told *Motor Cycle*. "I'll concentrate on bigger bikes – the Arter Matchless, factory Norton Commando in Production races, the Norton special for the 750 class."

The week the season began, Alan Barnett announced he was leaving the Kirby team, effective immediately. "I feel a fresh start would be a good idea," Barnett said. "There's no bad feeling, I just felt I was losing my identity."

"I'm mystified," said Kirby. "Up until Friday we were planning a very full season. I was doing everything I could to get Alan a ride with an Italian factory."

British racing got going at Mallory Park on 1 March with another initiative from the former colonies, the clutch start. Its champions recommended it as a safer, fairer means of getting under way than the traditional push, and Mallory tried it for the damp 500 final, with the major beneficiary proving to be Bob Heath on BSA's single. Cooper, Chandler and the Kuhn twins, Andrew and new recruit Mahoney, all tried to reel him in without success, and Chandler came home best of the rest from Andrew and Mahoney. The race also confirmed Croxford's suspicions – that he was riding the wrong 500. "I just couldn't seem to get used to it," he said. The Manx returned to Ray Petty's workshop while Croxford went hunting for a Seeley.

The world got its first glimpse of Cooper's new ride in the 350 race. He led early and looked a winner until the Yamsel jumped out of fourth gear, allowing Tony Rutter's Yamaha past. Cooper hung on for second from Chatterton's Yamaha, and claimed the fastest lap while Dave Croxford, giving his new bike its debut, retired when the ex-Gould TR2 seized.

BSA-Triumph was offering for sale kits of goodies, including a mighty Fontana ten-inch front brake, Quaife five-speed gear cluster and exhaust, that would convert their new three-cylinder roadsters, the Triumph Trident and BSA Rocket 3, into 'Production racers a la Daytona.' Meanwhile, Mike Daniels checked in from Rye to report that the Weslake engine would be raced in 1970: "We're making real progress," he said.

Now the weather weighed in on an untidy start to the season, with snow forcing postponement of the opening British championship rounds at Oulton Park and Cadwell. Alan Barnett might have been glad of the delay. He was back in business in the 500cc class with a Seeley from his pre-Kirby sponsor, Brian Coleshill; but he had no 350.

Honda's much-rumoured newcomer, the CB750, was meanwhile elbowing everything else out of the headlines. Dick Mann rode the racing version to victory in the Daytona 200, his CR750 developing 90+bhp compared with the road bike's 67 and weighing 385lb (175kg), rather less than the roadster's 480lb (218kg), but the point was made – and underlined when *Motor Cycle* posted a two-way mean standing quarter-mile time of 12.6 seconds on its test bike. There was even a race kit available. Small wonder Paul Dunstall was taking an interest.

Racing resumed at Easter with Pat Mahoney becoming the new King of Brands, (the meeting doubled as the opening round of the British championships) beating John Taylor by one point. Kuhn team-mate Mick Andrew shared the headlines by giving his 750 Kuhn Seeley a win in the 1300cc race after early leader Malcolm Uphill retired when the gearbox of his 500 Manx failed; through burst Andrew, chased home by Charlie Sanby and Mahoney to make a clean sweep for the Kuhn outfit. Andrew also led the Production race until his Kuhn Commando's transmission went the way of Uphill's, letting Commando-

Ken Redfern slips through the Croft chicane. In 1970 he became a full member of the Dunstall team and patrolled the north of England very successfully for his new outfit. (Courtesy Spencer Oliver)

propelled Brian Kemp through to win by a hundred yards – and then fall off at Paddock after taking the chequered flag.

Rutter's was the pick of the Yamahas in the 350 race, leading home Croxford and Chatterton, while Barnett comfortably won the opening round of the 500cc British Championship, going away from Uphill's Norton, while defending champion Croxford came fourth behind John Taylor's Seeley. Title aspirant Peter Williams was sixth, following Mahoney home after being caught up in the tightest scrap of the afternoon.

Low sides

On Easter Saturday, Ken Redfern gave his new 750 Dunstall a shakedown win at Croft from Tony Jefferies, then joined the southern stars at Mallory Park on Easter Sunday. John Cooper chose the meeting to reveal the full worth of his new Yamsel, cleaning up in both the 350 race (from Rutter) and the 1000cc race from Redfern. He was in bruising form again at Oulton Park on the Monday, fighting a reluctant Yamsel engine to cut through the 350 field and catch leader Rutter on the fourth lap of ten. The pair played cat and mouse for three laps before Cooper headed for the horizon. He did the same on his Seeley in the third round of the Shell Championship, bickering with Peter Williams on 'Wagon Wheels' and Barry Randle's Seeley, but getting home first just the same. Mahoney gave his Commando-engined Kuhn Seeley a win in the 750 race, wresting control from early leader Kemp at half distance and pulling away.

So far Percy Tait had had a quiet season, picking up a couple of minor places in Production events and not much more; but he'd been left largely to his own devices by Triumph. With a drive at corporate level to make a dent in the American market and road racing resources going into the three-cylinder racers for Daytona (Gene Romero had qualified fastest at 157mph for the Daytona 200 on one of BSA-Triumph's Rob Northframed triples and finished second, a couple of seconds behind Mann's Honda), Tait was supplied with parts then left to build his own bike with help from sidecar ace Owen Greenwood, using T120 cases, a short-stroke crankshaft, Rickman-Weslake eight-valve top-end, Quaife five-speed 'box, 18-in wheels and a Métisse frame.

Barnett, yet again a contender for the 500cc British title, now looked a better bet for the 350 class with the news that he'd be riding an Aermacchi for Syd Lawton. At Thruxton a week after Easter he tightened his grip on the 500cc championship by winning the title event after a poor start. With his customary blend of style and efficiency he worked up through the field, picking off Andrew and then leader Williams on the ninth damp lap of 12. So that was two from two. He led the 350 title race as well, but fell on an oily patch at the exit of the chicane two laps from home, leaving Croxford to take the flag after beating Chatterton in the battle of the TR2s. Brian Lee was third on a Lawton Aermacchi and Andrew fourth, recovering from a bad start. Charlie Sanby won the 1000cc race with team-mate Andrew third, and Barnett putting his 500 Seeley between the two 750s. Andrew was denied the chance to continue his meteoric improvement. Just a week later he died in a road crash on a Norton Commando, close to the Kuhn showroom in Stockwell, south London. He was 24.

As Croxford and Barnett prepared to do battle at Castle Combe for third round of the British championships, it began to look as though they wouldn't be at Mallory Park for the fourth; they pointed to a substantial cut in prize money as the cause. "I can't afford to go," said Croxford. "It makes a mockery of the championships." The news didn't affect either rider's form. Croxford bagged the 350 championship race in Wiltshire after passing early leader Dave Browning and easing away. In the 500 race, Barnett threaded his way deftly though the field to take the lead with two laps left, while Williams kept his title hopes alive with second place, ahead of Percy May's Petty Norton.

At Cadwell the following day Cooper bagged another 350/1000cc double on his remarkable Yamsel. Small wonder he was organising the sale of replica frame kits, or that Phil Read's was among his first enquiries. In each race he was chased home by Chatterton's TR2 but had, it seemed, enough in reserve to take untroubled wins. Brian Kemp won the Production race on his Norton Commando, beating home Tony Jefferies' Triumph, but then crashed his 750 Curley Norton in the 1000cc race, breaking a collarbone.

May opened with more bad news: Rob Fitton died at the Nürburgring during practice for the West German GP. Witnesses said he fell from his 350 Norton in a fast corner and struck a guard rail. He died in a Bonn hospital a few hours later. Yorkshireman Edwin Robin Fitton was 42 and a local government engineer. He'd been racing since 1947. "I've never been a potential star," he once said. "I'm just a holiday racer."

Home truth

The TT boasted a record 667 entries for 1970 and important changes to the race

Kuhn Seeley-mounted Pat Mahoney storms Cadwell Park's Mountain. Initially hired for just a month early in 1970, he took third for the team in the 500cc British Championship. (Courtesy Paul McElvie)

programme included a longer, five-lap Production race with an increase in prize money. Before that, however, there was Whitsun, and, after Peter Williams and Charlie Sanby won the Thruxton 500-miler for Norton, the stars regrouped at Mallory Park on Whit Sunday for the fourth round of the British championships, though without Alan Barnett who was riding at the North West 200. In Barnett's absence, Mahoney won the 500cc title race, closing the gap between them to just six points. He was followed home by Micky Collins' Seeley, while Cooper, who'd been shadowing them on his Seeley, stopped with an unspecified mechanical malady. There were no problems with the Yamsel; Cooper cleaned up in the 350 race, the clutch of Yamahas to his rear headed by Chatterton's.

Chatterton was in the money again the following day at Cadwell Park, winning the 1000cc Coronation Trophy when Redfern's Dunstall spluttered to a halt after leading for nine laps of the allotted ten. Chatterton also won the 350 race on his TR2 from Billie Nelson's, this time with Redfern's Aermacchi getting among the Yamahas in third place. Cooper, meanwhile, was at Brands for the Evening News International, demonstrating his Yamsel to sceptical southerners. The lesson started in the 350 race, where Smart, Read and Cooper battled throughout the early laps. Read fell at Paddock while trying to wrest the lead from Smart, whose gearbox failed a lap later to leave Cooper in control for his first win of the day. Paul Smart's moment in the sun came in the 500 race, getting the better of a long scrap with Mahoney and Collins, who ran out of fuel and allowed North West

Peter Williams (Arter Matchless), pictured here climbing away from Ramsey Hairpin, battled hard with Alan Barnett in the 1970 Senior TT, but ran in an untroubled second after the Seeley rider fell on melting tar. (Courtesy Paul McElvie)

200 winner Peter Williams into third. Read was a scratching from the 1000cc race after damaging a hand in his 350 fall, but Martyn Ashwood (700 Rickman-Weslake Métisse) took his place and vied for the lead with Cooper and Smart, who again retired. At the flag Cooper fended off Ashwood while Mahoney put his 750 Kuhn Seeley into third.

Croxford, out of the results and plainly struggling with his 350 Yamaha, decided a break was called for. "I may race again but I feel like a rest," he told *Motor Cycle*. "What I really need is a sponsor. You've got to have a Yamaha [TR2] but I can't afford to run one on the money being paid these days."

The last port of call before the TT migration was Oulton Park for the British championship round postponed from March. Cooper again won the 350 race and with Croxford absent, Tony Rutter's second place was enough to give him an eight-point lead in the title standings after five rounds. Cooper looked set to win the 500 race as well. Lap after lap he, Williams and Barry Ditchburn (Seeley) circulated in close company. They were caught eventually by Barnett, who took third while Williams slipped past Cooper to claim the win.

However you looked at it, 1970 was a bad year for the TT. Micky Collins died in practice, running wide and going through the fence at the Verandah; Spanish youngster Santiago Herrero died after sliding off at the 13th Milestone; Brian Steenson died after a crash on the Mountain during the Senior. Altogether six people lost their lives at the TT and more were hurt. Criticism bordered on open revolt. "The circuit is in bad condition," said Rod Gould. "It's very dangerous." Certainly, the hot weather had softened the tar in places, as some of the casualties would freely confirm. Stan Woods fell in Herrero's crash, breaking a leg, ankle and a collarbone; Barnett crashed in the Senior, sustaining facial injuries; and Malcolm Uphill injured a foot in practice.

Uphill won his second Production TT just the same, bringing home his Triumph Trident by just 1.6 seconds from Peter Williams' Norton Commando. Ray Pickrell finished third on a Dunstall Norton, continuing his gradual return to form, while Paul Smart pulled the move of the week, by bringing his Trident safely to a standstill after collecting a front wheel puncture at Quarry Bends.

The Junior and Senior both belonged to Ago, of course, though with different supporting casts. In the 350, Alan Barnett rode Syd Lawton's Aermacchi into a good second, posting a 99mph lap and displacing both Smart (Yamaha) and Kel Carruthers, whose much faster factory Benelli stretched its drive chain. In the Senior, Peter Williams took second after a long duel with Barnett, who crashed at Doran's Bend. "Alan went in very fast," Williams explained. "The tar was terrible there and the bike just shot out from under him at around 100mph."

At Mallory Park for the Post-TT meeting Cooper's triumphant run on the Yamsel was finally halted in the 1000cc race, but it took Giacomo Agostini and his 500 MV to do it. The Italian had a slightly easier run in the 500 race, winning comfortably from Smart's Seeley and Williams' Arter Matchless, and Phil Read had a win in the 350 class after Cooper's Yamsel had seized.

Rocking the boat

Thruxton's June national heralded the summer break, but noise continued to come from Hampshire long after Ken Redfern had collected his prize money for winning the 1000cc race. Hampshire County Council said that the BARC (British Automobile Racing Club) lacked planning permission for its new grandstands and race control tower, and that they had to be demolished. The BARC replied that they needed no planning permission, that it was all covered in the provisions of an agreement reached a dozen years earlier. The scuffle attracted the attention of the Ministry of Housing, which promptly announced an enquiry to settle the future of the circuit, which would roll on into 1971.

Weslake, quiet since the beginning of the year, now announced that a revised engine, containing many modifications aimed at cutting friction and improving cooling, would soon be ready for testing. There was a new 180-degree crankshaft running on roller main bearings. "Getting it right is a matter of pride," said a spokesman – though the next silence would be long indeed. Meanwhile Rickman had gone into the complete engine business, announcing the imminent release of its first full powerplant, using the Rickman-Weslake eight-valve head on a new bottom end. As announced, the engine was apparently good for a "genuine 76bhp," with more to come. Hefted into a Métisse frame, it weighed 315lb without streamlining and, said Percy Tait after sampling the product, was, "about as fast as my Daytona Trident."

Peter Williams gave his British title campaign extra impetus with a win at the Cadwell Park round, postponed from March. Cooper resumed his winning ways on the Yamsel, to lead home title aspirant Derek Chatterton in the 350 race. Title leader Tony Rutter ran a big end, and with two rounds of the championship remaining, now led Chatterton 50 points to 46. In the 500 race Williams beat Barnett, closing the gap to just eight points – Barnett 67, Williams 59.

The future came upon us by stealth. A week on from Francis Beart's announcement that he would withdraw from sponsorship – "it's no longer fun" – after providing Clive Brown with a 350 Aermacchi for the Manx Grand Prix, Brands Hatch revealed it would run a 'Daytona-style' race, under American regulations, at the Race of the South meeting in October. The event would be for production street bikes with extensive engine modifications and special frames, and attracted interest from BSA-Triumph and Norton-Villiers – though not the FIM, as the body didn't permit Daytona/AMA rules under the racing it governed. All the same, Formula 750 was clearly on its way – although not before the Hutch, where

the key issue was whether Cooper and his Yamsel could be stopped. The answer was no, yes and no, as Cooper won the 350 race and the second leg of the Evening News Trophy, but yielded the first leg win to Read after muffing the start and battling through to third behind Sanby's 750 Kuhn Seeley. Of the new 700 Rickman not much was seen, though Martyn Ashwood offered an indication of its worth by vying for the lead in the opening leg of the Evening News Trophy until he slid off.

Rod Gould took the 1970 250cc World Championship on a factory-supported TD2 Yamaha much improved by electronic ignition and re-ported barrels. Mechanic Nobby Clark stands by. (Courtesy Elwyn Roberts Collection)

Ken Redfern (Dunstall Domiracer) and Peter Williams (Arter Matchless) went head to head at the Croft round of the 1970 500cc British Championship. Williams won. (Courtesy Spencer Oliver)

The last international of the season at Snetterton, the Race of Aces meeting, naturally belonged to the Yamahas, arguing among themselves for supremacy, and in Norfolk Read licked Gould (Yamaha) and Redfern (750 Dunstall) in the title event, while Carruthers took the 350 race. Among the 500s Barnett put it across Williams in the sprint to the line, with Brian Kemp (Higley Seeley) third.

Ago came calling again on August Bank Holiday Monday at Oulton Park for the Daily Express International – and took a pocketful of cash home to Bergamo. Of his two comfortable wins the 350 was the more challenging, with a clutch of Yamahas hounding him all the way, led first by Kent Andersson's factory-supported bike, then by Cooper's Yamsel, then by Carruthers. Cooper did best, muscling Carruthers back to third.

In the 500 race Cooper put his Seeley in front of Ago for a couple of laps. Sure enough, the Italian swept by and made for the hills, but an enthralling scrap developed behind him with Cooper leading from Williams, Barnett, Seeley-mounted Tommy Robb and Croxford, back in the fray on Dr Blair's Seeley-framed two-stroke twin, the QUB. Williams found the groove while Cooper retired, setting him up nicely for the penultimate round of the British titles, at Croft.

Countdown

While Barry Sheene won the 125 championship at Croft and Steve Machin the 250, the 350 and 500cc titles were as tight at the end of the day as they'd been at the beginning. In the battle of the Yamahas for the 350 class, title front-runners Chatterton and Rutter broke from the field early. Chatterton had to break the lap record to be sure of the win, but he bagged the full 15 points to leave the circuit with a four-point break over his rival.

The 500 championship struggle between Williams and Barnett was tighter still, at Croft with the added complication of Ken Redfern. Riding his RJ Dunstall Domiracer with an engine from Dunstall himself, Redfern tailed Williams for two laps, then passed to lead for a further three. The pair circulated with the thickness of a Rizla Green between them, "Ken's circuit knowledge making up for the superior speed of the Matchless," recalled Mike Redfern. Towards the end of the race, while braking hard for a corner, they came together and Redfern ran wide allowing Williams to get clear for the win and Barnett into second. Redfern regained the track to finish third. Taking their best five results, Barnett now led Williams by two points; everything would be settled at Snetterton.

In September, Colin Seeley announced that an initial batch of a dozen Mk 3 500 Seeleys were in the build for 1971, and three months ahead of schedule; but, he said: "we've stopped making the 350, though we'll continue to supply spares and do engine rebuilds." The dance was fast coming to an end for four-stroke singles. Throughout the year Syd Lawton's Aermacchi had routinely been the quickest four-stroke in 350 racing, but even so majestic a talent as Alan Barnett's struggled to break through the stream of TR2s and put it into the top six.

Cooper was in magnificent form for the Race of the Year, winning the 500 race on his Seeley and chalking up two more to the Yamsel in the 350cc event and the main race. The meeting was without Ago for a change, but included a couple of North American visitors – former AMA No 1 plate-holder Gary Nixon and Yvon Duhamel on a Deeley TR2. Nixon was given a Percy Tait Triumph Trident for meeting, to which he fitted Goodyear tyres and had the head angle of Rob North's frame modified. The tweaks worked. Nixon was in the leading bunch behind Cooper from the opening laps, though dropped back a little as Cooper, Read, Gould, Jefferies (Norton Métisse) and Redfern (Dunstall Domiracer), broke away. Gould was second when his ignition failed, giving Read a clear shot at Cooper – but the Derby man was in a class of his own and led Read home from Paul Smart, who'd come through the pack to relegate Nixon in the closing laps. Redfern retired, but had already bagged the 1000cc race.

As the year wound down Phil Read came to a parting of the ways with sponsor Joe Henderson and was now looking for a TR2 to fill in until his 1971-spec bikes arrived. He was also looking for a new mechanic, no longer having Ron Herring's services. Ray Pickrell, who'd had a poor season compared with his stellar 1968 and early 1969, left Paul Dunstall's team and was offered the factory Trident Gary Nixon rode in the Race of the

Year. Reg Curley too had offered him a bike, the 750 Norton Brian Kemp had ridden throughout the season. Kemp had fallen at Oulton Park on August Bank Holiday Monday, and though the initial diagnosis of a broken thigh was later moderated to a chipped and dislocated hip, he'd be out for the rest of the year. So Curley approached Pickrell. "I reckon Ray can still beat them all," he said.

The last internationals of the year, at Cadwell and at Brands for the Race of the South, were about Yamsel-equipped Cooper doing his best to keep Ago's MVs in sight, though with one key exception. At Brands there was that 15-lapper for 'Daytona-style' bikes, which in effect meant Triumph triples, the odd Norton Commando and an assortment of Yamahas. In the event Smart and Pickrell, both Triumph-mounted, went head to head and broke away from the field to stage a fast, noisy and exciting dice that went Smart's way, albeit after Pickrell had posted the fastest lap. Tait, a lonely third, completed an all-Triumph podium. As a spectacle it was modest enough; but it pointed loudly towards a future of slick, fast, competitive racing that required neither grand prix bikes nor a gridful of two-strokes to be exciting.

Exit

Snetterton, 18 October 1970, the final round of the British championships: the numbers weren't easy to calculate and in the end the titles went to those who kept going. Early in the 350 race Chatterton and Rutter battled hard; Smart passed them both for the lead and Chatterton came under pressure from Steve Machin. The title contenders were tied on points then, and only a countback on second places would have separated them; but Rutter rolled to a stop, his engine "just died on him" and with it his championship hopes. Chatterton eased home in second behind Smart, with a championship-winning margin of six points.

Williams, swapping the Arter G50's 'Wagon Wheels' for spokes in a last-minute bid to cure below-par handling, broke with title rival Barnett at the start of the 500 race. Williams held a narrow lead – with Barnett tucked in behind, looking cool and confident. Barry Randle (Seeley) and Percy May (Petty Norton) vied for third, but the excitement was at the front. If positions stayed as they were, the title went to Williams. Barnett knew as much, and on the last lap tried to pass at Riches, the fast right-hander at the end of the start-finish straight, and slid off. Williams ran home to become champion by three points, and Barnett runner-up for the third year in a row.

Mist rose over the waterways of Norfolk, bikes disappeared into their vans, victors and vanquished went their separate ways: the end of another season. Except that this one wasn't quite like its predecessors. British 350 singles had all but disappeared at national level, and while the 500s would return their numbers were declining; soon they'd disappear from open racing altogether, along with the men who'd coaxed the best from them.

In September, Francis Beart lay in a hospital bed recovering from a haemorrhage, while Clive Brown gave the veteran tuner his last Manx Grand Prix triumph, putting his 350 Aermacchi into a race-winning lead after Gordon Pantall's Yamaha expired. Tom Kirby, already struggling with a shoulder injury from a bad fall, would sell his business in 1971, declaring himself uninterested in two-strokes. Having no spares for them, he broke up his two exotic 7R engines and gave away many of their parts as gifts. Steve Lancefield, whose last great triumph had been Steve Spencer's third place in the 1967 Senior TT, faded from the business; but Ray Petty soldiered on. In 1971 Percy May took the last 500cc British Championship to be won on a British bike, and did it on one of Petty's Nortons; but, by then, the headline races were in other classes, and more riders drifted away to ride 350 Yamahas or 750s. The first F750 TT was held in 1971, although the long road to the modern superbike can be traced back to the successes of Doug Hele's experimental Domiracer a decade earlier.

The final entry in the ledger went to Peter Williams. Long after Alan Barnett had parked his Brian Coleshill Seeley, Williams wheeled out the Arter Matchless one last time at the 1973 Senior TT, and rode a tense race to finish second behind Jack Findlay's TR500 Suzuki. Despite a deficit of 20bhp and as many miles an hour, Williams rode superbly, keeping in touch with second-placed Findlay by cornering on the sidewalls of his tyres. Mick Grant, riding a 354 Yamaha, was flying in the lead, but then slid off on oil at Parliament Square, and the G50's last great grand prix duel began.

As early as the second lap, a slide at Barregarrow warned Williams that brake fluid was leaking onto his rear tyre; but even when taking it easy on left-handers he was just four seconds adrift of the Suzuki as they pitted, and after a much faster stop than Findlay, led by 17 seconds as they started lap four. By Ballacraine Williams, now tiring, had had his lead cut to eight seconds; at the Bungalow, after he had been slowed by a dog on the road, they were neck and neck. Findlay, too, had his problems, the Suzuki being far too stiffly suspended for Manx roads; but he gradually eased away, and by race end had a lead of more than a minute. Williams was exhausted, but he had another second place – his fourth – in the Senior TT on a Tom Arter G50. Fifteen years after Jack Williams, Peter's dad, had watched Jack Ahearn coax the G50 prototype into an unpromising 29th place in the 1958 Senior TT, the era of the British racing single had come to an end.

Chapter 15

The Results

1960

8 April, Silverstone – Hutchinson 100

350 BMCRC Championship (15 laps, 43.9 miles): 1 Bob McIntyre (AJS), 92.6mph, 2 Mike Hailwood (AJS), 3 Phil Read (Norton), 4 Alan Shepherd (AJS), 5 J Lewis (Norton), 6 Bob Rowe (Norton). Fastest lap: McIntyre, 1m 51.8s, 94.25mph.

500 BMCRC Championship (15 laps): 1 McIntyre (Norton), 95.37mph, 2 Hailwood (Norton), 3 Frank Perris (Norton), 4 Bill Smith (Matchless), 5 Bob Anderson (Norton), 6 Tom Thorp (Matchless). Fastest lap: McIntyre, 1m 48.2s, 97.39mph.

15 April, Brands Hatch

350 (20 laps, 24.8 miles): 1 Derek Minter (Norton), 73.50mph, 2 Mike Hailwood (AJS), 3 Phil Read (Norton), 4 Bob Rowe (Norton), 5 John Lewis (Norton), 6 Tom Thorp (AJS). Fastest lap: Minter, 75.41mph (record)

500 (20 laps): 1 Minter (Norton), 74.71mph, 2 Hailwood (Norton), 3 Ron Langston (Matchless), 4 Rowe (Norton), 5 Ginger Payne (Norton), 6 Bruce Daniels (Norton). Fastest lap: Minter, 76.97mph (record)

1000 (20 laps): 1 Minter (Norton), 75.68mph, 2 Hailwood (Norton), 3 Thorp (Matchless).

17 April, Snetterton

350: (10 laps, 27.1 miles): 1 Derek Minter (Norton), 87.29mph, 2 Phil Read (Norton), 3 Ron Langston (AJS). Fastest lap: Minter, 89.83mph (record)

500 (10 laps): 1 Minter (Norton), 91.19mph, 2 Read (Norton), 3 Tommy Robb (Matchless). Fastest lap: Minter, 92.91mph (record)

18 April, Crystal Palace

350 (10 laps, 13.9 miles): 1 Bob Rowe (Norton), 73.98mph, 2 Brian Setchell (Norton), 3 Ned Minihan (Norton). Fastest lap: Minihan, 76.05mph.

500 (10 laps): 1 Minihan (Norton), 75.85mph, 2 Rowe (Norton), 3 A Gearing (Matchless). Fastest lap: Minihan, 78.68mph.

18 April, Oulton Park

350 (19 laps, 52.4 miles): 1 Bob McIntyre (AJS), 85.26mph, 2 Derek Minter (Norton), 3 Alan Shepherd (AJS), 4 Phil Read (Norton), 5 Bob Anderson (Norton), 6 Bill Smith (Matchless). Fastest lap: McIntyre, Minter: 1m 55s, 86.43mph (record).

500 (19 laps): 1 Minter (Norton), 86.96mph, 2 McIntyre (Norton), 3 Anderson (Norton), 4 Ron Langston (Matchless), 5 Read (Norton), 6 Dan Shorey (Norton). Fastest lap: Minter 1m 52s, 88.75mph (record).

23 April, Castle Combe

350 (10 laps, 18.4 miles): 1 Mike Hailwood (AJS), 83.67mph, 2 Derek Minter (Norton), 3 Phil Read (Norton), 4 Dan Shorey (Norton), 5 Brian Setchell (Norton), 6 Ginger Payne (AJS). Fastest lap: Hailwood, 85.79mph (record)

500 (10 laps): 1 Minter (Norton), 85.92mph, 2 Read (Norton), 3 Hailwood (Norton), 4 Shorey (Norton), 5 Tony Godfrey (Norton), 6 Dave Williams (Norton). Fastest lap: Minter, 88.31mph

30 April, Aberdare

350 (12 laps, 9 miles): 1 Ron Langston (AJS), speed n/a, 2 Dan Shorey (Norton). Fastest lap: Mike Hailwood, 57.48mph (equals record)

500 (12 laps): 1 Hailwood (Norton), speed n/a, 2 Tony Godfrey (Norton), 3 Shorey (Norton). Fastest lap: Hailwood, 57.97mph (record)

1000 (15 laps): 1 Hailwood (Norton), speed n/a, 2 Godfrey (Norton), 3 Langston (Matchless). Fastest lap: Hailwood, 57.97mph (equals record)

1 May, Mallory Park

350 (20 laps, 27 miles): 1 Bob McIntyre (AJS), 84.10mph, 2 Phil Read (Norton), 3 Bruce Daniels (Norton), 4 Brian Setchell (Norton), 5 Fred Neville (Norton), 6 Dan Shorey (Norton). Fastest lap: Mike Hailwood, 87.10mph (record)

500 (20 laps): 1 Hailwood (Norton), 85.67mph, 2 McIntyre (Norton), 3 Read (Norton), 4 Bill Smith (Matchless), 5 Terry Shepherd (Norton), 6 Daniels (Norton). Fastest lap: Hailwood, 88.37mph (record)

7 May, Scarborough – Cock o' the North

350 (15 laps, 36.15 miles): 1 Mike Hailwood (AJS), 65.94mph, 2 Alan Shepherd (AJS), 3 Dan Shorey (Norton), 4 George Catlin (AJS), 5 S Pratt (Norton), 6 Fred Rutherford (BSA). Fastest lap: Hailwood, 67.05mph (record)

500 (15 laps): 1 Shepherd (Matchless), 64.90mph, 2 Hailwood (Norton), 3 Shorey (Norton), 4 Rob Fitton (Norton), 5 Catlin (Matchless), 6 Ned Minihan (Norton). Fastest lap: Shepherd, 69.29mph (equals record)

14 May, Aintree, Red Rose

350 (10 laps, 30 miles): 1 Mike Hailwood (AJS), 75.89mph, 2 Phil Read (Norton), 3 Bill Smith (AJS), 4 Ray Fay (Norton), 5 Rob Fitton (Norton), 6 Dennis Pratt (Norton). Fastest lap: Hailwood, 78.37mph.

500 (10 laps): 1 Read (Norton), 83.08mph, 2 Hailwood (Norton), 3 Fred Stevens (Norton), 4 Dan Shorey (Norton), 5 Fitton (Norton), 6 Dennis Pratt (Norton). Fastest lap: Hailwood, 84.38mph.

15 May, Brands Hatch

350 (20 laps, 24.8 miles): 1 Mike Hailwood (AJS), 73.57mph, 2 Ginger Payne (Norton), 3 Dan Shorey (Norton), 4 Mike O'Rourke (Norton), 5 J Cripps (Norton), 6 P Horton (Norton). Fastest lap: Hailwood, 75.15mph.

500 leg 1 (20 laps): 1 Derek Minter (Norton), 75.27mph, 2 Mike Hailwood (Norton), 3 Ginger Payne (Matchless), 4 Alan Thurgood (Norton), 5 J Wright (Norton). Fastest lap: Minter, 77.23mph.

500 leg 2 (20 laps): 1 Minter (Norton), 75.81mph, 2 Payne (Matchless), 3 Hailwood (Norton), 4 Shorey (Norton), 5 J Wright (Norton), 6 Lewis Young (BSA). Fastest lap: Minter, 77.77mph (record).

28 May, Silverstone, Silverstone Saturday

350 (17 laps, 49.76 miles): 1 Derek Minter (Norton), 94.08mph, 2 John Hartle (Norton), 3 Phil Read (Norton), 4 John Lewis (Norton), 5 Alan Rutherford (Norton), 6 Bill Siddles (Norton). Fastest lap: Minter, 98.48mph (record).

500 (17 laps): 1 Mike Hailwood (Norton), 98.22mph, 2 Minter (Norton), 3 Tommy Robb (Matchless), 4 Bob Anderson (Matchless), 5 Dickie Dale (Norton), 6 Alan Shepherd (Matchless). Fastest lap: Hailwood, 100.16mph (record).

6 June, Cadwell Park

350 (12 laps, 15 miles): 1 Bill Siddles (Norton), 60.34mph, 2 Louis Carr (AJS), 3 M Hancock (Norton). Fastest lap: Siddles, 62.50mph.

500 (12 laps): 1 Dennis Pratt (Norton), speed 62.43mph, 2 Lewis Young (Norton), 3 Derek Phillips (Norton). Fastest lap: n/a.

6 June, Blandford

350 (16 laps, 50.24 miles): 1 Phil Read (Norton), 84.90mph, 2 Jack Adam (Norton), 3 Ned Minihan (Norton), 4 Alan Rutherford (Norton), 5 D Chapman (Norton), 6 Dan Shorey (Norton). Fastest lap: Adam, 86.17mph.

500 (16 laps): 1 Ron Langston (Matchless), 89.07mph, 2 Read (Norton), 3 Shorey (Norton), 4 Ned Minihan (Norton), 5 Mike Brookes (Norton), 6 Bert Schneider (Norton). Fastest lap: Read, 90.44mph.

19 June, Mallory Park

350 (20 laps, 27 miles): 1 Mike Hailwood (AJS), 84.04mph, 2 Bob McIntyre (Norton), 3 Dickie Dale (Norton), 4 Bob Brown (Norton), 5 Mike Brookes (Norton) 6 Phil Read (Norton). Fastest lap: Dale, 85.86mph.

500 (20 laps): 1 Bob McIntyre (Norton), 85.58mph, 2 Mike Hailwood (Norton), 3 Ron Langston (Matchless), 4 Read (Norton), 5 Paddy Driver (Norton), 6 Dale (Norton). Fastest lap: McIntyre, Hailwood, 87.73mph.

25 June, Thruxton

500 Miles: 1 Ron Langston/ D Chapman (AJS 31CSR), 2 Dan Shorey/Ginger Payne (Triumph Bonneville), 3 John Holder/P Webb (Triumph Bonneville).

26 June, Cadwell Park

350 (8 laps, 10 miles): 1 Tony Sugden (AJS), 62mph, 2 George Catlin (AJS), 3 Lewis Young (Norton). Fastest lap: n/a.

500 (12 laps): 1 Dan Shorey (Norton), 62.6mph, 2 Alan Trow (Norton), 3 Tony Sugden (Norton).

2 July, Crystal Palace

350 (15 laps, 20.85 miles): 1 Ned Minihan (Norton), 74.76mph, 2 Tom Thorp (AJS), 3 Michael O'Rourke (Norton). Fastest lap: Thorp, 76.98mph.

1000 (15 laps): 1 Minihan (Norton), 76.70mph, 2 Ron Langston (Matchless), 3 Bob Rowe (Norton). Fastest lap: Minihan, 78.60mph.

9 July, Brands Hatch (first motorcycle meeting on 2.65-mile track)

350 (20 laps, 53 miles): 1 Mike Hailwood (AJS), 73.17mph, 2 Ron Langston (AJS), 3 Tom Thorp (AJS), 4 Mike O'Rourke (Norton), 5 Phil Read (Norton), 6 Alan Trow (Norton). Fastest lap: Derek Minter (Norton), 76.44mph (record).

500 (20 laps): 1 Hailwood (Norton), 77.84mph, 2 Fred Neville (Matchless), 3 John Hartle (Norton), 4 Alan Shepherd (Matchless), 5 Ron Langston (Matchless), 6 Mike Brookes (Norton). Fastest lap: Hartle, 80.71mph.

16 July, Castle Combe

350 (10 laps, 18.4 miles): 1 Phil Read (Norton), 82.58mph, 2 Brian Setchell (Norton), 3 Mike Hailwood (Norton), 4 Dan Shorey (Norton), 5 Fred Neville (Norton), 6 Bill Siddles (Norton). Fastest lap: Neville, 84.91mph.

500 (10 laps): 1 Hailwood (Norton), 85.83mph, 2 Read (Norton), 3 Tony Godfrey (Norton), 4 Shorey (Norton), 5 Neville (Matchless) 6 Lewis Young (Norton). Fastest lap: Hailwood, 87.84mph.

17 July, Mallory Park

350 (20 laps, 27 miles): 1 Bob McIntyre (AJS), 77.53mph, 2 Terry Shepherd (Norton), 3 Phil Read (Norton), 4 Bill Siddles (Norton), 5 Mike Hailwood (AJS), 6 Peter Chatterton (AJS). Fastest lap: McIntyre, Shepherd, 82.93mph.

500 (20 laps): 1 Mike Hailwood (Norton), 88.10mph, 2 McIntyre (Norton), 3 Ray Fay (Norton), 4 Alan Shepherd (Matchless), 5 Tom Thorp (Matchless), 6 Mike Brookes (Norton). Fastest lap: Hailwood, McIntyre, 87.41mph.

24 July, Snetterton

350 (10 laps, 27.1 miles): 1 Mike Hailwood (AJS), 88.10mph, 2 Phil Read (Norton), 3 John Lewis (Norton), 4 Tom Thorp (AJS), 5 Tony Sugden (AJS), 6 Ron Langston (AJS). Fastest lap: Hailwood, 90.16mph (record).

500 (10 laps): 1 Read (Norton), 89.83mph, 2 Tony Godfrey (Norton), 3 Langston (Matchless), 4 Lewis Young (Norton), 5 Ned Minihan (Norton), 6 Dave Williams (Norton). Fastest lap: Read, 91.69mph.

1 August, Oulton Park – British Championships

350 (30 laps, 82.8 miles): 1 Bob McIntyre (AJS), 85.01mph, 2 Alan Shepherd (AJS), 3 Dickie Dale (Norton), 4 Terry Shepherd (Norton), 5 Fred Stevens (Norton), 6 Ray Fay (Norton). Fastest lap: McIntyre, 86.28mph.

500 (30 laps): 1 McIntyre (Norton), 85.46mph, 2 Mike Hailwood (Norton), 3 Shepherd (Matchless), 4 John Hartle (Norton), 5 Stevens (Norton), 6 Fay (Norton). Fastest lap: McIntyre, 88.59mph.

Les Graham Memorial Trophy (10 laps): 1 McIntyre (Norton), 83.73mph, 2 Hailwood (Norton), 3 Fay (Norton), 4 T Charnley (Norton), 5 Stevens (Norton), 6 Ginger Payne (Matchless). Fastest lap: Hailwood, 88.59mph.

1 August, Thruxton – Commonwealth Trophy

350 (10 laps, 22.75 miles): 1 Tom Phillis (Norton), 77.47mph, 2 Hugh Anderson (Norton), 3 Paddy Driver (Norton), 4 Tony Godfrey, 5 Peter Pawson (AJS), 6 Peter Darvill (AJS). Fastest lap: Anderson, Phillis, 79.5mph.

500 (10 laps): 1 Godfrey (Norton), 79.9mph, 2 Anderson (Norton), 3 Phillis (Norton), 4 Dave Williams (Norton), 5 Pawson (Norton), 6 V Cottle (Norton). Fastest lap: Anderson, 82.56mph.

1 August, Crystal Palace

350 (12 laps, 16.68 miles): 1 Phil Read (Norton), 74.21mph, 2 Ned Minihan (Norton), 3 Bob Rowe (Norton), 4 Mike O'Rourke (Norton), 5 Frank Perris (Norton), 6 Dave Degens (AJS). Fastest lap: n/a.

1000 (12 laps): Abandoned due to crashes.

13 August, Aberdare

350 (12 laps, 9 miles): 1 Mike Hailwood (Norton), 50.4mph, 2 Tony Godfrey (Norton), 3 Bill Siddles (BSA), 4 J Buxton ((Norton), 5 John Cooper (Norton), 6 Malcolm Uphill (Norton). Fastest lap: Hailwood, 53.65mph

500 (12 laps): 1 Hailwood (Norton), speed n/a, 2 Godfrey (Norton), 3 John Buxton (Norton), 4 Mike Brookes (Norton), 5 Bill Siddles (BSA), 6 Louis Carr (AJS). Fastest lap: Hailwood, 54.72mph.

1000 (15 laps, 11.25 miles): 1 Hailwood (Norton), 51.75mph, 2 Godfrey (Norton), 3 W Siddles (BSA), 4 Brookes (Norton), 5 Lewis Young (Norton), 6 V Cottle (Norton). Fastest lap: Hailwood, 53.65mph

21 August, Brands Hatch

350 (20 laps, 24.8 miles): 1 Mike Hailwood (AJS), 75.46mph, 2 Derek Minter (Norton), 3 John Hempleman (Norton), 4 Brian Setchell (Norton), 5 Tom Phillis (Norton), 6 Bruce Daniels (Norton). Fastest lap: Hailwood, 77.77mph (record).

500 (20 laps): 1 Minter (Norton), 76.24mph, 2 Tom Thorp (Matchless), 3 Hailwood (Norton), 4 Hempleman (Norton), 5 Ginger Payne (Norton), 6 Bob Rowe (Norton). Fastest lap: Minter, Hailwood: 78.59mph (record).

1000 (20 laps): 1 Minter (Norton), 76.87mph, 2 Hailwood (Norton), 3 Thorp (Matchless), 4 Daniels (Norton), 5 Phillis (Norton), 6 Lewis Young (Norton). Fastest lap: Minter, 79.15mph (record).

4 September, Snetterton

350 (10 laps, 27.1 miles): 1 Derek Minter (Norton), 87.91mph, 2 Tom Thorp (AJS), 3 Brian Setchell (Norton), 4 Trevor Pound (Norton), 5 V Cottle (Norton), 6 Dave Degens (AJS). Fastest lap: Minter, 89.83mph.

500 (10 laps): 1 Minter (Norton), 90.43mph, 2 Tony Godfrey (Norton), 3 Mike Hailwood (Norton), 4 Tom Thorp (Matchless), 5 Bruce Daniels (Norton), 6 Trevor Charnley (Norton). Fastest lap: Hailwood, 92.55mph

11 September, Cadwell Park

350 (12 laps, 15 miles): 1 Alan Shepherd (AJS), 62.79mph, 2 Roy Mayhew (AJS), 3 Dennis Pratt (Norton), 4 Lewis Young (Norton), 5 Fred Neville (AJS), 6 Trevor Pound (Norton). Fastest lap: n/a.

500 (20 laps): 1 Shepherd (Matchless), 64.90mph, 2 Dan Shorey (Norton), 3 Peter Middleton (Norton), 4 Trevor Charnley (Norton), 5 Mayhew (Matchless), 6 Pratt (Norton). Fastest lap: n/a.

15-17 September, Scarborough

350 (16 laps, 38.56 miles): 1 Alan Shepherd (AJS), 59.69mph, 2 John Hartle (Norton), 3 Louis Carr (AJS), 4 Peter Middleton (Norton), 5 John Nutter (AJS), 6 Ralph Rensen (Norton). Fastest lap: Shepherd, 62.42mph.

500 (16 laps): 1 Hartle (Norton), 66.66mph, 2 Dennis Pratt (Norton), 3 Peter Middleton (Norton), 4 Ray Fay (Norton), 5 Ginger Payne (Matchless), 6 Dan Shorey (Norton). Fastest lap: Hartle, Shepherd, 67.99mph.

18 September, Brands Hatch

350 (10 laps, 26.5 miles): 1 Mike Hailwood (AJS), 82.45mph, 2 Phil Read (Norton), 3 Tom Thorp (AJS), 4 John Hempleman (Norton), 5 Tom Phillis (Norton), 6 Hugh Anderson (Norton). Fastest lap: Hailwood, 84.27mph (record).

500 (10 laps): 1 Hailwood (Norton), 84.64mph, 2 Read (Norton), 3 Paddy Driver (Norton), 4 Bob Rowe, 5 Alan Trow (Norton), 6 John Hempleman (Norton). Fastest lap: Hailwood, 87.20mph (record).

1000 (10 laps): 1 Hailwood (499 Norton), 85.53mph, 2 Read (499 Norton), 3 Thorp (496 Matchless), 4 Trow (499 Norton), 5 Rowe (499 Norton), 6 Fred Neville (496 Matchless). Fastest lap: Hailwood, 87.20mph.

24 September, Aintree Century

350 (5 laps, 15 miles): 1 John Hartle (Norton), 81.75mph, 2 Bob McIntyre (AJS), 3 Mike Hailwood (AJS), 4 Phil Read (Norton), 5 Alan Shepherd (AJS), 6 Ray Fay (Norton). Fastest lap: Hartle, 84.24mph (record)

500 (5 laps): 1 Hartle (Norton), 83.80mph, 2 Hailwood (Norton), 3 McIntyre (Norton), 4 Tom Thorp (Matchless), 5 Shepherd (Matchless), 6 Trevor Charnley (Norton). Fastest lap: Fay (Norton), 86.40mph (record).

5000 Aintree Century (21 laps): 1 Thorp (Matchless), 83.31mph, 2 Hartle (Norton), 3 Shepherd (Matchless), 4 Dennis Pratt (Norton), 5 Tony Godfrey (Norton), 6 Charnley (Norton). Fastest lap: Hartle, 85.58mph.

25 September, Mallory Park – Race of the Year

350 (25 laps, 33.75 miles): 1 Bob McIntyre (AJS), 85.39mph, 2 Mike Hailwood (AJS), 3 Dickie Dale (Norton), 4 Phil Read (Norton), 5 John Buxton (Norton), 6 Peter Chatterton (Norton). Fastest lap: McIntyre, Hailwood, 87.41mph (record)

500 (25 laps): 1 McIntyre (Norton), 85.42mph, 2 Paddy Driver (Norton), 3 Ray Fay (Norton), 4 Bob Anderson (Matchless), 5 Alan Shepherd (Matchless), 6 Read (Norton). Fastest lap: Hailwood (Norton), 89.00mph
Race of the Year (40 laps): 1 Hailwood (499 Norton), 86.32mph, 2 Terry Shepherd (499 Norton), 3 Ron Langston (Matchless), 4 Bob Anderson (Matchless), 5 Dale (Norton), 6 Alan Shepherd (Matchless). Fastest lap: Hailwood (Norton), 89.00mph (record).

8 October, Oulton Park
350 (6 laps, 16.56 miles): 1 John Hartle (Norton), 74.01mph, 2 Alan Shepherd (AJS), 3 Ron Langston (AJS), 4 Peter Bettison (Norton), 5 John Buxton (Norton), 6 Fred Stevens (Norton). Fastest lap: Hartle, 76.58mph.
500 (6 laps): 1 Alan Shepherd (Matchless), 75.62mph, 2 Hartle (Norton), 3 Langston (Matchless), 4 Buxton (Norton), 5 Hailwood (Norton), 6 Keith Terretta (Norton). Fastest lap: Langston, 77.65mph.

9 October, Brands Hatch
350 (12 laps, 31.8 miles): 1 Mike Hailwood (AJS), 77.07mph, 2 Phil Read (Norton), 3 John Hartle (Norton), 4 Ron Langston (AJS). Fastest lap: n/a.
1000 (12 laps): 1 Hartle (499 Norton), 79.61mph, 2 Hailwood (499 Norton), 3 Alan Shepherd (496 Matchless), 4 Derek Minter (Norton). Fastest lap: n/a.

1960 ACU Road Racing Stars:
350: 1 Mike Hailwood, 2 Phil Read, 3 Bob McIntyre
500 1 Hailwood, 2 Derek Minter, 3 Read

1961
31 March, Brands Hatch
350 (10 laps, 26.5 miles): 1 Mike Hailwood (AJS), 83.42mph, 2 Phil Read (Norton), 3 John Hartle (Norton), 4 Derek Minter (Norton), 5 Paddy Driver (Norton), 6 Dickie Dale (Norton). Fastest lap: Hailwood, 85.17mph (record).
Over 350 (10 laps): 1 Minter (Norton), 85.51mph, 2 Read (Norton), 3 Driver (Norton), 4 Dan Shorey (Norton), 5 Joe Dunphy (Norton), 6 Dale (Norton). Fastest lap: Hailwood (Norton), Minter, 87.68mph (record).
Over 250 (15 laps): 1 Hailwood (499 Norton), 87.91mph, 2 Minter (499 Norton), 3 Read (499 Norton), 4 Dale (499 Norton), 5 Hartle (499 Norton), 6 Driver (Norton). Fastest lap: Hailwood, 89.15mph (record)

2 April, Snetterton
350 (10 laps, 27.1 miles): 1 Mike Hailwood (AJS), 85.12mph, 2 Derek Minter (Norton), 3 Bruce Daniels (Norton), 4 Tony Godfrey (Norton), 5 R Jones (Norton), 6 Lewis Young (AJS). Fastest lap: Hailwood, Minter, 88.37mph.
500: 1 Minter (Norton), 91.74mph, 2 Hailwood (Norton), 3 Dan Shorey (Norton), 4 Godfrey (Norton), 5 Peter Darvill (Norton), 6 Ron Langston (Norton). Fastest lap: Minter, 94.90mph (record).

3 April, Oulton Park
350 (19 laps, 52.44 miles): 1 Derek Minter (Norton), 85.48mph, 2 Phil Read (Norton), 3 John Hartle (Norton), 4 Alistair King (Norton), 5 Fred Neville (AJS), 6 Ginger Payne (Norton). Fastest lap: Minter, 87.19mph (record).
500 (19 laps): 1 Minter (Norton), 87.79mph, 2 Read (Norton), 3 Neville (Matchless), 4 Payne (Norton), 5 Dan Shorey (Norton), 6 Roy Mayhew (Matchless). Fastest lap: Minter, 89.22mph (record).

3 April, Thruxton – Commonwealth Trophy
350 (10 laps, 22.75 miles): 1 Mike Hailwood (AJS), 71.09mph, 2 Hugh Anderson (Norton), 3 Dickie Dale (Norton), 4 Roy Ingram (Norton), 5 Tony Godfrey (Norton), 6 V Cottle (Norton). Fastest lap: Hailwood 72.61mph.
500 Commonwealth Trophy (12 laps): 1 Hailwood (Norton), 71.78mph, 2 Dale (Norton), 3 Paddy Driver (Norton), 4 Hugh Anderson (Norton), 5 Frank Perris (Norton), 6 Dave Williams (Norton). Fastest lap: Hailwood, 74.45mph.

3 April, Cadwell Park
350 (8 laps, 10 miles): 1 Dennis Pratt (Norton), 60.5mph, 2 Louis Carr (AJS), 3 Peter Middleton (Norton), 4 Lewis Young (AJS), 5 T Sugden (AJS), 6 Norman Storer (Norton). Fastest lap: Pratt, 62.67mph.
1000 (12 laps): 1 Pratt (Norton), 61.93mph, 2 Lewis Young (Norton), 3 Middleton (Norton), 4 Peter Chatterton (Norton), 5 Billie Nelson (348 Norton), 6 Sugden (349 AJS). Fastest lap: Pratt, 63.55mph.

3 April, Crystal Palace
350 (10 laps, 13.9 miles): 1 Robin Dawson (AJS), 65.50mph, 2 Ted Wooder (AJS), 3 Brian Setchell (Norton), 4 J N Wright (Norton). Fastest lap: Dawson, 67.99mph.
500 (10 laps): 1 Joe Dunphy (Norton), 66.25mph, 2 Wooder (Matchless), 3 Dawson (Matchless), 4 G Young (Norton). Fastest lap: Dunphy, 67.99mph.

8 April, Silverstone – Hutchinson 100
350 BMCRC Championship (15 laps, 43.9 miles): 1 Derek Minter (Norton), 95.39mph, 2 Phil Read (Norton), 3 Alan Shepherd (AJS), 4 Fred Neville (AJS), 5 Bob McIntyre (AJS), 6 Alistair King (Norton). Fastest lap: Minter, 96.99mph.
500 BMCRC Championship (15 laps): 1 John Hartle (Norton), 98.37mph, 2 McIntyre (Norton), 3 Neville (Matchless), 4 Tom Thorp (Norton), 5 Bob Anderson (Norton), 6 Dan Shorey (Norton). Fastest lap: Hartle/Minter (Norton), 100.74mph (record)

9 April, Mallory Park
350 (25 laps, 33.75 miles): 1 Phil Read (Norton), 85.03mph, 2 Bob McIntyre (AJS), 3 Mike Hailwood (AJS), 4 Dickie Dale (Norton), 5 Alan Shepherd (AJS), 6 Alistair King (Norton). Fastest lap: Hailwood, 87.09mph.
500 (25 laps): 1 Hailwood (Norton), 87.88mph, 2 Dickie Dale (Norton), 3 McIntyre (Norton), 4 Read (Norton), 5 Bob Anderson (Norton), 6 Fred Neville (Matchless). Fastest lap: Hailwood, 89.33mph (record).

30 April, Brands Hatch
350 (18 laps, 47.7 miles): 1 Derek Minter (Norton), 84.81mph, 2 Phil Read (Norton), 3 Fred Neville (AJS), 4 Bruce Daniels (Norton), 5 Ron Langston (AJS), 6 Dave Degens (Norton). Fastest lap: Minter, 86.41mph (record).
500 (20 laps): 1 Minter (Norton), 87.54mph, 2 Neville (Matchless), 3 Robb (Matchless), 4 Joe Dunphy (Norton), 5 Roy Mayhew (Matchless), 6 R Harper (Norton). Fastest lap: Minter, 89.15mph (equals record).

13 May, Aberdare
350 (12 laps, 9.12 miles): 1 Tony Godfrey (Norton), 54.48mph, 2 Robin Dawson (AJS), 3 Norman Storer (Norton), 4 Dan Shorey (Norton), 5 Mike Brookes (Norton), 6 Malcolm Uphill (Norton). Fastest lap: Godfrey, 56.06mph.
500 (12 laps): 1 Godfrey (Norton), 55.76mph, 2 Dawson (Matchless), 3 Tony Brookes (Norton), 4 Lewis Young (Norton), 5 John Cooper (Norton), 6 Shorey (Norton). Fastest lap: Godfrey, 57mph.
1000 (15 laps): 1 Godfrey (499 Norton), 55.46mph, 2 Dawson (496 Matchless), 3 John Cooper (499 Norton), 4 Shorey (499 Norton), 5 Young (499 Norton), 6 Uphill (348 Norton). Fastest lap: Godfrey, 55.84mph.

14 May, Mallory Park
350 (25 laps, 33.75 miles): 1 Phil Read (Norton), 84.08mph, 2 Fred Neville (AJS), Alistair King (Norton), 4 Peter Middleton (Norton), 5 Lewis Young (Norton), 6 T Sugden (Norton). Fastest lap: Read, 86.78mph
500 (25 laps): 1 Read (Norton), 86.15mph, 2 Neville (Matchless), 3 King (Norton), 4 Joe Dunphy (Norton), 5 Peter Chatterton (Norton), 6 Bruce Daniels (Norton). Fastest lap: Read 88.36mph.

22 May, Aintree, Red Rose
350 (12 laps, 19.68 miles): 1 Fred Stevens (Norton), 81.42mph, 2 Brian Carr (AJS), 3 Noel Wright (Norton). Fastest lap: n/a.
500 (15 laps): 1 Ray Fay (Norton), 85.17mph, 2 George Young (Norton), 3 Geoff Smith (Norton). Fastest lap: n/a.

22 May, Brands Hatch
350 (20 laps, 24.8 miles): 1 Fred Neville (AJS), 73.55mph, 2 Ron Langston (AJS), 3 Bruce Daniels (Norton). Fastest lap: n/a.
500 (20 laps): 1 Neville (Matchless), 76.64mph, 2 Joe Dunphy (Norton), 3 Ron Grant (Norton), 4 Daniels (Norton), 5 Dave Degens (Norton), 6 Ron Langston (Matchless). Fastest lap: n/a.
1000 (20 laps): 1 Dunphy (499 Norton), 75.31mph. 2 Grant (499 Norton), 3 Jack Simmonds (496 Matchless), 4 Degens (499 Norton), 5 H King (499 Norton), 6 Griff Jenkins (Norton). Fastest lap: n/a.

22 May, Cadwell Park
350 (8 laps, 10 miles): 1 Dennis Pratt (Norton), 62.76mph, 2 Lewis Young (AJS), 3 John Cooper (Norton). Fastest lap: Pratt, 64.66mph.
500 (12 laps): 1 Pratt (Norton), 64.19mph, 2 Young (Norton), 3 Peter Middleton (Norton). Fastest lap: Pratt, 66.77mph.

22 May, Thruxton
350 (22 laps, 50.05 miles): 1 Derek Minter, 79.15mph, 2 Phil Read (Norton), 3 Tony Godfrey (Norton), 4 Roy Mayhew (AJS), 5 Ginger Payne (Norton), 6 Mike Duff (AJS). Fastest lap: Minter, 80.29mph (record).
500 (22 laps): 1 Minter (Norton), 82.15mph, 2 Read (Norton), 3 Mayhew (Matchless), 4 Godfrey (Norton), 5 Alistair King (Norton), 6 Dan Shorey (Norton). Fastest lap: Minter, Mayhew, 82.89mph (equals record).

27 May, Castle Combe
350 (10 laps, 18.4 miles): 1 Ginger Payne (Norton), 82.17mph, 2 Tony Godfrey (Norton), 3 Louis Carr (AJS), 4 Lewis Young (AJS), 5 Selwyn Griffiths (AJS), 6 Peter Darvill (AJS). Fastest lap: Godfrey, 85.57mph.
500 (10 laps): 1 Mike Hailwood (Norton), 80.59mph, 2 Godfrey (Norton), 3 Payne (Norton), 4 Young (Norton), 5 Dan Shorey (Norton), 6 P Stacey (Norton). Fastest lap: Hailwood, 84.05mph.

3 June, Scarborough – Cock o' the North
350 (15 laps, 36.15 miles): 1 Dennis Pratt (Norton), 64.17mph, 2 Ginger Payne (Norton), 3 Louis Carr (AJS), 4 John Cooper (Norton), 5 Rob Fitton (AJS), 6 Ray Fay (Norton). Fastest lap: Pratt, 65.72mph.
500 (15 laps): 1 Payne (Norton), 66.84mph, 2 Robin Dawson (Matchless), 3 Rob Fitton (Norton), 4 Ray Fay (Norton), 5 Fred Stevens (Norton), 6 J Stancer (Matchless). Fastest lap: Payne, 66.84mph.

18 June, Mallory Park
350 (25 laps, 33.75 miles): 1 Bob McIntyre (AJS), 85.13mph, 2 Mike Hailwood (AJS), 3 Phil Read (Norton), 4 Paddy Driver (AJS), 5 Ginger Payne (Norton), 6 Percy Tait (Norton). Fastest lap: McIntyre, 86.48mph.
500 (25 laps): 1 McIntyre (Norton), 85.99mph, 2 Alistair King (Norton), 3 Ginger Payne (Norton), 4 Read (Norton), 5 Driver (Norton), 6 Fred Neville (Matchless). Fastest lap: McIntyre, 87.73mph.

8 July, Thruxton
500-mile: 1 Tony Godfrey/John Holder (650 Triumph Bonneville).

9 July, Brands Hatch
350 (10 laps, 26.5 miles): 1 Phil Read (Norton), 83.38mph, 2 Fred Neville (AJS), 3 Derek Minter (Norton), 4 Mike Hailwood (AJS), 5 Ginger Payne (Norton), 6 Tom Thorp (AJS). Fastest lap: Read and Neville, 85.48mph.
350-1000 (10 laps): 1 Minter (499 Norton), 85.82mph, 2 Read (499 Norton), 3 John Hartle (499 Norton), 4 Ginger Payne (499 Norton), 5 Neville (496 Matchless), 6 Dan Shorey (499 Norton). Fastest lap: n/a.
250-1000 15 laps): 1 Minter (499 Norton), 86.20mph, 2 Read (499 Norton), 3 Neville (596 Dunstall Domiracer), 4 Payne (499 Norton), 5 Roy Mayhew (496 Matchless), 6 Shorey (499 Norton). Fastest lap: n/a.

15 July, Castle Combe
350 (10 laps, 18.4 miles) 1 Derek Minter (Norton), 77.01mph, 2 Tony Godfrey (Norton), 3 Louis Carr (AJS), 4 R Jones (Norton), 5 Roy Ingram (Norton). Fastest lap: Minter, 80.77mph.
500 (10 laps): 1 Mike Hailwood (Norton), 81.79mph, 2 Minter (Norton), 3 Godfrey (Norton), 4 Fred Neville (Matchless), 5 Dan Shorey (Norton). Fastest lap: Minter, 85.57mph.

30 July, Snetterton
350 (10 laps, 27.1 miles): 1 Phil Read (Norton), 86.52mph, 2 Tony Godfrey (Norton), 3 Michael O'Rourke (Norton), 4 Dave Degens (Norton), 5 Brian Setchell (Norton), 6 B Clark (Norton). Fastest lap: Read, 89.01mph.
500 (10 laps): 1 Derek Minter (Norton), 92.04mph, 2 Read (Norton), 3 Godfrey (Norton), 4 Tom Thorp (Norton), 5 Roy Ingram (Norton), 6 Lewis Young (Norton). Fastest lap: Minter, 94.35mph.

7 August, Oulton Park – British Championships
350 (30 laps, 82.8 miles): 1 John Hartle (Norton), 85.13mph, 2 Bob McIntyre (Norton), 3 Phil Read (Norton), 4 Fred Neville (AJS), 5 Alistair King (Norton), 6 Alan Shepherd (AJS). Fastest lap: Derek Minter (Norton), 87.34mph (record).
500 (30 laps): 1 Minter (Norton), 86.43mph, 2 Neville (Matchless), 3 Mike Hailwood (Norton), 4 King (Norton), 5 Shepherd (Matchless), 6 Read (Norton). Fastest: King, 88.91mph.
Les Graham Memorial Trophy (10 laps): 1 Alistair King (Norton), 88.33mph, 2 Minter (Norton), 3 John Hartle (Norton), 4 Shepherd (Matchless), 5 Neville (Matchless), 6 Tom Thorp (Norton). Fastest lap: Minter, 90.02mph (record).

7 August, Crystal Palace
350 (10 laps, 13.9 miles): 1 Ned Minihan (AJS), 74.29mph, 2 Robin Dawson (AJS), 3 R. Foster (AJS). Fastest lap: Minihan, 75.82mph.
1000 (10 laps): 1 Minihan (Norton), 75.07mph, 2 Ernie Wooder (Matchless), 3 Dawson (Matchless). Fastest lap: Wooder, 77.7mph.

7 August, Cadwell Park (new 2.25-mile circuit)
350 (6 laps, 13.5 miles): 1 Dennis Pratt (Norton), 66.15mph, 2 John Cooper (Norton), 3 Peter Middleton (Norton), 4 Lewis Young (AJS), 5 Carl Ward (AJS), 6 Norman Storer (Norton). Fastest lap: Middleton, 68.88mph (record).
500 Coronation Cup (10 laps): 1 Pratt (Norton), 67.57mph, 2 Young (Norton), 3 Storer (Norton), 4 Middleton (Norton), 5 R Cousins (Norton), 6 Cooper (Norton). Fastest lap: Pratt, 71.93mph (record).

7 August, Thruxton
350 (10 laps, 22.75 miles): 1 Tony Godfrey (Norton), 77.38mph, 2 Roy Mayhew (AJS), Roy Ingram (Norton), 4 Dave Degens (Norton), 5 Dave Williams (Norton), 6 J Holder (AJS). Fastest lap: Mayhew, 79.06mph.
500 (10 laps): 1 Godfrey (Norton), 80.90mph, 2 Mayhew (Matchless), 3 Ingram (Norton), 4 Degens (Norton), 5 Tom Phillips (Norton), 5 W Rudd (Norton). Fastest lap: Godfrey, 83.06mph.

20 August, Brands Hatch
350 (12 laps, 31.8 miles): 1 Mike Hailwood (AJS), 85.40mph, 2 Fred Neville (AJS), 3 Phil Read (Norton), 4 Tom Thorp (AJS), 5 Dave Degens (Norton), 6 Mike Duff (AJS). Fastest lap: Read, 87.52mph (record).
500 (12 laps): 1 Read (Norton), 86.52mph, 2 Derek Minter (Norton), 3 Neville (Matchless), 4 Dan Shorey (Norton), 5 Thorp (Norton), 6 Duff (AJS). Fastest lap: Minter, Read, 87.68mph (record).
1000 (12 laps): 1 Neville (647 Dunstall Domiracer), 86.59mph, 2 Tom Thorp (496 Matchless), 3 Mike Duff (496 Matchless), 4 Shorey (499 Norton), 5 Degens (499 Norton), 6 Alan Thurgood (Matchless). Fastest lap: Neville, 88.17mph.

26 August, Aberdare
350 (12 laps, 9.1 miles): 1 Mike Hailwood (AJS), speed n/a, 2 Tony Godfrey (Norton), 3 Norman Surtees (Norton), 4 Dan Shorey (Norton), 5 Norman Storer (Norton), 6 John Cooper (Norton). Fastest lap: Hailwood, 58.46mph (record).
500 (12 laps): 1 Hailwood (Norton), speed n/a, 2 Godfrey (Norton), 3 Dan Shorey (Norton), 4 Jack Bullock (Norton), 5 Storer (Norton), 6 Lewis Young (Norton). Fastest lap: Hailwood, 59.22mph (record)
1000 (15 laps): 1 Godfrey (499 Norton), speed n/a, 2 Shorey (499 Norton), 3 Bullock (499 Norton), 4 Young (499 Norton), 5 Storer (499 Norton), 6 Cooper (499 Norton). Fastest lap: Godfrey, 58.46mph (record).

3 September, Snetterton
350 (7 laps, 18.97 miles): 1 Derek Minter (Norton), 82.61mph, 2 Tony Godfrey (Norton), 3 Lewis Young (AJS), 4 Dave Degens (Norton), 5 Dan Shorey (Norton), 6 B Clark (Norton). Fastest lap: Minter, 88.53mph.
500 (10 laps): 1 Godfrey (Norton), 77.51mph, 2 Young (Norton), 3 Dan Shorey (Norton), 4 Degens (Norton), 5 L Kempster (Norton), 6 L Cross (Norton). Fastest lap: Godfrey, 81.30mph.

10 September, Cadwell Park
350 (12 laps, 27 miles): 1 John Hartle (Norton), 70.28mph, 2 John Cooper (Norton), 3 Dan Shorey (Norton), 4 Peter Middleton (Norton), 5 Roy Mayhew (AJS), 6 Rob Fitton (AJS). Fastest lap: Hartle, 71.54mph (record).
500 (12 laps): 1 Hartle (Norton), 71.95mph, 2 Alan Shepherd (Matchless), 3 Dan Shorey (Norton), 4 Dennis Pratt (Norton), 5 Mayhew (Matchless), 6 Norman Storer (Norton). Fastest lap: Hartle, Mayhew, 72.84mph (record).

15/16 September, Scarborough
350 (14 laps, 33.74 miles): 1 John Cooper (Norton), 58.96mph, 2 Peter Middleton (Norton), 3 Jack Brett (AJS), 4 Dennis Pratt (Norton), 5 Dan Shorey (Norton), 6 Roy Mayhew (AJS). Fastest lap: Cooper, 60.34mph.
500 (16 laps): 1 Dennis Pratt (Norton), 67.11mph, 2 Dan Shorey (Norton), 3 Middleton (Norton), 4 Dennis Greenfield (Norton), 5 Robin Dawson (Norton), 6 Rob Fitton (Norton). Fastest lap: Pratt, 68.42mph.

194

17 September, Brands Hatch
350 (10 laps, 26.5 miles): 1 Derek Minter (Norton), 74.18mph, 2 Phil Read (Norton), 3 Roy Mayhew (AJS), 4 Lewis Young (AJS), 5 Dave Degens (Norton), 6 Hugh Anderson (AJS). Fastest lap: n/a.
351-1000 (10 laps): 1 Minter (499 Norton), 82.59mph, 2 Lewis Young (499 Norton), 3 Mayhew (496 Matchless), 4 Degens (Norton), 5 Chris Conn (499 Norton), 6 Anderson (499 Norton). Fastest lap: n/a.
251-1000 (10 laps): 1 Minter (499 Norton), 82.62mph, 2 Mayhew (496 Matchless), 3 Young (499 Norton), 4 Conn (499 Norton), 5 Anderson (499 Norton), 6 C Williams (499 Norton). Fastest lap: n/a.

24 September, Mallory Park – Race of the Year
350 (20 laps, 27 miles): 1 Mike Hailwood (AJS), 84.33mph, 2 Alan Shepherd (AJS), 3 Phil Read (Norton), 4 Roy Mayhew (AJS), 5 Dan Shorey (Norton), 6 John Holder (Norton). Fastest lap: Hailwood, 86.17mph.
500 (25 laps): 1 Gary Hocking (MV), 87.64mph, 2 Hailwood (Norton), 3 Shepherd (Matchless), 4 Alistair King (Norton), 5 Mayhew (Matchless), 6 Read (Norton). Fastest lap: Hocking, 89.00mph.
Race of the Year (40 laps): 1 Hocking (MV), 87.72mph, 2 Hailwood (Norton), 3 Shepherd (Matchless), 4 Mayhew (Matchless), 5 Read (Norton), 6 Jim Redman (250 Honda). Fastest lap: Hocking, 89.66mph.

30 September, Aintree, Aintree Century
350 (5 laps, 15 miles): 1 Mike Hailwood (AJS), 2 Tony Godfrey (Norton), 3 Alan Shepherd (AJS), 4 Lewis Young (AJS), 5 Derek Minter (Norton), 6 Tommy Robb (AJS). Fastest lap: Hailwood, 83.2mph.
500 (5 laps): 1 Hailwood (Norton), 2 Dennis Pratt (Norton), 3 Phil Read (Norton), 4 Alan Shepherd (Matchless), 5 Tony Godfrey (Norton), 6 Derek Minter (Norton). Fastest lap: Hailwood, 85.31mph.
500 Aintree Century (21 laps): 1 Hailwood (499 Norton), 2 Shepherd (496 Matchless), 3 Pratt (499 Norton), 4 Read (499 Norton), 5 Robb (Matchless), 6 Godfrey (499 Norton). Fastest lap: Hailwood, 86.4mph (record).

7 October, Oulton Park
350 (10 laps, 27.6 miles): 1 Alan Shepherd (AJS), 82.55mph, Brian Carr (AJS), 3 Dennis Greenfield (Norton), 4 Fred Stevens (Norton), 5 Freddie Fisher (Norton), 6 Peter Darvill (AJS). Fastest lap: Derek Minter (Norton), 83.95mph
500 (10 laps): 1 Mike Hailwood (Norton), 86.82mph, 2 Phil Read (Norton), 3 Shepherd (Matchless), 4 Minter (Norton), 5 Stevens (Norton), 6 Rob Fitton (Norton). Fastest lap: Hailwood, 88.43mph.

8 October, Brands Hatch
350 (10 laps, 26.5 miles): 1 Derek Minter (Norton), 83.43mph, 2 Phil Read (AJS), 3 Mike Duff (AJS), 4 Roy Mayhew (AJS), 5 R Minto (AJS), 6 Dave Degens (Norton). Fastest lap: n/a.
500 (10 laps): 1 Minter (Norton), 76.87mph, 2 Read (Matchless), 3 Mike Hailwood (Norton), 4 Chris Conn (Norton), 5 Alan Thurgood (Matchless), 6 Roy Mayhew (Matchless). Fastest lap: n/a.
251-1000 (10 laps): 1 Read (496 Matchless), 76.50mph, 2 Minter (597 Dunstall Domiracer), 3 Mayhew (496 Matchless), 4 Conn (499 Norton), 5 Thurgood (496 Matchless), 6 Ron Grant (Norton). Fastest lap: n/a.

1961 ACU Road Racing Stars
350: 1 Phil Read, 2 Mike Hailwood, 3 Tony Godfrey
500: 1 Hailwood, 2 Derek Minter, 3 Read

1962

1 April, Mallory Park
350 (20 laps, 27 miles): 1 Derek Minter (Norton), 82.84mph, 2 Alan Shepherd (AJS), 3 Alistair King (Norton), 4 Phil Read (Norton), 5 Peter Middleton (Norton), 6 Lewis Young (AJS). Fastest lap: Minter, 85.26mph.
500 (25 laps): 1 Mike Hailwood (Norton), 79.30mph, 2 Shepherd (Matchless), 3 Minter (Norton), 4 Phil Read (Norton), 5 Roy Mayhew (Matchless), 6 Chris Conn (Norton). Fastest lap: Minter, 82.37mph.

7 April, Silverstone – Hutchinson 100
350 BMCRC Championship (15 laps, 43.9 miles): 1 Derek Minter (Norton), 92.59mph, 2 Mike Hailwood (AJS), 3 Alan Shepherd (AJS), 4 Hugh Anderson (AJS), 5 Tony Godfrey (Norton), 6 Roy Mayhew (AJS). Fastest lap: Minter, Hailwood, 94.42mph.
500 BMCRC Championship (15 laps): 1 Hailwood (Norton), 96.65mph, 2 Bob McIntyre (Matchless), 3 Shepherd (Matchless), 4 Anderson (Norton), 5 Mayhew (Matchless), 6 Phil Read (Norton). Fastest lap: Hailwood, McIntyre, 98.30mph

20 April, Brands Hatch
350 (10 laps, 26.5 miles): 1 Mike Hailwood (AJS), 82.76mph, 2 Derek Minter (Norton), 3 Phil Read (Norton), 4 Alan Shepherd (AJS), 5 Hugh Anderson (AJS), 6 Roy Mayhew (AJS) Fastest lap: n/a.
500 Redex Trophy (10 laps): 1 Derek Minter (Norton), 84.92mph, 2 Read (Norton), 3 Anderson (Norton), 4 Shepherd (Matchless), 5 Hailwood (Norton), 6 Mayhew (Matchless) Fastest lap: n/a.
Over 250 (15 laps): 1 Minter (600 Domiracer), 87.27mph, 2 Hailwood (499 Norton), 3 Shepherd (496 Matchless), 4 Mayhew (496 Matchless), 5 Tony Godfrey (499 Norton), 6 J Cripps (Norton). Fastest lap: n/a.

21 April, Scarborough
350 (12 laps, 28.92 miles): 1 Peter Middleton (Norton), 59.71mph, 2 Brian Hornby (Norton), 3 John Nutter (AJS), 4 Dave King (Norton), 5 Peter Bettison (Norton), 6 Louis Carr (AJS). Fastest lap: Middleton, 61.54mph
500 (12 laps): 1 Middleton (Norton), 61.01mph, 2 Billie Nelson (Norton), 3 Louis Carr (Matchless), 4 Tom Phillips (Norton), 5 Fred Stevens (Norton), 6 Derek Phillips (Norton). Fastest lap: Middleton, 62.24mph.

22 April, Snetterton
350 (10 laps, 27.1 miles): 1 Mike Hailwood (MV Agusta), 90.05mph, 2 Roy Mayhew (AJS), 3 Derek Minter (Norton), 4 Dan Shorey (Norton), 5 Lewis Young (AJS), 6 Tony Godfrey (Norton). Fastest lap: Hailwood, 92.55mph (record).
500 (10 laps): 1 Hailwood (MV Agusta), 94.02mph, 2 Mayhew (Matchless), 3 Godfrey (Norton), 4 Minter (Norton), 5 Shorey (Norton), 6 Dave Degens (Matchless). Fastest lap: Hailwood, 96.21mph (record).

23 April, Oulton Park
350 (19 laps, 52.44 miles): 1 Alan Shepherd (AJS), 85.25mph, 2 Phil Read (Norton), 3 Alistair King (Norton), 4 Derek Minter (Norton), 5 Fred Stevens (Norton), 6 Freddie Fisher (Norton). Fastest lap: Bob McIntyre (285 Honda), 87.19mph
500 (19 laps): 1 McIntyre (Matchless), 88.28mph, 2 Shepherd (Matchless), 3 Minter (Norton), 4 Read (Norton), 5 King (Norton), 6 Fisher (Norton). Fastest lap: McIntyre, 90.36mph (record).

23 April, Crystal Palace
350 (10 laps, 13.9 miles): 1 Joe Dunphy (Norton), 74.25mph, 2 Ned Minihan (Norton), 3 Noel Wright (Norton), 4 Ernie Wooder (AJS). Fastest lap: Minihan, 76.98mph.
500 (10 laps): 1 Dunphy (Norton), 77.05mph, 2 Minihan (Norton), 3 Robin Dawson (Norton), 4 J R Cripps (Norton). Fastest lap: Dunphy, 79.43mph (record).

23 April, Thruxton – Commonwealth Trophy
350 (10 laps, 22.75 miles): 1 Mike Hailwood (MV Agusta), 82.47mph, 2 Hugh Anderson (AJS), 3 Tony Godfrey (Norton), 4 Mike Duff (AJS), 5 B Williams (Norton), 6 Peter Darvill (AJS). Fastest lap: n/a.
Commonwealth Trophy (10 laps): 1 Hailwood (MV Agusta), 85.54mph, 2 Godfrey (Norton), 3 Anderson (Norton), 4 Duff (Matchless), 5 B Williams (Norton), 6 R Burgess (Norton). Fastest lap: n/a.

23 April, Cadwell Park
350 (8 laps, 18 miles): 1 Roy Mayhew (AJS), 70.14mph, 2 Lewis Young (AJS), 3 John Cooper (Norton), 4 Dennis Pratt (Norton), 5 Peter Middleton (AJS), 6 T Sugden (AJS). Fastest lap: Mayhew, 71.93mph
500 (8 laps): 1 Mayhew (Matchless), 72.03mph, 2 Pratt (Norton), 3 Middleton (Norton), 4 P R Evans (Matchless), 5 Dennis Greenfield (Norton), 6 Billie Nelson (Norton). Fastest lap: Mayhew, 73.9mph (record).

29 April, Mallory Park
350 (20 laps, 27 miles): 1 Bob McIntyre (285 Honda), 85.46mph, 2 Alan Shepherd (AJS), 3 Derek Minter (Norton), 4 Roy Mayhew (AJS), 5 Phil Read (Norton), 6 Alistair King (Norton). Fastest lap: McIntyre, 87.41mph
500 (25 laps): 1 McIntyre (Matchless), 87.41mph, 2 Shepherd (Matchless), 3 Minter (Norton), 4 Read (Norton), 5 Tony Godfrey (Norton), 6 Joe Dunphy (Norton). Fastest lap: McIntyre, 89.34mph.

5 May, Castle Combe
350 (10 laps, 18.4 miles): 1 Derek Minter (Norton), 76.48mph, 2 Tony Godfrey (Norton), 3 Noel Wright (Norton). Fastest lap: Minter, Godfrey, 79.03mph.
500 (10 laps): 1 Minter (Norton), 77.95mph, 2 Godfrey (Norton), 3 Tom Phillips (Norton). Fastest lap: Minter, 80.57mph.

12 May, Aberdare
350 (12 laps, 9.1 miles): 1 Tony Godfrey (Norton), 56.14mph, 2 John Cooper (Norton), 3 Robin Dawson (AJS), 4 Roger Hunter (AJS), 5 Malcolm Uphill (Norton), 6 R Foster (Norton). Fastest lap: Godfrey, 57.48mph.
500 (12 laps): 1 Godfrey (Norton), 56.35mph, 2 Cooper (Norton), 3 Dawson (Norton), 4 Hunter (Matchless), 5 Tom Phillips (Norton), 6 Peter Darvill (Norton). Fastest lap: n/a.
1000 (15 laps): 1 Godfrey (499 Norton), 56.20mph, 2 Cooper (499 Norton), 3 Dawson (499 Norton), 4 Phillips (499 Norton), 5 Chris Conn (499 Norton), 6 Uphill (499 Norton). Fastest lap: Godfrey, 58.71mph (record).

13 May, Brands Hatch
350 (10 laps, 26.5 miles): 1 Derek Minter (Norton), 82.21mph, 2 Tony Godfrey (Norton), 3 Roy Mayhew (AJS), 4 Joe Dunphy (Norton), 5 Noel Wright (Norton), 6 Dave Degens (Norton). Fastest lap: n/a.
500 Redex Trophy (10 laps): 1 Minter (Norton), 83.04mph, 2 Godfrey (Norton), 3 Dunphy (Norton), 4 Mayhew (Matchless), 5 Griff Jenkins (Norton), 6 C J Williams (Norton). Fastest lap: n/a.
1000 (15 laps): 1 Minter (650 Domiracer), 86.03mph, 2 Dunphy (499 Norton), 3 Godfrey (499 Norton), 4 Williams (499 Norton), 5 Jack Simmonds (496 Matchless), 6 Ron Chandler (496 Matchless). Fastest lap: n/a.

20 May, Snetterton
350 (10 laps, 27.1 miles): 1 Derek Minter (Norton), 89.51mph, 2 Tony Godfrey (Norton), 3 Dan Shorey (Norton), 4 Rudi Thalhammer (Norton), 5 Peter Darvill (AJS), 6 Dave Degens (Norton). Fastest lap: Minter, 91.35mph.
500 Molyslip (10 laps): 1 Minter (Norton), 93.34mph, 2 Godfrey (Norton), 3 Degens (Matchless), 4 Alistair King (Norton), 5 Shorey (Norton), 6 Phil Read (Norton). Fastest lap: Minter, 95.46mph.

9 June, Mallory Park
350 (20 laps, 27 miles): 1 Mike Hailwood (MV Agusta), 85.88mph, 2 Alistair King (Norton), 3 Paddy Driver (Norton), 4 Phil Read (Norton), 5 Hugh Anderson (AJS), 6 Tony Godfrey (Norton). Fastest lap: Hailwood, 88.69mph (record).
500 (25 laps): 1 Hailwood (MV Agusta), 88.59mph, 2 Gary Hocking (MV Agusta), 3 Bob McIntyre (Matchless), 4 Anderson (Norton), 5 King (Norton), 6 Dave Degens (Matchless). Fastest lap: Hailwood, 91.70mph (record).

10 June, Brands Hatch
350 (20 laps, 53 miles): 1 Phil Read (Norton), 82.94mph, 2 Hugh Anderson (AJS), 3 Paddy Driver (AJS), 4 Mike Hailwood (MV Agusta), 5 Joe Dunphy (Norton), 6 Tom Thorp (AJS). Fastest lap: Hailwood, 86.41mph.
500 (20 laps): 1 Hailwood (MV Agusta), 85.94mph, 2 Read (Norton), 3 Anderson (Norton), 4 Dave Degens (Matchless), 5 Driver (Matchless), 6 Griff Jenkins (Norton). Fastest lap: Hailwood, 88.17mph.

10 June, Cadwell Park
350 (8 laps, 18 miles): 1 Lewis Young (AJS), 70.14mph, 2 John Cooper (Norton), 3 Peter Middleton (Norton). Fastest lap: Cooper, 72.06mph (record).
500 (8 laps): 1 Dennis Pratt (Norton), 71.49mph, 2 Middleton (Norton), 3 Alistair King (Norton). Fastest lap: King, 72.97mph.
Over 200 Invitation (10 laps) 1 Pratt (Norton), 71.89mph, 2 King (Norton), 3 Young (Matchless). Fastest lap: King, 73.36mph.

10 June, Thruxton
350 (10 laps, 22 miles): 1 Mike Duff (AJS), 82.71mph, 2 Tony Godfrey (Norton), 3 Peter Darvill (AJS), 4 Dave Williams (Norton), 5 Selwyn Griffiths (AJS), 6 Roy Ingram (Norton). Fastest lap: Duff, 84.25mph.
1000 (12 laps): 1 Godfrey (499 Norton), 85.16mph, 2 Duff (496 Matchless), 3 Williams (499 Norton), 4 Ingram (499 Norton), 5 Griffiths (496 Matchless), 6 Richard Difazio (499 Norton). Fastest lap: Godfrey, 88.00mph (record).

11 June, Aintree – Red Rose
350 (15 laps, 45 miles): 1 Derek Woodman (AJS), 82.29mph, 2 Robin Dawson (AJS), 3 Peter Bettison (Norton). Fastest lap: Tom Phillips (Norton) 83.10mph.
500 (15 laps): 1 Phillips (Norton), 85.09mph, 2 Noel Wright (Norton), 3 Dawson (Norton). Fastest lap: Phillips 86mph.

15/16 June, Scarborough – Cock 'o the North
350 (14 laps, 33.74 miles): 1 Peter Middleton (Norton), 65.59mph, 2 Dennis Pratt (Norton), 3 Robin Dawson (AJS), 4 John Cooper (Norton), 5 Rob Fitton (Norton), 6 Billie Nelson. Fastest lap: Middleton, 66.84mph.
500 (14 laps): 1 Middleton (Norton), 67.25mph, 2 Pratt (Norton), 3 Cooper (Norton), 4 Dawson (Norton), 5 Jack Bullock (Norton), 6 Fitton (Norton). Fastest lap: Middleton, 68.63mph.

23 June, Thruxton – *Motor Cycle* 500-mile Grand Prix
1 Phil Read/Brian Setchell (650SS Norton), 2 Roy Ingram/Fred Swift (88SS Norton), 3 Ellis Boyce/Tom Phillips (499 Velocette).

8 July, Brands Hatch
350 (10 laps, 26.5 miles): 1 Derek Minter (Norton), 84.43mph, 2 Phil Read (Norton), 3 Lewis Young (AJS), 4 Tom Thorp (AJS), 5 Ian Goddard (AJS), 6 Noel Wright (Norton). Fastest lap: Minter, Read, 86.88mph.
500 Redex Trophy (10 laps): Minter (Norton), 87.31mph, 2 Read (Norton), 3 Young (Matchless), 4 Joe Dunphy (Norton), 5 John Cripps (Norton), 6 Griff Jenkins (Norton). Fastest lap: Minter, 88.82mph.
1000 (15 laps): 1 Minter (650 Domiracer), 87.21mph, 2 Read (499 Norton), 3 Young (496 Matchless), 4 Dunphy (499 Norton), 5 Tom Thorp (499 Norton), 6 Chris Conn (499 Norton). Fastest lap: Minter, 89.32mph.

21 July, Castle Combe
350 (10 laps, 18.4 miles): 1 Derek Minter (Norton), 82.99mph, 2 Tony Godfrey (Norton), 3 Mike Hailwood (AJS), 4 Tom Phillips (Norton), 5 Selwyn Griffiths (AJS), 6 Ray Watmore (AJS). Fastest lap: Hailwood, 85.97mph.
500 (10 laps): 1 Minter (Norton), 87.17mph, 2 Hailwood (Norton), 3 Godfrey (Norton), 4 Chris Conn (Norton), 5 Noel Wright (Norton), 6 C J Williams (Norton). Fastest lap: Minter, 90.00mph.

29 July, Snetterton
350 (10 laps, 27.1 miles): 1 Phil Read (Norton), 89.34mph, 2 Lewis Young (AJS), 3 Peter Darvill (AJS), 4 Selwyn Griffiths (AJS), 5 Brian Dennehy (Norton), 6 Dan Shorey (Norton). Fastest lap: Derek Minter (Norton), 92.21mph.
500 (7 laps, rain shortened): 1 Minter (Norton), 72.93mph, 2 Young (Matchless), 3 Darvill (Norton), 4 Chris Conn (Norton), 5 Selwyn Griffiths (Matchless), 6 Tom Thorp (Norton). Fastest lap: Conn, 76.10mph.

6 August, Oulton Park – British Championships
350 (30 laps, 82.8 miles): 1 Derek Minter (Norton), 87.18mph, 2 Mike Hailwood (AJS), 3 Phil read (Norton), 4 Hugh Anderson (AJS), 5 Alan Shepherd (AJS), 6 Mike Duff (AJS). Fastest lap: Bob McIntyre (285 Honda), 88.59mph (record).
500 (30 laps): 1 Minter (Norton), 79.71mph, 2 Read (Norton), 3 Hailwood (Norton), 4 Freddie Fisher (Norton), 5 Anderson (Norton), 6 Duff (Matchless). Fastest lap: Minter, 82.69mph.
Les Graham Memorial Trophy (10 laps): 1 Shepherd (Matchless), 77.52mph, 2 John Nutter (Norton), 3 W Fulton (Norton), 4 David Downer (348 Norton). Fastest lap: Shepherd, 80.42mph.

6 August, Cadwell Park
350 (8 laps, 18 miles): 1 Peter Middleton (Norton), 71.59mph, 2 Tony Godfrey (Norton), 3 Lewis Young (AJS), 4 Rob Fitton (AJS), 5 John Cooper (Norton), 6 D Greenfield (Norton). Fastest lap: Middleton, 73.14mph.
500 (8 laps): 1 Middleton (Norton), 69.51mph, 2 Cooper (Norton), 3 Godfrey (Norton), 4 Young (Matchless), 5 Chris Conn (Norton), 6 Billie Nelson (Norton). Fastest lap: Middleton, 71.68mph.

6 August, Crystal Palace
350 (12 laps): 1 Robin Dawson (AJS), 58.38mph, 2 C J Williams (AJS), 3 Roger Hunter (AJS), 4 Ian Goddard (Norton). Fastest lap: Dawson, 67.80mph.

1000 (12 laps): 1 Joe Dunphy (499 Norton), 69.28mph, 2 Williams (Norton), 3 Dawson (Matchless), 4 Ernie Wooder (Matchless). Fastest lap: Dunphy, 71.90mph

19 August, Brands Hatch
350 (10 laps, 26.5 miles): 1 Phil Read (Norton), 82.02mph, 2 Rex Butcher (AJS), 3 Tony Godfrey (Norton), 4 Joe Dunphy (Norton), 5 David Downer (Norton), 6 Dennis Ainsworth (Norton). Fastest lap: Read, 84.57mph.
500 Redex Trophy (10 laps): 1 Lewis Young (Matchless), 84.09mph, 2 Dunphy (Norton), 3 Chris Conn (Norton), 4 J R Cripps (Norton), 5 Godfrey (Norton), 6 Butcher (Norton). Fastest lap: Young, Dunphy, 86.56mph.
1000 (15 laps): 1 Downer (650 Dunstall Domiracer), 85.43mph, 2 Godfrey (650 Norton), 3 Conn (499 Norton), 4 Butcher (499 Norton), 5 Young (496 Matchless), 6 Griff Jenkins (Norton). Fastest lap: Downer, 86.56mph.

25 August, Aberdare
350 (10 laps, 9.1 miles): 1 Tony Godfrey (Norton), 56.05mph, 2 John Cooper (Norton), 3 Chris Conn (Norton), 4 Dan Shorey (Norton), 5 Malcolm Uphill (Norton), 6 Lewis Young (AJS). Fastest lap: Shorey, 57.97mph.
500 (12 laps): 1 Cooper (Norton), 55.99mph, 2 Godfrey (Norton), 3 Shorey (Norton), 4 Young (Matchless), 5 Louis Carr (Matchless), 6 D Filler (Norton). Fastest lap: Shorey, 58.90mph.
1000 (15 laps): 1 Godfrey (499 Norton), 56.68mph, 2 Cooper (499 Norton), 3 Shorey (499 Norton), 4 Conn (348 Norton), 5 Uphill (348 Norton), 6 Carr (496 Matchless). Fastest lap: Godfrey, 58.21mph.

9 September, Snetterton
350 (10 laps, 27.1 miles): 1 Tom Thorp (AJS), 87.26mph, 2 Brian Dennehy (Norton), 3 Chris Conn (Norton), 4 Selwyn Griffiths (Norton), 5 Roy Ingram (Norton), 6 R Foster (AJS). Fastest lap: Griffiths, 89.35mph.
500 (10 laps): 1 Conn (Norton), 90.09mph, 2 Dave Strickland (Norton), 3 Noel Wright (Norton), 4 Griffiths (Matchless), 5 S R Robinson (Norton), 6 Ray Pickrell (Norton). Fastest lap: Conn, 93.09mph.

16 September, Cadwell Park
350 (12 laps, 27 miles): 1 Phil Read (Norton), 71.41mph, 2 Peter Middleton (Norton), 3 Tony Godfrey (Norton), 4 Hugh Anderson (AJS), 5 Dan Shorey (Norton), 6 John Cooper (Norton). Fastest lap: Godfrey, 73.10mph (equals record).
500 (12 laps): 1 Read (Norton), 73.06mph, 2 Godfrey (Norton), 3 Anderson (Norton), 4 Middleton (Norton), 5 Tom Phillips (Norton), 6 Billie Nelson (Norton). Fastest lap: Chris Conn (Norton), 74.86mph (record).

22 September, Scarborough
350 (16 laps, 38.56 miles): 1 Dan Shorey (AJS), 65.95mph, 2 Fred Stevens (Norton), 3 Chris Conn (Norton), 4 John Cooper (Norton), 5 Tom Phillips (Norton), 6 J Rae (Norton). Fastest lap: Shorey, 67.25mph (record).
500 (16 laps): 1 Peter Middleton (Norton), 68.41mph, 2 Phillips (Norton), 3 Stevens (Norton), 4 Rob Fitton (Norton), 5 Cooper (Norton), 6 Conn (Norton). Fastest lap: Middleton, 69.51mph.

23 September, Brands Hatch
350 Fred Neville Trophy (10 laps, 26.5 miles): 1 Derek Minter (Norton), 85.46mph, 2 Phil Read (Norton), 3 Dan Shorey (AJS), 4 Tony Godfrey (Norton), 5 Rex Butcher (JS Special), 6 Paddy Driver (Norton). Fastest lap: Minter, 87.36mph (record).
500 Redex Trophy (10 laps): 1 Minter (Norton), 88.18mph, 2 Read (Norton), 3 Godfrey (Norton), 4 Joe Dunphy (Norton), 5 Shorey (Matchless), 6 J Cripps (Norton). Fastest lap: Minter, Read, 89.83mph (record).
1000 (15 laps): 1 Minter (650 Domiracer), 87.52mph, 2 David Downer (650 Dunstall Domiracer), 3 Read (499 Norton), 4 Godfrey (499 Norton), 5 Shorey (496 Matchless), 6 Driver (Norton). Fastest lap: Minter, 88.82mph.

29 September, Aintree – Aintree Century
350 (5 laps, 15 miles): 1 Dan Shorey (AJS), 80.72mph, 2 Derek Minter (Norton), 3 Fred Stevens (Norton), 4 Peter Middleton (Norton), 5 David Downer (Norton), 6 Chris Conn (Norton). Fastest lap: Minter, 82.95mph.
500 (5 laps): 1 Minter (Norton), 83.63mph, 2 Alan Shepherd (Matchless), 3 Middleton (Norton), 4 Stevens (Norton), 5 Shorey (Norton), 6 Tom Phillips (Norton). Fastest lap: Minter, 85.58mph.
Aintree Century (21 laps): 1 Minter (499 Norton), 84.84mph, 2 Shepherd (496 Matchless), 3 Stevens (499 Norton), 4 Rob Fitton (499 Norton), 5 Phillips (499 Norton), 6 Conn (499 Norton). Fastest lap: Minter, 85.85mph.

30 September, Mallory Park – Race of the Year
350 (25 laps, 33.75 miles): 1 Phil Read (Norton), 83.31mph, 2 Alan Shepherd (AJS), 3 Dan Shorey (AJS), 4 Derek Minter (Norton), 5 Brian Setchell (Norton), 6 Chris Conn (Norton). Fastest lap: Shepherd, Shorey, 85.86mph
500 (25 laps): 1 Minter (Norton), 83.13mph, 2 Read (Norton), 3 Shepherd (Matchless), 4 Joe Dunphy (Norton), 5 John Cooper (Norton), 6 Shorey (Matchless). Fastest lap: Read, 86.78mph.
Race of the Year (40 laps): 1 Minter (499 Norton), 86.35mph, 2 Shepherd (496 Matchless), 3 Cooper (499 Norton), 4 Jim Redman (250 Honda), 5 Dan Shorey (496 Matchless), 6 Setchell (Norton). Fastest lap: Minter, 90.00mph.

6 October, Oulton Park
350 (10 laps, 27.6 miles): 1 Derek Minter (Norton), 86.16mph, 2 Fred Stevens (Norton), 3 Dan Shorey (AJS), 4 Freddie Fisher (Norton), 5 Mike Duff (AJS), 6 David Downer (Norton). Fastest lap: Minter, 89.87mph (record).
500 (10 laps): 1 Minter (Norton), 87.37mph, 2 Duff (Matchless), 3 Shorey (Matchless), 4 Roger Hunter (Matchless), 5 Rob Fitton (Norton), 6 J R Cripps (Norton). Fastest lap: Minter, 89.06mph.

14 October, Brands Hatch
350 (10 laps, 26.5 miles): 1 Derek Minter (Norton), 84.62mph, 2 Tony Godfrey (Norton), 3 Mike Duff (AJS), 4 Paddy Driver (AJS), 5 Chris

Conn (Norton), 6 J R Cripps (Norton). Fastest lap: n/a.
500 Redex Trophy (10 laps): 1 Paddy Driver (Matchless), 85.48mph, 2 Joe Dunphy (Norton), Duff (Matchless), 4 Godfrey (Norton), 5 Conn (Norton), 6 Griff Jenkins (Norton). Fastest lap: n/a.
Over 250 (10 laps): 1 Godfrey (650 Domiracer), 85.62mph, 2 Duff (496 Matchless), 3 Driver (496 Matchless), 4 Dunphy (499 Norton), 5 Cripps (499 Norton), Griff Jenkins (Norton). Fastest lap: n/a.
ACU Road Racing Stars: Derek Minter, 350, 500

1963
31 March, Mallory Park
350 (20 laps, 27 miles): 1 Derek Minter (Norton), 82.92mph, 2 Mike Duff (AJS), 3 Chris Conn (Norton), 4 Monty Buxton (Norton), 5 Paddy Driver (AJS), 6 Dave Degens (Norton). Fastest lap: Minter, 85.87mph.
500 (25 laps): 1 Minter (Norton), 86.93mph, 2 Mike Hailwood (Norton), 3 Phil Read (Norton), 4 Duff (Matchless), 5 Joe Dunphy (Norton), 6 Dave Williams (Norton). Fastest lap: Minter, 89.01mph.

6 April, Silverstone – Hutchinson 100
350 BMCRC Championship (18 laps, 52.69 miles): 1 Mike Hailwood (AJS), 92.47mph, 2 Mike Duff (AJS), 3 Phil Read (Norton), 4 Paddy Driver (AJS), 5 Peter Preston (Norton), 6 David Downer (Norton). Fastest lap: Read, 94.25mph.
500 BMCRC Championship (18 laps): 1 Derek Minter (Gilera), 97.54mph, 2 John Hartle (Gilera), 3 Phil Read (Norton), 4 Mike Hailwood (Norton), 5 Joe Dunphy (Norton), 6 Duff (Matchless). Fastest lap: Minter, 99.41mph.

12 April, Brands Hatch
350 (10 laps, 26.5 miles): 1 Derek Minter (Norton), 84.57mph, 2 Mike Duff (AJS), 3 Phil Read (Norton), 4 John Hartle (Norton), 5 Paddy Driver (AJS), 6 Joe Dunphy (Norton). Fastest lap: n/a.
500 Redex Trophy (10 laps): 1 Minter (Gilera), 87.29mph, 2 Read (Norton), 3 Driver (Matchless), 4 David Downer (Norton), 5 Dunphy (Norton), 6 Ron Chandler (Matchless). Fastest lap: n/a.
1000 (15 laps): 1 Minter (Gilera), 87.95mph, 2 Hartle (Gilera), 3 Read (Norton), 4 Duff (Matchless), 5 Driver (Matchless), 6 G C Young (Norton). Fastest lap: Minter, 90.34mph (record).

13 April, Scarborough – Cock o' The North
350 (12 laps, 28.92 miles): 1 Monty Buxton (Norton), 61.52mph, 2 Barry Walker (Norton), 3 John Nutter (AJS), 4 D King (Norton), 5 Peter Bettison (Norton), 6 M Hodges (Norton). Fastest lap: Buxton, 62.96mph.
500 (12 laps): 1 Tom Phillips (Norton), 62.93mph, 2 Billie Nelson (Norton), 3 Louis Carr (Matchless), 4 Nutter (Matchless), 5 Dave King (Norton), 6 Bettison (Norton). Fastest lap: Phillips, 64.27mph.

14 April, Snetterton
350 (10 laps, 27.1 miles): 1 Mike Duff (AJS), 82.30mph, 2 Selwyn Griffiths (AJS), 3 Tony Godfrey (Norton), 4 Dave Dicker (AJS), 5 Peter Darvill (AJS), 6 Dave Degens (Norton). Fastest lap: Duff, 85.28mph
500 Molyslip Trophy (10 laps): 1 Sven-Olov Gunnarsson (Norton), 80.01mph, 2 Dave Degens (Matchless), 3 David Downer (Norton), 4 Lewis Young (Matchless), 5 Paddy Driver (Matchless), 6 Roger Hunter (Matchless). Fastest lap: Downer, 82.68mph.

15 April, Oulton Park
350 (19 laps, 52.44 miles): 1 Derek Minter (Norton), 86.76mph, 2 Phil Read (Norton), 3 John Hartle (Norton), 4 John Rae (Norton), 5 Fred Stevens (Norton), 6 Dennis Ainsworth (AJS). Fastest lap: Minter, 88.59mph (equals record).
500 (19 laps): 1 Minter (Gilera), 89.74mph, 2 Hartle (Gilera), 3 Read (Norton), 4 Downer (Norton Domiracer), 5 Bill Smith (Matchless), 6 Derek Woodman (Matchless). Fastest lap: Minter, 91.86mph (record).

15 April, Thruxton – Commonwealth Trophy
350 (10 laps, 22 miles): 1 Mike Duff (AJS), 80.82mph, 2 Peter Preston (Norton), 3 Dave Williams (AJS), 4 Selwyn Griffiths (AJS), 5 Peter Darvill (AJS), 6 Tony Godfrey (Norton). Fastest lap: Duff, 83.72mph.
500 Commonwealth Trophy (12 laps): 1 Duff (Matchless), 83.84mph, 2 Williams (Norton), 3 Tom Phillips (Norton), 4 John Jacques (Norton), 5 Darvill (Norton), 6 Griffiths (Matchless). Fastest lap: Williams, 85.52mph.

15 April, Crystal Palace
350 (10 laps, 13.9 miles): 1 Joe Dunphy (Norton), 74.38mph, 2 Griff Jenkins (AJS), 3 Roger Hunter (AJS), 4 B J Weller (Norton), 5 R Langland (AJS), 6 Jack Simmonds (AJS). Fastest lap: Dunphy, 76.28mph.
500 (10 laps): 1 Jenkins (Norton), 76.40mph, 2 Dunphy (Norton), 3 Hunter (Matchless), 4 Simmonds (Matchless), 5 G Young (Norton), 6 J Wright (Norton). Fastest lap: Dunphy, 76.99mph.

15 April, Cadwell Park
350 (8 laps, 18 miles): 1 John Cooper (Norton), 64.17mph, 2 Billie Nelson (Norton), 3 R Macgregor (Norton), 4 Derek Phillips (Norton), 5 J Simpson (Norton), 6 J Morgan (AJS). Fastest lap: Cooper, 67.05mph
500 (8 laps): 1 Cooper (Norton), 67.30mph, 2 Derek Phillips (Norton), 3 Tony Willmott (Triumph), 4 Norman Archard (Matchless), 5 B Dennehy (Norton), 6 Sid Mizen (Matchless). Fastest lap: Cooper, 69.23mph.

20 April, Castle Combe
350 (10 laps, 18.4 miles): 1 Selwyn Griffiths (AJS), 75.75mph, 2 David Downer (Norton), 3 Ray Watmore (Norton), 4 Peter Darvill (Norton), 5 Noel Wright (Norton), 6 C Howard (Norton). Fastest lap: Griffiths, 77.40mph.
500 (10 laps): 1 Tom Phillips (Norton), 77.43mph, 2 Griffiths (Matchless), 3 Downer (Domiracer), 4 Louis Carr (Matchless), 5 Wright (Norton), 6 Darvill (Norton). Fastest lap: Phillips, 79.62mph.

28 April, Mallory Park

350 (20 laps, 27 miles): 1 Phil Read (Norton), 82.61mph, 2 Griff Jenkins (AJS), 3 Joe Dunphy (Norton), 4 Chris Conn (Norton), 5 Brian Setchell (Norton), 6 John Cooper (Norton). Fastest lap: Read, 88.36mph.

500 (25 laps): 1 Read (Norton), 85.59mph, 2 Dunphy (Norton), 3 David Downer (Domiracer), 4 Jenkins (Norton), 5 Conn (Norton), 6 Cooper (Norton). Fastest lap: Read, 88.36mph.

12 May, Brands Hatch

350 (10 laps, 26.5 miles): 1 Phil Read (Norton), 85.16mph, 2 Derek Minter (Norton), 3 Peter Preston (AJS), 4 David Downer (Norton), 5 Joe Dunphy (Norton), 6 Ian Goddard (AJS). Fastest lap: Read, 87.04mph.

500 Redex Trophy 2 (10 laps): 1 Minter (Norton), 87.20mph, 2 Read (Norton), 3 Downer (Domiracer), 4 Dave Degens (Matchless), 5 Griff Jenkins (Norton), 6 Joe Dunphy (Norton). Fastest lap: Minter, 88.66mph.

1000 (15 laps): 1 Degens (Norton), 85.43mph, 2 Dunphy (Norton), 3 Ron Chandler (Matchless), 4 Lewis Young (Matchless), 5 Rex Butcher (Norton), 6 Dave Williams (Norton). Fastest lap: Minter (Norton), 90.00mph.

3 June, Brands Hatch

350 (20 laps, 53 miles): 1 Griff Jenkins (AJS), 82.74mph, 2 Ian Goddard (AJS), 3 Peter Preston (AJS), 4 Rex Butcher (Norton), 5 Rudi Thalhammer (Norton), 6 Sven-Olov Gunnarsson (Norton). Fastest lap: Jenkins, 84.87mph.

500 (20 laps): 1 Preston (Norton), 83.95mph, 2 Dennis Ainsworth (Matchless), 3 Ron Chandler (Matchless), 4 Jenkins (Norton), 5 Butcher (Norton), 6 Gunnarsson (Norton). Fastest lap: Preston, 86.10mph.

3 June, Cadwell Park

350 (8 laps, 18 miles): 1 John Cooper (Norton), 70.57mph, 2 Tom Phillips (Norton), 3 Selwyn Griffiths (AJS), 4 M Bancroft (AJS), 5 Tony Willmott (AJS), 6 Billie Nelson (Norton). Fastest lap: Cooper, 72.41mph.

500 (8 laps): 1 Cooper (Norton), 72.68mph, 2 Griffiths (Matchless), 3 Phillips (Norton), 4 Nelson (Norton), 5 Derek Phillips (Norton), 6 Willmott (500 A&A Special). Fastest lap: Cooper, 75.14mph.

16 June, Mallory Park

350 (15 laps, 20.25 miles): 1 Dan Shorey (Norton), 82.09mph, 2 Joe Dunphy (Norton), 3 Dave Degens (Norton), 4 Ron Chandler (AJS), 5 Paddy Driver (AJS), 6 Tom Phillips (Norton). Fastest lap: Dunphy, Phil Read (Norton), 84.37mph.

500 (20 laps): 1 Phil Read (Norton), 77.97mph, 2 Dunphy (Norton), 3 Mike Duff (Matchless), 4 Phillips (Norton), 5 Lewis Young (Matchless), 6 Griff Jenkins (Norton). Fastest lap: Read, Dunphy, 79.41mph.

22 June, Scarborough – Cock o' the North

350 (14 laps, 33.74 miles): 1 John Cooper (Norton), 64.03mph, 2 Rob Fitton (Norton), 3 B J Walker (Norton), 4 Dave King (Norton), 5 A J Reed (AJS), 6 Norman Archard (AJS). Fastest lap: Cooper, Tom Phillips (Norton), 65.33mph.

500 (14 laps): 1 Fitton (Norton), 67.05mph, 2 Cooper (Norton), 3 Billie Nelson (Norton), 4 Derek Phillips (Norton), 5 Selwyn Griffiths (Matchless), 6 M L Bennett (Norton). Fastest lap: Fitton, Cooper 67.99mph.

22 June, Thruxton 500

1 Phil Read/Brian Setchell (Norton 650SS), 2 Sid Mizen/John Holder (Triumph Bonneville), 3 J Bowman/Ron Chandler (Triumph Bonneville).

30 June, Cadwell Park

350 (8 laps, 18 miles): 1 Lewis Young (AJS), 63.61mph, 2 Selwyn Griffiths (AJS), 3 Tom Phillips (Norton), 4 Joe Dunphy (Norton), 5 Chris Conn (Norton), 6 B J Walker (Norton). Fastest lap: Griffiths, 66.50mph.

500 (4 laps – rain shortened): 1 Phillips (Domiracer), 64.19mph, 2 Young (Matchless), 3 Rob Fitton (Norton), 4 John Jacques (Matchless), 5 John Cooper (Norton), 6 Dave Degens (Norton). Fastest lap: Phillips, 67.52mph.

Invitation (5 laps): 1 Cooper (Norton), 66.18mph, 2 Roger Hunter (Matchless), 3 Griffiths (Matchless), 4 Tom Phillips (Norton), 5 Derek Phillips (Norton), 6 Young (Matchless). Fastest lap: Griffiths, 70.07mph.

14 July, Brands Hatch

350 (10 laps, 26.5 miles): 1 Phil Read (Norton), 83.56mph, 2 Joe Dunphy (Norton), 3 Dan Shorey (Norton), 4 Chris Conn (Norton), 5 Griff Jenkins (AJS), 6 Lewis Young (AJS). Fastest lap: Read, Shorey, 85.33mph.

500 Redex Trophy, 3 (10 laps): 1 Read (Norton), 85.48mph, 2 Dunphy (Norton), 3 Dennis Ainsworth (Matchless), 4 Jenkins (Norton), 5 Ron Chandler (Matchless), 6 Peter Preston (Norton). Fastest lap: Read, 87.52mph.

1000 Alan Trow Memorial (15 laps): 1 Read (499 Norton), 85.56mph, 2 Dunphy (499 Norton), 3 Ainsworth (496 Matchless), 4 Chandler (496 Matchless), 5 Roger Hunter (Matchless), 6 Young (Matchless). Fastest lap: n/a.

20 July, Castle Combe

350 (10 laps): 1 Dan Shorey (Norton), 82.82mph, 2 Selwyn Griffiths (AJS), 3 Tom Phillips (Norton), 4 Ray Watmore (AJS), 5 Peter Darvill (AJS). Fastest lap: Shorey, 85.16mph.

500 (10 laps): 1 Phillips (Domiracer), 84.68mph, 2 Chris Conn (Norton), 3 Shorey (Norton), 4 Selwyn Griffiths (Matchless), 5 Richard Difazio (Norton). Fastest lap: Phillips, 86.94mph.

21 July, Mallory Park

350 (20 laps, 27 miles): 1 Phil Read (Norton), 84.28mph, 2 John Cooper (Norton), 3 Alan Shepherd (AJS), 4 Dan Shorey (Norton), 5 Roger Hunter (AJS), 6 Griff Jenkins (AJS). Fastest lap: Shepherd, 85.87mph.

500 (25 laps): 1 Read, 85.60mph, 2 Shepherd (Matchless), 3 Joe Dunphy (Norton), 4 Cooper (Norton), 5 Chris Conn (Norton), 6 Hunter (Matchless). Fastest lap: Shepherd, Dunphy, 87.73mph.

28 July, Snetterton
350 (10 laps, 27.1 miles): 1 Joe Dunphy, 88.77mph, 2 Peter Darvill (AJS), 3 Lewis Young (AJS), 4 Roger Hunter (AJS), 5 Selwyn Griffiths (AJS), 6 Brian Davis (AJS). Fastest lap: Dunphy, 90.33mph.
500 (10 laps): 1 Young (Matchless), 91.98mph, 2 Dunphy (Norton), 3 Griffiths (Matchless), 4 Hunter (Matchless), 5 Shorey (Norton), 6 R Macgregor (BSA). Fastest lap: Young, Dunphy 93.27mph.

5 August, Oulton Park – British Championships
350 (30 laps, 82.8 miles): 1 Phil Read, 85.22mph, 2 Alan Shepherd (AJS), 3 Dan Shorey (Norton), 4 Dennis Ainsworth (AJS), 5 Fred Stevens (Norton), 6 Jack Ahearn (Norton). Fastest lap: Read, 87.19mph.
500 (30 laps): 1 Derek Minter (Gilera), 90.62mph, 2 Read (Norton), 3 Shepherd (Matchless), 4 Jack Findlay (Matchless), 5 Mike Duff (Matchless), 6 Gyula Marsovszky (Matchless). Fastest lap: Minter, 92.03 (record).
Les Graham Memorial Trophy (10 laps): 1 Minter (Gilera), 89.30mph, 2 Shorey (Norton), 3 Duff (Matchless), 4 Ainsworth (Matchless), 5 Stevens (Norton), 6 Derek Woodman (Matchless). Fastest lap: Minter, 91.19mph.

5 August, Crystal Palace
350 (12 laps, 16.68 miles): 1 Joe Dunphy (Norton), 71.64mph, 2 Roger Hunter (AJS), 3 Griff Jenkins (AJS), 4 Brian Davis (AJS), 5 Peter Preston (Norton), 6 Ron Chandler (AJS). Fastest lap: Dunphy, 76.51mph.
1000 (12 laps): 1 Dunphy (Norton), 77.82mph, 2 Hunter (Matchless), 3 Jenkins (Norton), 4 Preston (Norton), 5 J C Wilkinson (Norton), 6 Chandler (Matchless). Fastest lap: Dunphy, 80.19mph (record).

5 August, Cadwell Park
350 (8 laps, 18 miles): 1 John Cooper (Norton), 67.01mph, 2 Lewis Young (AJS), 3 Billie Nelson (Norton), 4 M Bancroft (AJS), 5 Tony Willmott (AJS), 6 Roly Capper (AJS). Fastest lap: Cooper, 68.88mph.
500 Coronation Trophy (12 laps, 27 laps): 1 Young (Matchless), 68.55mph, 2 Cooper (Norton), 3 Chris Conn (Norton), 4 Nelson (Norton), 5 Derek Phillips (Norton), 6 M L Bennett (Norton). Fastest lap: Young, 70.31mph.

5 August, Thruxton – Britannia Gold Vase
350 (10 laps, 22 miles): 1 Paddy Driver (AJS), 77.83mph, 2 Tom Phillips (Norton), 3 Dave Williams (Norton), 4 Peter Darvill (AJS), 5 Sid Mizen (AJS), 6 Richard Difazio (Norton). Fastest lap: Williams, 79.68mph.
500 Britannia Gold Vase (12 laps): 1 Driver (Matchless), 82.49mph, 2 Selwyn Griffiths (Matchless), 3 John Jacques (Norton), 4 Mizen (Matchless), 5 Darvill (Norton), 6 Louis Carr (Matchless). Fastest lap: Driver, 84.44mph.

24 August, Aberdare
350 (12 laps, 9.1 miles): 1 John Cooper (Norton), 55.68mph, 2 Selwyn Griffiths (AJS), 3 Tom Phillips (Norton), 4 Malcolm Uphill (Norton), 5 R W Watts (Norton), 6 Carl Ward (Norton). Fastest lap: Cooper, 57.48mph.
500 (12 laps): 1 Cooper (Norton), 56.82mph, 2 Griffiths (Matchless), 3 Dan Shorey (Matchless), 4 Uphill (Norton), 5 Chris Conn (Norton), 6 Louis Carr (Matchless). Fastest lap: Cooper, 58.46mph.
1000 (15 laps): 1 Cooper (499 Norton), 56.83mph, 2 Phillips (650 Domiracer), 3 Shorey (496 Matchless), 4 Griffiths (496 Matchless), 5 Conn (499 Norton), 6 Uphill (Norton). Fastest lap: Cooper, 58.46mph.

25 August, Brands Hatch
350 (10 laps, 26.5 miles): 1 Dennis Ainsworth (AJS), 74.69mph, 2 John Blanchard (AJS), 3 Dan Shorey (AJS), 4 Tom Phillips (Norton), 5 Joe Dunphy (Norton), 6 Jack Smith (Norton). Fastest lap: n/a.
500 Redex Trophy (10 laps): 1 Dunphy (Norton), 77.02mph, 2 Sid Mizen (Domiracer), 3 Phillips (Domiracer), 4 Ainsworth (Matchless), 5 Peter Preston (Norton), 6 Chris Conn (Norton). Fastest lap: n/a.
1000 (10 laps): 1 Dunphy (499 Norton), 75.22mph, 2 Mizen (Domiracer), 3 Preston (499 Norton), 4 Phillips (650 Domiracer), 5 Bill Ivy (Monard), 6 G Young (Norton). Fastest lap: n/a.

8 September, Snetterton
350 (8 laps, 21.68 miles): 1 Joe Dunphy (Norton), 76.97mph, 2 Roger Hunter (AJS), 3 Selwyn Griffiths (AJS), 4 Tom Phillips (Norton), 5 Peter Preston (Norton), 6 Ray Watmore (AJS). Fastest lap: Dunphy, 78.80mph.
500 (8 laps): 1 Dunphy (Norton), 80.16mph, 2 John Cooper (Norton), 3 Hunter (Matchless), 4 Dave Degens (Norton), 5 A Fullerton (Norton), 6 Richard Difazio (Norton). Fastest lap: Dunphy, 82.40mph.

15 September, Cadwell Park
350 (12 laps, 27 miles): 1 John Cooper (Norton), 71.86mph, 2 Joe Dunphy (Norton), 3 Tom Phillips (Norton), 4 Tony Willmott (AJS), 5 Chris Conn (Norton), 6 Rob Fitton (Norton). Fastest lap: Cooper, 73.10mph.
500 (12 laps): 1 Fitton (Norton), 72.60mph, 2 Dunphy (Norton), 3 Derek Phillips (Norton), 4 Selwyn Griffiths (Matchless), 5 Dave Degens (Matchless), 6 Tom Phillips (Domiracer). Fastest lap: Griffiths, 74.72mph.

20 September, Scarborough
350 (16 laps, 38.56 miles): 1 John Cooper (Norton), 66.33mph, 2 Tom Phillips (Norton), 3 Derek Minter (Norton), 4 Billie Rae (Norton), 5 Rob Fitton (AJS), 6 Dan Shorey (AJS). Fastest lap: Minter, 66.33mph.
500 (16 laps): 1 Phil Read (Gilera), 67.14mph, 2 Cooper (Norton), 3 Phillips (Domiracer), 4 Shorey (Matchless), 5 George Buchan (Norton), 6 Billie Nelson (Norton). Fastest lap: Read, 68.31mph.

22 September, Brands Hatch
350 Fred Neville Memorial (10 laps, 26.5 miles): 1 Mike Duff (AJS), 83.11mph, 2 Joe Dunphy (Norton), 3 Phil Read (Norton), 4 Dennis

Ainsworth (AJS), 5 Sid Mizen (AJS), 6 Tom Phillips (Norton). Fastest lap: n/a.
500 Redex Trophy (10 laps): 1 Derek Minter (Gilera), 87.95mph, 2 Read (Gilera), 3 Duff (Matchless), 4 Dunphy (Norton), 5 Paddy Driver (Matchless), 6 Ainsworth (Matchless). Fastest lap: n/a.
1000 (15 laps): 1 Minter (499 Gilera), 88.11mph, 2 Read (499 Gilera), 3 Dunphy (499 Norton), 4 Duff (496 Matchless), 5 Ainsworth (496 Matchless), 6 Driver (496 Matchless). Fastest lap: n/a.

29 September, Mallory Park – Race of the Year
350 (25 laps, 33.75 miles): 1 Jim Redman (340 Honda), 84.40mph, 2 Alan Shepherd (AJS), 3 Dennis Ainsworth (Norton), 4 Derek Minter (Norton), 5 Griff Jenkins (AJS), 6 John Cooper (Norton). Fastest lap: Redman, 87.10mph.
500 (25 laps): 1 Mike Hailwood (MV), 83.84mph, 2 Shepherd (Matchless), 3 Minter (Gilera), 4 Phil Read (Gilera), 5 John Cooper (Norton), 6 Mike Duff (Matchless). Fastest lap: Hailwood, 86.48mph.
Race of the Year (40 laps): 1 Hailwood (MV), 89.12mph, 2 Minter (Gilera), 3 Shepherd (Matchless), 4 Read (Gilera), 5 Redman (340 Honda), 6 Cooper (Norton). Fastest lap: Hailwood, 90.68mph.

5 October, Oulton Park
350 (8 laps, 22.08 miles): 1 Phil Read (Norton), 85.21mph, 2 Derek Minter (Norton), 3 Mike Duff (AJS), 4 Tom Phillips (Norton), 5 Keith Heckles (Norton), 6 Fred Stevens (Norton). Fastest lap: Read, 86.58mph.
500: (8 laps): 1 Read (Norton), 87.86mph, 2 Minter (Norton), 3 Duff (Matchless), 4 Dennis Ainsworth (Norton), 5 Rex Butcher (Norton), 6 Billie Rae (Norton). Fastest lap: Minter, 88.91mph.
350 Bob McIntyre Handicap (8 laps): 1 Dan Shorey (AJS), 82.59mph, 2 Chris Conn (Norton), 3 Peter Bettison (Norton), 4 Butcher (Norton), 5 G Morgan (AJS), 6 Peter Preston (Norton). Fastest lap: Read (Norton), 86.73mph.

13 October, Brands Hatch
350 (10 laps, 26.5 miles): 1 Phil Read (Norton), 85.13mph, 2 Derek Minter (Norton), 3 John Hartle (Norton), 4 Dennis Ainsworth (Norton), 5 Joe Dunphy (Norton), 6 Paddy Driver (AJS). Fastest lap: n/a.
500 Redex Trophy (10 laps): 1 Read (Norton), 87.74mph, 2 Minter (Norton), 3 Dunphy (Norton), 4 Duff (Matchless), 5 Ainsworth (Norton), 6 Dave Degens (Matchless). Fastest lap: n/a.
1000 (15 laps): 1 Minter (Norton), 86.88mph, 2 Ainsworth (Norton), 3 Dunphy (499 Norton), 4 Degens (496 Matchless), 5 Rex Butcher (Norton), 6 Duff (496 Matchless). Fastest lap: n/a.

ACU Road Racing Stars:
350: 1 Phil Read, 2 Joe Dunphy, 3 John Cooper
500: 1 Read, 2 Dunphy, 3 Cooper

1964
22 March, Mallory Park
350 (15 laps, 20.25 miles): 1 John Hartle (Norton), 80.52mph, 2 Derek Minter (Norton), 3 John Cooper (Norton), 4 Mike Duff (AJS), 5 Phil Read (AJS), 6 Tom Phillips (Aermacchi). Fastest lap: Minter, Duff, 83.50mph.
500 (20 laps): 1 Minter (Norton), 84.13mph, 2 Read (Matchless), 3 Hartle (Norton), 4 Duff (Matchless), 5 Cooper (Norton), 6 Carl Ward (Norton). Fastest lap: Minter, 87.41mph.

27 March, Brands Hatch
350 (10 laps, 26.5 miles): 1 Phil Read (AJS), 83.33mph, 2 John Hartle (Norton), 3 Dennis Ainsworth (Norton), 4 Rex Butcher (Norton), 5 Paddy Driver (AJS), 6 Lewis Young (AJS). Fastest lap: n/a.
500 Redex Trophy (10 laps): 1 Minter (Norton), 77.09mph, 2 Read (Matchless), 3 Hartle (Norton), 4 Dave Degens (Matchless), 5 Joe Dunphy (Norton), 6 Young (Matchless). Fastest lap: n/a.
1000 (15 laps): 1 Minter (499 Norton), 77.55mph, 2 Read (496 Matchless), 3 Degens (496 Matchless), 4 Mike Duff (496 Matchless), 5 Griff Jenkins (499 Norton), 6 Young (496 Matchless). Fastest lap: n/a.

29 March, Snetterton
350 (10 laps, 27.1 miles): 1 John Hartle (Norton), 87.52mph, 2 Othmar Drixl (Aermacchi), 3 Tom Phillips (Aermacchi), 4 Dan Shorey (AJS), 5 Dennis Ainsworth (Norton), 6 Joe Dunphy (Norton). Fastest lap: Hartle, 89.83mph.
500 (10 laps): 1 Derek Minter (Norton), 90.84mph, 2 Hartle (Norton), 3 Gyula Marsovszky (Matchless), 4 Chris Conn (Norton), 5 Tom Phillips (Norton), 6 J Smith (Norton). Fastest lap: Hartle, Conn, 92.38mph.

30 March, Oulton Park
350 (19 laps, 52.44 miles): 1 Phil Read (Norton), 84.17mph, 2 John Hartle (Norton), 3 Dennis Ainsworth (Norton), 4 Derek Woodman (AJS), 5 J Evans (Norton), 6 Dan Shorey (Norton). Fastest lap: Read, 85.69mph.
500 (19 laps): 1 Read (Norton), 86.64mph, 2 Hartle (Norton), 3 Ainsworth (Norton), 4 Brian Warburton (Norton), 5 Woodman (Matchless), 6 George Buchan (Norton). Fastest lap: Read, 88.59mph.

30 March, Thruxton – Commonwealth Trophy
350 (10 laps, 22 miles): 1 Dave Williams (MW Special), 80.92mph, 2 Ray Pickrell (AJS), 3 Ray Watmore (AJS), 4 Maurice Low (AJS), 5 B Davies (AJS), 6 Sid Mizen (AJS). Fastest lap: Williams, 83.2mph.
500 Commonwealth Trophy (12 laps): 1 Mike Duff (Matchless), 83.21mph, 2 Tom Phillips (Norton), 3 Williams (Norton), 4 Low (Norton), 5 Ginger Molloy (Norton), 6 Ray Pickrell (Norton). Fastest lap: Duff, 85.34mph.

30 March, Crystal Palace
350 (8 laps, 11.12 miles): 1 Jack Simmonds (AJS), 73.10mph, 2 Griff Jenkins (AJS), 3 Joe Dunphy (AJS), 4 Peter Williams (Norton),

202

5 R Flack (Norton), 6 Alan Peck (Norton). Fastest lap: Young, 68.94mph.
500 (8 laps): 1 Dunphy (Matchless), 70.30mph, 2 Roger Hunter (Matchless), 3 J Wilkinson (Norton), 4 Simmonds (Norton), 5 Dave Croxford (Matchless), 6 G Young (Norton). Fastest lap: Hunter, 72.52mph.

30 March, Cadwell Park
350 (8 laps, 18 miles): 1 Lewis Young (AJS), 64.90mph, 2 John Cooper (Norton), 3 Chris Conn (Norton), 4 Billie Nelson (Norton), 5 Rob Fitton (Norton), 6 M Bancroft (AJS). Fastest lap: Young, 68.94mph.
500 (8 laps): 1 Cooper (Norton), 65.18mph, 2 Young (Matchless), 3 Conn (Norton), 4 Nelson (Norton), 5 Selwyn Griffiths (Matchless), 6 Fitton (Norton). Fastest lap: Cooper, 67.50mph.

4 April, Silverstone – Hutchinson 100
350 (18 laps, 52.69 miles): 1 Jim Redman (Honda), 86.09mph, 2 Tom Phillips (Aermacchi), 3 Phil Read (AJS), 4 John Cooper (Norton), 5 Derek Minter (Norton), 6 Dave Williams (MW Special). Fastest lap: Redman, 88.70mph.
500 (15 lap – rain shortened): 1 Mike Hailwood (MV), 89.11mph, 2 Read (Matchless), 3 Phillips (Norton), 4 Cooper (Norton), 5 Carl Ward (Norton), 6 Chris Conn (Norton). Fastest lap: Hailwood, 93.75mph.

18 April, Castle Combe
350 (10 laps, 18.4 miles): 1 Ray Watmore (AJS), 86.06mph, 2 Chris Conn (Norton), 3 Tom Dickie (AJS), 4 A Fullerton (Norton), 5 Brian Davis (AJS). Fastest lap: Minter, 89.29mph (record).
500 (10 laps): 1 Phillips (Norton), 88.47mph, 2 Conn (Norton), 3 Jack Smith (Norton), 4 Selwyn Griffiths (Matchless), 5 Peter Darvill (Norton). Fastest lap: Phillips, 90.75mph (record).

19 April, Brands Hatch
350 (10 laps, 26.5 miles): 1 Derek Minter, 81.53mph, 2 Tom Phillips (Aermacchi), 3 Tom Dickie (AJS), 4 John Cooper (Norton), 5 Chris Conn (Norton), 6 Brian Davis (AJS). Fastest lap: n/a.
500 Redex Trophy (10 laps): 1 Phillips (Norton), 74.54mph, 2 Minter (Norton), 3 Dave Degens (Matchless), 4 D. Chester (Norton), 5 Cooper (Norton), 6 Griff Jenkins (Norton). Fastest lap: n/a.
1000 (10 laps): 1 Phillips (499 Norton), 75.29mph, 2 Cooper (499 Norton), 3 Minter (499 Norton), 4 Degens (649 Triton), 5 Bill Ivy (500 Monard), 6 Dave Croxford (496 Matchless). Fastest lap: n/a.

26 April, Snetterton
350 (10 laps, 27.1 miles): 1 Tom Phillips (Aermacchi), 89.12mph, 2 Derek Minter (Norton), 3 Dave Williams (MW Special), 4 Chris Conn (Norton), 5 Dave Degens (AJS), 6 Joe Dunphy (AJS). Fastest lap: Phillips, 91.35mph.
1000 Senior Service Trophy (10 laps): 1 Minter (499 Norton), 91.38mph, 2 Phillips (499 Norton), 3 Bill Ivy (650 Monard), 4 Peter Darvill (499 Norton), 5 Conn (499 Norton), 6 Ray Pickrell (499 Norton). Fastest lap: Minter, 93.27mph.

3 May, Mallory Park
350 (15 laps, 20.25 miles): 1 John Cooper (Norton), 83.39mph, 2 Griff Jenkins (AJS), 3 Derek Minter (Norton), 4 Dave Williams (Aermacchi), 5 Chris Conn (Norton), 6 Tom Phillips (Aermacchi). Fastest lap: Conn, 85.87mph.
500 (20 laps): 1 Cooper (Norton), 85.39mph, 2 Jenkins (Norton), 3 Conn (Norton), 4 Dave Degens (Matchless), 5 Ron Chandler (Matchless), 6 A Fullerton (Norton). Fastest lap: Cooper, 87.41mph.

9 May, Aberdare
350 (12 laps, 9.1 miles): 1 John Cooper (Norton), 55.63mph, 2 Malcolm Uphill (Norton), 3 Tom Phillips (Aermacchi), 4 Tony Willmott (Norton), 5 Dave Degens (AJS), 6 Billie Nelson (Norton). Fastest lap: Cooper, 57mph.
500 (12 laps): 1 Cooper (Norton), 56.51mph, 2 Uphill (Norton), 3 Griffiths (Matchless), 4 Phillips (Norton), 5 Nelson (Norton), 6 J C Buxton (Norton). Fastest lap: Cooper, 60.53mph (record).
1000 (15 laps): 1 Cooper (499 Norton), 57.16mph, 2 Uphill (499 Norton), 3 Phillips (650 Domiracer), 4 Griffiths (496 Matchless), 5 Willmott (Norton), 6 Dave Degens (650 Triumph). Fastest lap: Cooper, 58.46mph.

10 May, Snetterton
350 (10 laps, 27.1 miles): 1 Dennis Ainsworth (Norton), 88.04mph, 2 Chris Conn (Norton), 3 Lewis Young (AJS), 4 Rex Butcher (Norton), 5 Tom Dickie (AJS), 6 Derek Minter (Norton). Fastest lap: John Cooper (Norton), 90.5mph.
500 (10 laps): 1 Minter (Norton), 91.87mph, 2 Joe Dunphy (Norton), 3 Rex Butcher (Norton), 4 Cooper (Norton), 5 Conn (Norton), 6 Dave Degens (Norton). Fastest lap: Minter, 94.35mph.

16 May, Scarborough
350 (10 laps, 24.1 miles): 1 John Cooper (Norton), 65.46mph, 2 Chris Conn (Norton), 3 Billie Nelson (Norton), 4 Dan Shorey (Norton), 5 George Buchan (Norton), 6 Billie Rae (Norton). Fastest lap: Cooper, 66.23mph.
500 (10 laps): 1 Cooper (Norton), 66.56mph, 2 Conn (Norton), 3 Buchan (Norton), 4 Shorey (Norton), 5 Carl Ward (Norton), 6 M L Bennett (Norton). Fastest lap: Cooper, Nelson (Norton) 67.88mph.

18 May, Cadwell Park
350 (8 laps, 18 miles): 1 John Cooper (Norton), 71.65mph, 2 Tom Phillips (Aermacchi), 3 Lewis Young (AJS), 4 Chris Conn (Norton), 5 Roly Capper (AJS), 6 Carl Ward (Norton). Fastest lap: Cooper, 72.97mph.
500 (8 laps): 1 Cooper (Norton), 74.06mph, 2 Billie Nelson (Norton), 3 Conn (Norton), 4 Young (Matchless), 5 Ward (Norton), 6 Tony Willmott (Norton). Fastest lap: Cooper, 75.98mph.

18 May, Brands Hatch
350 (20 laps, 53 miles): 1 Phil Read (AJS), 83.06mph, 2 Paddy Driver (AJS), 3 Dave Williams (MW Special), 4 Rex Butcher (Norton), 5 Cyril Davey (Norton), 6 Griff Jenkins (AJS). Fastest lap: Read, 85.33mph.
500 (20 laps): 1 Derek Minter (Norton), 84.45mph, 2 Driver (Matchless), 3 Butcher (Norton), 4 Jenkins (Norton), 5 Roger Hunter (Matchless), 6 Dave Degens (Dunstall Domiracer). Fastest lap: Minter, 86.41mph

14 June, Mallory Park
350 (15 laps, 20.25 miles): 1 John Cooper (Norton), 84.12mph, 2 Phil Read (AJS), 3 Dave Williams (MW Special), 4 Chris Conn (Norton), 5 Derek Minter (Norton), 6 Carl Ward (Norton). Fastest lap: Cooper, Read, 85.87mph.
500 (20 laps): 1 Cooper (Norton), 86.12mph, 2 Williams (Norton), 3 Dunphy (Norton), 4 Griff Jenkins (Norton), 5 Rex Butcher (Norton), 6 Ron Chandler (Matchless). Fastest lap: Cooper, 88.36mph.

21 June, Brands Hatch
350 (10 laps, 26.5 miles): 1 Derek Minter (Norton), 83.13mph, 2 John Cooper (Norton), 3 Dave Degens (AJS), 4 Rex Butcher (Norton), 5 Bill Ivy (AJS), 6 Mike Duff (AJS). Fastest lap: n/a.
500 Redex Trophy (10 laps): 1 Minter (Norton), 87.15mph, 2 Cooper (Norton), 3 Griff Jenkins (Norton), 4 Degens (Dunstall Domiracer), 5 Joe Dunphy (Norton), 6 Duff (Matchless). Fastest lap: n/a.
1000 (10 laps): 1 Minter (499 Norton), 85.19mph, 2 Cooper (499 Norton), 3 Dunphy (499 Norton), 4 Butcher (499 Norton), 5 Duff (496 Matchless), 6 Dennis Ainsworth (Norton). Fastest lap: n/a.

26/27 June, Scarborough – Cock o' the North
350 (12 laps, 28.92 miles): 1 John Cooper (Norton), 64.52mph, 2 Rob Fitton (Norton), 3 Billie Nelson (Norton), 4 Norman Archard (AJS), 5 B.M. Walker (AJS), 6 A.J. Reed (AJS). Fastest lap: 65.43mph.
500 (12 laps): 1 Cooper (Norton), 66.45mph, 2 Fitton (Norton), 3 Nelson (Norton), 4 Rex Butcher (Norton), 5 Louis Carr (Matchless), 6 Dave King (Norton). Fastest lap: Cooper, 67.67mph.

12 July, Mallory Park
350 (15 lap, 20.25 miles): 1 John Cooper (Norton), 82.06mph, 2 John Blanchard (AJS), 3 Ron Chandler (AJS), 4 Derek Chatterton (Norton), 5 Norman Archard (AJS), 6 Peter Bettison (Norton). Fastest lap: Cooper, 84.37mph.
500 (20 laps): 1 Cooper (Norton), 83.63mph, 2 Carl Ward (Norton), 3 Rob Fitton (Norton), 4 Bettison (Norton), 5 J Sear (Matchless), 6 J Brillard (Norton). Fastest lap: Cooper, 86.48mph.

25 July, Castle Combe
350 (10 laps, 18.4 miles): 1 Derek Minter (Norton), 85.26mph, 2 Chris Conn (Norton), 3 Ray Watmore (AJS). Fastest lap: Minter, 87.87mph.
500 (10 laps): 1 Minter (Norton), 2 Conn (Norton), 3 Selwyn Griffiths (Matchless). Fastest lap: Minter, 91.25mph (record).

26 July, Snetterton
350 (10 laps, 27.1 miles): 1 Derek Minter (Norton), 88.02mph, 2 John Cooper (Norton), 3 Dave Williams (MW Special), 4 Rex Butcher (Norton), 5 Dave Degens (AJS), 6 Bill Ivy (Norton). Fastest lap: Williams, 91.18mph.
500 (10 laps): 1 Minter (Norton), 91.26mph, 2 Cooper (Norton), 3 Chris Conn (Norton), 4 Rex Butcher (Norton), 5 Jack Simmonds (Norton), 6 Dave Croxford (Matchless). Fastest lap: Minter, 93.27mph.

3 August, Oulton Park – British Championships
350 (25 laps, 69 miles): 1 Mike Duff (AJS), 82.04mph, 2 John Evans (Norton), 3 John Cooper (Norton), 4 Derek Woodman (AJS), 5 Peter Bettison (Norton), 6 Bill Ivy (Norton). Fastest lap: Bruce Beale (305 Honda), 85.39mph.
500 (25 laps): 1 Derek Minter (Norton), 86.41mph, 2 Woodman (Matchless), 3 Duff (Matchless), 4 Gyula Marsovszky (Matchless), 5 Dan Shorey (Norton), 6 Bettison (Norton). Fastest lap: Woodman, 87.96mph.
Les Graham Memorial Trophy (10 laps): 1 Cooper (Norton), 78.62mph, 2 Phil Read (Norton), 3 Ivy (Monard), 4 Brian Warburton (Norton), 5 Minter (Norton), 6 Woodman (Matchless). Fastest lap: Cooper, 79.64mph.

3 August, Crystal Palace
350 (12 laps, 16.68 miles): 1 Ron Chandler (AJS), 73.75mph, 2 Cyril Davey (Norton), 3 Roger Hunter (AJS), 4 Alan Peck (Norton), 5 Brian Davis (AJS), 6 Charlie Sanby (AJS). Fastest lap: Joe Dunphy (Norton), 76.51mph.
1000 (12 laps): 1 Jack Simmonds (Norton), 76.81mph, 2 Dunphy (Norton), 3 Hunter (Matchless), 4 Griff Jenkins (Norton), 5 K Inwood (Norton), 6 Davis (Matchless). Fastest lap: Dunphy, 78.43mph.

3 August Thruxton
350 (10 laps, 22 miles): 1 Alan Harris (Norton), 80.95mph, 2 Dave Williams (MW Special), 3 Ray Watmore (AJS), 4 Maurice Low (AJS), 5 John Williams (AJS), 6 Malcolm Uphill (Norton). Fastest lap: Dave Williams, Paddy Driver (AJS), 83.19mph.
500 (12 laps): 1 Driver (Matchless), 84.23mph, 2 Dave Williams (Norton), 3 Ray Pickrell (Norton), 4 W Molloy (Norton), 5 Watmore (Matchless), 6 Low (Norton). Fastest lap: Williams, 87.03mph.

3 August, Cadwell Park – Coronation Trophy
350 (8 laps, 18 miles): 1 Lewis Young (AJS), 69.32ph, 2 Chris Conn (Norton), 3 Billie Nelson (Norton), 4 Selwyn Griffiths (AJS), 5 Rod Gould (Norton). Fastest lap: Conn, 71.18mph.
Coronation Trophy (12 laps): 1 Conn (Norton), 72.05mph, 2 Rob Fitton (Norton), 3 Derek Phillips (Norton), 4 G Buxton (Norton), 5 M Bennett (Norton). Fastest lap: Phillips, 73.64mph.

16 August, Brands Hatch
350 (10 laps, 26.5 miles): 1 Derek Minter (Norton), 83.01mph, 2 Paddy Driver (AJS), 3 Chris Conn (Norton), 4 Mike Duff (AJS), 5 Rex Butcher (Norton), 6 Ray Pickrell (Norton). Fastest lap: n/a.
500 Redex Trophy (10 laps): 1 Minter (Norton), 84.51mph, 2 Paddy Driver (Matchless), 3 Dave Degens (Dunstall Domiracer), 4 Joe Dunphy (Norton), 5 Jack Smith (Norton), 6 Duff (Matchless). Fastest lap: n/a.

22 August, Aberdare
350 (12 laps, 9.1 miles): 1 John Cooper (Norton), 56.63mph, 2 Dan Shorey (Norton), 3 Malcolm Uphill (Norton), 4 Selwyn Griffiths (AJS), 5 Jack Smith (Norton), 6 Billie Nelson (Norton). Fastest lap: Cooper, 58.46mph (equals record).
500 (12 laps): 1 Selwyn Griffiths (Matchless), 56.86mph, 2 Shorey (Norton), 3 Chris Conn (Norton), 4 Nelson (Norton), 5 Carl Ward (Norton), 6 Tony Willmott (Norton). Fastest lap: Griffiths, 57.97mph.
1000 (15 laps): 1 Griffiths (496 Matchless), 56.83mph, 2 Shorey (499 Norton), 3 Uphill (499 Norton), 4 Willmott (Norton), 5 Ward (Norton), 6 Roly Capper (496 Matchless). Fastest lap: Uphill, 59.48mph (record).

30 August, Mallory Park
350 (15 laps, 20.25 miles): 1 John Cooper (Norton), 82.32mph, 2 Ray Watmore (AJS), 3 Norman Archard (AJS), 4 Jack Simmonds (Norton), 5 Carl Ward (Norton), 6 Bill Ivy (Norton). Fastest lap: Cooper, 85.26mph.
500 (20 laps): 1 Cooper (Norton), 84.00mph, 2 Ward (Norton), 3 Dave Strickland (Matchless), 4 Simmonds (Norton), 5 Ivy (Monard), 6 Dave Croxford (Matchless). Fastest lap: Cooper, 85.87mph.

5 September, Castle Combe
350 (10 laps, 18.4 miles): 1 John Cooper (Norton), 86.13mph, 2 Chris Conn (Norton), 3 Othmar Drixl (Aermacchi), 4 Ray Watmore (AJS), 5 Rod Gould (Norton), 6 A J Reed (Norton). Fastest lap: Conn, 88.10mph
500 (10 laps): 1 Cooper (Norton), 89.48mph, 2 Conn (Norton), 3 Ray Watmore (Matchless), 4 Selwyn Griffiths (AJS), 5 Derek Best (Norton), 6 Ron Chandler (Norton). Fastest lap: Conn, 91.25mph (equals record).

6 September, Snetterton
350 (10 laps, 27.1 miles): 1 Derek Minter (Norton), 88.81mph, 2 John Cooper (Norton), 3 Alan Peck (Norton), 4 Bill Ivy (Norton), 5 Chris Conn (Norton), 6 Ray Watmore (AJS). Fastest lap: Minter, 91.01mph.
500 (10 laps): 1 Minter (Norton), 91.14mph, 2 Conn (Norton), 3 Watmore (Matchless), 4 Cooper (Norton), 5 Jack Simmonds (Norton), 6 Joe Dunphy (Norton). Fastest lap: Minter, 94.35mph.

13 September, Cadwell Park
350 (12 laps, 27 miles): 1 Chris Conn (Norton), 71.44mph, 2 Rod Gould (Norton), 3 Lewis Young (AJS), 4 Rob Fitton (Norton), 5 Selwyn Griffiths (AJS), 6 Billie Nelson (Norton). Fastest lap: Cooper, 74.45mph.
500 (12 laps): 1 Conn (Norton), 72.95mph, 2 Bill Ivy (Monard), 3 Dan Shorey (Norton), 4 Joe Dunphy (Norton), 5 Griffiths (Matchless), 6 Tony Willmott (Norton). Fastest lap: Conn, 76.42mph (record).

18 September, Scarborough
350 (16 laps, 38.56 miles): 1 Phil Read (251 Yamaha), 65.89mph, 2 John Cooper (Norton), 3 Chris Conn (Norton), 4 George Buchan (Norton), 5 Dan Shorey (Norton), 6 Rex Butcher (Norton). Fastest lap: 67.15mph.
500 (16 laps): 1 Derek Woodman (Matchless), 67.45mph, 2 Conn (Norton), 3 Rob Fitton (Norton), 4 Shorey (Norton), 5 Dave King (Norton), 6 Carl Ward (Norton). Fastest lap: Conn, Woodman, 68.31mph.

20 September, Brands Hatch
350 (10 laps, 26.5 miles): 1 John Cooper (Norton), 83.36mph, 2 Paddy Driver (AJS), 3 Derek Minter (Norton), 4 Rex Butcher (Norton), 5 Dave Degens (AJS), 6 Griff Jenkins (Norton). Fastest lap: Minter, 84.87mph.
500 Redex Trophy (10 laps): 1 Minter (Norton), 84.92mph, 2 Joe Dunphy (Norton), 3 Paddy Driver (Matchless), 4 Cooper (Norton), 5 Ivy (Monard), 6 Jenkins (Norton). Fastest lap: Minter, 86.41mph.
1000 (10 laps): 1 Minter (499 Norton), 85.02mph, 2 Dave Degens (647 Dunstall Domiracer), 3 Cooper (Norton), 4 Driver (496 Matchless), 5 Dave Croxford (496 Matchless), 6 Chris Conn (Norton). Fastest lap: Minter, 87.52mph.

27 September, Mallory Park – Race of the Year
350 (25 laps, 33.75 miles): 1 Phil Read (251 Yamaha), 85.67mph, 2 Jim Redman (305 Honda), 3 John Cooper (Norton), 4 Derek Minter (Norton), 5 Derek Woodman (AJS), 6 Dan Shorey (Norton). Fastest lap: Read, 90.67mph (record).
500 (25 laps): 1 Mike Hailwood (MV), 87.74mph, 2 John Cooper (Norton), 3 Chris Conn (Norton), 4 Joe Dunphy (Norton), 5 Bill Ivy (Monard), 6 Derek Minter (Norton). Fastest lap: Hailwood, 90.00mph.
Race of the Year (40 laps): 1 Hailwood (MV), 87.09mph, 2 Cooper (Norton), 3 Minter (Norton), 4 Redman (305 Honda), 5 Dunphy (Norton), 6 Ivy (Monard). Fastest lap: Hailwood, 90.00mph.

3 October, Oulton Park
350 (8 laps, 22.08 miles): 1 John Cooper (Norton), 84.31mph, 2 Derek Minter (Norton), 3 Dan Shorey (Norton), 4 Rob Fitton (Norton), 5 Dave Simmonds (Honda), 6 Mike Duff (AJS). Fastest lap: Minter, 86.58mph.
500 Bob McIntyre Memorial (8 laps): 1 Minter (Norton), 86.26mph, 2 Cooper (Norton), 3 Dave Croxford (Matchless), 4 Bill Ivy (Monard), 5 Joe Dunphy (Norton), 6 J Evans (Norton). Fastest lap: Minter, 87.80mph.

11 October, Brands Hatch
350 (8 laps, 21.2 miles): 1 John Cooper (Norton), 82.54mph, 2 Mike Duff (AJS), 3 Derek Minter (Norton), 4 Dave Croxford (AJS), 5 Griff Jenkins (Norton), 6 Bill Ivy (Norton). Fastest lap: n/a.

500 Redex Trophy (10 laps): 1 Minter (Norton), 82.86mph, 2 Duff (Matchless), 3 Jenkins (Norton), 4 Joe Dunphy (Norton), 5 Croxford (Matchless), 6 Bill Ivy (Monard). Fastest lap: n/a.
1000 (10 laps): 1 Minter (499 Norton), 85.96mph, 2 Dave Degens (647 Dunstall Dominator), 3 Dunphy (499 Norton), 4 Bill Ivy (649 Triumph), 5 Griff Jenkins (499 Norton), 6 Croxford (496 Matchless). Fastest lap: n/a.

ACU Road Racing Stars:
350, 1 John Cooper, 2 Derek Minter, 3 Chris Conn
500, 1 Minter, 2 Cooper, 3 Conn

1965
7 March, Mallory Park
350 (10 laps, 13.5 miles): 1 John Cooper (Norton), 82.68mph, 2 Joe Dunphy (Norton), 3 Bill Ivy (Norton), 4 Derek Minter (Norton), 5 Rex Butcher (Norton), 6 Peter Williams (Norton). Fastest lap: Cooper, 85.26mph.
500 (15 laps): 1 Cooper (Norton), 85.58mph, 2 Minter (Norton), 3 Dunphy (Norton), 4 Dave Williams (Norton), 5 Dave Degens (Matchless), 6 Chris Conn (Norton). Fastest lap: Cooper, 87.73mph.

21 March, Brands Hatch
350 (10 laps, 26.5 miles): 1 Dave Degens (Aermacchi), 74.82mph, 2 Derek Minter (Norton), 3 John Cooper (Norton), 4 Dave Williams (AJS), 5 Bill Ivy (Norton), 6 Dave Croxford (AJS). Fastest lap: Degens, 76.93mph.
500 Redex Trophy (10 laps): 1 Minter (Norton), 81.20mph, 2 Degens (Dunstall Domiracer), 3 Joe Dunphy (Norton), 4 Dave Croxford (Matchless), 5 Lewis Young (Matchless), 6 Griff Jenkins (Norton). Fastest lap: Minter, 83.53mph.
1000 (10 laps): 1 Degens (647 Dunstall Domiracer), 82.78mph, 2 Minter (499 Norton), 3 Ivy (649 Monard), 4 Young (496 Matchless), 5 Dunphy (499 Norton), 6 Croxford (496 Matchless). Fastest lap: Degens, Minter, 84.12mph.

27 March, Snetterton
350 (10 laps, 27.1 miles): 1 Dan Shorey (Norton), 89.50mph, 2 John Cooper (Norton), 3 Derek Minter (Norton), 4 Bill Ivy (Norton), 5 Rod Gould (Norton), 6 Dave Croxford (AJS). Fastest lap: Minter, 92.04mph.
500 (10 laps): 1 Minter (Norton), 93.40mph, 2 Shorey (Norton), 3 Joe Dunphy (Norton), 4 Cooper (Norton), 5 Ivy (Monard), 6 Stuart Graham (Matchless). Fastest lap: Minter, Shorey, 95.27mph.

9 April, Scarborough
350 (10 laps, 24.1 miles): 1 Dan Shorey (Norton), 65.18mph, 2 John Cooper (Norton), 3 George Buchan (Norton), 4 Barry Randle (Norton), 5 Ray Watmore (AJS), 6 Selwyn Griffiths (AJS). Fastest lap: Shorey, 66.63mph.
500 (10 laps): 1 Cooper (Norton), 66.79mph, 2 Shorey (Norton), 3 Buchan (Norton), 4 Griffiths (Matchless), 5 Billie Nelson (Norton), 6 Watmore (Matchless). Fastest lap: Cooper, 67.78mph.

16 April, Brands Hatch – King of Brands
350 (10 laps, 26.5 miles): 1 Derek Minter, 83.39mph, 2 Mike Duff (AJS), 3 Dan Shorey (Norton), 4 Dave Croxford (AJS), 5 Jack Smith (Norton), 6 Paddy Driver (AJS). Fastest lap: Phil Read (254 Yamaha), 87.20mph.
500 Redex Trophy (10 laps): 1 Minter (Norton), 86.03mph, 2 Bill Ivy (Monard), 3 Dave Degens (Dunstall Domiracer), 4 Paddy Driver (Matchless), 5 Dave Croxford (Matchless), 6 Smith (Norton). Fastest lap: Minter, Croxford, 87.20mph.
1000 King of Brands (10 laps): 1 Derek Minter (499 Norton), 86.64mph, 2 Read (254 Yamaha), 3 Joe Dunphy (499 Norton), 4 Paddy Driver (496 Matchless), 5 Dave Croxford (496 Matchless), 6 John Cooper (499 Norton). Fastest lap: Minter, 88.00mph.

18 April, Snetterton – Race of Aces
350 (10 laps, 27.1 miles): 1 Phil Read (254 Yamaha), 91.18mph, 2 Dan Shorey (Norton), 3 Derek Minter (Norton), 4 John Cooper (Norton), 5 Dave Croxford (AJS), 6 Mike Hailwood (AJS). Fastest lap: Read, 92.73mph (record).
500 Race of Aces (10 laps): 1 Hailwood (Norton), 91.88mph, 2 Shorey (Norton), 3 Dave Degens (Dunstall Domiracer), 4 Derek Minter (Norton), 5 Lewis Young (Matchless), 6 Bill Ivy (Monard). Fastest lap: Hailwood, 93.99mph.

19 April, Oulton Park
350 (19 laps, 52.44 miles): 1 Derek Minter (Norton), 83.50mph, 2 Dan Shorey (Norton), 3 Mike Duff (AJS), 4 Bill Ivy (Norton), 5 Dennis Ainsworth (Norton), 6 John Cooper (Norton). Fastest lap: Minter, 86.43mph.
500 (19 laps): 1 Cooper (Norton), 86.19mph, 2 Minter (Norton), 3 Shorey (Norton), 4 Dave Degens (Dunstall Domiracer), 5 Joe Dunphy (Norton), 6 Griff Jenkins (Norton). Fastest lap: Cooper, 90.86mph.

19 April, Cadwell Park
350 (8 laps, 18 miles): 1 Tom Phillips (Aermacchi), 63.75mph, 2 Rod Gould (Norton), 3 Billie Nelson (Norton), 4 Rob Fitton (Norton), 5 Lewis Young (AJS), 6 Carl Ward (Norton). Fastest lap: Phillips, 65.75mph.
500 (12 laps): 1 Nelson (Norton), 62.92mph, 2 Phillips (Norton), 3 Young (Matchless), 4 Chris Conn (Norton), 5 A Georgeades (Norton), 6 Selwyn Griffiths (Matchless). Fastest lap: Phillips, 64.80mph.

19 April, Thruxton – Commonwealth Trophy
350 (10 laps, 22 miles): 1 Dave Williams (MW Special), 79.18mph, 2 Ray Watmore (AJS), 3 Ray Pickrell (Norton), 4 Paddy Driver (AJS), 5 John Williams (AJS), 6 Brian Kemp (Norton). Fastest lap: Williams, 80.82mph.
500 Commonwealth Trophy (12 laps): 1 Williams (Norton), 82.40mph, 2 Watmore (Matchless), 3 Pickrell (Norton), 4 R Burgess (Norton), 5 Paddy Driver (Matchless), 6 Derek Best (Norton). Fastest lap: Williams, 84.26mph.

206

19 April, Crystal Palace
350 (8 laps, 11.12 miles): 1 John Blanchard (Aermacchi), 73.35mph, 2 Reg Everett (301 Yamaha), 3 Roger Hunter (AJS), 4 Ron Chandler (AJS), 5 Cyril Davey (Norton), 6 Charlie Sanby (AJS). Fastest lap: Blanchard, 75.59mph.
500 (8 laps): 1 Ron Chandler (Matchless), 74.11mph, 2 Peter Williams (Norton), 3 D Chester (Norton), 4 J Elvin (Norton), 5 K Inwood (Norton), 6 Roger Hunter (Norton). Fastest lap: Chandler, Williams, 78.28mph.

20 April, Mallory Park
350 (15 laps, 20.25 miles): 1 John Cooper (Norton), 76.61mph, 2 Rod Gould (Norton), 3 Ray Watmore (AJS), 4 Roger Hunter (AJS), 5 Rob Fitton (Norton), 6 Tony Ward (Norton). Fastest lap: Cooper, 79.16mph.
500 (15 laps): 1 Cooper (Norton), 83.89mph, 2 Joe Dunphy (Norton), 3 Dave Degens (Dunstall Domiracer), 4 Watmore (Matchless), 5 Jack Smith (Norton), 6 Dan Shorey (Norton). Fastest lap: Degens, 86.48mph.

1 May, Castle Combe
350 (10 laps, 18.4 miles): 1 Derek Minter (Norton), 85.64mph, 2 Rod Gould (Norton), 3 Selwyn Griffiths (AJS), 4 John Williams (AJS), 5 Tony Rutter (Norton), 6 Barry Randle (Norton). Fastest lap: Minter, 87.63mph.
500 (10 laps): 1 Minter (Norton), 87.70mph, 2 Peter Williams (Norton), 3 Dave Croxford (Matchless), 4 Griffiths (Matchless), 5 Malcolm Uphill (Norton), 6 Dave Degens (Dunstall Domiracer). Fastest lap: Minter, 91.00mph.

9 May, Brands Hatch
350 (10 laps, 26.5 miles): 1 Derek Minter (Norton), 83.70mph, 2 Dan Shorey (Norton), 3 Bill Ivy (AJS), 4 Paddy Driver (AJS), 5 John Cooper (Norton), 6 Dave Williams (MW Special). Fastest lap: Minter, 85.79mph.
500 Redex Trophy (10 laps): 1 Bill Ivy (Matchless), 86.03mph, 2 John Cooper (Norton), 3 Paddy Driver (Matchless), 4 Joe Dunphy (Norton), 5 Dave Croxford (Matchless), 6 Minter (Norton). Fastest lap: Minter, 87.84mph.
1000 (10 laps): 1 Minter (499 Norton), 86.31mph, 2 Driver (496 Matchless), 3 Ivy (496 Matchless), 4 Griff Jenkins (Norton), 5 Dan Shorey (Norton), 6 Croxford (Matchless). Fastest lap: Minter, 88.50mph.

16 May, Snetterton
350 (10 laps, 27.1 miles): 1 Ray Watmore (AJS), 87.31mph, 2 Joe Dunphy (Norton), 3 Dan Shorey (Norton), 4 Ron Chandler (AJS), 5 John Cooper (Norton), 6 Chris Conn (Norton). Fastest lap: Chandler (AJS), 90.00mph.
500 Great Eastern Trophy (10 laps): 1 Bill Ivy (Matchless), 90.93mph, 2 Ray Watmore (Matchless), 3 John Cooper (Norton), 4 Derek Minter (Norton), 5 Peter Williams (Norton), 6 Dave Croxford (Matchless). Fastest lap: Ivy, 94.17mph.

23 May, Mallory Park
350 (15 laps, 20.25 miles): 1 Derek Minter (Norton), 84.2mph, 2 John Cooper (Norton), 3 Bill Ivy (AJS), 4 Tony Ward (AJS), 5 Joe Dunphy (Norton), 6 Jack Smith (Norton). Fastest lap: Minter, 86.48mph.
500 (20 laps): 1 Ivy (Matchless), 86.65mph, 2 Cooper (Norton), 3 Dave Degens (Dunstall Domiracer), 4 Peter Willliams (Norton), 5 Ron Chandler (Matchless), 6 Minter (Norton). Fastest lap: Ivy, 89.01mph.

4 June, Scarborough – Cock o' the North
350 (12 laps, 28.82 miles): 1 Dan Shorey (Norton), 66.19mph, 2 George Buchan (Norton), 3 Billie Nelson (Norton), 4 S Hodges (Norton), 5 Rod Gould (Norton), 6 Selwyn Griffiths (AJS). Fastest lap: Buchan, 67.26mph.
500 (12 laps): 1 Shorey (Norton), 67.36mph, 2 Buchan (Norton), 3 Peter Williams (Norton), 4 Nelson (Norton), 5 Griffiths (Matchless), 6 Derek Phillips (Norton). Fastest lap: Buchan, 68.63mph.

7 June, Cadwell Park
350 (8 laps, 18 miles): 1 Billie Nelson (Norton), 65.31mph, 2 Rod Gould (Norton), 3 Tom Phillips (Aermacchi), 4 George Buchan (Norton), 5 Chris Conn (Norton), 6 Selwyn Griffiths (AJS). Fastest lap: Nelson, 67.05mph.
500 (12 laps): 1 Nelson (Norton), 72.71mph, 2 Chris Conn (Norton), 3 Phillips (Norton), 4 Buchan (Norton), 5 Derek Phillips (Norton), 6 Griffiths (Matchless). Fastest lap: Conn, 74.86mph.

20 June, Mallory Park
350 (15 laps, 20.25 miles): 1 Jim Redman (Honda), 84.65mph, 2 Bill Ivy (AJS), 3 Mike Duff (AJS), 4 Dan Shorey (Norton), 5 Dennis Ainsworth (Norton), 6 Griff Jenkins (Norton). Fastest lap: Redman, 86.79mph.
500 (20 laps): 1 Mike Hailwood (MV), 87.30mph, 2 Ivy (Matchless), 3 John Cooper (Norton), 4 Joe Dunphy (Norton), 5 Ron Chandler (Matchless), 6 Chris Conn (Norton). Fastest lap: Hailwood, 89.34mph.

27 June, Brands Hatch
350 (10 laps, 26.5 miles): 1 Derek Minter (Arter AJS), 84.39mph, 2 Bill Ivy (AJS), 3 Ron Chandler (AJS), 4 Griff Jenkins (Norton), 5 Joe Dunphy (Norton), 6 Cyril Davey (Norton). Fastest lap: Minter, 85.79mph.
500 Redex Trophy (10 laps): 1 Ivy (Matchless), 86.68mph, 2 Derek Minter (Norton), 3 Jenkins (Norton), 4 Dave Croxford (Matchless), 5 Paddy Driver (Matchless), 6 Dave Degens (Norton). Fastest lap: Ivy, 88.83mph.

10 July, Castle Combe
1st 350 (8 laps, 14.72 miles): 1 Ray Watmore (AJS), 84.56mph, 2 Tony Ward (Norton), 3 Barry Randle (Norton), 4 Richard Difazio (Norton), 5 Selwyn Griffiths (AJS), 6 A Monk (BSA). Fastest lap: Watmore, 87.63mph.
2nd 350 (8 laps): 1 Derek Minter (Norton), 86.01mph, 2 Brian Kemp (Norton), 3 John Williams (AJS), 4 Clive Brown (Norton), 5 A Copeland (Norton), 6 T Packer (Norton). Fastest lap: Minter, 89.04mph.
1st 500 (8 laps): 1 Dave Croxford (Matchless), 85.57mph, 2 Selwyn Griffiths (Matchless), 3 Watmore (Matchless), Louis Carr (AJS), 5 Difazio (Norton), 6 J Brillard (Norton). Fastest lap: Croxford, 89.77mph.

2nd 500 (8 laps): 1 Minter (Norton), 87.86mph, 2 Martin Watson (Norton), 3 D Chester (Norton), 4 Tony Ward (Norton), 5 Steve Spencer (Norton), 6 T Gill (Matchless). Fastest lap: Minter, 91.50mph.

Avon Trophy (27 laps, 49.68 miles): 1 Watmore (Matchless), 89.18mph, 2 Croxford (Matchless), 3 Watson (Norton), 4 Minter, 5 Steve Spencer (Norton), 6 Godfrey Nash (Norton). Fastest lap: Minter, 91.76mph (record).

1 August, Thruxton
350 (10 laps, 22 miles): 1 Ray Pickrell (Norton), 81.85mph, 2 Dave Williams (MW Special), 3 John Blanchard (Norton), 4 Paddy Driver (AJS), 5 Brian Kemp (Norton), 6 Richard Difazio (Norton). Fastest lap: Willliams, 83.90mph.
500 Wills Trophy (12 laps): 1 Driver (Matchless), 84.45mph, 2 Pickrell (Norton), 3 Williams (MW Norton), 4 A Prange (Matchless), 5 S Brillard (Norton), 6 R Mahon (Norton). Fastest lap: Driver, 86.66mph.

1 August, Cadwell Park
Experts Invitation (12 laps, 27 miles): 1 John Cooper (499 Norton), 72.07mph, 2 Rob Fitton (499 Norton), 3 Billie Nelson (499 Norton), 4 Dan Shorey (499 Norton), 5 Tom Phillips (MW Norton), 6 George Buchan (Norton). Fastest lap: Shorey, 74.31mph.
Experts Invitation Handicap (12 laps): 1 Shorey (499 Norton), 74.10mph, 2 Cooper (499 Norton), 3 Selwyn Griffiths (349 AJS), 4 Nelson (499 Norton), 5 John Ashworth (250 Yamaha), 6 Derek Chatterton (250 Yamaha). Fastest lap: Cooper, 76.27mph.

14 August, Silverstone – Hutchinson 100
350 (20 laps, 58.54 miles): 1 Mike Hailwood (AJS), 94.50mph, 2 John Cooper (Norton), 3 Derek Minter (Norton), 4 Mike Duff (AJS), 5 Chris Conn (Norton), 6 Bill Ivy (AJS). Fastest lap: Minter, 98.48mph (equals record).
500 (25 laps): 1 Hailwood (MV), 97.49mph, 2 Bill Ivy (Matchless), 3 Cooper (Norton), 4 Paddy Driver (Matchless), 5 Phil Read (250 Yamaha), 6 Fred Stevens (Matchless). Fastest lap: Hailwood, 99.41mph.
Production (15 laps): 1 Hailwood (654 BSA), 83.14mph, 2 Phil Read (649 Triumph), 3 Percy Tait (649 Triumph), 4 Rod Gould (654 BSA), 5 Driver (750 Matchless), 6 Tom Phillips (499 Velocette). Fastest lap: Hailwood, 85.81mph.

15 August, Brands Hatch (short circuit)
350 (15 laps, 18.6 miles): 1 Derek Minter (Norton), 74.15mph, 2 John Cooper (Norton), 3 Bill Ivy (AJS), 4 Jack Smith (Norton), 5 Chris Conn (Norton), 6 Dave Croxford (AJS). Fastest lap: Minter, Cooper, 76.44mph.
500 Redex Trophy (15 laps): 1 Ivy (Matchless), 75.06mph, 2 Minter (Norton), 3 Cooper (Norton), 4 Griff Jenkins (Norton), 5 Paddy Driver (Matchless), 6 Dave Degens (Matchless). Fastest lap: Ivy, 77.50mph.

30 August, Oulton Park – British Championships
350 (19 laps, 52.44 miles): 1 Dan Shorey (Norton), 86.08mph, 2 Mike Duff, (AJS), 3 Derek Minter (Norton), 4 Bill Ivy (AJS), 5 Griff Jenkins (Norton), 6 Joe Dunphy (Norton). Fastest lap: Phil Read (Yamaha), 89.55mph.
500 (19 laps): 1 Ivy (Matchless), 88.24mph, 2 Minter (Norton), 3 Jenkins (Norton), 4 Shorey (Norton), 5 M Watson (Norton), 6 John Cooper (Norton). Fastest lap: Ivy, 90.36mph.
Les Graham Trophy (8 laps): 1 Minter (Norton), 87.70mph, 2 Paddy Driver (Matchless), 3 Shorey (Norton), 4 Ivy (Matchless), 5 Jenkins (Norton), 6 Dave Croxford (Matchless). Fastest lap: Ivy, 89.87mph.

30 August, Cadwell Park
350 (8 laps, 18 miles): 1 Selwyn Griffiths (AJS), 71.44mph, 2 Rod Gould (Norton), 3 Billie Nelson (Norton), 4 Tom Phillips (Norton), 5 Roger Hunter (AJS), 6 J Ashworth (Yamaha). Fastest lap: Gould, 74.31mph.
500 (12 laps): 1 Griffiths (Matchless), 72.71mph, 2 Rob Fitton (Norton), 3 Phillips (MW Norton), 4 Peter Richards (Norton), 5 C Burton (Matchless), 6 C Wray (Matchless). Fastest lap: Griffiths, 75mph.

30 August, Crystal Palace
350 (12 laps, 16.68 miles): 1 John Blanchard (Norton), 75.3mph, 2 Ron Chandler (AJS), 3 Jack Simmonds (Norton), 4 Godfrey Nash (Norton), 5 H W Rayner (AJS), 6 J M Dodsworth (AJS). Fastest lap: Blanchard, 77.46mph.
1000 (12 laps): 1 Chandler (Matchless), 75.93mph, 2 Simmonds (Norton), 3 B Burgess (Norton), 4 D Chester (Norton), 5 Nash (Norton), 6 John Samways (Norton). Fastest lap: Chandler, 77.94mph.

4 September, Castle Combe
350 (10 laps, 18.4 miles): 1 Derek Minter (Norton), 85.97mph, 2 Rod Gould (Norton), 3 Selwyn Griffiths (AJS), 4 Tom Phillips (Norton), 5 R J Flack (Norton), 6 Tony Rutter (Norton). Fastest lap: Minter, 88.80mph.
500 (10 laps): 1 Minter (Norton), 89.29mph, 2 Brian Kemp (Norton), 3 Ray Pickrell (Norton), 4 Phillips (Norton), 5 John Samways (Norton), 6 Godfrey Nash (Norton). Fastest lap: Minter, 91.50mph.

5 September, Snetterton
350 (7 laps, 18.97 miles): 1 Derek Minter (Norton), 82.93mph, 2 Martin Watson (Norton), 3 Chris Conn (Norton), 4 Joe Dunphy (Norton), 5 Bill Ivy (AJS), 6 Ron Chandler (AJS). Fastest lap: Minter, 84.67mph.
500 (7 laps): 1 Ivy (Matchless), 85.09mph, 2 Dave Degens (Matchless), 3 Watson (Norton), 4 Minter (Norton), 5 Tom Phillips (Norton), 6 Dunphy (Norton). Fastest lap: Minter (Norton), 87.73mph.

12 September, Cadwell Park
350 (12 laps, 27 miles): 1 Phil Read (254 Yamaha), 72.94mph, 2 John Cooper (Norton), 3 Chris Conn (Norton), 4 Rod Gould (Norton), 5 Tom Phillips (Norton), 6 Bill Ivy (AJS). Fastest lap: Cooper, 74.59mph (record).
Invitation (20 laps): 1 Cooper (Norton), 71.48mph, 2 Read (254 Yamaha), 3 Phillips (Norton), 4 Conn (Norton), 5 Billie Nelson (Norton), 6 Selwyn Griffiths (Matchless). Fastest lap: Read, 74.86mph.

17 September, Scarborough
350 (12 laps, 28.82 miles): 1 John Cooper (Norton), 60.57mph, 2 Phil Read (254 Yamaha), 3 Billie Nelson (Norton), 4 Peter Williams (AJS), 5 Dan Shorey (Norton), 6 Selwyn Griffiths (AJS). Fastest lap: Read, 61.89mph.
500 (16 laps): 1 Cooper (Norton), 68.69mph, 2 Williams (Dunstall Domiracer), 3 Shorey (Norton), 4 Nelson (Norton), 5 Rob Fitton (Norton), 6 Griffiths (Matchless). Fastest lap: Cooper, 70.18mph (record).

19 September, Brands Hatch
Fred Neville Trophy 350 (10 laps, 26.5 miles): 1 Bill Ivy (254 Yamaha), 84.46mph, 2 Derek Minter (Norton), 3 Paddy Driver (AJS), 4 John Cooper (Norton), 5 Dave Croxford (AJS), 6 Roger Hunter (AJS). Fastest lap: Ivy, 85.94mph.
500 Redex Trophy (10 laps): 1 Minter (Norton), 86.08mph, 2 Ivy (Matchless), 3 Cooper (Norton), 4 Driver (Matchless), 5 Griff Jenkins (Norton), 6 Dan Shorey (Norton). Fastest lap: Driver, 88mph.
1000 (10 laps): 1 Minter (499 Norton), 85.1mph, 2 Driver (496 Matchless), 3 Jenkins (Norton), 4 Cooper (499 Norton), 5 Ivy (496 Matchless), 6 Shorey (499 Norton). Fastest lap: Minter, Ivy, 87.52mph.

26 September, Mallory Park – Race of the Year
350 (20 laps, 27 miles): 1 Dave Degens (AJS), 75.89mph, 2 Peter Williams (AJS), 3 John Cooper (Norton), 4 Paddy Driver (AJS), 5 Ron Chandler (AJS), 6 Stuart Graham (AJS). Fastest lap: Phil Read (254 Yamaha) 80.73mph.
500 (25 laps): 1 Mike Hailwood (MV), 87.69mph, 2 Bill Ivy (Matchless), 3 John Cooper (Norton), 4 Paddy Driver (Matchless), 5 Ron Chandler (Matchless), 6 Peter Williams (Dunstall Domiracer). Fastest lap: Hailwood, 90mph.
Race of the Year (30 laps): 1 Cooper (Norton), 80.52mph, 2 Read (254 Yamaha), 3 Ivy (Matchless), 4 Driver (Matchless), 5 Hailwood (MV), 6 Degens (Matchless). Fastest lap: Cooper, 82.37mph.

2 October, Oulton Park
350 (6 laps, 16.26 miles – rain shortened): 1 John Cooper (Norton), 72.53mph, 2 Stuart Graham (AJS), 3 Dave Degens (AJS), 4 Bill Ivy (AJ), 5 Dan Shorey (Norton), 6 Billie Nelson (Norton). Fastest lap: Cooper, 74.51mph.
500 Bob McIntyre Trophy (6 laps): 1 Ivy (Matchless), 76.99mph, 2 Fred Stevens (Matchless), 3 Malcolm Uphill (Norton), 4 Graham (Matchless), 5 Tom Phillips (Norton), 6 Shorey (Norton). Fastest lap: Ivy, 79.01mph.

10 October, Brands Hatch
350 (20 laps, 53 miles): 1 Dave Degens (AJS), 82.76mph, 2 Paddy Driver (AJS), 3 Cyril Davey (Norton), 4 Ray Pickrell (Norton), 5 Mike Hailwood (AJS), 6 Dave Croxford (AJS). Fastest lap: Driver, 85.79mph.
500 Evening News Trophy (20 laps): 1 Hailwood (Matchless), 85.74mph, 2 Ivy (Matchless), 3 Driver (Matchless), 4 Croxford (Matchless), 5 Griff Jenkins (Dunstall Domiracer), 6 John Blanchard (Monard). Fastest lap: Hailwood, Ivy, 87.20mph.
500 Redex Trophy (10 laps): 1 Ivy (Matchless), 84.29mph, 2 Driver (Matchless), 3 Jenkins (Dunstall Domiracer), 4 Croxford (Matchless), 5 Ron Chandler (Matchless), 6 Errol Cowan (Matchless). Fastest lap: Jenkins, 85.79mph.

31 October, Mallory Park
350 (10 laps): 1 Peter Williams (AJS), 74.13mph, 2 Stuart Graham (AJS), 3 Dave Degens (AJS), 4 Tony Ward (Norton), 5 Dan Shorey (Norton), 6 Chris Conn (AJS). Fastest lap: Graham, 78.38mph.
500 (10 laps): 1 Bill Ivy (Matchless), 76.29mph, 2 Chris Conn (Matchless), 3 Graham (Matchless), 4 C Dixon (Norton), 5 Shorey (Norton), 6 Ward (Norton). Fastest lap: Ivy, Conn, 78.13mph.

1965 ACU Road Racing Stars:
350: 1 Derek Minter, 2 John Cooper, 3 Rob Gould
500: 1 Bill Ivy, 2 Minter, 3 Cooper

1966
6 March, Mallory Park
350 Birmingham Cup (10 laps, 13.5 miles): 1 Dave Degens (Norton), 82.82mph, 2 John Cooper (Norton), 3 Dan Shorey (Norton), 4 Bill Ivy (AJS), 5 Stuart Graham (AJS), 6 Ray Pickrell (Norton). Fastest lap: Degens, 86.48mph.
500 (15 laps): 1 Ivy (Matchless), 86.62mph, 2 Degens (Matchless), 3 Derek Minter (Seeley Matchless), 4 Griff Jenkins (Dunstall Domiracer), 5 Cooper (Norton), 6 Chris Conn (Matchless). Fastest lap: Ivy, 88.68mph.

13 March, Brands Hatch
350 (10 laps, 26.5 miles): 1 Bill Ivy (AJS), 82.97mph, 2 Dave Degens (Norton), 3 John Cooper (Norton), 4 Dan Shorey (Norton), 5 Dave Croxford (AJS), 6 Ron Chandler (AJS). Fastest lap: Degens, 85.03mph.
500 Redex Trophy (12 laps): 1 Derek Minter (Seeley Matchless), 85.71mph, 2 Griff Jenkins (Dunstall Domiracer), 3 Cooper (Norton), 4 Degens (Matchless), 5 Ivy (Matchless Métisse), 6 Rex Butcher (Norton). Fastest lap: Minter, 87.84mph.
1000 (10 laps): 1 Butcher (647 Dunstall Domiracer), 85.71mph, 2 Ivy (496 Matchless Métisse), 3 Cooper (499 Norton), 4 Minter (496 Seeley Matchless), 5 Jenkins (497 Dunstall Domiracer), 6 Chandler (496 Matchless). Fastest lap: Jenkins, 88.66mph.

20 March, Snetterton
350 (10 laps, 27.1 miles): 1 Derek Minter (Seeley AJS), 83.28mph, 2 Dave Degens (Aermacchi), 3 Dave Simmonds (Honda), 4 John Cooper (Norton), 5 Rod Gould (Norton), 6 Dan Shorey (Norton). Fastest lap: Degens, 84.83mph.
500 (10 laps): 1 Cooper (Norton), 86.30mph, 2 Minter (Seeley Matchless), 3 Shorey (Norton), 4 Ron Chandler (AJS), 5 Rex Butcher (497 Dunstall Domiracer), 6 Chris Conn (Matchless). Cooper, 87.89mph.

8 April, Brands Hatch – King of Brands
350 (10 laps, 26.5 miles): 1 Mike Hailwood (Honda), 83.42mph, 2 Bill Ivy (AJS), 3 Peter Williams (AJS), 4 Dave Degens (Norton), 5 Joe

Dunphy (Norton), 6 Derek Minter (Seeley AJS). Fastest lap: Hailwood, 85.17mph.

500 Redex Trophy (10 laps): 1 Degens (Norton), 84.98mph, 2 Griff Jenkins (Dunstall Domiracer), 3 Minter (Seeley Matchless), 4 Dave Croxford (Matchless), 5 Ray Pickrell (Norton), 6 Rex Butcher (Norton). Fastest lap: Degens, Jenkins, 86.72mph.

1000 King of Brands (15 laps): 1 Ivy (496 Matchless), 85.55mph, 2 Degens (650 Dresda Triton), 3 Hailwood (Honda), 4 Croxford (496 Matchless), 5 Peter Williams (496 Matchless), 6 Dan Shorey (Norton). Fastest lap: Degens, 87.52mph.

10 April, Snetterton – Race of Aces
350 (4 laps, 10.84 miles – rain shortened): 1 Peter Williams (AJS), 70.20mph, 2 Bill Ivy (AJS), 3 Dan Shorey (Norton), 4 Tony Rutter (Norton), 5 Ray Pickrell (Norton), 6 Marty Lunde (Norton). Fastest lap: Williams, 72.48mph.

500 Race of Aces (8 laps): 1 Dave Degens (Matchless), 84.06mph, 2 Bill Ivy (Matchless), 3 Dave Croxford (Matchless), 4 Rex Butcher (Norton), 5 Williams (Matchless), 6 Tom Phillips (Norton). Fastest lap: Ivy, 86.49mph.

11 April, Oulton Park
350 (19 laps, 52.44 miles): 1 Mike Hailwood (Honda), 84.77mph, 2 Derek Minter (Seeley AJS), 3 John Cooper (Norton), 4 Peter Williams (AJS), 5 Bill Ivy (AJS), 6 Dave Simmonds (Honda). Fastest lap: Hailwood, 86.28mph.

500 (19 laps): 1 Minter (Seeley Matchless), 85.48mph, 2 Cooper (Norton), 3 Griff Jenkins (Dunstall Domiracer), 4 Malcolm Uphill (Norton), 5 Ivy (Matchless), 6 Stuart Graham (Matchless). Fastest lap: Cooper, Jenkins, 87.04mph.

11 April, Cadwell Park
350 (8 laps, 18 miles): 1 Selwyn Griffiths (AJS), 70.80mph, 2 Rod Gould (Norton), 3 Billie Nelson (Norton), 4 Rex Butcher (Norton). Fastest lap: Gould, 73.50mph.

500 (12 laps): 1 Griffiths (Matchless), 72.32mph, 2 Butcher (Norton), 3 Nelson (Norton), 4 Peter Richards (Norton). Fastest lap: Griffiths, 73.64mph.

11 April, Crystal Palace
350 (8 laps, 11.12 miles): 1 John Blanchard (Norton), 66.60mph, 2 Ron Chandler (AJS), 3 Charlie Sanby (AJS), 4 Godfrey Nash (Norton), 5 D Filler (AJS), 6 G Brown (Norton). Fastest lap: Blanchard, 68.17mph.

500 (8 laps): 1 Chandler (Matchless), 68.24mph, 2 Sanby (Norton), 3 George Young (Norton), 4 Blanchard (Monard), 5 Graham Sharp (Norton), 6 Selwyn Griffiths (Matchless). Fastest lap: Chandler, 69.89mph.

12 April, Mallory Park
350 (15 laps, 20.25 miles): 1 John Cooper (Norton), 80.06mph, 2 Dave Simmonds (Honda), 3 Dan Shorey (Norton), 4 Ron Chandler (AJS), 5 Rex Butcher (Norton), 6 Joe Dunphy (Norton). Fastest lap: Cooper, 82.37mph.

500 (15 laps): 1 Dave Croxford (Matchless), 83.26mph, 2 Griff Jenkins (Dunstall Domiracer), 3 Chandler (Matchless), 4 Rex Butcher (Norton), 5 Shorey (Norton), 6 Tony Ward (Norton). Fastest lap: Croxford, Jenkins, 85.87mph.

30 April, Castle Combe
350 (10 laps, 18.4 miles): 1 Selwyn Griffiths (AJS), 86.16mph, 2 Derek Minter (Seeley AJS), 3 Dave Croxford (Lyster Norton), 4 Rod Gould (Norton), 5 Ray Pickrell (Norton), 6 Tom Phillips (Ducati). Fastest lap: Gould, 88.56mph.

500 (10 laps): 1 Croxford (Matchless), 88.36mph, 2 Griffiths (Matchless), 3 Phillips (Norton), 4 Gould (Norton), 5 Pickrell (Norton), 6 Minter (Seeley Matchless). Fastest lap: Gould, Croxford, 90.99mph.

1 May, Brands Hatch (short track)
350 (15 laps, 18.6 miles): 1 Dave Degens (Aermacchi), 72.06mph, 2 Peter Williams (AJS), 3 John Cooper (Norton), 4 Rex Butcher (Norton), 5 Dave Simmonds (Honda), 6 Derek Minter (Seeley AJS). Fastest lap: Butcher, Williams, 74.65mph.

500 Redex Trophy (15 laps): 1 Degens (Matchless), 73.82mph, 2 Minter (Seeley Matchless), 3 Dave Croxford (Matchless), 4 Tom Phillips (Norton), 5 Cooper (Norton), 6 Butcher (Norton). Fastest lap: Degens, 75.92mph.

1000 (20 laps): 1 Cooper (499 Norton), 73.62mph, 2 Minter (496 Seeley Matchless), 3 Butcher (647 Dunstall Domiracer), 4 Croxford (496 Matchless), 5 Phillips (499 Norton), 6 Martin Watson (Norton). Fastest lap: Cooper, 76.70mph.

22 May, Mallory Park – Derby Cup
350 (15 laps, 20.25 miles): 1 Rod Gould (Norton), 76.67mph, 2 Dave Degens (Aermacchi), 3 Tony Ward (Norton), 4 Ron Chandler (AJS), 5 Griff Jenkins (AJS), 6 Martin Watson (Norton). Fastest lap: Gould, 79.67mph.

500 (10 laps): 1 Dave Croxford (Matchless), 76.32mph, 2 Gould (Norton), 3 Griff Jenkins (Dunstall Domiracer), 4 Ray Pickrell (Norton), 5 Charlie Sanby (Norton), 6 Dave Degens (DW Special). Fastest lap: Gould, 79.42mph.

28 May, Scarborough
350 (12 laps, 28.92 miles): 1 Dan Shorey (Norton), 64.26mph, 2 George Buchan (Norton), 3 Rod Gould (Norton), 4 Steve Spencer (Norton), 5 Carl Ward (AJS), 6 Marty Lunde (AJS). Fastest lap: Shorey, 66.33mph.

500 (12 laps): 1 Peter Williams (Matchless), 66.88mph, 2 Shorey (Norton), 3 Buchan (Norton), 4 Barry Scully (Norton), 5 Dave King (Norton), 6 G Fish (Norton). Fastest lap: Williams, Shorey, Buchan, 68.09mph.

29 May, Snetterton
350 (8 laps, 21.68 miles): 1 Dave Simmonds (Honda), 87.22mph, 2 Joe Dunphy (Norton), 3 Peter Williams (AJS), 4 Martin Watson (Norton), 5 Dan Shorey (Norton), 6 Ray Pickrell (Norton). Fastest lap: Simmonds, 89.51mph.

500 (8 laps): 1 John Cooper (Norton), 91.39mph, 2 Dave Croxford (Matchless), 3 Rex Butcher (Norton), 4 Williams (Matchless), 5 Peter Richards (Norton), 6 B Davies (Matchless). Fastest lap: Williams, 93.99mph.

30 May, Brands Hatch
350 (10 laps, 26.5 miles): 1 Phil Read (251 Yamaha), 83.04mph, 2 Jim Redman (350 Honda), 3 Bill Ivy (AJS), 4 Derek Minter (Seeley AJS),

5 Ron Chandler (AJS), 6 Ray Pickrell (Norton). Fastest lap: Read, 84.87mph.
500 Redex Trophy (10 laps): 1 Peter Williams (Matchless), 84.65mph, 2 Dave Croxford (Matchless), 3 Bill Ivy (Matchless), 4 Chandler (Matchless), 5 Dan Shorey (Norton), 6 Ray Pickrell (Norton). Fastest lap: Williams, 86.10mph.
1000 Evening News Trophy (20 laps): 1 Mike Hailwood (350 Honda), 85.60mph, 2 Williams (496 Matchless), 3 Croxford (496 Matchless), 4 Ivy (496 Matchless Métisse), 5 Minter (Seeley Matchless), 6 Chandler (496 Matchless). Fastest lap: Hailwood, 87.52mph.

30 May, Cadwell Park
350 (8 laps, 18 miles): 1 Rod Gould (Norton), 71.90mph, 2 Selwyn Griffiths (AJS), 3 John Cooper (Norton), 4 Billie Nelson (Norton), 5 Martin Watson (Norton), 6 Stuart Graham (AJS). Fastest lap: Gould, Griffiths, 73.37mph.
500 Middleton Trophy (12 laps): 1 Cooper (Norton), 71.37mph, 2 Gould (Norton), 3 Graham (Matchless), 4 Steve Spencer (Norton), 5 Watson (Norton), 6 Charlie Sanby (Norton). Fastest lap: Cooper, 72.58mph.

18 June, Croft
350 (16 laps, 28 miles): 1 John Cooper (Norton), 73.74mph, 2 George Buchan (Norton), 3 Malcolm Uphill (Norton), 4 Rob Fitton (Norton), 5 Tony Rutter (Norton), 6 Alan Barnett (AJS). Fastest lap: Cooper, Buchan, 75.54mph.
500 (16 laps): 1 Cooper (Norton), 75.72mph, 2 Uphill (Norton), 3 Buchan (Norton), 4 Fitton (Norton), 5 Barry Scully (Norton), 6 Barnett (Matchless). Fastest lap: Cooper, Uphill, Buchan, 77.21mph.

19 June, Mallory Park – Post non-TT International
350 (15 laps, 20.25 miles): 1 Mike Hailwood (Honda), 85.83mph, 2 Phil Read (251 Yamaha), 3 John Cooper (Norton), 4 Peter Williams (AJS), 5 Rod Gould (Norton), 6 Dan Shorey (Norton). Fastest lap: Hailwood, 88.04mph.
500 (20 laps): 1 Cooper (Norton), 86.95mph, 2 Dave Croxford (Matchless), 3 Williams (Matchless), 4 Griff Jenkins (Dunstall Domiracer), 5 Gyula Marsovszky (Matchless), 6 Chris Conn (Norton). Fastest lap: Cooper, 89.01mph.

26 June, Brands Hatch – 500-mile Grand Prix
1 Dave Degens/Rex Butcher (Triumph Bonneville), 2 Phil Read/Percy Tait (Triumph Bonneville), 3 Griff Jenkins/David Dixon (Norton 650SS).

9 July, Castle Combe
350 (10 laps, 18.4 miles): 1 Derek Minter (Norton), 85.67mph, 2 Peter Williams (AJS), 3 Barry Randle (Norton), 4 Reg Everett (Yamaha), 5 Tom Dickie (AJS), 6 Clive Brown (Norton). Fastest lap: Minter, 88.09mph.
500 Avon Trophy (10 laps): 1 Williams (Matchless), 89.08mph, 2 Minter (Seeley Matchless), 3 Malcolm Uphill (Norton), 4 Alan Barnett (Matchless), 5 Selwyn Griffiths (Matchless), 6 Barry Scully (Norton). Fastest lap: Griffiths, 90.99mph.

7 August, Cadwell Park
750 Experts Invitation (10 laps, 22.5 miles): 1 Peter Williams (Matchless), 64.42mph, 2 Malcolm Uphill (Norton), 3 Dan Shorey (Norton), 4 Tom Phillips (Norton), 5 Roger Bowring (650 Triumph), 6 Derek Chatterton (250 Yamaha). Fastest lap: Williams, 65.64mph.

14 August, Brands Hatch – Hutchinson 100
350 BMCRC Championship (20 laps, 53 miles): 1 Mike Hailwood (Honda), 85.89mph, 2 Derek Minter (Norton), 3 John Blanchard (Seeley AJS), 4 Dave Degens (Aermacchi), 5 Dan Shorey (Norton), 6 Kel Carruthers (Norton). Fastest lap: Hailwood, 87.36mph.
500 BMCRC Championship (25 laps): 1 John Cooper (Norton), 83.53mph, 2 Shorey (Norton), 3 Gyula Marsovszky (Matchless), 4 Lance Weil (Norton), 5 John Dodds (Norton), 6 Rex Butcher (Matchless Métisse). Fastest lap: Hailwood (350 Honda), 86.41mph.

20 August, Croft
350 (10 laps, 17.5 miles): 1 Reg Everett (251 Yamaha), 72.09mph, 2 G Bell (AJS), 3 Jack Smith (AJS), 4 B Palmer (AJS), 5 C M Thompson (Norton). Fastest lap: Derek Chatterton (Chat Yamaha), 74.82mph.
500 (10 laps): 1 Alan Baker (Matchless), 74.18mph, 2 Martin Watson (Norton), 3 J Richards (Norton), 4 Carl Ward (Norton), 5 S Hedges (Norton). Fastest lap, Baker, 76.27mph.

21 August, Mallory Park
350 (10 laps, 13.5 miles): 1 John Cooper (Norton), 71.47mph, 2 Dave Croxford (AJS), 3 Rod Gould (Norton), 4 Dave Degens (Aermacchi), 5 A Ward (Norton), 6 Tom Phillips (Aermacchi). Fastest lap: Cooper, 74.77mph.
750 (10 laps): 1 Croxford (Matchless), 73.48mph, 2 Martin Watson (Norton), 3 Gould (Norton), 4 Ron Chandler (Matchless), 5 Degens (650 Dresda Métisse), 6 Richard Difazio (Norton). Fastest lap: Croxford, 75.47mph.

29 August, Oulton Park
350 (19 laps, 52.44 miles): 1 John Cooper (Norton), 73.19mph, 2 Dan Shorey (Norton), 3 Jack Ahearn (Norton), 4 Malcolm Uphill (Norton), 5 Chris Conn (Norton), 6 Rob Fitton (Norton). Fastest lap: Cooper, 74.37mph.
500 (19 laps): 1 Ahearn (Norton), 76.09mph, 2 Uphill (Norton), 3 Cooper (Norton), 4 Dave Degens (Matchless Métisse), 5 Shorey (Norton), 6 Fitton (Norton). Fastest lap: Ahearn, 78.14mph.
Les Graham Memorial Trophy (8 laps, 22 miles): 1 Shorey (Norton), 84.32mph, 2 Degens (Matchless Métisse), 3 Conn (Norton), 4 Rex Butcher (Norton), 5 Alan Baker (Matchless), 6 Keith Heckles (Norton). Fastest lap: Conn, 86.13mph.

29 August, Crystal Palace
350 (8 laps, 11.12 miles): 1 Trevor Barnes (Moto Guzzi), 73.94mph, 2 Alan Peck (Norton), 3 Dave Elvin (AJS), 4 Reg Everett (Yamaha), 5 Brian Davis (AJS), 6 John Blanchard (Seeley AJS). Fastest lap: Barnes, 76.51mph.
1000 (12 laps): 1 Lance Weil (Norton), 67.55mph, 2 Davis (Matchless), 3 Peter Butler (649 Triumph), 4 Declan Doyle (750 Taraton), 5 J Brillard (Norton), 6 Martyn Ashwood (Matchless). Fastest lap: Weil, 69.50mph.

29 August, Cadwell Park – Cadwell Conqueror
350 (8 laps, 18 miles): 1 Martin Watson (252 Bultaco), 70.29mph, 2 Rod Gould (Norton), 3 Billie Nelson (Norton), 4 Tom Phillips (Ducati), 5 Tony Willmott (Norton), 6 Derek Chatterton (251 Yamaha). Fastest lap: Watson, 72.71mph.
500 (8 laps): 1 Gould (Norton), 67.47mph, 2 Billie Nelson (Norton), 3 Phillips (Norton), 4 Peter Richards (Norton), 5 Steve Spencer (Norton), 6 Barry Scully (Norton). Fastest lap: Gould, 70.43mph.
Cadwell Conqueror (12 laps): 1 Nelson (Norton), 72.76mph, 2 Watson (Norton), 3 Chatterton (251 Yamaha), 4 Scully (Norton), 5 Willmott (Norton), 6 Richards (Norton). Fastest lap: Gould, 74.59mph.
Production (8 laps): 1 Gould (654 BSA), 68.78mph, 2 Spencer (Norton), 3 John Hedger (Norton), 4 Tony Smith (654 BSA), 5 Chris Hopes (649 Triumph), 6 D Vickers (649 Triumph). Fastest lap: Spencer, 71.80mph.

10 September, Castle Combe
350 (10 laps, 18.4 miles): 1 Dave Simmonds (305 Honda), speed 85.21mph, 2 Reg Everett (251 Yamaha), 3 Rod Gould (Norton), 4 Charlie Sanby (AJS), 5 Tony Rutter (Norton), 6 Dave Elvin (AJS). Fastest lap: Simmonds, 87.62mph.
500 (10 laps): 1 Dave Croxford (Matchless), 88.46mph, 2 Gould (Norton), 3 Tom Phillips (Norton), 4 Malcolm Uphill (Norton), 5 C Burton (Matchless), 6 Charlie Sanby (Norton). Fastest lap: Gould, Croxford, 90.25mph.

7 September, Croft
350 (12 laps, 21 miles): 1 Dennis Gallagher (AJS), 73.28mph 2 Tony Rutter (Norton), 3 Phil Read (Norton), 4 Reg Everett (Yamaha), 5 Tom Armstrong (Norton), 6 R Wilson (Norton). Fastest lap: Gallagher, 75.54mph.
500 (15 laps): 1 Rob Fitton (Norton), 74.51mph, 2 Read (Norton), 3 Peter Richards (Norton), 4 Wilson (Norton), 5 Carl Ward (Norton), 6 R Humble (Norton). Fastest lap: Read, 76.64mph.

18 September, Cadwell Park
350 (12 laps, 27 miles): 1 Dan Shorey (Norton), 72.03mph, 2 Peter Williams (AJS), 3 Rod Gould (Norton), 4 Billie Nelson (Norton), 5 Tony Willmott (Norton), 6 Dave Degens (Aermacchi). Fastest lap: Shorey, 75.98mph (record).
Experts Invitation (20 laps): 1 Mike Hailwood (250 Honda), 74.92mph, 2 John Cooper (Norton), 3 Shorey (Norton), 4 Phil Read (250 Yamaha), 5 Gould (Norton), 6 Malcolm Uphill (Norton). Fastest lap: Hailwood, 76.42mph.

24 September, Scarborough
350 (12 laps, 28.92 miles): 1 Dan Shorey (Norton), 65.87mph, 2 Dennis Gallagher (AJS), 3 Steve Spencer (Norton), 4 John Blanchard (Seeley AJS), 5 George Fogarty (AJS), 6 Dave King (Norton). Fastest lap: Shorey, 67.15mph.
500 (12 laps): 1 Shorey (Norton), 66.83mph, 2 Spencer (Norton), 3 Blanchard (Seeley Matchless), 4 Barry Scully (Norton), 5 Roly Capper (Matchless), 6 Charlie Sanby (Norton). Fastest lap: Shorey, 68.42mph.

25 September, Mallory Park – Race of the Year
350 (10 laps, 13.5 miles): 1 Giacomo Agostini (MV), 85.44mph, 2 Dan Shorey (Norton), 3 Peter Williams (AJS), 4 Joe Dunphy (Norton), 5 John Cooper (Norton), 6 Chris Conn (Norton). Fastest lap: Agostini, 87.41mph.
500 (10 laps): 1 Agostini (MV), 87.94mph, 2 Williams (Matchless), 3 Dave Croxford (Matchless), 4 Cooper (Norton), 5 Dunphy (Norton), 6 Shorey (Norton). Fastest lap: Agostini, 89.67mph.
Race of the Year (30 laps, 40.5 miles): 1 Agostini (500 MV), 88.87mph, 2 Bill Ivy (250 Yamaha), 3 Mike Duff (250 Yamaha), 4 Williams (496 Matchless), 5 Cooper (Norton), 6 Ron Chandler (Matchless). Fastest lap: Agostini, 91.70mph (equals record).

1 October, Oulton Park
350 (6 laps, 16.56 miles): 1 John Cooper (Norton), 82.65mph, 2 Dan Shorey (Norton), 3 Peter Williams (AJS), 4 C Wild (Aermacchi), 5 Tom Dickie (AJS), 6 Rod Gould (Norton). Fastest lap: Shorey, Williams, 85.07mph.
500 (6 laps): 1 Cooper (Norton), 85.88mph, 2 Shorey (Norton), 3 Williams (Matchless), 4 Keith Heckles (Norton), 5 Dave Croxford (Matchless), 6 Alan Barnett (Matchless). Fastest lap: Williams, 87.65mph.

9 October, Brands Hatch – Race of the South
350 (10 laps, 26.5 miles): 1 Giacomo Agostini (MV), 85.53mph, 2 Mike Duff (254 Yamaha), 3 Peter Williams (AJS), 4 Dan Shorey (Norton), 5 Dave Croxford (AJS), 6 John Blanchard (Seeley AJS). Fastest lap: Duff, 87.04mph.
Redex Trophy 500 (10 laps): 1 Agostini (MV), 86.18mph, 2 Croxford (Matchless), 3 Shorey (Norton), 4 Dave Degens (Matchless Métisse), 5 Ron Chandler (Matchless), 6 Williams (Matchless). Fastest lap: Agostini, 88.66mph.
750 Race of the South (20 laps): 1 Agostini (500 MV), 86.26mph, 2 Croxford (496 Matchless), 3 Chandler (496 Matchless), 4 Williams (496 Matchless), 5 Shorey (499 Norton), 6 Griff Jenkins (750 Dunstall Métisse). Fastest lap: Agostini, 87.84mph.

23 October, Snetterton
350 (7 laps, 18.97 miles): 1 Dan Shorey (Norton), 88.49mph, 2 Martin Watson (252 Bultaco), 3 John Blanchard (Seeley AJS), 4 John Cooper (Norton), 5 Alan Barnett (AJS), 6 Joe Dunphy (Norton). Fastest lap: Shorey, Cooper, Watson, 90.00mph.
500 (7 laps): 1 Cooper (Norton), 91.32mph, 2 Rod Gould (Norton), 3 Dave Degens (Matchless Métisse), 4 John Blanchard (Seeley Matchless), 5 Chris Conn (Norton), 6 Rex Butcher (Norton). Fastest lap: Cooper, 93.81mph.

30 October, Mallory Park
350 (10 laps, 13.5 miles): 1 Dan Shorey (Norton), 83.85mph, 2 John Cooper (Norton), 3 Ron Chandler (AJS), 4 Martin Watson (252 Bultaco), 5 Rod Gould (Norton), 6 Rex Butcher (Norton). Fastest lap: Chandler, 86.48mph.
500 (15 laps): 1 Cooper (Norton), 87.35mph, 2 Chandler (Matchless), 3 Gould (Norton), 4 Shorey (Norton), 5 Dave Degens (Matchless Métisse), 6 John Blanchard (Seeley Matchless). Fastest lap: Cooper, Croxford, Chandler, Gould, 89.34mph.

212

British Championships
350: 1 John Cooper, 2 Rod Gould, 3 Dan Shorey
500: 1 Cooper, 2 Dave Croxford, 3 Gould

1967

5 March, Mallory Park
350 (10 laps, 13.5 miles): 1 Peter Williams (Arter AJS), 81.65mph, 2 Dave Croxford (AJS), 3 Paul Smart (Aermacchi), 4 Rex Butcher (Norton), 5 Joe Dunphy (Norton), 6 Dave Degens (AJS Métisse). Fastest lap: Dunphy, 86.17mph.
500 (15 laps): 1 Ron Chandler (Matchless), 86.35mph, 2 Alan Barnett (Matchless), 3 Derek Minter (Norton), 4 Steve Spencer (Norton), 5 Percy Tait (Triumph), 6 Rex Butcher (Norton). Fastest lap: John Cooper (Norton), 89.01mph.

12 March, Snetterton
350 (7 laps, 18.97 miles): 1 John Cooper (Norton), 87.11mph, 2 John Blanchard (Seeley AJS), 3 Dan Shorey (Norton), 4 Alan Barnett (AJS), 5 Paul Smart (Aermacchi), 6 Derek Minter (Norton). Fastest lap: Cooper, Shorey, 89.01mph.
500 (7 laps): 1 Shorey (Norton), 89.67mph, 2 Blanchard (Seeley Matchless), 3 Dave Croxford (Matchless), 4 Rod Gould (Norton), 5 Chandler (Matchless), 6 Minter (Norton). Fastest lap: Shorey, 92.04mph.

24 March, Brands Hatch – King of Brands
350 (10 laps, 26.5 miles): 1 John Blanchard (Seeley AJS), 83.22mph, 2 Dan Shorey (Norton), 3 Derek Minter (Norton), 4 Dave Croxford (AJS), 5 John Cooper (Norton). Fastest lap: Blanchard, 85.18mph.
500 Redex Trophy (10 laps): 1 Blanchard (Seeley Matchless), 85.81mph, 2 Dave Degens (Matchless Métisse), 3 Croxford (Matchless), 4 Chandler (Matchless), 5 Pat Mahoney (Matchless), 6 Dan Shorey (Norton). Fastest lap: Blanchard, 87.84mph.
750 King of Brands (15 laps): 1 Chandler (496 Matchless), 85.89mph, 2 Blanchard (496 Seeley Matchless), 3 Rex Butcher (750 Domiracer), 4 Shorey (499 Norton), 5 Alan Barnett (496 Matchless), 6 John Hartle (650 Triumph Métisse). Fastest lap: Chandler, Barnett, 87.38mph.
750 (10 laps): 1 Chandler (496 Matchless), 85.36mph, 2 Croxford (496 Matchless), 3 Butcher (750 Domiracer), 4 Peter Williams (496 Matchless), 5 Hartle (650 Triumph Métisse), 6 Degens (650 Triumph Métisse). Fastest lap: Croxford, 87.04mph.

26 March, Mallory Park – Master of Mallory
Master of Mallory (30 laps, 40.5 miles): 1 John Cooper (Norton), 81.74mph, 2 Ron Chandler (Matchless), 3 Pat Mahoney (Matchless Métisse), 4 Peter Williams (Matchless), 5 Rod Gould (Norton), 6 Alan Barnett (Matchless). Fastest lap: Cooper, 87.41mph.
Solo Handicap (15 laps): 1 Joe Dunphy (499 Norton), 85.6mph, 2 Rex Butcher (750 Domiracer), 3 Chris Conn (499 Norton), 4 Gould (499 Norton), 5 Cooper (499 Norton), 6 Chandler (496 Matchless). Fastest lap: Dunphy, 88.36mph.

27 March, Oulton Park – Race of the North
350 (19 laps, 52.44 miles): 1 Mike Hailwood (Honda), 84.94mph, 2 Derek Minter (Norton), 3 John Cooper (Norton), 4 Peter Williams (AJS), 5 Dan Shorey (Norton), 6 John Hartle (AJS). Fastest lap: Hailwood, 87.96mph.
500 Race of the North (19 laps, 52.44 miles): 1 Minter (Norton), 86.42mph, 2 Williams (Matchless), 3 Steve Spencer (Norton), 4 Griff Jenkins (Norton), 5 Barry Randle (Norton), 6 Malcolm Uphill (Norton). Fastest lap: Minter, 88.12mph.
750 (9 laps): 1 Hartle (650 Triumph Métisse), 85.16mph, 2 Rex Butcher (750 Domiracer), 3 Dan Shorey (540 Norton), 4 Tony Smith (654 BSA), 5 Percy Tait (649 Triumph). Fastest lap: Butcher, 87.96mph.

27 March, Crystal Palace
350 (8 laps, 11.12 miles): 1 Ron Chandler (AJS), 67.12mph, 2 Alan Peck (Norton), 3 Reg Everett (270 Yamaha), 4 Charlie Sanby (AJS), 5 Paul Smart (Aermacchi), 6 Brian Davis (AJS). Fastest lap: Peck, 72.10mph.
500 (8 laps): 1 Chandler (Matchless), 73.13mph, 2 Sanby (Norton), 3 Godfrey Nash (Norton), 4 Alan Peck (AJS), 5 G Young (Norton), 6 Graham Sharp (Norton). Fastest lap: Chandler, 76.51mph.

27 March, Cadwell Park
350 (8 laps, 18 miles): 1 Rod Gould (Norton), 70.15mph, 2 Billie Nelson (Norton), 3 Ginger Molloy (252 Bultaco), 4 Tony Willmott (Norton), 5 Pat Mahoney (AJS Métisse), 6 Rob Fitton (Norton). Fastest lap: Gould, 71.84mph.
500 (12 laps): 1 Gould (Norton), 72.79mph, 2 Dave Degens (Matchless Métisse), 3 Tom Phillips (Norton), 4 Pat Mahoney (Matchless Métisse), 5 Alan Barnett (Matchless), 6 C Burton (Matchless). Fastest lap: Gould, Degens, 74.04mph.

29 April, Castle Combe
350 (10 laps, 18.4 miles): 1 Rod Gould (Norton), 86.70mph, 2 Dave Croxford (AJS), 3 Paul Smart (Aermacchi), 4 G Daniels (AJS), 5 Alan Peck (Norton), 6 Alan Barnett (AJS). Fastest lap: Gould, 88.79mph.
500 (10 laps): 1 Croxford (Matchless), 89.10mph, 2 Percy Tait (Triumph), 3 Barry Randle (Norton), 4 Tom Phillips (Norton), 5 Selwyn Griffiths (Matchless). Fastest lap: Tait, Randle, 91.75mph (equals record).

27 May, Scarborough – Cock o' The North
350 (8 laps, 19.28 miles): 1 Dan Shorey (Norton), 57.78mph, 2 Tom Phillips (Ducati), 3 Tom Armstrong (Norton), 4 Bill Crozier (AJS), 5 J Learmonth (Norton), 6 D Sellars (Norton). Fastest lap: Phillips, 59.76mph.
250-750 (8 laps): 1 Shorey (Norton), 58.93mph, 2 Rob Fitton (Norton), 3 Crozier (Matchless), 4 D Saville (650 Sabre), 5 Barry Scully (Norton), 6 Alan Jefferies (650 Triumph). Fastest lap: Fitton, 61.45mph.

28 May, Mallory Park
350 (15 laps, 20.25 miles): 1 Ron Chandler (AJS), 84.69mph, 2 Pat Mahoney (AJS Métisse), 3 Paul Smart (Aermacchi), 4 John Cooper (Norton), 5 Dan Shorey (Norton), 6 Joe Dunphy (Norton). Fastest lap: Chandler, Ray Pickrell (Norton), 86.78mph.

500 (15 laps): 1 Peter Williams (Matchless), 86.46mph, 2 Cooper (Norton), 3 Percy Tait (Triumph), 4 John Blanchard (Seeley Matchless), 5 Rod Gould (Norton), 6 Dunphy (Norton). Fastest lap: Cooper, 88.68mph.

29 May, Brands Hatch – Evening News Trophy
350 (10 laps, 26.5 miles): 1 Pat Mahoney (AJS Métisse), 82.84mph, 2 Paul Smart (Aermacchi), 3 Peter Williams (AJS), 4 Fred Stevens (Paton), 5 John Cooper (Norton), 6 Ron Chandler (AJS). Fastest lap: Mahoney, 85.18mph.
500 Redex Trophy, 2 (10 laps): 1 Williams (Matchless), 85.73mph, 2 Cooper (Norton), 3 Dave Croxford (Matchless), 4 Ron Chandler (Matchless), 5 Dan Shorey (Norton). Fastest lap: Hailwood, 87.36mph.
1000 Evening News Trophy (20 laps): 1 Hailwood (250 Honda), 86.39mph, 2 Williams (496 Matchless), 3 Dave Degens (650 Dresda Triumph), 4 Croxford (496 Matchless), 5 Shorey (499 Norton), 6 Derek Minter (499 Norton). Fastest lap: Hailwood, 88.17mph.

29 May, Cadwell Park – Cadwell Conqueror
350 (8 laps, 18 miles): 1 Steve Jolly (Aermacchi), 71.70mph, 2 Rod Gould (Norton), 3 Derek Chatterton (Chat Yamaha), 4 Billie Nelson (Norton), 5 Malcolm Uphill (Norton), 6 Charlie Sanby (AJS). Fastest lap: Gould, 74.04mph.
500 (8 laps): 1 Nelson (Norton), 72.99mph, 2 Tom Phillips (Norton), 3 Uphill (Norton), 4 Gould (Norton), 5 Sanby (Norton), 6 Steve Jolly (Matchless). Fastest lap: Nelson, 74.59mph.
250-750 Cadwell Conqueror (12 laps): 1 Nelson (499 Norton), 73.01mph, 2 Phillips (499 Norton), 3 Tom Dickie (496 Matchless), 4 Barry Scully (499 Norton), 5 Joe Dunphy (499 Norton), 6 Jolly (344 Aermacchi). Fastest lap: Nelson, 75.14mph.

18 June, Mallory Park – Post-TT International
350 (15 laps, 20.25 miles): 1 Pat Mahoney (Aermacchi), 85.48mph, 2 Derek Chatterton (251 Yamaha), 3 Paul Smart (Aermacchi), 4 Mike Duff (Aermacchi Métisse), 5 Dave Degens (Aermacchi), 6 John Cooper (Seeley). Fastest lap: Mahoney, John Hartle (Aermacchi Métisse), 87.73mph.
500 (20 laps): 1 Giacomo Agostini (MV), 88.15mph, 2 Hartle (Matchless Métisse), 3 Peter Williams (Matchless), 4 Pat Mahoney (Matchless Métisse), 5 Malcolm Uphill (Norton), 6 Tom Phillips (Norton). Fastest lap: Agostini, 90.67mph.
250-750 (20 laps): 1 Agostini (500 MV), 88.47mph, 2 Degens (650 Dresda Triumph), 3 Hartle (496 Matchless Métisse), 4 Mahoney (496 Matchless Métisse), 5 Ron Chandler (Matchless), 6 Joe Dunphy (499 Norton). Fastest lap: Agostini, 91.01mph.

24 June, Oulton Park
350 (6 laps, 16.56 miles – rain shortened): 1 Dave Croxford (AJS), 75.30mph, 2 Steve Jolly (Aermacchi), 3 Malcolm Uphill (Norton), 4 Brian Kemp (Norton), 5 Clive Padgett (Yamaha), 6 Brian Ball (Yamaha). Fastest lap: Croxford, 75.27mph.
500, heat 1 (4 laps – final abandoned, flooded track): 1 Croxford (Matchless), 2 Uphill (Norton), 3 Rutter (Norton), 4 Pat Mahoney (Matchless Métisse). Fastest lap: Croxford, 75.19mph.
500, heat 2 (4 laps): 1 F Moss (Norton-BSA), 2 Ray Pickrell (Monard), 3 Jolly (Matchless), 4 Tom Phillips (Norton). Fastest lap: D Rae (Velocette), 67.07mph.

1 July, Castle Combe
350 (10 laps, 18.4 miles): 1 Dave Croxford (AJS), 86.34mph, 2 Tom Phillips (Aermacchi), 3 Paul Smart (Aermacchi), 4 Brian Kemp (Norton), 5 Tony Rutter (Norton), 6 G Daniels (AJS). Fastest lap: Phillips, 88.56mph.
500 Avon Trophy (10 laps): 1 Barry Randle (Norton), 89.08mph, 2 Rutter (Norton), 3 Phillips (Norton), 4 Tom Dickie (Matchless), 5 Smart (Triumph), 6 Percy May (Norton). Fastest lap: Randle, 91.49mph.

30 July, Snetterton
350 (7 laps, 18.97 miles): 1 Dave Simmonds (Kawasaki), 87.22mph, 2 Tom Phillips (Aermacchi), 3 John Cooper (Norton), 4 Dave Croxford (AJS), 5 Barry Randle (Norton), 6 Paul Smart (Aermacchi). Fastest lap: Simmonds, 89.35mph.
500 (7 laps): 1 Derek Minter (Norton), 89.1mph, 2 Cooper (Norton), 3 Dan Shorey (Norton), 4 Tom Phillips (Norton), 5 Smart (Triumph), 6 Charlie Sanby (Norton). Fastest lap: Minter, Cooper, 91.01mph.
250-1000 (6 laps): 1 Ray Pickrell (748 Domiracer), 88.96mph, 2 Phillips (748 Dunstall Norton Métisse), 3 Cooper (499 Norton), 4 Shorey (499 Norton), 5 Rex Butcher (748 Dunstall Norton), 6 Minter (499 Norton). Fastest lap: Cooper, 91.18mph.

13 August, Brands Hatch – Hutchinson 100
350 (10 laps, 26.5 miles): 1 Dan Shorey (Norton), 82.69mph, 2 Rex Butcher (Norton), 3 Dave Croxford (AJS), 4 Dave Degens (Aermacchi), 5 Griff Jenkins (Norton), 6 Rod Gould (Norton). Fastest lap: Shorey, 84.57mph.
750 leg 1 (15 laps): 1 Mike Hailwood (297 Honda), 85.65mph, 2 Ray Pickrell (745 Dunstall Atlas), 3 Shorey (499 Norton), 4 John Cooper (496 Seeley), 5 Dave Croxford (496 Matchless), 6 Charlie Sanby (499 Norton). Fastest lap: Hailwood, 88.01mph.
750 leg 2 (15 laps): 1 Hailwood, 85.99mph, 2 Pickrell, 3 Shorey, 4 Cooper, 5 Croxford, 6 Rod Gould (499 Norton). Fastest lap: Hailwood, 88.17mph (record for reverse circuit).
Production (20 laps): 1 John Hartle (649 Triumph Bonneville), 83.87mph, 2 Gould (649 Triumph Bonneville), 3 Pickrell (745 Dunstall Norton), 4 Paul Smart (745 Dunstall Norton), 5 Mick Andrew (649 Triumph Bonneville), 6 Tony Smith (654 BSA Spitfire). Fastest lap: Hartle, 85.64mph.

20 August, Mallory Park
350 (15 laps, 20.25 miles): 1 Rod Gould (Norton), 85.08mph, 2 Dave Degens (Aermacchi), 3 Dave Croxford (AJS), 4 Pat Mahoney (AJS Métisse), 5 John Cooper (Norton), 6 Griff Jenkins (Norton). Fastest lap: Croxford, Degens, Gould, 86.48mph.
500 (15 laps): 1 Cooper (Seeley), 88.26mph, 2 Barry Randle (Norton), 3 Ron Chandler (Matchless), 4 Dan Shorey (Norton), 5 Gould (Norton), 6 Mahoney (Matchless Métisse). Fastest lap: Cooper, 90.38mph.

26 August, Scarborough – International Gold Trophy
350 (10 laps, 24.1 miles): 1 Dan Shorey (Norton), 64.98mph, 2 Billie Nelson (Norton), 3 Chris Conn (Norton), 4 Steve Spencer (Norton),

5 John Cooper (Norton), 6 John Hartle (Aermacchi Métisse). Fastest lap: Shorey, 66.84mph.
500 Gold Trophy (10 laps): 1 Cooper (Seeley), 68.35mph, 2 Shorey (Norton), 3 Hartle (Matchless), 4 Dave Croxford (Matchless), 5 Peter Richards (Norton), 6 Spencer (Norton). Fastest lap: John Blanchard (URS), 69.96mph.

27 August, Snetterton – Daily Mail Race of Aces
350 (10 laps, 27.1 miles): 1 Kel Carruthers (Aermacchi), 86.71mph, 2 Dan Shorey (Norton), 3 Tom Phillips (Aermacchi), 4 Brian Kemp (Norton), 5 Rex Butcher (Norton), 6 Tony Rutter (Norton). Fastest lap: Mike Hailwood (Honda), 90.16mph (record for modified track).
500 (10 laps): 1 Dan Shorey (Norton), 89.2mph, 2 Barry Randle (Norton), 3 Rod Gould (Norton), 4 Rex Butcher (Norton), 5 Ron Chandler (Matchless), 6 Peter Richards (Norton). Fastest lap: Shorey, 91.69mph.
250-1000 Daily Mail Race of Aces (10 laps): 1 Shorey (499 Norton), 90.13mph, 2 Dave Croxford (496 Matchless), 3 Chandler (496 Matchless), 4 John Cooper (496 Seeley), 5 Gould (499 Norton), 6 Randle (499 Norton). Fastest lap: Shorey, 92.55mph (record for modified track).

28 August, Cadwell Park – Coronation Trophy
350 (8 laps, 18 miles): 1 Rod Gould (Norton), 70.67mph, 2 Billie Nelson (Norton), 3 Tony Willmott (Norton), 4 Barry Scully (Norton), 5 Selwyn Griffiths (AJS), 6 Tom Phillips (Norton). Fastest lap: Griffiths, Willmott, 72.19mph.
500 Coronation Trophy (10 laps): 1 Peter Richards (Norton), 73.41mph, 2 Nelson (Norton), 3 Scully (Norton), 4 Willmott (Norton), 5 Arthur Giles (Norton), 6 Derek Phillips (Norton). Fastest lap: Nelson, 75.14mph.

28 August, Oulton Park
350 (19 laps, 52.44 miles): 1 Kel Carruthers (Aermacchi Métisse), 84.73mph, 2 Derek Minter (Norton), 3 Steve Spencer (Norton), 4 John Hartle (Aermacchi Métisse), 5 Dan Shorey (Norton), 6 Chris Conn (Norton). Fastest lap: Carruthers, 86.13mph.
500 Avon Gold Cup (19 laps): 1 John Cooper (Seeley), 81.49mph, 2 Hartle (Matchless), 3 Shorey (Norton), 4 Steve Jolly (Matchless), 5 Rex Butcher (Norton), 6 Malcolm Uphill (Norton). Fastest lap: Cooper, 84.66mph.
500 Les Graham Memorial Trophy (8 laps): 1 Cooper, 88.43mph, 2 Minter (Norton), 3 Hartle (Matchless), 4 Jolly (Matchless), 5 Butcher (Norton), 6 Spencer (Norton). Fastest lap: Hartle, 89.71mph.
Hailwood 250 class and outright lap record, 97.07mph

28 August, Crystal Palace
350 (12 laps, 16.68 miles): 1 Charlie Sanby (AJS), 74.41mph, 2 Martyn Ashwood (AJS), 3 D Filler (AJS), 4 Ron Chandler (AJS), 5 H Rayner (AJS), 6 Reg Everett (Broad Yamaha). Fastest lap: Ashwood, 76.75mph.
1000 (12 laps): 1 Chandler (496 Matchless), 77.36mph, 2 Joe Dunphy (499 Norton), 3 Ashwood (Matchless), 4 Peter Butler (649 Triumph), 5 B Burgess (499 Norton), 6 A Rogers (650 Norton). Fastest lap: Chandler, 79.68mph.

3 September, Brands Hatch
350 (10 laps, 26.5 miles): 1 John Cooper (Norton), 76.64mph, 2 Dave Croxford (AJS), 3 Ron Chandler (AJS), 4 Derek Minter (Norton), 5 Brian Kemp (Norton), 6 Malcolm Uphill (Norton). Fastest lap: Cooper, 79.76mph.
500 Redex Trophy 3 (10 laps): 1 Minter (Norton), 85.04mph, 2 Croxford (Matchless), 3 Cooper (Seeley), 4 Dave Degens (Dresda Triumph), 5 John Taylor (Matchless), 6 Alan Barnett (Matchless). Fastest lap: Minter, 87.04mph.
1000, race 1 (10 laps): 1 Cooper (496 Seeley), 74.26mph, 2 Croxford (496 Matchless), 3 Steve Ellis (Matchless), 4 Martyn Ashwood (Matchless), 5 Chandler (496 Matchless), 6 Taylor (Matchless). Fastest lap: Cooper, 76.32mph.
1000, race 2 (10 laps): 1 Cooper, 84.5mph, 2 Croxford, 3 Chandler, 4 Charlie Sanby (Norton), 5 Tony Rutter (Norton), 6 Ashwood. Fastest lap: Croxford, 85.95mph.

10 September, Cadwell Park
350 (12 laps, 27 miles): 1 Mike Hailwood (297 Honda), 74.80mph, 2 Dan Shorey (Norton), 3 Billie Nelson (Norton), 4 John Cooper (Norton), 5 Derek Chatterton (251 Yamaha), 6 Rod Gould (Norton). Fastest lap: Hailwood, 76.70mph (record).
175-750 Invitation (20 laps): 1 Hailwood (297 Honda), 75.85mph, 2 Bill Ivy (250 Yamaha), 3 Shorey (499 Norton), 4 Gould (499 Norton), 5 Nelson (499 Norton), 6 Rob Fitton (499 Norton). Fastest lap: Hailwood, 78.79mph (record).

17 September, Mallory Park – Race of the Year
350 (15 laps, 20.25 miles): 1 Mike Hailwood (297 Honda), 90.40mph, 2 Giacomo Agostini (MV), 3 Phil Read (251 Yamaha), 4 Paul Smart (Aermacchi Métisse), 5 Griff Jenkins (Norton), 6 Ron Chandler (AJS). Fastest lap: Hailwood, 92.40mph (record).
1000 (20 laps): 1 Agostini (420 MV), 89.30mph, 2 John Cooper (496 Seeley), 3 Ray Pickrell (748 Dunstall Domiracer), 4 Dave Croxford (496 Matchless), 5 Percy Tait (490 Triumph), 6 Barry Randle (499 Norton). Fastest lap: Agostini, 91.35mph.
Race of the Year (30 laps): 1 Hailwood (297 Honda), 91.31mph, 2 Agostini (420 MV), 3 Read (251 Yamaha), 4 Cooper (496 Seeley), 5 Ivy (251 Yamaha), 6 Croxford (496 Matchless). Fastest lap: Hailwood, 93.46mph (record).

1 October, Brands Hatch – Race of the South
350 (10 laps, 26.5 miles): 1 Mike Hailwood (297 Honda), 86.57mph, 2 Giacomo Agostini (MV), 3 Dan Shorey (Norton), 4 Derek Minter (Norton), 5 Dave Croxford (AJS), 6 Rex Butcher (Norton). Fastest lap: Hailwood, 87.84mph (record).
500 Redex Trophy 4 (10 laps): 1 Shorey (Norton), 86.21mph, 2 Minter (Norton), 3 Croxford (496 Matchless), 4 Ron Chandler (Matchless), 5 Steve Spencer (Norton), 6 Alan Barnett (Matchless). Fastest lap: Shorey, 88.17mph.
Evening News Race of the South (20 laps): 1 Hailwood (297 Honda), 87.44mph, 2 Phil Read (248 Yamaha), 3 Minter (499 Norton), 4 Shorey (499 Norton), 5 Chandler (496 Matchless), 6 Barnett (496 Matchless). Fastest lap: Hailwood, 90.17mph.

15 October, Snetterton
350 (7 laps, 18.97 miles): 1 Dan Shorey (Norton), 86.8mph, 2 Dave Croxford (AJS), 3 Dave Degens (Aermacchi), 4 Derek Minter (Norton), 5 Derek Chatterton (251 Yamaha), 6 Tony Rutter (Norton). Fastest lap: Croxford, Shorey, Degens, 88.69mph.

500 (7 laps): 1 Minter (Norton), 84.42mph, 2 Ron Chandler (Matchless), 3 Alan Barnett (Matchless Métisse), 4 Rod Gould (Norton), 5 Joe Dunphy (Norton), 6 Dan Shorey (Norton). Fastest lap: Minter, 92.40mph (record – in heat).
1000 (6 laps): 1 Ray Pickrell (750 Dunstall), 90.78mph, 2 Shorey (499 Norton), 3 Chandler (496 Matchless), 4 Croxford (496 Matchless), 5 Rex Butcher (Norton), 6 Rob Fitton (499 Norton). Fastest lap: Pickrell, 93.63mph (record).

22 October, Brands Hatch
350 (8 laps, 21.2 miles): 1 Derek Minter (Norton), 83.11mph, 2 Dan Shorey (Norton), 3 Dave Croxford (AJS), 4 Rex Butcher (Norton), 5 Griff Jenkins (Norton), 6 Derek Chatterton (Kawasaki). Fastest lap: Shorey, 85.18mph.
500 (8 laps): 1 Shorey (Norton), 85.26mph, 2 Minter (Norton), 3 John Cooper (Seeley), 4 Ron Chandler (Matchless), 5 Alan Barnett (Matchless Métisse), 6 Kel Carruthers (Matchless Métisse). Fastest lap: Shorey, 87.36mph.
1000 (8 laps): 1 Minter (647 Curtis Norton), 83.83mph, 2 Cooper (496 Seeley), 3 Ray Pickrell (745 Dunstall Domiracer), 4 Dave Degens (649 Dresda Métisse), 5 Croxford (496 Matchless), 6 Chandler (496 Matchless). Fastest lap: Minter, 86.97mph.

29 October, Mallory Park
350 (10 laps, 13.5 miles): 1 John Cooper (255 Yamaha), 74.45mph, 2 Dave Croxford (AJS), 3 Rod Gould (Norton), 4 John Samways (Bultaco), 5 Dan Shorey (Norton), 6 Alan Barnett (AJS). Fastest lap: Samways, 77.89mph.
500 (15 laps): 1 Percy Tait (490 Triumph), 83.05mph, 2 Cooper (Seeley), 3 Gould (Norton), 4 Croxford (Matchless), 5 Ron Chandler (Matchless), 6 Barry Randle (Norton). Fastest lap: Tait, 87.10mph.

British Championships:
350: 1 Dave Croxford, 2 Rob Gould, 3 John Cooper
500: 1 Ron Chandler, 2 Cooper, 3 Derek Minter

1968
3 March, Mallory Park
350 (10 laps, 20.25 miles): 1 John Hartle (Aermacchi Métisse), 83.19mph, 2 Rex Butcher (Kawasaki), 3 Ron Chandler (Seeley), 4 Dan Shorey (Norton), 5 Griff Jenkins (Norton), 6 Tony Rutter (Norton). Fastest lap: Chandler, 86.70mph.
Unlimited (30 laps): 1 Ray Pickrell (745 Dunstall Domiracer), 84.79mph, 2 Chandler (496 Matchless), 3 Dave Croxford (636 Matchless), 4 Shorey (545 Norton), 5 Steve Spencer (Norton), 6 John Cooper (Seeley). Fastest lap: Pickrell, 89.34mph.

10 March, Cadwell Park
350 (8 laps, 18 miles): 1 Tom Armstrong (Norton), 63.62mph, 2 Dave Foulkes (Norton), 3 Trevor Burgess (Greeves), 4 P Malkinson (AJS), 5 Gordon Pantall (AJS), 6 Rob Fitton (Norton). Fastest lap: Dave Croxford (AJS), Pantall, 65.43mph.
500 (10 laps): 1 John Cooper (Seeley), 72.13mph, 2 Steve Spencer (Norton), 3 Steve Jolly (Matchless), 4 Croxford (Seeley), 5 Barry Scully (Norton), 6 Arthur Giles (Norton). Fastest lap: Cooper, 74.18mph.

10 March, Brands Hatch
350 (10 laps, 26.5 miles): 1 Alan Barnett (AJS Métisse), 82.86mph, 2 John Hartle (Aermacchi Métisse), 3 Derek Chatterton (275 Chat Kawasaki), 4 Dan Shorey (Petty Norton), 5 Tony Rutter (Norton), 6 Griff Jenkins (Norton). Fastest lap: Barnett, 84.42mph.
500 Redex Grand National (40 laps): 1 Hartle (Matchless Métisse), 80.27mph, 2 Martyn Ashwood (Arter Matchless), 3 Pat Mahoney (Matchless), 4 Ron Chandler (Matchless), 5 Malcolm Uphill (Norton), 6 Tom Dickie (Matchless). Fastest lap: Hartle, 85.95mph.
1300 (10 laps): 1 Ray Pickrell (745 Dunstall Domiracer), 82.68mph, 2 Mahoney (647 Curtis Domiracer), 3 Hartle (496 Matchless Métisse), 4 Chandler (496 Matchless), 5 Rex Butcher (647 Francis Domiracer), 6 Ashwood (496 Arter Matchless). Fastest lap: Pickrell, Barnett (496 Matchless Métisse), 87.04mph.

17 March, Snetterton
350 (7 laps, 18.97 miles): 1 Dan Shorey (Petty Norton), 84.62mph, 2 Derek Chatterton (275 Chat Kawasaki), 3 Rex Butcher (Kawasaki), 4 Alan Barnett (AJS Métisse), 5 Bob Grimson (Norton), 6 Tom Phillips (Aermacchi). Fastest lap: Butcher, 86.79mph.
500 (7 laps): 1 Shorey (Petty Norton), 86.49mph, 2 Percy Tait (Triumph), 3 John Cooper (Seeley), 4 Dave Croxford (Matchless), 5 Barnett (Matchless Métisse), 6 Barry Scully (Norton). Fastest lap: Tait, 90.16mph.
1000 (20 laps): 1 Cooper (647 Curtis Domiracer), 88.04mph, 2 Tait (490 Triumph), 3 Shorey (499 Norton), 4 Barnett (496 Matchless Métisse), 5 Barry Randle (499 Norton), 6 Butcher (647 Francis Domiracer). Fastest lap: Shorey, 91.01mph.

30 March, Oulton Park
350 (8 laps, 22.08 miles): 1 Dave Simmonds (Kawasaki), 85.15mph, 2 Dan Shorey (Petty Norton), 3 Tony Rutter (Norton), 4 Rex Butcher (Kawasaki), 5 Barry Randle (Norton), 6 Steve Spencer (Norton). Fastest lap: Butcher, 87.65mph.
1000 (8 laps): 1 Shorey (499 Norton), 86.75mph, 2 Percy Tait (490 Triumph), 3 Dave Croxford (636 Matchless), 4 Griff Jenkins (745 Curley Norton), 5 Rex Butcher (647 Francis Domiracer), 6 Malcolm Uphill (499 Norton). Fastest lap: Tait, 88.75mph.

7 April, Cadwell Park – Woodlands National
350 (6 laps, 13.5 miles): 1 Alan Barnett (AJS Métisse), 64.88mph, 2 Clive Padgett (305 Yamaha), 3 Tony Smith (BSA), 4 Dave Foulkes (Norton), 5 Derek Chatterton (275 Chat Kawasaki), 6 Tony Willmott (Norton). Fastest lap: Barnett, 67.42mph.
650 (6 laps): 1 Barnett (496 Matchless Métisse), 65.66mph, 2 Smith (BSA), 3 Hall (649 Triton), 4 Foulkes (499 Norton), 5 Geoff Barry (499 Norton), 6 Brian Clarke (Métisse). Fastest lap: Barnett, 69.23mph.

12 April, Brands Hatch – King of Brands
350 Castrol Challenge (15 laps, 39.75 miles): 1 Martin Carney (Kawasaki), 82.86mph, 2 Alan Barnett (AJS Métisse), 3 Dave Simmonds (Kawasaki), 4 Dave Croxford (AJS), 5 Griff Jenkins (Norton), 6 Derek Chatterton (275 Chat Kawasaki). Fastest lap: Barnett, 84.72mph.
500 (15 laps): 1 Croxford (Seeley), 86.71mph, 2 Malcolm Uphill (Norton), 3 Rod Gould (Norton), 4 Griff Jenkins (Norton),

5 Pat Mahoney (Matchless), 6 Martyn Ashwood (Arter Matchless). Fastest lap: Croxford, 87.84mph.

1300 (15 laps): 1 Uphill (499 Norton), 85.48mph, 2 Croxford (496 Seeley), 3 Gould (499 Norton), 4 Barnett (496 Matchless Métisse), 5 Ashwood (496 Arter Matchless), 6 Geoff Barry (499 Norton). Fastest lap: Ray Pickrell (745 Dunstall Norton), 87.36mph.

Production (10 laps): 1 Colin Dixon (649 Triumph), 80.85mph, 2 John Hedger (649 Triumph), 3 Peter Butler (649 Triumph). Fastest lap: Pickrell (745 Dunstall Norton), 86.73mph.

14 April, Mallory Park – Master of Mallory

350 Castrol Challenge (15 laps, 20.25 miles): 1 Kel Carruthers (Drixton Aermacchi), 85.91mph, 2 Tony Rutter (Norton), 3 Barry Randle (Norton), 4 Dave Croxford (AJS), 5 Rod Gould (Norton), 6 Malcolm Uphill (Norton). Fastest lap: Carruthers, 88.36mph.

500 (15 laps): 1 Croxford (Seeley), 88.13mph, 2 Gould (Norton), 3 Randle (Norton), 4 Percy Tait (Triumph), 5 Uphill (Norton), 6 Griff Jenkins (Norton). Fastest lap: Gould, 90.33mph. Master of Mallory placings: 1 Croxford, 2 Gould, 3 Randle.

15 April, Oulton Park – Race of the North

350 Castrol Challenge (15 laps, 41.4 miles): 1 Kel Carruthers (Drixton Aermacchi), 85.34mph, 2 Barry Randle (Norton), 3 Tony Rutter (Norton), 4 Bill Smith (305 Honda), 5 Tom Dickie (Norton), 6 Rob Fitton (Norton). Fastest lap: Carruthers, 86.58mph.

500 (15 laps): 1 Percy Tait (Triumph), 87.75mph, 2 Malcolm Uphill (Norton), 3 Randle (Norton), 4 Derek Woodman (Matchless), 5 Carruthers (Norton), 6 Brian Ball (Seeley). Fastest lap: Tait, 88.75mph.

750 (10 laps): 1 Ray Pickrell (745 Dunstall), 88.04mph, 2 Dave Croxford (636 Matchless), 3 Pat Mahoney (496 Oakley Matchless), 4 L Geeson (499 Norton), 5 A Cooper (647 Norton), 6 Tait (649 Triumph). Fastest lap: Pickrell, 89.38mph.

15 April, Crystal Palace

350 (10 laps, 13.9 miles): 1 Clive Brown (Norton), 74.05mph, 2 Godfrey Nash (Norton), 3 Alan Barnett (AJS Métisse), 4 Alan Peck (Norton), 5 Mick Andrew (Norton), 6 Paul Smart (Aermacchi). Fastest lap: Barnett, Nash, 77.22mph.

Player's No.6 Championship (10 laps): 1 Paul Smart (745 Curtis Norton), 77.63mph, 2 Martyn Ashwood (496 Arter Matchless), 3 Barnett (496 Matchless Métisse), 4 Charlie Sanby (499 Norton), 5 Brown (Norton), 6 Graham Sharp (Norton). Fastest lap: Smart, 80.45mph (record).

21 April, Thruxton

350 (8 laps, 18.85 miles): 1 Alan Barnett (AJS Métisse), 84.88mph, 2 Malcolm Uphill (Norton), 3 Paul Smart (Aermacchi), 4 Tom Dickie (AJS), 5 A Monk (BSA Special), 6 Jack Smith (AJS). Fastest lap: Barnett, 86.55mph.

500 (10 laps): 1 Dave Croxford (Seeley), 88.20mph, 2 Uphill (Norton), 3 Barnett (Matchless Métisse), 4 Percy Tait (Triumph), 5 Tony Godfrey (Norton), 6 Tom Dickie (Petty Norton). Fastest lap: Croxford, 90.81mph.

27 April, Castle Combe

350 (10 laps, 28.4 miles): 1 Tony Rutter (Norton), 76.60mph, 2 Barry Randle (Norton), 3 Malcolm Uphill (Norton), 4 Colin Thompson (Norton), 5 Tony Mark (BSA), 6 Stan Woods (BSA). Fastest lap: Rutter, 79.62mph.

500 (10 laps): 1 Percy Tait (Triumph), 78.28mph, 2 Dave Croxford (Seeley), 3 Tom Phillips (Norton), 4 Tom Dickie (Petty Norton), 5 Mike Hatherill (Matchless Métisse), 6 Derek Filler (Norton). Fastest lap: Croxford, 82.18mph.

5 May, Mallory Park – Derby Cup

350 (15 laps, 2.25 miles): 1 Jim Curry (Aermacchi), 85.42mph, 2 Barry Randle (Norton), 3 Alan Barnett (AJS Métisse), 4 Pat Mahoney (Oakley AJS), 5 Steve Spencer (Norton), 6 Tony Smith (BSA). Fastest lap: Curry, 87.73mph.

500 Derby Cup (30 laps): 1 Dave Croxford (Seeley), 88.47mph, 2 Randle (Norton), 3 Percy Tait (Triumph), 4 Barnett (Matchless Métisse), 5 Spencer (Norton), 6 Mahoney (Oakley Matchless). Fastest lap: Croxford, Randle, 90.00mph.

12 May, Thruxton

Motorcycle 500 GP: 1 Dave Nixon/ Peter Butler (Triumph T100), 2 Gordon Keith/Brian Ball (Suzuki T20), 3 Tom Dickie/Chas Mortimer (250 Ducati).

19 May, Cadwell Park

350 Castrol Challenge (8 laps, 18 miles): 1 Mike Hailwood (297 Honda), 75.24mph, 2 Phil Read (251 Yamaha), 3 Dan Shorey (Norton), 4 Kel Carruthers (Aermacchi Métisse), 5 Billie Nelson (Norton), 6 Martin Carney (Kawasaki). Fastest lap: Hailwood 78.64mph (record).

500 Middleton Trophy (15 laps): 1 Read (251 Yamaha), 65.84mph, 2 John Cooper (Seeley), 3 Dave Croxford (Seeley), 4 Hailwood (500 Honda), 5 Tom Phillips (Norton), 6 Shorey (Norton). Fastest lap: Read, 68.18mph.

Production (8 laps): 1 Ray Pickrell (745 Dunstall Dominator), 62.62mph, 2 Chris Hopes (649 Triumph), 3 Steve Spencer (745 Norton), 4 Peter Davies (650 Triumph), 5 B Richards (250 Bultaco), 6 L Porter (654 BSA). Fastest lap: Pickrell, 65.22mph

1 June, Scarborough

350 (8 laps, 18 miles): 1 Dan Shorey (Norton), 61.84mph, 2 Tom Phillips (Aermacchi), 3 Dave Foulkes (Norton), 4 S Wright (305 Yamaha), 5 Tom Goodfellow (Norton), 6 J Swannack (Norton). Fastest lap: 63.33mph.

1000 (8 laps): 1 Shorey (499 Norton), 63.94mph, 2 Barry Scully (499 Norton), 3 Bill Crozier (Matchless), 4 Paul Cott (498 Triumph), 5 A Moses (650 Tribsa), 6 John Barton (498 Triumph). Fastest lap: Shorey, 65.23mph.

2 June, Mallory Park

350 (15 laps, 20.25 miles): 1 Dan Shorey (Norton), 85.81mph, 2 Jim Curry (Aermacchi), 3 Kel Carruthers (Aermacchi Métisse), 4 Tony Mark (BSA), 5 Griff Jenkins (Norton), 6 Barry Randle (Norton). Fastest lap: Shorey, Jenkins, 88.04mph.

500 (15 laps): 1 Dave Croxford (Seeley), 88.24mph, 2 Peter Williams (Arter Matchless), 3 Shorey (Norton), 4 Rod Gould (Norton), 5 Randle (Norton), 6 Ron Chandler (Seeley). Fastest lap: Croxford, Williams, Gould, 90.67mph.

Production (30 laps): 1 Ray Pickrell/Croxford (745 Dunstall Norton), 83.25mph, Martyn Ashwood/Joe Dunphy (649 Triumph), 3 Tony Smith/Mick Andrew (654 BSA). Fastest lap: n/a.

3 June, Brands Hatch – Evening News Trophy
350 (10 laps, 26.5 miles): 1 Kel Carruthers (Aermacchi Métisse), 71.47mph, 2 Gordon Keith (Yamaha), 3 Dave Croxford (Seeley), 4 Pat Mahoney (AJS), 5 Griff Jenkins (Norton), 6 Jim Curry (Aermacchi). Fastest lap: Carruthers, 77.01mph.
500 Redex Trophy (10 laps): 1 Croxford (Seeley), 78.11mph, 2 Peter Williams (Arter Matchless), 3 Martyn Ashwood (Matchless), 4 Mahoney (Matchless), 5 Ron Chandler (Seeley), 6 D Miller (Norton). Fastest lap: Croxford, Williams, 80.44mph.
1000 Evening News Trophy (20 laps): 1 Ray Pickrell (745 Dunstall), 87.31mph, 2 Jenkins (745 Curley Norton), 3 Croxford (496 Seeley), 4 Mahoney (745 Curley Norton), 5 Williams (496 Arter Matchless), 6 Chandler (496 Seeley). Fastest lap: Pickrell, 88.99mph.

3 June, Cadwell Park
350 (8 laps, 18 miles): 1 Tom Phillips (Aermacchi), 70.24mph, 2 Steve Jolly (Aermacchi), 3 Jack Smith (AJS), 4 Clive Brown (Norton), 5 D Thomas (Aermacchi), 6 Steve Machin (Aermacchi). Fastest lap: Smith, 72.45mph.
500 (8 laps): 1 John Cooper (Seeley), 72.32mph, 2 Jolly (Norton), 3 Tony Willmott (Norton), 4 Barry Scully (Norton), 5 Paul Cott (Norton), 6 Gordon Pantall (Norton). Fastest lap: Cooper, 74.18mph
Player's No.6 Championship (10 laps): 1 Cooper (496 Seeley), 72.5mph, 2 Tom Phillips (499 Norton), 3 Jolly (499 Norton), 4 Willmott (499 Norton), 5 Scully (499 Norton), 6 Cott (499 Norton). Fastest lap: Cooper, 74.18mph.

16 June, Mallory Park – Post-TT International
350 Castrol Challenge (15 laps, 20.25 miles): 1 Mike Hailwood (297 Honda), 89.73mph, 2 Phil Read (251 Yamaha), 3 Jim Curry (Aermacchi Métisse), 4 Brian Ball (Yamaha), 5 Stan Woods (Yamaha), 6 Tony Smith (BSA). Fastest lap: Read, 92.05mph.
500 (20 laps): 1 Giacomo Agostini (MV), 89.28mph, 2 Alan Barnett (Matchless Métisse), 3 John Cooper (Seeley), 4 Rod Gould (Norton), 5 Pat Mahoney (Matchless), 6 Ron Chandler (Matchless). Fastest lap: Barnett, 92.05mph.
1000 (20 laps): 1 Hailwood (297 Honda), 90.40mph, 2 Agostini (500 MV), 3 Read (251 Yamaha), 4 Barnett (496 Matchless Métisse), 5 Mahoney (496 Matchless), 6 Gyula Marsovszky (496 Matchless). Fastest lap: Hailwood, 93.10mph.

16 June, Silloth
350 (10 laps, 11 miles): 1 Rob Fitton (Norton), 67.25mph, 2 Jack Smith (AJS), 3 John Findlay (Norton), 4 Barry Scully (Norton) 5 A Myers (AJS), 6 L Trotter (Norton). Fastest lap: Findlay, 69.23mph.
500 (10 laps): 1 Fitton (Norton), 69.27mph, 2 Scully (Norton), 3 Martyn Ashwood (Matchless), 4 Findlay (Norton), 5 M Moffat (NorBSA), 6 George Fogarty (Matchless). Fastest lap: Fitton, 71.22mph.
Player's No.6 Championship (10 laps): 1 Fitton (499 Norton), 69.84mph, 2 Chris Hopes (499 Norton), 3 Findlay (499 Norton), 4 George Fogarty (496 Matchless), 5 Moffat (499 NorBSA), 6 Fogarty (496 Matchless). Fastest lap: Fitton, 71.73mph.

23 June, Snetterton
350 Castrol Challenge (10 laps, 13.5 miles): 1 Kel Carruthers (Aermacchi Métisse), 89.67mph, 2 John Cooper (Seeley), 3 Peter Williams (Arter AJS), 4 Tony Smith (BSA), 5 Alan Peck (Norton), 6 Mick Andrew (Aermacchi). Fastest lap: Smith, 89.01mph.
1000 Snetterton 150 (50 laps): 1 Cooper (496 Seeley), 88.29mph, 2 Percy Tait (490 Triumph), 3 Carruthers (499 Norton), Dave Nixon (649 Triumph), 5 Barry Scully (499 Norton), 6 Bert Clark (496 Matchless Métisse). Fastest lap: Ray Pickrell (745 Dunstall), 92.55mph.

23 June, Thruxton
350 (8 laps, 18.85 miles): 1 Alan Barnett (AJS Métisse), 86.11mph, 2 Tom Dickie (Petty Norton), 3 Jim Curry (Aermacchi), 4 Dave Croxford (Seeley), 5 Brian Hunter (AJS), 6 D Palmer (Aermacchi). Fastest lap: Barnett, 87.81mph (record).
500 (10 laps): 1 Barnett (Matchless Métisse), 88.52mph, 2 Malcolm Uphill (Norton), 3 Dickie (Petty Norton), 4 Hunter (Coleshill Matchless), 5 John Taylor (Kirby Matchless), 6 M Hunt (Triumph). Fastest lap: Barnett, 90.23mph.
Players No.6 Championship (15 laps): 1 Barnett (654 BSA Métisse), 88.07mph, 2 Uphill (649 Triumph Métisse), 3 Dickie (499 Petty Norton), 4 Hunter (496 Matchless), 5 Brian Hussey (496 Matchless), 6 Gordon Pantall (499 Norton). Fastest lap: Barnett, 89.85mph.

30 June, Brands Hatch
350 (10 laps, 26.5 miles): 1 Jim Curry (Aermacchi Métisse), 82.67mph, 2 Brian Ball (Yamaha), 3 John Taylor (AJS Métisse), 4 Tony Rutter (Norton), 5 Martin Carney (Kawasaki), 6 Martyn Ashwood (AJS). Fastest lap: Curry, Ball 83.98mph.
500 Redex Trophy (10 laps): 1 Dave Croxford (Seeley), 84.72mph, 2 Alan Barnett (Matchless Métisse), 3 Pat Mahoney (Matchless Métisse), 4 Taylor (Matchless Métisse), 5 Tom Dickie (Petty Norton), 6 Nigel Palmer (Matchless Métisse). Fastest lap: Barnett, 87.52mph.
1300 (10 laps): 1 Ray Pickrell (745 Dunstall), 85.04mph, 2 Mahoney (745 Curley Norton), 3 Paul Smart (647 Curtis Norton), 4 Croxford (496 Seeley), 5 Brian Hunter (Coleshill Matchless), 6 Malcolm Uphill (649 Triumph Métisse). Fastest lap: Pickrell, 86.88mph.

13 July, Croft
350 (10 laps, 17.5 miles): 1 Dennis Gallagher (AJS), 71.1mph, 2 J Griffiths (Greeves), 3 Malcolm Uphill (Norton), 4 John Swannack (Norton), 5 Carl Ward (Bultaco), 6 Barry Scully (Scott). Fastest lap: Gallagher, Griffiths, 75.54mph.
500 (10 laps): 1 Uphill (Norton), 76.62mph, 2 Brian Ball (Seeley), 3 Findlay (Norton), 4 Gallagher (Matchless), 5 Tom Armstrong (Norton), 6 Scully (Norton). Fastest lap: Uphill, 78.36mph.
750 (10 laps): 1 Tom Dickie (649 Triton), 68.21mph, 2 F Wyatt (650 Triumph), 3 B Birkett (650 Triton), 4 Armstrong (650 Triumph), 5 I Bowerbank (Triton), 6 D Clarkson (650 BSA). Fastest lap: Dave Foulkes (740 Norton), 74.82mph.

20 July, Castle Combe
350 (10 laps, 18.4 miles): 1 Jim Curry (Aermacchi), 86.05mph, 2 Barry Randle (Norton), 3 Tom Dickie (Petty Norton), 4 Tony Rutter (Norton), 5 D Palmer (Aermacchi), 6 Brian Hunter (Coleshill AJS). Fastest lap: Randle, 88.32mph.
500 (10 laps): 1 Dave Croxford (Seeley), 89.06mph, 2 Randle (Norton), 3 Dickie (Petty Norton), 4 Hunter (Coleshill Matchless), 5 Percy Tait (Triumph), 6 Nigel Palmer (Matchless). Fastest lap: Croxford, 91.75mph (equals record).

218

28 July, Crimond
350 (12 laps, 21.6 miles): 1 Denis Gallagher (AJS), 2 John Findlay (Norton), 3 Malcolm Uphill (Norton).

4 August, Snetterton
350 (7 laps, 18.97 miles): 1 John Cooper (Seeley), 86.69mph, 2 Ian Richards (252 Yamaha), 3 Tony Rutter (Norton), 4 Barry Randle (Norton), 5 Ray Pickrell (Aermacchi Métisse), 6 Dan Shorey (Norton). Fastest lap: Richards, 89.18mph.
500 (7 laps): 1 Percy Tait (Triumph), 87.44mph, 2 Percy May (Norton), 3 Derek Best (Norton), 4 Brian Ball (Seeley), 5 Tom Dickie (Petty Norton), 6 John Taylor (Matchless Métisse). Fastest lap: Best, 90.5mph.
1000 (10 laps): 1 Cooper (496 Seeley), 90.89mph, 2 Paul Smart (647 Curtis Norton), 3 Derek Chatterton (275 Chat Kawasaki), 4 Dickie (499 Petty Norton), 5 Ball (496 Seeley), 6 Taylor (496 Matchless Métisse). Fastest lap: Ray Pickrell (745 Dunstall), 93.27mph.

11 August, Brands Hatch – Hutchinson 100
350 Castrol Challenge (10 laps, 26.5 miles): 1 Mike Hailwood (297 Honda), 87.17mph, 2 Kel Carruthers (Aermacchi Métisse), 3 Rod Gould (Aermacchi Métisse), 4 John Cooper (Seeley), 5 Dave Simmonds (Kawasaki), 6 Martin Carney (Kawasaki). Fastest lap: Hailwood, 88.33mph (record).
1000, leg 1 (15 laps): 1 Hailwood (297 Honda), 87.27mph, 2 Renzo Pasolini (348 Benelli), 3 Phil Read (251 Yamaha), 4 Bill Ivy (248 Yamaha), 5 John Cooper (496 Seeley), 6 Barry Randle (745 Curley Norton). Fastest lap: Hailwood, 88.33mph.
1000, leg 2 (15 laps): 1 Hailwood (29 Honda), 87.94mph, 2 Read (251 Yamaha), 3 Ivy (248 Yamaha), 4 Ray Pickrell (745 Dunstall), 5 Rod Gould (750 Dunstall), 6 Percy Tait (649 Triumph). Fastest lap: Hailwood, 89.49mph (record, reverse circuit).
Production (20 laps): 1 Pickrell (745 Dunstall Norton), 84.97mph, 2 Gould (649 Triumph), 3 Malcolm Uphill (649 Triumph), 4 Tony Smith (654 BSA), 5 Tait (649 Triumph), 6 Peter Butler (649 Triumph). Fastest lap: Gould, 86.10mph.

25 August, Mallory Park
350 (30 laps, 40.5 miles): 1 Barry Randle (Norton), 85.17mph, 2 Jim Curry (Aermacchi Métisse), 3 Alan Barnett (AJS Métisse), 4 Ron Chandler (Seeley), 5 Pat Mahoney (Oakley AJS), 6 Dan Shorey (Norton). Fastest lap: Curry, 88.04mph.
500 (15 laps): 1 Barnett (Matchless Métisse), 88.15mph, 2 Dave Croxford (Seeley), 3 Mahoney (Oakley Matchless), 4 Percy Tait (Triumph), 5 Randle (Norton), 6 Ray Pickrell (Dunstall Domiracer). Fastest lap: Barnett, Mahoney, 91.35mph.

31 August, Scarborough
350 (8 laps, 19.28 miles): 1 Jim Curry (Aermacchi Métisse), 65.76mph, 2 Billie Nelson (Norton), 3 Dennis Gallagher (AJS), 4 Dan Shorey (Norton), 5 Barry Randle (Norton), 6 Rob Fitton (Norton). Fastest lap: Curry, 66.33mph.
500 (8 laps): 1 Nelson (Norton), 67.73mph, 2 Dave Croxford (Seeley), 3 Shorey (Norton), 4 Randle (Norton), 5 Gallagher (Matchless), 6 Fitton (Norton). Fastest lap: Nelson, Croxford, 68.85mph.

1 September, Snetterton – Race of Aces
350 (10 laps, 27.1 miles): 1 Mike Hailwood (297 Honda), 83.52mph, 2 Kel Carruthers (Aermacchi Métisse), 3 Peter Williams (Arter AJS), 4 Barry Randle (Norton), 5 Tony Rutter (Norton), 6 Tom Dickie (Petty Norton). Fastest lap: Hailwood, 88.53mph.
500 (10 laps): 1 Hailwood (Honda), 92.56mph, 2 Alan Barnett (Matchless Métisse), 3 Dave Croxford (Seeley), 4 John Cooper (Seeley), 5 Percy Tait (Triumph), 6 Pat Mahoney (Oakley Matchless). Fastest lap: Hailwood, 93.81mph (record).
1000 Race of Aces (10 laps): 1 Hailwood (297 Honda), 93.56mph, 2 Phil Read (248 Yamaha), 3 Ray Pickrell (745 Dunstall), 4 Tait (649 Triumph), 5 Barnett (654 BSA Métisse), 6 Croxford (Seeley). Fastest lap: Hailwood, 95.65mph (record).

2 September, Oulton Park – Avon Trophy
350 Castrol Challenge (19 laps, 52.44 miles): 1 Mike Hailwood (297 Honda), 86.90mph, 2 Kel Carruthers (Aermacchi Métisse), 3 Ginger Molloy (Bultaco), 4 Malcolm Stanton (Ducati), 5 Rob Fitton (Norton), 6 Dave Simmonds (Kawasaki). Fastest lap: Hailwood, 92.20mph (record).
500 Avon Trophy (19 laps): 1 Hailwood (Seeley), 82.55mph, 2 John Cooper (Seeley), 3 Percy Tait (Triumph), 4 Peter Williams (Arter Matchless), 5 Fitton (Norton), 6 Bill Smith (Matchless). Fastest lap: Hailwood, 86.28mph
Les Graham Memorial Trophy (8 laps): 1 Tait (490 Triumph), 87.38mph, 2 Williams (496 Arter Matchless), 3 Cooper (496 Seeley), 4 Fitton (499 Norton), 5 Pat Mahoney (Quaife Matchless), 6 Dan Shorey (499 Norton). Fastest lap: Tait, Williams, 89.87mph.

2 September, Cadwell Park
350 (8 laps, 18 miles): 1 Steve Jolly (Higley Aermacchi), 70.59mph, 2 Billie Nelson (Norton), 3 Derek Chatterton (275 Chat Kawasaki), 4 John Swannack (Norton), 5 Tom Armstrong (Aermacchi), 6 Dave Foulkes (Norton). Fastest lap: Jolly, 72.19mph.
1000 (10 laps): 1 Tony Smith (654 BSA), 67.33mph, 2 Nelson (499 Norton), 3 Jolly (496 Higley Matchless), 4 Chatterton (275 Chat Kawasaki), 5 Chris Hopes (649 Triumph), 6 Foulkes (499 Norton). Fastest lap: Smith, 72.97mph.

2 September, Crystal Palace
350 (10 laps, 13.9 miles): 1 Ron Chandler (Seeley), 73.74mph, 2 Rex Butcher (Kawasaki), 3 Martyn Ashwood (AJS), 4 Chris Singleton (Aermacchi) 5 Paul Smart (Ducati), 6 Malcolm Uphill (Norton). Fastest lap: Chandler, Butcher, 76.75mph.
Player's No.6 Championship (10 laps): 1 Ray Pickrell (745 Dunstall), 77.49mph, 2 Chandler (496 Matchless), 3 Uphill (499 Norton), 4 Ashwood (Arter Matchless), 5 Smart (647 Curtis Norton), 6 Mick Andrew (745 Norton). Fastest lap: Pickrell, 79.94mph.
Production (8 laps): 1 Pickrell (745 Dunstall Norton), 76.22mph, 2 Ashwood (649 Triumph), 3 Peter Butler (649 Triumph), 4 Dave Nixon (649 Triumph), 5 Andrew (745 Norton), 6 P Davies (649 Triumph). Fastest lap: Pickrell, 78.19mph.

8 September, Brands Hatch – Derek Minter Benefit
350 (10 laps, 12.4 miles): 1 Ron Chandler (Seeley), 72.04mph, 2 Dave Croxford (Seeley), 3 Ray Pickrell (Aermacchi), 4 Alan Peck (Norton), 5 Tony Rutter (Norton), 6 Paul Smart (Ducati). Fastest lap: Chandler, 76.07mph.
500 Redex Trophy (10 laps): 1 Alan Barnett (Matchless Métisse), 75.27mph, 2 Brian Hunter (Coleshill Matchless), 3 Pat Mahoney (Oakley Matchless), 4 Percy May (Norton), 5 Martyn Ashwood (Arter Matchless), 6 Ron Chandler (Seeley). Fastest lap: Barnett, 77.77mph.

1000 (15 laps): 1 Pickrell (750 Dunstall), 75.29mph, 2 Barnett (496 Matchless Métisse), 3 Roy Francis (649 Monard), 4 Mahoney (496 Oakley Matchless), 5 Ashwood (496 Arter Matchless), 6 Chandler (496 Seeley). Fastest lap: Pickrell, 78.04mph.

22 September, Mallory Park – Race of the Year
350 Castrol Challenge (15 laps, 20.25 miles): 1 Mike Hailwood (297 Honda), 82.81mph, 2 Giacomo Agostini (MV), 3 Jim Curry (Aermacchi Métisse), 4 Kel Carruthers (Aermacchi Métisse), 5 Barry Randle (Norton), 6 Nigel Palmer (Aermacchi). Fastest lap: Hailwood, 92.05mph.
350-1000 (20 laps): 1 Agostini (500 MV), 89.75mph, 2 Alan Barnett (496 Matchless Métisse), 3 Peter Williams (Arter Matchless), 4 Randle (Norton), 5 Gyula Marsovszky (496 Matchless), 6 Percy Tait (Triumph). Fastest lap: Agostini, 92.49mph.
1000 Race of the Year (30 laps): 1 Hailwood (297 Honda), 82.16mph, 2 Agostini (500 MV), 3 Randle (499 Norton), 4 Barnett (496 Matchless Métisse), 5 Tait (749 Triumph), Dave Croxford (Seeley). Fastest lap: Hailwood, 88.04mph.

28 September, Croft:
350 (10 laps, 17.5 miles): 1 Rob Fitton (Norton), 73.84mph, 2 Stan Woods (Dugdale Yamaha), 3 Jim Curry (Aermacchi), 4 Vin Duckett (Aermacchi), 5 Malcolm Uphill (Norton), 6 A Myers (AJS). Fastest lap: Fitton, 75.18mph.
1000 (10 laps): 1 Fitton (499 Norton), 74.45mph, 2 Ken Redfern (647 Norton), 3 Duckett (496 Matchless), 4 Brian Kemp (499 Norton), 5 Dave Foulkes (499 Norton), 6 Allan Jefferies (490 Triumph). Fastest lap: Redfern, 77.02mph.

29 September, Cadwell Park
350 (8 laps, 18 miles): 1 Rob Fitton (Norton), 66.28mph, 2 Alan Barnett (AJS Métisse), 3 Steve Jolly (Aermacchi), 4 Billie Nelson (Norton), 5 Barry Scully (Scott), 6 Dan Shorey (Norton). Fastest lap: Jolly, 70.07mph.
1000 Invitation (10 laps): 1 Peter Williams (Arter Matchless), 72.12mph, 2 Fitton (Norton), 3 Ken Redfern (647 Norton), 4 Percy Tait (749 Triumph), 5 Barry Randle (499 Norton), 6 Nigel Palmer (496 Matchless Métisse). Fastest lap: Tony Smith (654 BSA), 74.86mph.
1000 Player's No.6 Championship final (12 laps): 1 Barnett (496 Matchless Métisse), 70.94mph, 2 Scully (499 Norton), 3 Jolly (496 Matchless), 4 Fitton (499 Norton), 5 Tom Dickie (499 Norton), 6 Malcolm Uphill (Norton). Fastest lap: Barnett, 73.37mph.

6 October Brands Hatch – Race of the South
350 Castrol Challenge (10 laps, 26.5 miles): 1 Mike Hailwood (297 Honda), 88.01mph, 2 Giacomo Agostini (MV), 3 Kel Carruthers (Aermacchi Métisse), 4 Alan Barnett (AJS Métisse), 5 Dave Croxford (Seeley), 6 Tony Rutter (Norton). Fastest lap: Hailwood, 89.46mph.
500 Redex Trophy (10 laps): 1 Agostini (MV), 86.64ph, 2 Barnett (Matchless Métisse), 3 Croxford (Seeley), 4 Bill Ivy (Seeley), 5 Pat Mahoney (Oakley Quaife), 6 Martyn Ashwood (Arter Matchless). Fastest lap: Agostini, 88.83mph.
1000 Race of the South (20 laps): 1 Hailwood (297 Honda), 89.24mph, 2 Agostini (500 MV), 3 Phil Read (251 Yamaha), 4 Ray Pickrell (745 Dunstall), 5 Tony Smith (654 BA), 6 Alan Barnett (496 Matchless Métisse). Fastest lap: Hailwood, 90.86mph (record).

13 October, Snetterton
350 (7 laps, 18.97 miles): 1 Alan Barnett (AJS Métisse), 87.58mph, 2 Rod Gould (Aermacchi), 3 Jim Curry (Aermacchi Métisse), 4 Pat Mahoney (Aermacchi), 5 Tony Rutter (Norton), 6 Tom Dickie (Norton). Fastest lap: Barnett, 90.00mph.
500 (7 laps): 1 Percy Tait (Triumph), 90.69mph, 2 Barnett (Matchless Métisse), 3 Barry Randle (Norton), 4 Brian Hunter (Coleshill Matchless), 5 Ron Chandler (Seeley), 6 Tony Smith (BSA). Fastest lap: Randle, 92.55mph.
1000 Squire of Snetterton (10 laps): 1 Ray Pickrell (745 Dunstall), 91.93mph, 2 Tait (490 Triumph), 3 Randle (499 Norton), 4 Barnett (496 Matchless Métisse), 5 Smith (654 BSA), 6 Hunter (496 Coleshill Matchless). Fastest lap: Smith, 93.81mph.

20 October, Mallory Park
350 (10 laps, 13.5 miles): 1 John Cooper (Seeley), 80.09mph, 2 Dave Croxford (Seeley), 3 Paul Smart (Ducati), 4 Pat Mahoney (Aermacchi), 5 Alan Barnett (AJS Métisse), 6 Barry Randle (Norton). Fastest lap: Cooper, Croxford, 82.93mph.
500 (15 laps): 1 Cooper (Seeley), 86.01mph, 2 Percy Tait (Triumph), 3 Barnett (Matchless Métisse), 4 Barry Randle (Norton), 5 Brian Hunter (Coleshill Matchless), 6 Ron Chandler (Seeley). Fastest lap: Cooper, 88.68mph.

27 October, Brands Hatch
350 (10 laps, 12.4 miles): 1 Dave Simmonds (Kawasaki), 74.37mph, 2 Alan Barnett (AJS Métisse), 3 Pat Mahoney (Aermacchi Métisse), 4 Brian Hunter (Yamaha), 5 Ray Pickrell (Aermacchi), 6 Jim Curry (Aermacchi). Fastest lap: Simmonds, Barnett, 76.70mph.
500 Redex Trophy (10 laps): 1 Dave Croxford (Seeley), 75.89mph, 2 Ray Pickrell (497 Dunstall), 3 Barnett (Matchless Métisse), 4 Hunter (Coleshill Matchless), 5 Ron Chandler (Seeley), 6 Mick Andrew (Seeley). Fastest lap: Croxford, Pickrell, 77.77mph.
1300 (10 laps): 1 Pickrell (745 Dunstall), 75.91mph, 2 Croxford (745 Curley Norton), 3 Mick Andrew (745 Kuhn Commando), 4 Martyn Ashwood (501 Arter Matchless), 5 Tony Smith (654 BSA) 6 Brian Kemp (745 Curley Norton). Fastest lap: Pickrell, 78.32mph.

British Championships:
350: 1 Alan Barnett, 2 Jim Curry, 3 Dan Shorey
500: 1 Dave Croxford, 2 Barnett, 3 Percy Tait

1969
2 March, Brands Hatch
350 (10 laps, 12.4 miles): 1 Pat Mahoney (Aermacchi), 72.82mph, 2 Alan Barnett (AJS Métisse), 3 Derek Chatterton (Chat Kawasaki), 4 Peter Williams (Arter AJS), 5 Jim Curry (Aermacchi), 6 J Wade (Aermacchi). Fastest lap: Mahoney, 77.50mph.
500 Redex Trophy (10 laps): 1 Dave Croxford (Kuhn Seeley), 74.6mph, 2 Ray Pickrell (Dunstall Domiracer), 3 Martyn Ashwood (Arter Matchless), 4 Mick Andrew (Kuhn Seeley), 5 Brian Hunter (Coleshill Matchless), 6 Tony Smith (BSA). Fastest lap: Croxford, Pickrell, 77.23mph.
1300 (10 laps): 1 Pickrell (745 Dunstall), 74.7mph, 2 Smith (654 BSA), 3 John Taylor (496 Matchless), 4 Ashwood (496 Arter Matchless), 5 Barry Ditchburn (649 Triton), 6 Hunter (745 Curley Norton). Fastest lap: Pickrell, 78.32mph.

8 March, Oulton Park

350 British Championship, Rd 1 (8 laps): 1 Tommy Robb (Aermacchi), 84.3mph, 2 Pat Mahoney (Aermacchi), 3 Alan Barnett (AJS Métisse), 4 Dave Croxford (Kuhn Seeley), 5 Brian Steenson (Aermacchi), 6 Barry Randle (Norton). Fastest lap: Robb, Mahoney, 85.83mph.

500 British Championship, Rd 1 (8 laps): 1 Barnett (Kirby Métisse), 84.63mph, 2 Croxford (Kuhn Seeley), 3 Andrew (Kuhn Seeley), 4 Malcolm Uphill (Norton), 5 Randle (Norton), 6 Robin Duffty (Norton). Fastest lap: Barnett, 86.88mph.

9 March, Snetterton

350 (7 laps, 18.97 miles): 1 Jim Curry (Aermacchi), 85.83mph, 2 Peter Williams (Arter AJS), 3 Percy May (Norton), 4 Graham Sharp (Aermacchi), 5 T Parker (Aermacchi), 6 Barry Sheene (Bultaco). Fastest lap: Williams, 87.73mph.

500 (7 laps): 1 Ray Pickrell (Dunstall), 89.2mph, 2 Williams (Arter Matchless), 3 Dave Croxford (Kuhn Seeley), 4 Mick Andrew (Kuhn Seeley), 5 S Hudson (Matchless), 6 P Gibson (Matchless). Fastest lap: Pickrell, Williams, 91.01mph.

1000 (10 laps): 1 Pickrell (745 Dunstall), 90.2mph, 2 Croxford (496 Kuhn Seeley), 3 Williams (496 Arter Matchless), 4 Andrew (745 Kuhn Commando), 5 L Geeson (745 Norton), 6 Ron Wittich (648 TSR Norton). Fastest lap: Pickrell, 92.55mph.

16 March, Mallory Park

350 (15 laps, 20.25 miles): 1 Alan Barnett (AJS Métisse), 84.00mph, 2 Pat Mahoney (Aermacchi), 3 Dave Croxford (Kuhn Seeley), 4 Jim Curry (Aermacchi), 5 Dennis Trollope (Aermacchi), 6 Ray Pickrell (Aermacchi). Fastest lap: Barnett, Mahoney, 87.78mph.

1000 (15 laps): 1 Tony Smith (654 BSA), 86.13mph, 2 Percy Tait (490 Triumph), 3 Barnett (Matchless Métisse), 4 Pickrell (745 Dunstall), 5 Robin Duffty (499 Petty Norton), 6 Brian Kemp (745 Curley Norton). Fastest lap: Tait, Croxford, 88.68mph.

4 April, Brands Hatch – King of Brands

350 British Championship, Rd 2 (10 laps, 26.5 miles): 1 Rod Gould (Yamaha), 84.29mph, 2 Alan Barnett (AJS Métisse), 3 Pat Mahoney (Aermacchi), 4 Dave Simmonds (Kawasaki), 5 Jim Curry (Aermacchi Métisse), 6 Ron Chandler (Seeley). Fastest lap: Gould, 86.10mph.

500 British Championship, Rd 2 (10 laps): 1 Barnett (Matchless Métisse), 86.07mph, 2 Peter Williams (Arter Matchless), 3 Dave Croxford (Kuhn Seeley), 4 Malcolm Uphill (Norton), 5 Tony Smith (BSA), 6 Rex Butcher (Matchless). Fastest lap: Barnett, 87.52mph.

1300 (10 laps): 1 Ray Pickrell (745 Dunstall), 86.02mph, 2 Williams (496 Arter Matchless), 3 Croxford (496 Kuhn Seeley), 4 Uphill (499 Norton), 5 Paul Smart (745 Francis Norton), 6 Mick Andrew (745 Kuhn Commando). Fastest lap: Pickrell, 88.99mph.

5 April, Croft

350 (10 laps, 17.5 miles): 1 Ken Redfern (Aermacchi), 73.56mph, 2 Rob Fitton (Norton), 3 Tom Armstrong (Aermacchi), 4 Vin Duckett (Aermacchi), 5 D Boxhall (Honda), 6 Jack Smith (AJS). Fastest lap: Redfern, 75.00mph.

Unlimited (10 laps): 1 Redfern (499 Norton), 75.34mph, 2 Armstrong (649 Triumph), 3 J Barton (649 Triumph), 4 John Findlay (499 Norton), 5 Dave Foulkes (496 Seeley), 6 Duckett (496 Seeley). Fastest lap: Chris Hopes (649 Triumph), 77.21mph.

13 April, Thruxton

350 (8 laps, 18.85 miles): 1 Pat Mahoney (Aermacchi), 84.77mph, 2 Dave Croxford (Kuhn Seeley), 3 Ray Pickrell (Aermacchi), 4 Brian Lee (Aermacchi), 5 Jim Curry (Aermacchi), 6 Graham Sharp (Aermacchi). Fastest lap: Mahoney, 86.60mph.

500 (10 laps): 1 Percy Tait (Triumph), 87.71mph, 2 Croxford (Kuhn Seeley), 3 Brian Hunter (Seeley), 4 Mick Andrew (Kuhn Seeley), 5 Ken Redfern (Norton), 6 Tony Rutter (Norton). Fastest lap: Tait, 89.85mph.

1000 Wills Jubilee Goblets (15 laps): 1 Pickrell (745 Dunstall), 89.06mph, 2 Tait (490 Triumph), 3 Croxford (745 Kuhn Commando), 4 Brian Kemp (745 Curley Norton), 5 Tom Dickie (499 Petty Norton), 6 Malcolm Uphill (499 Norton). Fastest lap: Pickrell, 91.00mph.

26 April, Castle Combe

350 British Championship, Rd 3 (10 laps, 18.4 miles): 1 Mick Andrew (Kuhn Seeley), 82.31mph, 2 Pat Mahoney (Aermacchi), 3 Alan Barnett (AJS Métisse), 4 Dave Croxford (Kuhn Seeley), 5 P Casey (Aermacchi), 6 Martin Carney (Chat Kawasaki). Fastest lap: Mahoney, 85.80mph.

500 British Championship, Rd 3 (10 laps): 1 Croxford (Kuhn Seeley), 88.56mph, 2 Percy Tait (Triumph), 3 Barnett (Matchless Métisse), 4 Robin Duffty (Petty Norton), 5 Andrew (Kuhn Seeley), 6 Mahoney (382 Aermacchi). Fastest lap: Tait, 91.24mph.

4 May, Cadwell Park

350 (8 laps, 18 miles): 1 Dan Shorey (Aermacchi), 72.58mph, 2 John Cooper (Wraggs Seeley), 3 Mick Andrew (Kuhn Seeley), 4 Peter Williams (Arter AJS), 5 Derek Chatterton (Chat Seeley), 6 Rex Butcher (Oakley Seeley). Fastest lap: Shorey, 74.28mph.

1000 (10 laps): 1 Stuart Graham (350 Yamaha), 74.48mph, 2 Tony Smith (654 BSA), 3 Alan Barnett (496 Matchless Métisse), 4 Andrew (Kuhn Seeley), 5 Butcher (496 Oakley Quaife), 6 Barry Scully (499 Norton). Fastest lap: Shorey (496 Oakley Matchless), Graham, 76.42mph.

10 May, Thruxton – Motor Cycle 500-mile Grand Prix

1 Percy Tait/Malcolm Uphill (Triumph), 2 John Cooper/Steve Jolly (Triumph), 3 L Phelps/Cliff Carr (Triumph), 4 Tony Smith/Pat Mahoney (BSA).

11 May, Scarborough

350 British Championship, Rd 4 (8 laps, 19.28 miles): 1 Terry Grotefeld (Aermacchi), 56.14mph, 2 Barry Scully (Scott), 3 Mike Bennett (Norton), 4 Geoff Barry (AJS), 5 John Swannack (Norton), 6 V Wright (Greeves). Fastest lap: Grotefeld, 61.54mph.

1000 – inc. 500 British Championship, Rd 4 (8 laps): 1 Barry Scully (499 Norton), 60.63mph, 2 Barry (496 Matchless), 3 Bennett (499 Norton), 4 H Porter (650 Norton), 5 Paul Cott (499 Norton), 6 Mick Grant (499 Velocette). Fastest lap: Scully, 62.06mph.

25 May, Mallory Park

350 (15 laps, 20.25 miles): 1 Cliff Carr (Yamaha), 85.26mph, 2 Pat Mahoney (Aermacchi), 3 Ray Pickrell (Aermacchi), 4 Dave Simmonds (Kawasaki), 5 Chris Hopes (Norton), 6 Barry Randle (Norton). Fastest lap: Carr, 88.36mph.

1000 (15 laps): 1 Dave Croxford (496 Kuhn Seeley), 88.17mph, 2 Paul Smart (750 Francis Norton), 3 Alan Barnett (496 Matchless Métisse), 4 Rex Butcher (496 Oakley Quaife), 5 Tony Rutter (499 Norton), 6 Brian Hussey (496 Matchless). Fastest lap: Pickrell (745 Dunstall), 89.14mph.
Production (30 laps): 1 Croxford (745 Kuhn Commando), 85.26mph, 2 Pickrell (Dunstall Norton), 3 Peter Davies (649 Triumph), 4 Dave Browning (T500 Suzuki), 5 J Judge (490 Triumph), 6 H Robinson (649 Triumph). Fastest lap: Pickrell, 88.36mph.

26 May, Brands Hatch (short track) – Evening News International
350 (15 laps, 18.6 miles): 1 Phil Read (Yamaha), 76.53mph, 2 Rod Gould (Yamaha), 3 Dave Croxford (Kuhn Seeley), 4 Mick Andrew (Kuhn Seeley), 5 Ron Chandler (Seeley), 6 Rex Butcher (Seeley). Fastest lap: Read, 79.15mph (record).
500 (20 laps): 1 Croxford (Kuhn Seeley), 76.74mph, 2 Alan Barnett (Matchless Métisse), 3 Chandler (Seeley), 4 Butcher (Oakley Quaife), 5 Andrew (Kuhn Seeley), 6 Brian Hunter (Coleshill Seeley). Fastest lap: Barnett, 78.59mph (equals record).
Evening News 1000, Leg 1 (20 laps): 1 Ray Pickrell (745 Dunstall), 77.74mph, 2 Croxford (496 Kuhn Seeley), 3 Barnett (496 Matchless Métisse), 4 Chandler (496 Seeley), 5 Butcher (496 Oakley Quaife), 6 Hunter (496 Coleshill Seeley). Fastest lap: Read (348 Yamaha), 79.43mph (record).
Leg 2 (20 laps): 1 Pickrell, 77.06mph, 2 Croxford, 3 Chandler, 4 Butcher, 5 Hunter, 6 Martyn Ashwood (496 Arter Matchless). Fastest lap: Pickrell, Croxford, 78.87mph.

15 June, Mallory Park – Post-TT International
350 (15 laps, 20.25 miles): 1 Rod Gould (Yamaha), 87.52mph, 2 Derek Chatterton (Chat Yamaha), 3 Phil Read (Yamaha), 4 Kel Carruthers (Aermacchi), 5 Pat Mahoney (Aermacchi), 6 Cliff Carr (Yamaha). Fastest lap: Read, 90.00mph.
500 (15 laps): 1 Giacomo Agostini (MV), 86.05mph, 2 Robin Duffty (Petty Norton), 3 Rex Butcher (Oakley Seeley), 4 John Samways (Norton), 5 Barry Randle (Norton), 6 Gyula Marsovszky (Matchless). Fastest lap: Agostini, 87.73mph.
1000 (20 laps): 1 Gould (348 Yamaha), 87.71mph, 2 Agostini (500 MV), 3 Dave Croxford (496 Kuhn Seeley), 4 Mick Andrew (745 Kuhn Commando), 5 Butcher (496 Oakley Seeley), 6 Duffty (545 Petty Norton). Fastest lap: Ago, 93.46mph (equals record).

22 June, Thruxton
350 British Championship, Rd 5 (10 laps, 23.56 miles): 1 Derek Chatterton (Chat Yamaha), 87.21mph, 2 Cliff Carr (Yamaha), 3 Martin Carney (Shepherd Kawasaki), 4 Alan Barnett (AJS Métisse), 5 Mick Andrew (Kuhn Seeley), 6 Paul Smart (Aermacchi). Fastest lap: Chatterton, 89.09mph (record).
500 British Championship, Rd 5 (12 laps): 1 Barnett (Matchless Métisse), 88.52mph, 2 Dave Croxford (Kuhn Seeley), 3 Percy Tait (490 Triumph), 4 Robin Duffty (Petty Norton) and Rex Butcher (Oakley Quaife), 6 Percy May (Petty Norton). Fastest lap: Barnett, 90.62mph.

28 June, Croft
350 British Championship, Rd 6 (15 laps, 26.25 miles): 1 Derek Chatterton (Chat Yamaha), 75.53mph, 2 Martin Carney (Yamaha), 3 Pat Mahoney (Aermacchi), 4 Mick Andrew (Kuhn Seeley), 5 Tom Armstrong (Aermacchi Métisse), 6 Peter Berwick (Aermacchi). Fastest lap: Chatterton, 77.97mph.
500 British Championship, Rd 6 (15 laps): Andrew (Kuhn Seeley), 75.95mph, 2 Ken Redfern (Norton), 3 Dave Croxford (Kuhn Seeley), 4 Nigel Rollason (Seeley), 5 Robin Duffty (Petty Norton), 6 Mick Grant (Velocette). Fastest lap: Redfern, 77.97mph.

19 July, Castle Combe
350 (10 laps, 18.4 miles): 1 Tony Rutter (Yamaha), 88.75mph, 2 Pat Mahoney (Yamaha), 3 Cliff Carr (Yamaha), 4 Mick Andrew (Kuhn Seeley), 5 Barry Sheene (Bultaco), 6 Percy May (Petty Norton). Fastest lap: Rutter, 91.24mph (record).
500 (10 laps): 1 Dave Croxford (Kuhn Seeley), 88.06mph, 2 Percy Tait (Triumph), 3 Percy May (Petty Norton), 4 John Samways (Norton), 5 Nigel Palmer (Matchless Métisse), 6 May (Petty Norton). Fastest lap: Tait, 90.74mph.

10 August, Brands Hatch – Hutchinson 100
350 (10 laps, 26.5 miles): 1 Mick Andrew (Kuhn Seeley), 82.48mph, 2 Alan Barnett (AJS Métisse), 3 Peter Williams (Arter AJS), 4 Cliff Carr (Yamaha), 5 Dave Croxford (Kuhn Seeley), 6 Paul Smart (Yamaha). Fastest lap: Rod Gould (Yamaha), 88.99mph.
Evening News Trophy, Leg 1 (15 laps): 1 Gould (348 Yamaha), 86.09mph, 2 Andrew (745 Kuhn Commando), 3 Smart (745 Francis Norton), 4 Rex Butcher (700 Rickman Métisse), 5 Tony Smith (654 BSA), 6 Croxford (496 Kuhn Seeley). Fastest lap: Gould, 88.07mph.
Evening News Trophy, Leg 2 (15 laps): 1 Gould, 86.06mph, 2 Andrew, 3 Barnett (700 Rickman Métisse), 4 Smart, 5 Santiago Herrero (250 Ossa), 6 Charlie Sanby (745 Kuhn Commando). Fastest lap: Gould, Andrew, 87.52mph.
Production (20 laps): 1 Andrew (745 Kuhn Commando), 84.34mph, 2 Smith (654 BSA), 3 Gould (649 Triumph), 4 Ray Pickrell (750 Dunstall Dominator), 5 Peter Williams (745 Norton Commando), 6 Tait (741 Triumph Trident). Fastest lap: Smith, 86.57mph (record).

31 August, Snetterton – Race of Aces
350 (10 laps, 27.1 miles): 1 Cliff Carr (Yamaha), 88.2mph, 2 Barry Sheene (Bultaco), 3 Mike Hatherill (Aermacchi), 4 Peter Williams (Arter AJS), 5 John Samways (Bultaco), 6 Barry Ditchburn (Aermacchi Métisse). Fastest lap: Carr, Sheene, 89.67mph.
500 (10 laps): 1 Percy Tait (Triumph), 81.49mph, 2 Dave Degens (Dresda Triumph), 3 Paul Smart (Seeley), 4 John Cooper (Honda), 5 Geoff Barry (Matchless), 6 Nigel Palmer (Matchless Métisse). Fastest lap: Tait, Cooper, 83.38mph.
1000 Race of Aces (10 laps): 1 Rod Gould (348 Yamaha), 93.84mph, 2 Tony Rutter (348 Yamaha), 3 Dave Croxford (496 Kuhn Seeley), 4 Cooper (500 Honda), 5 Tait (649 Triumph), 6 Brian Steenson (496 Seeley). Fastest lap: Gould, 95.83mph (record).

1 September, Oulton Park
350 (19 laps, 52.44 miles): 1 Giacomo Agostini (MV), 89.50mph, 2 Phil Read (Yamaha), 3 Marty Lunde (Yamaha), 4 Brian Steenson (Aermacchi), 5 Cliff Carr (Yamaha), 6 Jim Curry (Aermacchi Métisse). Fastest lap: Agostini, 91.52mph (record).
500 (19 laps): 1 Agostini (MV), 88.61mph, 2 Nigel Palmer (Matchless Métisse), 3 Peter Williams (Arter Matchless), 4 Malcolm Uphill (Norton), 5 John Williams (Matchless), 6 Percy Tait (Triumph). Fastest lap: Agostini, 91.52mph.
Les Graham Memorial Trophy (8 laps): 1 Rod Gould (348 Yamaha), 87.15mph, 2 Tait (Triumph), 3 Williams (Arter Matchless), 4 Rob Fitton (Norton), 5 Palmer (Matchless Métisse), 6 Uphill (Norton). Fastest lap: Gould, 88.75mph.

1 September, Crystal Palace
350 British Championship, Rd 7 (12 laps, 16.68 miles): 1 Ron Chandler (Seeley), 75.19mph, 2 Charlie Sanby (AJS), 3 Graham Sharp (Aermacchi), 4 Pat Mahoney (Seeley), 5 Martyn Ashwood (Aermacchi), 6 Dave Degens (Ducati). Fastest lap: Chandler, 76.75mph.
500 British Championship, Rd 7 (15 laps): 1 Chandler (Seeley), 78.17mph, 2 Paul Smart (Francis Seeley), 3 Dave Croxford (Kuhn Seeley), 4 Ashwood (Arter Matchless), 5 Rex Butcher (Oakley Quaife), 6 Ian Ratcliffe (Seeley). Fastest lap: Chandler, 80.19mph (equals record).

6 September, Croft
350 (10 laps, 17.5 miles): 1 Tony Rutter (Yamaha), 75.86mph, 2 Ken Redfern (Aermacchi), 3 Barry Sheene (Bultaco),4 Peter Berwick (Aermacchi), 5 Dave Browning (Yamaha), 6 D Boxhall (Honda). Fastest lap: Rutter, 77.4mph.
1000 (10 laps): 1 Redfern (750 Norton), 76.96mph, 2 Allan Jefferies (750 Métisse), 3 Tom Armstrong (750 Norton), 4 Stan Woods (499 Norton), 5 Ivan Hackman (496 E.D. Seeley), 6 Chris Hopes (649 Triumph). Fastest lap: Redfern, 78.26mph (equals record).

13 September, Scarborough – International Gold Cup
350 (8 laps, 19.28 miles): 1 Jim Curry (Aermacchi), 60.66mph, 2 Rob Fitton (Norton), 3 Steve Machin (275 Kawasaki), 4 Dave Croxford (Kuhn Seeley), 5 Steve Jolly (Seeley), 6 Dave Degens (Ducati). Fastest lap: Curry, 61.97mph.
500 International Gold Cup (8 laps): 1 Degens (Dresda), 65.71mph, 2 Fitton (Norton), 3 Jolly (Seeley), 4 Geoff Barry (Oakley Matchless), 5 Bill Crosier (Matchless), 6 George Fogarty (Matchless). Fastest lap: Degens, 67.99mph.

14 September, Cadwell Park
350 (8 laps, 18 miles): 1 Phil Read (348 Yamaha), 68.31mph, 2 Giacomo Agostini (MV), 3 Ken Redfern (Aermacchi), 4 Tony Rutter (Yamaha), 5 Stuart Graham (Yamaha), 6 Dave Croxford (Kuhn Seeley). Fastest lap: Read, 71.81mph.
1000 Wills Trophy (10 laps): 1 Agostini (500 MV), 74.39mph, 2 Redfern (750 Norton), 3 Croxford (496 Seeley), 4 Tony Jefferies (750 Norton Métisse), 5 John Hedger (650 Métisse), 6 Paul Smart (496 Seeley). Fastest lap: Agostini, Read (348 Yamaha), 77.00mph.

21 September, Mallory Park – Race of the Year
350 (15 laps, 20.25 miles): 1 Giacomo Agostini (MV), 90.4mph, 2 Rod Gould (Yamaha), 3 Phil Read (Yamaha), 4 Cliff Carr (Yamaha), 5 Tony Rutter (Yamaha), 6 Kel Carruthers (Aermacchi). Fastest lap: Agostini, 92.4mph.
1000 (20 laps): 1 Agostini (MV), 89.98mph, 2 Percy Tait (700 Rickman Métisse), 3 Mike Hailwood (496 Seeley), 4 Malcolm Uphill (700 Rickman Métisse), 5 Ron Chandler (496 Seeley), 6 Rex Butcher (496 Seeley). Fastest lap: Agostini, 92.5mph.
Race of the Year (30 laps): 1 Agostini (500 MV), 91.21mph, 2 Ken Redfern (750 Norton), 3 Dave Croxford (750 Kuhn Norton), 4 Malcolm Uphill (700 Rickman Métisse), 5 Hailwood (496 Seeley), 6 Paul Smart (750 Francis Norton). Fastest lap: Agostini, 93.1mph.

5 October, Brands Hatch – Race of the South
350 (10 laps, 26.5 miles): 1 Phil Read (Yamaha), 86.41mph, 2 Giacomo Agostini (MV), 3 Derek Chatterton (Chat Yamaha), 4 Chas Mortimer (Yamaha), 5 Martin Carney (Shepherd Kawasaki), 6 Jim Curry (Aermacchi). Fastest lap: Read, 87.84mph.
500 Redex Trophy (10 laps): 1 Agostini (MV), 87.37mph, 2 Paul Smart (Seeley), 3 Mick Andrew (Seeley), 4 Dave Croxford (Seeley), 5 Rex Butcher (Quaife Métisse), 6 Nigel Palmer (Matchless Métisse). Fastest lap: Agostini, 87.84mph.
1000 Race of the South (20 laps): 1 Agostini (500 MV), 87.21mph, 2 Andrew (750 Kuhn Commando), 3 Read (348 Yamaha), 4 John Hedger (649 Triumph Métisse), 5 Mortimer (650 Curtis Norton), 6 Bob Heath (654 BSA). Fastest lap: Agostini, 88.86mph.

British Championships:
350 1 Pat Mahoney, 2 Derek Chatterton, 3 Alan Barnett
500 1 Dave Croxford, 2 Barnett, 3 Mick Andrew

1970
1 March, Mallory Park
350 (15 laps, 20.25 miles): 1 Tony Rutter (Yamaha), 85.86mph, 2 John Cooper (Yamsel), 3 Derek Chatterton (Yamaha), 4 Brian Kemp (Aermacchi Métisse), 5 Cliff Carr (Yamaha), 6 Jim Curry (Aermacchi Métisse). Fastest lap: Cooper, 88.68mph.
500 Shell Championship (15 laps): 1 Bob Heath (BSA), 81.25mph, 2 Ron Chandler (Seeley), 3 Mick Andrew (Kuhn Seeley), 4 Pat Mahoney (Kuhn Seeley), 5 Cooper (Seeley), 6 Robin Duffty (Petty Norton). Fastest lap: Chandler, Andrew, 85.87mph.

27 March, Brands Hatch
350 British Championship, Rd 1 (10 laps): 1 Tony Rutter (Yamaha), 82.86mph, 2 Dave Croxford (Yamaha), 3 Derek Chatterton (Yamaha), 4 Martin Carney (Shepherd Kawasaki), 5 Jim Curry (Aermacchi), 6 John Taylor (Aermacchi). Fastest lap: Rutter, 85.03mph.
500 British Championship, Rd 1 (10 laps): 1 Alan Barnett (Seeley), 84.95mph, 2 Malcolm Uphill (Norton), 3 Taylor (Seeley), 4 Croxford (Seeley), 5 Pat Mahoney (Kuhn Seeley), 6 Peter Williams (Arter Matchless). Fastest lap: Barnett, Taylor, 86.73mph.
1300 (10 laps): Andrew (750 Kuhn Seeley), 85.38mph, 2 Charlie Sanby (750 Kuhn Seeley), 3 Mahoney (750 Kuhn Seeley), 4 Rex Butcher (348 Ivy Yamaha), 5 Williams (496 Arter Matchless), 6 Brian Kemp (750 Curley Norton). Fastest lap: Sanby, Butcher, 87.52mph.
Production (10 laps): 1 Kemp (745 Norton Commando), 82.71mph, 2 Bob Heath (741 BSA), 3 Dave Nixon (741 Triumph), 4 Percy Tait (649 Triumph), 5 Peter Butler (649 Triumph), 6 Paul Davies (649 Triumph). Fastest lap: Kemp, 85.33mph.

28 March, Croft
350 (8 laps, 14 miles): 1 Ken Redfern (Aermacchi), 67.92mph, 2 Peter Berwick (Aermacchi), 3 Jack Smith (AJS), 4 Rob Fitton (Norton), 5 P Welfare (Honda), 6 B Cammack (Ducati). Fastest lap: Redfern, 70.31mph.
1000 (8 laps): 1 Redfern (750 Dunstall), 67.43mph, 2 Allan Jefferies (750 Norton Métisse), 3 Ivan Hackman (496 Seeley), 4 Mick Grant (499 Velocette), 5 R Sutton (499 Norton), 6 F Moss (649 Triton). Fastest lap: Redfern, 70.00mph.

29 March, Mallory Park
350 (15 laps, 20.25 miles): 1 John Cooper (Yamsel), 85.85mph, 2 Tony Rutter (Yamaha), 3 Alan Barnett (Aermacchi), 4 Ken Redfern (Aermacchi), 5 Mick Andrew (Kuhn Seeley), 6 Bob Haldane (Yamaha). Fastest lap: Cooper, 88.04mph.
500 Shell Championship (15 laps): 1 Ivan Hackman (Seeley), 77.95mph, 2 Bob Heath (BSA), 3 Pat Mahoney (Kuhn Seeley), 4 Barry Randle (Seeley), 5 Geoff Barry (Oakley Matchless), 6 Stan Woods (Norton). Fastest lap: Mahoney, 81.54mph.
1000 (15 laps): 1 Cooper (348 Yamsel), 86.6mph, 2 Redfern (745 Dunstall), 3 Mahoney (496 Kuhn Seeley), 4 Randle (496 Seeley), 5 Paul Smart (496 Seeley), 6 Peter Williams (496 Arter Matchless). Fastest lap: Cooper, Redfern, Randle, 88.6mph.

30 March, Oulton Park
350 (10 laps, 27.6 miles): 1 John Cooper (Yamsel), 86.36mph, 2 Tony Rutter (Yamaha), 3 K Daniels (Yamaha), 4 Theo Bult (Yamaha), 5 Peter Berwick (Aermacchi), 6 Jim Curry (Honda). Fastest lap: Rutter, 89.38mph.
500 Shell Championship (10 laps): 1 Cooper (Seeley), 85.67mph, 2 Peter Williams (Arter Matchless), 3 Barry Randle (Seeley), 4 Robin Duffty (Petty Norton), 5 Gordon Pantall (Seeley), 6 Cliff Carr (Kawasaki). Fastest lap: Williams, 86.88mph.
750 (6 laps): 1 Pat Mahoney (745 Kuhn Seeley), 82.10mph, 2 Brian Kemp (745 Curley Norton), 3 Duffty (600 Norton), 4 Bill Crosier (Rutherford Norton), 5 Nigel Rollason (700 Weslake Métisse), 6 L Geeson (Norton). Fastest lap: Mahoney, 85.1mph.

30 March, Crystal Palace
350 (10 laps, 13.9 miles): 1 Chas Mortimer (Broad Yamaha), 67.39mph, 2 Alan Barnett (Aermacchi), 3 Roger Bowler (Bultaco), 4 Barry Ditchburn (Aermacchi), 5 Clive Brown (Norton), 6 G Gibson (Yamaha). Fastest lap: Barnett, 71.49mph.
500 (10 laps): 1 John Blanchard (Chuck Seeley), 71.21mph, 2 Barnett (Seeley), 3 Ron Chandler (Kirby Triumph), 4 Ditchburn (Seeley), 5 Brown (Norton), 6 Martin Carney (405 Shepherd Kawasaki). Fastest lap: Blanchard, 74.24mph.
1000 (8 laps): 1 Charlie Sanby (745 Kuhn Seeley), 76.86mph, 2 Carney (405 Shepherd Kawasaki), 3 Paul Smart (750 Norton), 4 Graham Sharp (750 Kuhn Seeley), 5 Rex Butcher (348 Ivy Yamaha), 6 Martyn Ashwood (700 Rickman Métisse). Fastest lap: Sanby, 79.18mph.

12 April, Thruxton
350 British Championship, Rd 2 (10 laps): 1 Dave Croxford (Yamaha), 76.95mph, 2 Derek Chatterton (Chat Yamaha), 3 Brian Lee (Lawton Aermacchi), 4 Mick Andrew (Kuhn Seeley), 5 Chas Mortimer (Broad Yamaha), 6 Tony Rutter (Yamaha). Fastest lap: Barnett, 81.87mph.
500 British Championship, Rd 2 (12 laps): 1 Barnett (Seeley), 80.19mph, 2 Peter Williams (Arter Matchless), 3 Mick Andrew (Kuhn Seeley), 4 Robin Duffty (Petty Norton), 5 Pat Mahoney (Kuhn Seeley), 6 Barry Ditchburn (Seeley). Fastest lap: Barnett, 82.62mph.
1000 (6 laps – rain shortened): 1 Charlie Sanby (745 Kuhn Seeley), 83.84mph, 2 Barnett (496 Seeley), 3 Andrew (745 Kuhn Seeley), 4 V Chivers (499 Norton), 5 Graham Sharp (499 Norton), 6 Brian Hussey (Métisse). Fastest lap: Sanby, 87.44mph.

25 April, Castle Combe
350 British Championship, Rd 3 (10 laps, 18.4 miles): 1 Dave Croxford (Yamaha), 79.65mph, 2 Dave Browning (Yamaha), 3 Tony Rutter (Yamaha), 4 Brian Kemp (Aermacchi Métisse), 5 Martin Carney (Shepherd Kawasaki), 6 Pat Mahoney (Kuhn Seeley). Fastest lap: Croxford, 82.18mph.
500 British Championship, Rd 3 (10 laps): 1 Alan Barnett (Seeley), 81.96mph, 2 Pat Mahoney (Kuhn Seeley), 3 Peter Williams (Arter Matchless), 4 Percy May (Petty Norton), 5 Barry Ditchburn (Seeley), 6 Barry Randle (Seeley). Fastest lap: Barnett, 85.58mph.

26 April, Cadwell Park
350 (8 laps, 18 miles): 1 John Cooper (Yamsel), 70.42mph, 2 Derek Chatterton (Chat Yamaha), 3 Dave Browning (Yamaha), 4 Brian Kemp (Aermacchi Métisse), 5 Peter Williams (Arter AJS), 6 Brian Steenson (Seeley). Fastest lap: Chatterton, 72.06mph.
1000 (10 laps): 1 Cooper (348 Yamsel), 73.57mph, 2 Chatterton (348 Chat Yamaha), 3 John Barton (649 Triumph), 4 Steenson (496 Seeley), 5 Nigel Palmer (496 Matchless), 6 Steve Machin (250 Yamaha). Fastest lap: Steenson, 75.14mph.
Production (8 laps): 1 Kemp (745 Norton), 67.63mph, 2 Allan Jefferies (649 Triumph), 3 Peter Davies (998 Vincent), 4 Pat Mahoney (745 Kuhn Commando), 5 Gary Green (649 Triumph), 6 Steenson (741 BSA). Fastest lap: Kemp, 70.19mph.

2 May, Croft
350 (10 laps, 17.5 miles): 1 Peter Berwick (Aermacchi), 74.2 miles, 2 Micky Collins (Seeley), 3 Steve Machin (Yamaha), 4 D Littler (Yamaha), 5 Ron Pladdys (Drixton), 6 T Parker (Aermacchi). Fastest lap: Andrew Manship (Yamaha), 76.09mph.
1000 (12 laps): 1 Allan Jefferies (745 Commando Métisse), 75.86mph, 2 Jeff Wade (998 Egli Vincent), 3 Bill Crosier (750 Norton), 4 Ivan Hackman (496 Seeley), 5 G Tilley (499 Norton), 6 B Swales (499 Norton). Fastest lap: Ken Redfern (745 Dunstall), 81.4mph (record).

10 May, Thruxton – *Motor Cycle* 500-mile Grand Prix
1 Peter Williams/Charlie Sanby (Norton Commando), 2 Frank Whiteway/Stan Woods (Suzuki T500), 3 Brian Steenson/Pat Mahoney (BSA Rocket 3).

24 May, Mallory Park
350 British Championship, Rd 4 (15 laps, 20.25 miles): 1 John Cooper (Yamsel), 85.78mph, 2 Derek Chatterton (Yamaha), 3 Cliff Carr (Yamaha), 4 Tony Rutter (Yamaha), 5 Bob Haldane (Yamaha), 6 Dave Browning (Aermacchi). Fastest lap: Cooper, 88.36mph.
500 British Championship, Rd 4 (15 laps): 1 Pat Mahoney (Kuhn Seeley), 87.22mph, 2 Micky Collins (Seeley), 3 Percy May (Petty Norton), 4 Brian Steenson (Seeley), 5 Charlie Sanby (Kuhn Seeley), 6 P Elmore (Matchless). Fastest lap: Collins, 89.34mph.
Production (20 laps): 1 Sanby (Kuhn Commando), 83.42mph, 2 Peter Davies (649 Triumph), 3 Barry Ditchburn (745 Norton), 4 Garry Green (649 Triumph), 5 Ron Wittich (750 Norton), 6 Ivan Hackman (750 Norton). Fastest lap: Ditchburn, 86.48mph.

25 May, Brands Hatch – Evening News International
350 (10 laps, 26.5 miles): 1 John Cooper (Yamsel), 85.71mph, 2 Rex Butcher (Ivy Yamaha), 3 Alan Barnett (Aermacchi), 4 Barry Ditchburn (Aermacchi Métisse), 5 Charlie Sanby (Kuhn Seeley), 6 Bob Haldane (Yamaha). Fastest lap: Phil Read (Yamaha), 88.83mph.
500 Shell Championship (10 laps): 1 Paul Smart (Francis Seeley), 84.74mph, 2 Pat Mahoney (Kuhn Seeley), 3 Peter Williams (Arter

Matchless), 4 Sanby (Kuhn Seeley), 5 Ray Pickrell (Dunstall Norton), 6 Rex Butcher (Matchless Métisse). Fastest lap: Smart, 87.04mph.
1000 Invitation (12 lap): 1 Cooper (348 Yamsel), 85.99mph, 2 Martyn Ashwood (700 Rickman Métisse), 3 Mahoney (745 Kuhn Seeley), 4 Williams (496 Arter Matchless), 5 Clive Brown (499 Norton), 6 Jim Harvey (496 Matchless Métisse). Fastest lap: Ashwood, 88.50mph.

25 May, Cadwell Park – Coronation Trophy
350 (8 laps, 18 miles): 1 Derek Chatterton (Chat Yamaha), 72.21mph, 2 Billie Nelson (Yamaha), 3 Ken Redfern (Aermacchi), 4 Cliff Carr (Yamaha), 5 V Wright (Greeves), 6 A Myers (Myers). Fastest lap: Nelson, 73.9mph.
1000 Coronation Trophy (10 laps): 1 Chatterton (348 Chat Yamaha), 74.01mph, 2 Nelson (348 Yamaha), 3 Steve Machin (250 Yamaha), 4 Geoff Barry (750 Oakley Commando), 5 Mick Chatterton (348 Padgett Yamaha), 6 A Moss (750 Triumph). Fastest lap: Redfern (745 Dunstall), 75.84mph.

30 May, Oulton Park
350 British Championship, Rd 5 (8 laps, 22.08 miles): 1 John Cooper (Yamsel), 86.5mph, 2 Tony Rutter (Yamaha), 3 Rex Butcher (Yamaha), 4 Bob Haldane (Yamaha), 5 Cecil Crawford (Aermacchi), 6 A Myers (AJS). Fastest lap: Cooper, 89.06mph.
500 British Championship Rd 5 (8 laps): 1 Peter Williams (Arter Matchless), 86.21mph, 2 Cooper (Seeley), 3 Alan Barnett (Seeley), 4 Barry Ditchburn (Seeley), 5 Brian Steenson (Seeley), 6 Stan Woods (Kawasaki). Fastest lap: Williams, Cooper, 87.8mph.

14 June, Mallory Park – Post-TT
350 (15 laps, 20.25 miles): 1 Phil Read (Yamaha), 88.66mph, 2 Rod Gould (Yamaha), 3 Derek Chatterton (Chat Yamaha), 4 Tony Rutter (Yamaha), 5 Peter Williams (Arter AJS), 6 Mahoney (Yamaha). Fastest lap: Read, 91.01mph.
500 Shell Championship (15 laps): 1 Giacomo Agostini (MV), 89.08mph, 2 Paul Smart (Seeley), 3 Williams (Arter Matchless), 4 John Cooper (Seeley), 5 Ron Chandler (Seeley), 6 Martin Carney (Kawasaki). Fastest lap: Agostini, 90.67mph.
1000 Carreras Trophy (20 laps): 1 Agostini (500 MV), 90.64mph, 2 Cooper (348 Yamsel), 3 Gould (348 Yamaha), 4 Ken Redfern (750 Dunstall), 5 Read (348 Yamaha), 6 Pat Mahoney (750 Kuhn Seeley). Fastest lap: Agostini, 92.40mph (record).

21 June, Thruxton
350 (10 laps, 18.4 miles): 1 Derek Chatterton (Chat Yamaha), 86.94mph, 2 Ken Redfern (Aermacchi), 3 Percy May (Petty Norton), 4 Clive Brown (Norton), 5 Peter Casey (Cowles Aermacchi), 6 T Boyes (Aermacchi). Fastest lap: Chatterton, 88.17mph.
500 (12 laps): 1 Paul Smart (Seeley), 88.26mph, 2 Brown (Norton), 3 Nigel Palmer (Matchless Métisse), 4 May (Petty Norton), 5 Nigel Rollason (Seeley Matchless), 6 Dave Best (Petty Norton). Fastest lap: Smart, 90.42mph.
1000 (12 laps): 1 Ken Redfern (745 Dunstall), 87.47mph, 2 John Hedger (700 Kilbourn Métisse), 3 H Robinson (649 Triumph), 4 L Geeson (750 Norton), 5 R Nicholls (649 Triumph), 6 Percy Tait (750 Triumph). Fastest lap: Redfern, 89.47mph.

18 July, Castle Combe
350 (10 laps, 18.4 miles): 1 Tony Rutter (Yamaha), 88.84mph, 2 Cliff Carr (Yamaha), 3 Dave Browning (Yamaha), 4 Nigel Rollason (Yamaha), 5 R Keating (Yamaha), 6 Peter Casey (Cowles Aermacchi). Fastest lap: Browning, 91.49mph (record).
500 (10 laps): 1 Brian Kemp (Higley Seeley), 88.39mph, 2 Percy May (Petty Norton), 3 Peter Williams (Arter Matchless), 4 Nigel Palmer (Matchless), 5 Barry Randle (Seeley), 6 Dave Best (Petty Norton). Fastest lap: May, 90.74mph.
501-1000 (10 laps): 1 Brian Kemp (750 Curley Commando), 90.69mph, 2 Percy Tait (750 Triumph), 3 John Hedger (700 Kilbourn Métisse), 4 Graham Sharp (750 Kuhn Seeley), 5 R Corbett (Corbett Domiracer), 6 K Sullivan (n/a). Fastest lap: Kemp, 92.27mph (record).

26 July, Cadwell Park
350 British Championship, Rd 6 (8 laps): 1 John Cooper (Yamsel), 68.5mph, 2 Derek Chatterton (Chat Yamaha), 3 Cliff Carr (Yamaha), 4 Alan Barnett (Aermacchi), 5 D Littler (Chat Yamaha), 6 Geoff Barry (Oakley AJS). Fastest lap: Cooper, 70.56mph.
500 British Championship, Rd 6 (10 laps): 1 Peter Williams (Arter Matchless), 67.42mph, 2 Barnett (Seeley), 3 Rex Butcher (Matchless Métisse), 4 Barry Ditchburn (Seeley), 5 Pat Mahoney (Kuhn Seeley), 6 B Adams (Norton). Fastest lap: Williams, 69.42mph.

8 August, Brands Hatch – Hutchinson 100
350 (12 laps, 31.8 miles): 1 John Cooper (Yamsel), 86.37mph, 2 Phil Read (Yamaha), 3 Paul Smart (Yamaha), 4 Kent Andersson (Yamaha), 5 Barry Ditchburn (Yamaha), 6 Derek Chatterton (Chat Yamaha). Fastest lap: Cooper, 87.52mph.
1000 Evening News Trophy, Leg 1 (15 laps, 39.75 miles): 1 Read (348 Yamaha), 84.64mph, 2 Charlie Sanby (750 Kuhn Seeley), 3 Cooper (348 Yamsel), 4 Pat Mahoney (750 Kuhn Seeley), 5 Smart (750 Francis Trident), 6 John Hedger (700 Kilbourn Métisse). Fastest lap: Read, 87.84mph.
1000 Evening News Trophy, Leg 2 (15 laps): 1 Cooper, 86.41mph, 2 Smart, 3 Read, 4 Sanby, 5 Peter Williams (496 Arter Matchless), 6 Ken Redfern (750 Dunstall). Fastest lap: Cooper, 87.84mph.
Overall: 1 Read, 2 Sanby, 3 Cooper, 4 Smart, 5 Redfern, 6 Andersson.
Production (20 laps): 1 Smart (Triumph Trident), 85.25mph, 2 Sanby (Kuhn Commando), 3 Percy Tait (Triumph Bonneville), 4 Ray Pickrell (Triumph Trident), 5 Bob Heath (BSA Rocket 3), 6 Brian Kemp (Curley Commando). Fastest lap: 87.36mph (record).

30 August, Snetterton – Race of Aces
350 (10 laps, 27.1 miles): 1 Phil Read (Yamaha), 93.47mph, 2 Kel Carruthers (Yamaha), 3 Derek Chatterton (Chat Yamaha), 4 Tony Rutter (Yamaha), 5 Cliff Carr (Yamaha), 6 Tony Smith (Yamaha). Fastest lap: Read, 95.65mph (record).
500 Shell Championship (10 laps): 1 Alan Barnett (Seeley), 91.16mph, 2 Peter Williams (Arter Matchless), 3 Brian Kemp (Seeley), 4 Pat Mahoney (Kuhn Seeley), 5 Jim Harvey (Matchless Métisse), 6 Percy Tait (Seeley). Fastest lap: Barnett, Williams, 92.91mph.
1000 Race of Aces (10 laps): 1 Read (348 Yamaha), 92.98mph, 2 Rod Gould (Yamaha), 3 Ken Redfern (750 Dunstall), 4 Tony Rutter (Norton), 5 John Hedger (700 Kilbourn Métisse), 6 Derek Chatterton (348 Chat Yamaha). Fastest lap: Read, 95.27mph.

31 August, Crystal Palace
350 (10 laps, 13.9 miles): 1 Paul Smart (Yamaha), 77.29mph, 2 Rex Butcher (Ivy Yamaha), 3 Ron Chandler (Yamaha), 4 Pat Mahoney

(Kuhn Seeley). Fastest lap: Smart, 79.94mph (record).

500 (6 laps): 1 Chandler (Seeley), 66.28mph, 2 Martin Carney (Kawasaki), 3 Mahoney (Kuhn Seeley), 4 Butcher (Oakley Métisse). Fastest lap: Mahoney, 81.49mph.

1000 (12 laps): 1 Smart (750 Triumph), 79.22mph, 2 Charlie Sanby (Kuhn Commando), 3 Barry Ditchburn (700 Ditchburn Triumph), 4 Ray Pickrell (750 Dunstall). Fastest lap: Smart, 81.49mph.

Production I (10 laps): 1 Pickrell (Dunstall Norton), 78.23mph, 2 Sanby (Kuhn Commando), 3 Ron Wittich (Kuhn Commando), 4 Dave Nixon (Triumph Trident). Fastest lap: Pickrell, 80.19mph.

Production II (10 laps): 1 Wittich, 76.73mph, 2 Nixon, 3 Peter Butler (750 Trident), 4 J Vincent (Triumph Bonneville). Fastest lap: Sanby, 79.68mph. (Paul Smart set new outright lap record of 82.25mph in supporting event.)

31 August, Oulton Park – Daily Express International

350 (15 laps, 41.4 miles): 1 Giacomo Agostini (MV), 89.9mph, 2 John Cooper (Yamsel), 3 Kel Carruthers (Yamaha), 4 Phil Read (Yamaha), 5 Kent Andersson (Yamaha), 6 Tony Rutter (Yamaha). Fastest lap: Agostini, 91.52mph.

500 Shell Championship (15 laps): 1 Agostini (MV), 88.05mph, 2 Peter Williams (Arter Matchless), 3 Tommy Robb (Seeley), 4 Dave Croxford (Seeley QUB), 5 Alan Barnett (Seeley), 6 Percy Tait (Seeley). Fastest lap: Agostini, 91.19mph.

5 September, Croft

350 British Championship, Rd 7 (10 laps, 17.5 miles): 1 Derek Chatterton (Chat Yamaha), 76.89mph, 2 Tony Rutter (Yamaha), 3 Allan Jefferies (Yamaha), 4 Cliff Carr (Yamaha), 5 Mick Grant (Yamaha), 6 Alan Barnett (Aermacchi). Fastest lap: Chatterton, 78.75mph.

500 British Championship, Rd 7 (10 laps): 1 Peter Williams (Arter Matchless), 77.22mph, 2 Barnett (Seeley), 3 Ken Redfern (RJ Dunstall), 4 Pat Mahoney (Kuhn Seeley), 5 Dennis Gallagher (Seeley), 6 Bob Heath (BSA). Fastest lap: Williams, 79.15mph (record).

1000 (10 laps): 1 Jefferies (750 Norton Métisse), 76.38mph, 2 Mahoney (750 Kuhn Seeley), 3 H Robinson (649 Triumph), 4 Grant (750 Norton), 5 I Bowerbank (700 Triumph), 6 A Fyffe (750 Seeley). Fastest lap: Jefferies, 78.95mph.

12 September, Scarborough

350 (8 laps, 19.28 miles): 1 John Cooper (Yamsel), 67.3mph, 2 Allan Jefferies (Yamaha), 3 Derek Chatterton (Chat Yamaha), 4 Jim Curry (Aermacchi), 5 Mick Grant (Yamaha), 6 Brian Lee (Aermacchi) Fastest lap: Jefferies, 69.62mph (record).

750 (8 laps): 1 Jefferies (750 Norton Métisse), 67.61mph, 2 Cooper (496 Seeley), 3 Barry Sheene (750 Kuhn Seeley), 4 John Findlay (499 Norton), 5 Grant (750 Norton), 6 Barry Randle (496 Seeley). Fastest lap: Jefferies, 69.55mph.

20 September, Mallory Park – Race of the Year

350 (15 laps, 20.25 miles): 1 John Cooper (Yamsel), 89.76mph, 2 Rod Gould (Yamaha), 3 Kel Carruthers (Yamaha), 4 Tony Rutter (Yamaha), 5 Paul Smart (Yamaha), 6 Rex Butcher (Ivy Yamaha). Fastest lap: Cooper, 91.69mph.

500 Shell Championship (15 laps): 1 Cooper (Seeley), 87.37mph, 2 Peter Williams (Arter Matchless), 3 Alan Barnett (Seeley), 4 Ron Chandler (Seeley), 5 Percy May (Petty Norton), 6 Paul Smart (Seeley). Fastest lap: Williams, 89.67mph.

1000 (15 laps): 1 Ken Redfern (750 Dunstall), 88.64mph, 2 Paul Smart (750 Triumph), 3 Allan Jefferies (750 Norton Métisse), 4 Dave Nixon (750 Triumph), 5 Charlie Sanby (750 Kuhn Seeley), 6 Pat Mahoney (750 Kuhn Seeley). Fastest lap: Smart, 91.01mph.

Race of the Year (30 laps): 1 Cooper (348 Yamsel), 89.81mph, 2 Phil Read (250 Yamaha), 3 Smart (750 Triumph), 4 Nixon (750 Triumph), 5 Jefferies (750 Norton Métisse), 6 Redfern (750 Dunstall). Fastest lap: Read, 93.1mph.

27 September, Cadwell Park

350 (8 laps, 18 miles): 1 John Cooper (348 Yamsel), 75.67mph, 2 Tony Rutter (Yamaha), 3 Steve Machin (Padgett Yamaha), 4 Cliff Carr (Yamaha), 5 Derek Chatterton (Chat Yamaha), 6 Allan Jefferies (Yamaha). Fastest lap: Steve Manship (Yamaha), Cooper, 77.74mph.

175-1000 (10 laps): 1 Giacomo Agostini (500 MV), 76.36mph, 2 Chatterton (348 Chat Yamaha), 3 John Hedger (700 Kilbourn Métisse), 4 Machin (348 Padgett Yamaha), 5 Carr (348 Yamaha), 6 Jefferies (750 Norton Métisse). Fastest lap: Agostini, 78.19mph.

4 October, Brands Hatch – Evening News Race of the South

350 (10 laps, 26.5 miles): 1 Giacomo Agostini (MV), 86.71mph, 2 John Cooper (Yamsel), 3 Phil Read (Yamaha), 4 Paul Smart (Yamaha), 5 Rex Butcher (Ivy Yamaha), 6 Rod Gould (Yamaha). Fastest lap: Cooper, 90.02mph (record).

500 Shell Championship (10 laps): 1 Agostini (MV), 86.28mph, 2 Peter Williams (Arter Matchless), 4 Paul Smart (Seeley), 5 Pat Mahoney (Seeley), 6 Barry Randle (Seeley). Fastest lap: Agostini, 87.84mph.

Evening News Race of the South (12 laps): 1 Agostini (500 MV), 87.7mph, 2 Cooper (Yamsel), 3 Read (348 Yamaha), 4 Gould (348 Yamaha), 5 Smart (750 Daytona Triumph), 6 Ray Pickrell (750 Triumph). Fastest lap: Agostini, 90.34mph.

251-750 Daytona Race (15 laps): 1 Smart (750 Daytona Triumph), 86.39mph, 2 Pickrell (750 Triumph), 3 Percy Tait (750 Triumph), 4 Ron Chandler (348 Yamaha), 5 Dave Nixon (750 Boyer Triumph), 6 Mick Grant (750 Lee Commando). Fastest lap: Pickrell, 89.33mph.

18 October, Snetterton

350 British Championship, Rd 8 (7 laps, 18.97 miles): 1 Paul Smart (Yamaha), 92.02mph, 2 Derek Chatterton (Chat Yamaha), 3 Steve Machin (Padgett Yamaha), 4 Bill Henderson (Yamaha), 5 Cliff Carr (Yamaha), 6 Mick Grant (Lee Yamaha). Fastest lap: Chatterton, 94.33mph.

500 British Championship, Rd 8 (7 laps): 1 Peter Williams (Arter Matchless), 91.76mph, 2 Barry Randle (Seeley), 3 Percy May (Petty Norton), 4 Jim Harvey (Matchless Métisse), 5 Martin Carney (Kawasaki), 6 B Adams (Norton). Fastest lap: Williams, Randle, 93.63mph

British Championships:

350: 1 Derek Chatterton, 2 Tony Rutter, 3 John Cooper

500: 1 Peter Williams, 2 Alan Barnett, 3 Pat Mahoney

CUSTOM MOTORCYCLES

Italian Custom Motorcycles focuses exclusively on the Italian motorcycle-based chopper, bobber, trike, and quad custom bike scene. A book to inspire and entertain.
ISBN: 978-1-845843-94-6
Hardback • 25x25cm • £25* UK/$39.95* USA/ $43.95 CAN • 128 pages • 260 colour and b&w pictures

Solely devoted to the BMW custom bike scene, this book features stunning images of customised BMW singles, twins and fours, complemented by owners' stories and technical descriptions.
ISBN: 978-1-845843-25-0
Hardback • 25x25cm • £19.99* UK/$39.95* USA/ $43.95 CAN • 128 pages • 270 colour and b&w pictures

An insight into the growing trend of customising metric bikes into chopper, bobber et al – be they high-end bikes, garage built beauties, or more recent Japanese cruisers. Superbly illustrated, and featuring owner's stories and technical descriptions.
ISBN: 978-1-845845-30-8
Hardback • 25x25cm • £25* UK/$39.95* USA/ $43.95 CAN • 128 pages • 275 colour pictures

This book takes a look at some of the fantastic British-based custom bikes around the globe. A celebration of all things 'custom Brit,' it is the only book devoted entirely to the British custom motorcycle, revealing the innovative, fresh approach to British motorcycle-based custom bike building.
ISBN: 978-1-845846-21-3
Hardback • 25x25cm • £25* UK/$39.95* USA/ $43.95 CAN • 128 pages • 250 colour pictures

For more info on Veloce titles, visit our website at www.veloce.co.uk
• email: info@veloce.co.uk • Tel: +44(0)1305 260068
* prices subject to change, p&p extra

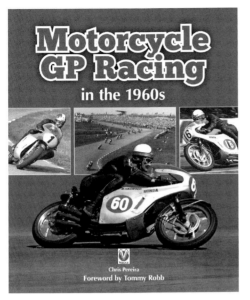

This book examines the classic period of Grand Prix racing from 1960 to 1969, and the men and machines involved. A fascinating exploration of the last decade of 'traditional' Grand Prix racing, before significant events changed the nature of the sport forever.

ISBN: 978-1-845844-16-5
Hardback • 25x20.7cm
• £30* UK/$49.95*
USA/$54.95 CAN • 176
pages • 177 colour and
b&w pictures

In this book, seasoned motorcycle restorer Ricky Burns takes you through each of the stages of real-life restorations. Aimed at enthusiasts of all abilities, from the total beginner to those with experience already, the reader is shown each stage and process in step-by-step detail, along with the techniques, tricks and tips used by experts. From choosing a project, setting up a workshop, and preparing a motorcycle, to sourcing parts, dismantling, restoring and renovating, this book is the perfect guide for the classic motorcycle restorer.

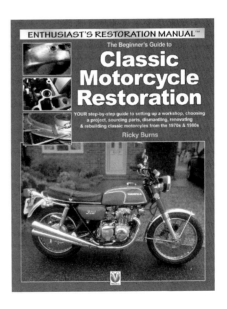

ISBN: 978-1-845846-44-2
Paperback • 27x20.7cm • 144 pages • 594 pictures •
£30* UK/$49.95* USA/$54.95 CAN

Index

230